ESSENTIALS OF COMMUNICATION RESEARCH

ESSENTIALS OF COMMUNICATION RESEARCH

Don W. Stacks
University of Miami

John E. Hocking
University of Georgia

HarperCollins*Publishers*

To Robin and Ruth, and Stacy, Katie, and Meg

Sponsoring Editor: Melissa A. Rosati
Project Editor: Robert Ginsberg
Design Supervisor: Heather A. Ziegler
Cover Design: Kay Cannizzaro
Production Manager/Assistant: Willie Lane/Sunaina Sehwani
Compositor: ComCom Division of Haddon Craftsmen, Inc.
Printer and Binder: R. R. Donnelley & Sons Company
Cover Printer: Phoenix Color Corp.

ESSENTIALS OF COMMUNICATION RESEARCH

Library of Congress Cataloging-in-Publication Data

Stacks, Don W.
    Essentials of communication research / Don W. Stacks, John E.
  Hocking
        p.   cm.
    Includes bibliographical references and index.
    ISBN 0-06-046424-0
    1. Communication—Research. I. Hocking, John E. II. Title.
  P91.3.S7 1992   91-3245
  302.2'072—dc20   CIP

91 92 93 94 9 8 7 6 5 4 3 2 1

Contents

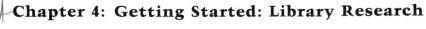

Chapter 5: Evaluating Sources: Historical/Critical Methodology   100

PART THREE ■ Modes of Analysis   273

Chapter 12: Descriptive Statistics   275

Chapter 13: Inferential Statistics   308

Preface

The importance of research in today's ever changing and more complex world cannot be overstated. We explain in the following section (To the Student) our ideas of how we should approach research and the role of research in contemporary communication. That role seems to be even more vital today.

This book is meant as a first introduction to the study of communication research. It is written for *communication* students employing *communication* examples. We truly believe that mastery of basic research skills is not only important, but ever more necessary as communication students seek answers to their questions. Research is a way of making sense out of the world, of relating to others. Regardless of what professional area the student ends in, he or she will be inundated with research, and most likely will be asked to analyze that research, possibly to conduct future research. Our goal is to provide the student with the means to do so.

Our organization is centered around the *process of research.* That is, we begin by focusing on the questions we ask and the role of theory in research. We introduce the topic of ethics in Chapter 3, believing it is important to study research ethics early in the course. In Part Two we turn to the various ways that research is conducted, beginning with the acquisition and evaluation of documents (library research). We then examine the various methods available to answer the research question or hypothesis of interest. Part Three introduces the student to data analysis, that is, making sense of the observations (data) collected and reporting those data and their significance to others.

We have employed certain pedagogical tools within each chapter. First, we provide a number of *probes*—questions for the student to consider, most of which have no "correct" answer—that serve to stimulate thinking about research. We also provide examples relevant to the many different types of research communication that students will read and conduct both in academic pursuit and in the "real world." We have attempted to establish realistic research guidelines. In sum, this book was written with the student in mind, with an expectation that he or she will be asked to conduct or analyze research based on any of the methods presented.

An Instructor's Manual is available upon adoption of the text.

ACKNOWLEDGMENTS

We would like to thank some significant others who made this book possible. They include Charles K. Atkin, Judee Burgoon, Michael Burgoon, Edward L. Fink, Mark Hickson, Jack Orwant, Cal Hylton, Gerald R. Miller, Don Richardson, Marvin Shaw, and John D. Stone. We also want to thank other research methods instructors with whom we have discussed both the project and our feelings about teaching the first course in research methods.

In writing this book we have been fortunate to work with a number of people who influenced not only how we approached research, but also the questions we personally address. Various stages of this book have been "pretested" on our students; we wish to acknowledge their anonymous contributions to the book. We also would like to thank Mark Hickson, University of Alabama at Birmingham, and Steve McDermott, California Polytechnic University, San Luis Obispo, for their contributed chapters. We are also grateful to the Literary Executor of the late Sir Ronald A. Fisher, F.R.S., to Dr. Frank Yates, F.R.S., and the Longman Group Ltd., London, for their permission to reprint Table 3 from their book *Statistical Tables for Biological, Agricultural and Medical Research,* Sixth Edition, 1974.

As we note in Chapter 2, research is a rigorous process. The process of writing this book has been no exception. We wish to acknowledge a number of people who not only reviewed earlier drafts of this book, but made us work harder to hone our own understanding of the research process. We gratefully appreciate the insight and stimulating questions provided by the following reviewers: William R. Cupach, Illinois State University; Michael D. Miller, University of Hawaii; Rebecca J.

Welch Cline, University of Florida; Andrew S. Rancer, Emerson College; Edward L. Fink, University of Maryland–College Park; Lawrence B. Rosenfeld, University of North Carolina at Chapel Hill; and Lloyd E. Rohler, University of North Carolina at Wilmington.

We also want to thank the people at HarperCollins for their contributions to this process: Melissa A. Rosati, Thomas R. Farrell, Robert Ginsberg, Barbara Cinquegrani, and Anne Smith. We appreciate their patient guiding hand in getting this project to press.

Finally, we would like to thank our families for their patience and understanding as this project went from stage to stage.

Don W. Stacks
John E. Hocking

To the Student

One of the major concerns faced by the graduate of any college or university today is the explosion of increasingly complex and varied information coming from myriad sources. More than ever, college graduates are becoming *consumers of knowledge.* To be good consumers of knowledge, however, they must first understand how that knowledge was generated and learn to be critical of the research methodology used in generating information, fact, and value statements. But these same consumers are increasingly becoming *suppliers* of knowledge; this necessitates not only being critical of method but also understanding how and why research is conducted. Today's college graduates must possess an understanding of the processes of research, be grounded in research methodology, and be prepared to examine knowledge based on research critically. Most fundamentally, they must understand that the types of *questions asked direct them to the appropriate methodology.*

Like other areas of academic study, communication research continues to become ever more complex and rigorous. This increased complexity creates the need for skilled knowledge generation and utilization. Undergraduate communication students must prepare for careers that compete with other disciplines in requiring that their students master research methodologies. If we are to compete, then, we must master research in a variety of contexts. Communication students, more than students of most other disciplines, must use a variety of methods, from historical to experimental, from quantitative to qualitative. A variety of appropriate analytical procedures must also become second nature to the communication student.

Knowing how to conduct research, analyze data and results, and interpret those findings does *not* require the learning of complex formulas or cumbersome methodology. In this text you are provided with the methodological tools needed to conduct and consume research in the library, the field, and the laboratory. The skills you begin to learn here will serve you well in such widely divergent communications-related fields as public relations, market analysis, advertising, human resource management, personnel, political communication, and general management.

A major concern for the neophyte methods student is understanding why research is conducted and what types of research questions are to be addressed. (What are you trying to find out? What type of question—fact, definition, value, or policy—is the research designed to answer?) The choice of the question will suggest the appropriate methodology. Thus a project is designed in such a way as to best answer your questions or test your predictions. The orientation here is practicality. Once you have specified method and design, you can collect and analyze your data.

A good researcher is also a good consumer of previous research. This includes the ability to critique past research for appropriateness in design and analysis. You must then understand research methodology well enough to conduct, analyze, and interpret the results, or to tell others how to do so.

This text is designed to provide the necessary materials to make such judgments. Because each research project you work on will be different, we present advantages and limitations of many methods and analytical tools. We also try to provide a grounded explanation of why we use certain procedures and methods, when they are appropriate, and how to interpret your findings.

Particular attention will be paid to establishing *models* of appropriate methodology. When appropriate, we provide actual questionnaires, examples of research designs, and computer-generated materials. The personal computer is an important tool in the research process, and, in an effort to provide you with samples for future use and comparison, computer-generated analyses will be presented and explained.

We have developed this book around the needs of a student with no background in theory or method. Obviously, if you have taken a communication theory course, you will be one step ahead of the game. If not, this book will be your introduction to both scientific and humanistic theory. Although our overall emphasis is on the methods used in studying human communication scientifically, we believe both approaches are valuable. We hope that this text—this course—will pique your interest enough to spur you on to a second or third course in the methodology—one that best suits your needs, that best answers the questions you want or will need to address.

The book begins with general considerations: What is science? How do we conduct research ethically? How does theory relate to method? In Part Two we present specific research methods—beginning in the library, moving on to historical/critical method, examining qualitative social scientific methodology, and then quantitative methodology, which describes, and, finally, examines laboratory and field experiments. Each method is related to, and in some way depends on, the methods that preceded it. We believe that the contemporary communication researcher should understand a little of all methods. All research, for example, begins in the library, with the researcher searching the past, using some of the tools of the historical/critical researcher, and then moves on to a particular method for gathering data for analysis. Part Three addresses the ways we can evaluate and analyze data, with emphasis on computer-assisted procedures and tools.

It is our hope that after you complete the course and the book you will be a better consumer of research, and that you will understand how research is conducted, why different researchers use different methods, and why they may come up with different results. We also hope that this book kindles an interest in research in general. And, we hope that we provide the material you will need in future courses, on the job, and as concerned, constructive citizens.

D.W.S.
J.E.H.

Theory and Research Methods

*T*his section serves as a general introduction to the study of communication theory and method. In a sense, it helps to establish a view of communication study. Research is only as good as the questions asked and, therefore, in establishing a base for research in communication we begin by considering the kinds of questions addressed. Asking a trivial question almost always ends in a bad research study regardless of the methodological sophistication of the attempt to answer it. Chapter 1 lays the foundation for asking *good* research questions, questions that concern communication. Chapter 1, then, discusses the process of inquiry in general.

Chapter 2 builds on this foundation by examining the study of *human* communication from a number of theoretical perspectives. The chapter begins with some general comments about research in communication and moves to-

ward an examination of science as one model of research and humanistic research as a second model. These two models are presented as different from,
yet complementary to, one another. In examining the two orientations, emphasis is placed on what each does best. Both serve as foundations for later discussion of more specific methods.

Chapter 3 takes a different perspective, one that moves from theory to
method. All good research meets certain ethical requirements, requirements
that are usually seen as the norms of research and, as such, are important in establishing what good research is. The discussion begins with the fundamental
rules of scholarship. Discussion then centers on the more specific questions of
what an ethical topic for research is and how we can ethically prepare, collect,
and analyze data. In the past there have been problems associated with the use
of human beings in research (communication researchers use *humans* as the
"subjects" of their studies either implicitly or explicitly), and, because of this,
we devote part of the chapter to a discussion of the ethical treatment of
human participants. Our purpose is to create a "social etiquette" for conducting research, regardless of the method chosen.

Part One establishes the reasons and the ground rules for conducting research. It should guide your later consideration of both methods and modes of
analysis. In establishing appropriate research methods and analytical procedures, we will refer back to Chapter 1 and Chapter 2 often.

Asking and Answering Questions

*T*he world was a lot different back in the 1950s. Dwight Eisenhower was president. Interstate highways did not exist. Rock 'n' roll was new and considered by many to be just a passing fad. Television was in black and white. College students did what they were told, asked few questions, were generally pleased with a grade of C, and never saw, or even imagined seeing, a teacher evaluation form. Speech students learned about public speaking and about great speakers and journalism students learned to write news stories.

Education, in general, was viewed largely as the learning of facts. An educated person was someone who knew lots of things and had lots of information stored away, ready for retrieval at the appropriate time. The symbol of this view of education was the television show "The $64,000 Question." Week after week, contestants were asked increasingly more difficult questions worth more and more money. "Geniuses," young and old, entered the isolation booth to rack their brains, strain showing on their faces, in an often successful effort to recall ever more obscure information. And their level of genius was viewed as directly proportional to the number of facts they could recall. The contestants were sometimes amazing. How could anyone be so smart, know so much, recall so many facts, have such a big brain, be *so well educated*? As it turned out, the show was a fraud; some contestants were given the answers ahead of time.

Needless to say, a lot has happened since those days. We have had several presidents, the majority of whom served only one term. Interstate highways, the largest construction project in the history of humankind, now crisscross the nation. Television is in color, except for the ubiquitous "Andy Griffith Show" and "Leave it to Beaver" episodes running in syndication, and rock music not only appears to be here to stay, but is available in color to viewers all over the country 24 hours a day on specialized networks. Today's college students ask lots and lots of questions, especially, Why do I need to know this? What is this good for? Will it help me get a job? They are usually displeased with a grade of C and fill out teacher evaluation forms routinely. "Speech" students are now "communication" students; journalism students study mass communication. And communication researchers and students study human verbal and nonverbal communications as symbolic transactions in every imaginable context. Education is no longer learning facts and storing them for later use. Education has changed from emphasizing the *storage* of information to emphasizing, indeed, demanding, the *processing* of information. Fundamentally, that is what this book is about. Instead of memorizing facts, we need to learn how to find out what is already known, how to understand and evaluate new information, and even how to discover things that were previously unknown. The purpose of this book is to provide a comprehensive introduction to the essential methods of research in Human Communication.

RESEARCH AND SOURCES OF INFORMATION

Social psychologist Elliot Aronson once wrote in tribute to his friend and mentor Leon Festinger: "I *could* say that he taught me all I know about social psychology, but that would be a lie. He taught me something much more valuable than that: he taught me to find out the things that neither I nor anybody else knew."[1]

Indeed! Much of the important information learned by students in the 1950s is now obsolete. And most of the information we learn today about human communication simply did not exist in the 1950s. More importantly, most of the information that will be known in ten years is not known today. How is this possible? Ours is an information age. Knowledge about human communication is growing exponentially. For many communication professionals, keeping up with this new information will be a critical determinant of career success. To find, evaluate, and use relevant information may be the single most valuable skill taught by colleges today. We will be so bold as to assert categorically that information *processing*—selectively choosing or discarding, combining or synthesizing, finding or creating, and most importantly, evaluating information to reach conclusions—will be the name of the game during the rest of your time in college, and in your careers in the 1990s and beyond.

Information comes, indeed, bombards us, from all directions. It comes from our personal experiences. It comes from family, friends, and work associates. It comes from the ancient sages Aristotle and Plato and from the more modern ones, McLuhan and Gerbner, Burke and Bitzer, McCroskey and Miller. It comes from the print and broadcast media. It is stored in archives and arrives with the evening news. But most importantly for our purposes here, it takes the form of *communication research*—the patient, systematic study to learn new "things" about human communication. Things, to paraphrase Aronson, that neither you nor I, nor anybody else, ever knew before. The modern student of human communication, regardless of his or her concentration, needs a grounding in understanding, planning, conducting, consuming, and evaluating communication research.

RESEARCH AND THE CONSUMPTION OF INFORMATION

More than ever before, today's college student (and graduate) is a hungry consumer of knowledge generated by diverse sources. To succeed in many upper-level communication courses, and in many postgraduate careers, skillful consumption of knowledge is paramount. In order to be a good consumer of knowledge, one must first know how that knowledge was generated, must learn to be critical of research methodology. It is equally important to note that with increasing frequency, this same consumer of knowledge is frequently a supplier of knowledge—for him- or herself, and for others. Thus, today's communication student and professional need to understand how and why research is conducted.

Scholars of human communication conduct research on many different subtopics using many different methods. These methods have some elements in common as well as some differences. Throughout this book we will be detailing these similarities and differences. Here, we will emphasize some very basic things that those of us who study communication all have in common.

1. *All methods of inquiry about human communication have as their ultimate goal the generation of knowledge that may then be used to improve the human condition.*

This will sound grandiose to some, pompous to others, and perhaps patently obvious to all. However, we feel that this point is so important that it deserves special emphasis, lest we lose sight of the big picture and get lost in the details of research procedures. Ideally the arts and the sciences exist to enrich lives, to make the world a better, more prosperous, fairer place. A particular scientist or artist might look at his or her creations as ends in themselves, but Art and Science, like other collective human endeavors such as government, exist and are worthy of our support because they can and often do make it a better world.

2. *All methods of inquiry about human communication involve studying how humans encode, transmit, and receive symbols to influence one another.*

The use of symbols, both verbal and nonverbal, is unique to our species. Our discipline focuses on symbol usage in all contexts, whether it be Johnny Carson telling a joke to millions, or a mother whispering to her child. To be sure, there is an overlap between what communication researchers study and what is studied by social psychologists, sociologists, political scientists, historians, and others. Knowledge does not always organize itself into the apparently discrete, but largely artificial categories between various academic disciplines reflected in academic departments. But whereas the social psychologist, for example, sometimes studies symbol usage, the communication researcher *always* has this as his or her focus.

3. *All methods of inquiry about human communication follow certain prescribed rules.*

Some of these rules are universally accepted as ethical absolutes, for example, providing credit and proper citations for the source of one's information and ideas. However, some of the rules are less explicit and vary with the type of research undertaken. For example, the methods of the communication researcher who takes a scientific approach generally dictate more explicit and stricter rules regarding research procedures than do the methods of the researcher who is engaging in textual criticism. Nonetheless, each method has a structure, a system of prescriptions about the right and wrong way to engage in research.

4. *All methods of inquiry about human communication involve the collection and analysis of data.*

The form the data take, the way they are analyzed, and the type of conclusions drawn may vary. The historian may gather newspaper accounts of an event, the rhetorical critic might gather the texts of a speech, and the social scientist might gather the responses to a questionnaire, but every communication researcher systematically and carefully collects and analyzes data in some form.

5. *All methods of inquiry about human communication begin with a question—an interrogative—asking about something that is unknown.*

At the core of any research project is a good research question, a question addressing an important aspect of human communication. Sometimes it is easy to get lost in a sea of detail about research procedures and to lose sight of this extremely important part of the process. If an important question is not being addressed, no matter how carefully the researcher proceeds to gather data, no matter how powerful and sophisticated the statistical or other analytic tools he or she applies, no matter how well written the paper that reports the research, the project is of little value, and the energies of all involved have been wasted. All good research begins with a *good* question, a question the researcher hopes to address through research that will advance his or her knowledge of the world. One of the hardest things in research is asking the *right* question, a question whose answer is important.

Let us start at the very beginning. Let us start our presentation of research methods about human communication with a discussion of the kinds of questions our field—communication—addresses.

ASKING QUESTIONS ABOUT HUMAN COMMUNICATION

Inquiry of any kind, regardless of the perspective from which it is conducted, has, at its core, the process of asking questions that the investigator uses to guide him- or herself through the research process. There are many kinds of questions that can be asked. Our primary aim in this section is to make what we consider to be the most fundamental distinction between the kinds of questions that can be asked about human communication, specifically, the distinction between questions of *fact* and questions of *value*. Later in this section we will discuss questions of *policy*. As we shall see, questions of policy require a blending of factual and value considerations before they can be adequately answered. Questions of *definition* are important regardless of the kind of inquiry. For this reason, we turn first to questions of definition.

Questions of Definition

Critically important to asking and answering questions about human communication is the definition of the terms used in the questions. Whether one is asking questions of fact, value, or policy, it is vital that the questioner, and others interested in the inquiry process, clearly understand what is being asked. If terms are not defined in an unambiguous way, the questioner cannot know exactly what question he or she is asking or even be confident that it has been adequately answered. Thus, we turn to an area that permeates all research about communication: questions of definition.

Abstraction Everything written in this book, including the questions to be posed, have been written in a language (English, obviously). Language is a system of symbols, and accompanying rules about how the symbols should be ordered, that is shared by those who understand the language. Communication is only possible if two users of the language share the same or similar meaning for the same symbol. Presumably, if you are reading this book, you are fluent in English, and therefore the ink on the page does not appear to you as random markings. A book written in a language in which you are not fluent, particularly one that did not use the 26 alphabetic characters of the English language, would literally be meaningless. There is no meaning in the ink on these pages. The meaning lies in those of us who are writing these sentences and those who are reading them.

Where do we learn meanings? We learn them from our parents, our playmates, our teachers and classmates, from authors, from friends and lovers, from movies and television, from music and art. We never stop learning meanings nor do the meanings we already have ever stop evolving and changing, albeit, usually in subtle ways. In short, we learn meanings from our past experiences.

No two people, however, have exactly the same past experiences, therefore no

two people will have exactly the same meaning for the same symbol. When someone says *dog*, you may think of your collie back home while he was thinking of
their neighbor's friendly little mixed breed, Suzie. But at least all were thinking
about four-legged animals that bark. You were not thinking about a tree while he
was thinking of Tuesday. Fortunately, we share considerable overlap in our meaning for most words, especially words with low levels of abstraction. The more
abstract the word, the more potential *referents*—specific meanings the word can
refer to—the word has. The word dog is a symbol with a low level of abstraction.
It can refer to many types and sizes of dog, but at least it does not refer to birds
as well. The word *pet* is more abstract because it might refer to dogs (in all
variations) or to birds, or to cats, or turtles, or whatever. The word *animal* is even
more abstract.

   As a general rule, the more abstract the word, the more important are clear
definitions to reduce potential for misunderstandings. Most of the questions communication researchers pose about human communication include abstract, equiv-
ocal, vague, or technical terms that require clear definition. There is a tendency
among all of us, including experienced communication researchers, to assume that
when we use a term in a particular way, others are using it in the same way. But
just as we think of two different dogs when we see the symbol, *dog*, we may have
different meanings for the terms in our important questions about values, facts, and
policy. What we mean by such abstract terms as social justice, ethically appropriate,
morally acceptable, TV ministry, lying, celebrity endorsement, greatest performer,
terrible-looking roommate, better painter, corporate divestment, date other people,
and so on, may or may not be what you mean by these terms. The bottom line is
that question-asking begins with definition. No question can be adequately answered unless everyone involved understands what is meant by the words in the
question.

Categorizing Definitions   There are many ways to categorize kinds of definitions and these will be discussed in more detail in later chapters. Here, it will suffice
to make a distinction between reportive definition and a stipulative definition.
Basically, a *reportive definition* reports how a particular term has been customarily
used, that is, what the conventional meaning for a term is. Dictionary definitions
can be thought of as reportive because they report to the reader how people in
general use a term.

   In contrast, a *stipulative definition* involves specifying how a term will be
used—to what it will be used to refer. In other words, the researcher stipulates what
he or she is referring to by using a particular word. For example, he or she might
say, ''by 'inappropriate self-disclosure,' I mean revealing highly personal information to someone who is known to the discloser for less than one hour.'' It is quite
silly to argue about whether a stipulated definition is true or false, right or wrong,
correct or incorrect. Stipulative definitions are thus not true or false, rather they
are statements or declarations about how a person intends to use a term. Stipulative
definitions should thus be judged on their *usefulness*. Do they effectively convey
a clear idea about the term being defined? Does a particular definition facilitate
answering some important research question? Later, in Chapter 2, we will discuss

in some detail a particular kind of stipulative definition, the *operational definition*, that defines variables with such specificity and concreteness that they make scientific research possible.

Questions of Value

Questions of value pose inquiries about whether an object, situation, or behavior is perceived as good or bad, right or wrong, beautiful or ugly. They concern the world as it *ought* to be, not necessarily as it is.[2] Let us examine some questions of value:

> Is Monet a better painter than Manet or Renoir?
>
> Is Bruce Springsteen the greatest rock 'n' roll performer ever?
>
> Was Ronald Reagan morally justified in selling weapons to Iran in the hopes of securing the release of American hostages?
>
> Is capital punishment wrong?
>
> Is it ethical to aim commercials advertising candy, toys, and cereal at children under seven years of age and who are predictably watching Saturday morning television?
>
> Is it ethically acceptable for various TV evangelists to tell people that good things will happen if they send money to the ministry?
>
> Is *Platoon* a better film about the Vietnam war than *Apocalypse Now, The Deer Hunter,* or the "Rambo" movies?
>
> Was Franklin Roosevelt's use of the radio, specifically his fireside chats, a more moral use of the mass media than George Bush's, specifically his short-notice press conferences?

All of these questions could be interesting to research. While all of them can be answered, will everyone agree about the answer? Probably not, because the answer to each of these questions of value lies to a great degree within the person who is asking and answering the question; that is, the answer lies in our internal mental judgments. Philosopher Dewit H. Parker writes that "values belong wholly to the inner world, to the world of the mind. . . . A value is always an experience, never a thing or an object. . . . We project into the external world."[3] This is why there is great disagreement regarding the answers to many questions of value.

Michael McGuire has written a very interesting essay about Bruce Springsteen's music in which he describes the music and identifies several central themes that Springsteen appears to return to again and again.[4] McGuire, who likes Springsteen, gives his opinion of the quality of the music. His essay is an excellent example of contemporary rhetorical criticism. If someone else wrote an analysis of Springsteen's music, would they write the same essay, identify the same themes, and have the same opinions about the quality of the music? Perhaps, but probably not.

Why? Because in McGuire's essay the reader learns about two very different things, in approximately equal amounts. First, of course, the reader learns something about Springsteen and his music. Second, and critically important to note, he or she learns a great deal about the essay's author. When he praises Springsteen's music, the statements he makes in doing so are more about himself than they are about Springsteen. When he says Springsteen is a great songwriter and performer he is really saying, *I believe* Springsteen is a great songwriter. *I like* Springsteen. The subject of these sentences is *I*—McGuire—not Springsteen. And to a greater or lesser degree, the same is true about all questions of value. Their answers lie largely within the person answering them.

We think McGuire's essay is excellent. However, a colleague of ours disagrees. In fact, he thinks that popular music is not an appropriate subject for rhetorical criticism. What do you think? As you think about it, you are looking within yourself to answer still another value question—one about the world of communication research as it *ought* to be.

Questions of value can be about big issues that affect society. They can also be about the small day-to-day judgments we make about what is right or wrong in our interpersonal interactions. Although debatable, we take the position that there are no absolute right or wrong answers to most questions of value. People will disagree about them, argue about them, sometimes resolve them temporarily, but the question remains, ultimately, open to debate. This is because the answer is within each of us. No two of us are exactly alike. We come into the world with a *tabula rasa*, a blank slate. We become what we are, think what we think, and have those values that we have as a result of our past experiences, but no two people have identical past experiences, therefore no two people's internal mental states will ever be exactly the same. Since we share a common culture and common language system, we share many of the same values. For example, it would be a safe bet that most people believe that human life is sacred, individual initiative is good, and education is important.

But our differences are profound. Some people believe in God, others do not. Some people believe that capital punishment is wrong, most people do not. The fact that American culture is pluralistic contributes to the diversity of our value systems. Ours is probably the most heterogeneous society in the world. All of us have different attitudes, opinions, beliefs, and values. Values are within us and it is ultimately within ourselves that we must turn for answers to questions of value.

Before leaving this discussion of questions of value, one final point deserves emphasis. Since the answers to questions of value lie largely within us, does this mean that all value judgments are equally good? That the answers to questions of value are equally valid? Some people argue for an extreme form of ethical relativism—the belief that all ethical judgments are equally valid because they depend on the situation in which the judgment is being made and the personal ethical beliefs of the individual making the judgment. This position would be in sharp contrast to *ethical absolutism*—the belief that ethical judgments are absolutely right or wrong, true or false, regardless of the situation or the beliefs of the individual.[5]

We prefer a middle ground between extreme forms of ethical relativism and absolutism. Not all value judgments are equally correct. Value judgments based on established principles that are widely accepted within a culture and that are advanced with thoughtful argument are much more likely to be correct judgments than those resulting from spontaneous emotional reactions. And, while value questions are internal mental judgments, the information on which these judgments are based certainly can be influenced by external sources. The Bible and other sources of moral authority provide guidance that aids many people in making these judgments. Similarly, many professions have codes of ethics that their members are required to follow. Simply knowing that almost everyone makes a similar value judgment may help us to make the same judgment.

What happens when a question of value requires the reconciliation of two deeply held values that come into conflict? For example, the belief that human life is sacred is believed almost universally, certainly within the western world. It follows from this that purposefully ending a human life is wrong. Here it appears that we are coming pretty close to a posture accepting ethical absolutism. Killing is wrong. Absolutely, and always. But what if the person who was killed had been suffering from some disease, and, after years and years of suffering, had begged to be killed? In this situation two powerful human values have come into conflict. Killing is wrong and should never be allowed. Terrible human suffering is wrong and should not be allowed. Perhaps in this situation causing the death of another person might be ethically appropriate. And many people, if apprised of the details, would agree. But not everyone. Even with careful study, thought, and use of ethical principles, people will often come up with different value judgments.

Questions of value deal with ethical, moral, aesthetic, and artistic concerns. There are many important and interesting questions of value that have to do with human communication. Communication researchers who take a humanistic (rhetorical/critical/historical) approach to inquiry spend much of their research energies and resources addressing questions of value. But questions of value influence all research projects.

Questions of Fact

Whereas questions of value deal with making *judgments* about the way the world ought to be, questions of fact are concerned with *describing the world as it is according to what we know at that time.* A question of fact poses an inquiry about the nature of the world that is external to our minds. And whereas the answers to questions of value are largely found within us, the answers to questions of fact are found "out there" in the observable environment. Questions of fact are often called *empirical* questions, capable of being verified or refuted by observation. The following questions are empirical:

Is the average cost of a Monet painting at auction higher than that of a painting by Manet or Renoir?

Did Bruce Springsteen sell over 10 million records in 1986?

Did Ronald Reagan give weapons to Iran in an effort to secure the release of American hostages?

Is capital punishment a deterrent to murder and other serious crimes?

Are commercials that advertise candy, toys, and cereal effective at changing the attitudes and behaviors of children under the age of seven?

If your roommate looks terrible for a date and you tell him so, what effect will this have on his self-concept, on his success during the date, and on your relationship with him?

How much money do people send in to the television evangelists as a result of hearing that good things will come if they send money?

Do Vietnam combat veterans believe that *Platoon* is a more realistic depiction of what it was like to be in combat in Vietnam than *Apocalypse Now* or *The Deer Hunter*?

Did more people listen to Franklin Roosevelt's fireside chats than see George Bush's spontaneous press conferences?

The answer to each can be found, at least potentially, through observation. If two people observe in the same way, that is, go through the same steps in the process of finding answers, follow the same observational rules, and if the rules are specific enough, they should arrive at the same answer. The answers are not within the researcher but rather are out there in the world. We can look for them and we can agree, at least theoretically, on what the answers are.

If these questions of fact were stated in the declarative form instead of their current interrogative form, these statements could, after appropriate research, be found to be true or false. Consider the statement, Bruce Springsteen sold fewer than 10 million records in 1986. This statement is true or false and it can, in fact, be determined to be so. He either sold this many records or he did not. It is one or the other. And what the researcher may think about Springsteen's music, or whether or not the researcher believes that human life is sacred, capital punishment is morally wrong, and so on, is not going to have any effect on how many records Springsteen sold in 1986. Contrast this with the value statement, Bruce Springsteen is the greatest performer in the history of rock music. This statement *cannot* be determined to be either true or false.

Questions of fact are amenable to empirical answers. This does not mean that they are easy to answer, nor does it mean that there will not be disagreements about the answers. Some questions of fact are complex, and despite being studied for years, different empirical studies may point to different answers.

Questions of fact may yield answers that seem contradictory. However, many questions of fact are answered by *different* people, using different methods, and different definitions.

For example, does the depiction of violent acts by the mass media contribute to violent behavior by those exposed to the media? This question has been studied empirically and the answers debated for over 30 years. The causes of violence in our society are many and sorting them out in a definitive way is an incredibly complex task. Think of all the other factors that may contribute to a violent act besides exposure to a Sylvester Stallone film or an episode of "Miami Vice." But ultimately, violence in the media either does or does not play some contributory role. The difficulty in answering a question does not determine whether the answer is out there in the external environment. It is possible to make observations relevant to the answer.

Questions of fact can be about the past, the present, or the future. Questions about the present and future lend themselves to *direct observation*. It is often possible to observe the answer first-hand. The Super Bowl is played every year. Who wins, what the score is, and how many people were at the game are all factual questions. We can observe the answers directly for games to be played in the future. Questions of fact about past events can only be observed indirectly.

When Franklin Roosevelt made his famous fireside chats in the 1930s, what was their impact? Did he restore national confidence at a time when it was at an all-time low? Did he energize people to apply themselves with new vigor to solving some of the great problems of the time? Even though these are questions of fact, we cannot *directly* observe the answers. Certainly there are historians who will assert that his chats did, in fact, have these effects. However, their assertions about these "facts" are based on *indirect observations*. They may have read newspaper accounts of the chats and the listeners' reactions to them. They may have interviewed people who were old enough to remember hearing the broadcasts. They may even have listened to tapes of the radio programs. Nonetheless, there will be historians who disagree and who have their own indirect observations to support opposite conclusions. Thus, while historians frequently deal with questions of fact, they use indirect observation methods to address such questions. The methods and limitations of historical research will be examined in Chapter 5.

Questions of fact can be answered in many ways and we will be discussing these later in the chapter. Communication researchers who address questions of fact about present and future events generally do so using the methods of *science*. Scientific research requires carefully controlled and defined observations that can be repeated again and again. The methods of science are designed to detect and correct mistakes in answering questions of fact. An assumption is that the individual human being is fallible, even prone to having biases and to making mistakes. Thus, the rules of science are designed to minimize these influences on descriptions of the world.

As noted earlier, deciding if an important question—or a good question—is being asked can be one of the most difficult and subjective parts of the research process. Students of human communication, whether they be neophytes taking their first course in the field or seasoned veterans of many research projects, spend great amounts of time deciding which questions are important and which are not. While there are no surefire principles for determining if an important question is being asked, there are some guidelines that may help. When trying to decide whether a question of fact is worthy of our research energies, the checklist in Box 1.1 may prove useful.

Before ending our discussion of questions of fact and value, a final point—a qualification—must be made. For clarity's sake, we have purposefully presented the distinction between questions of fact and questions of value in its simplest form, that is, as a dichotomy. However, this dichotomy is not quite as straightforward and tidy as our presentation has implied. While we can frequently distinguish

Box 1.1   Criteria for Evaluating Questions of Fact

1. Is it a factual question?

2. Is it about communication; that is, human symbolic transactions?

3. Is it clearly and unambiguously stated?

4. Is it about the relationship between two or more variables?

5. Is the question of potential theoretical interest? Is there reason to believe that the variables are related? Are there other variables possibly related to both? (Is there potential for the study to be published, and therefore the results becoming part of "public knowledge"?)

6. Is there previous research examining this or related questions?

7. Are we personally interested in devoting our energies to answering this question?

8. Would we be able to answer this question in an ethical way? Would our procedures pass the human subjects committee on campus?

9. Is it feasible for us to answer this question? That is, are we capable, given our resources, of doing the research? How would we operationalize the variables? What procedures would be necessary to address this question?

between a question of fact and a question of value, we cannot separate them completely. There is an interaction between facts and values. The researcher addressing a question of fact is not a totally objective seeker of the truth in the external world. He or she is a fallible and probably biased individual whose personal value judgments permeate all aspects of a research project. The specific factual questions addressed, and the procedures used to answer the question, are both influenced by the values they hold.

Nor is an individual whose concern is a question of value isolated from external and observable events. The observable characteristics of things enter into our evaluations of them. All knowledge is to some extent the result of a transaction between the internal mental states of the researcher and the outside observable world. Thus it is probably most useful to think of questions of fact and questions of value as falling along a continuum, as shown in Figure 1.1.

As shown, the extremes, which are anchored by "Answer Lies Purely Within the Questioner" and "Answer Lies Purely Within the External World," are never the realm in which the answer to either type of question lies. Rather, the answers to both questions of fact and value are found to varying degrees in the internal and external worlds, with the answers to questions of value tending to lie toward the

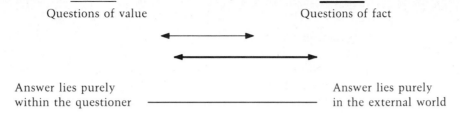

Figure 1.1 Locus of the answer to questions of fact and questions of value.

left of the center.[6] We shall have more to say about this issue in Chapter 5, in our discussion of historical/critical methods.

Questions of Policy

Questions of policy are concerned with deciding wise and prudent courses of action in the management of affairs. Policies prescribe what to do under certain circumstances. Policies take the form of formal or informal rules regarding courses of action or behavior. Usually when we think of policies we think of formal organizations such as governments, businesses, and educational institutions. Consider the following policy questions:

> Should the United States send troops into Central America to aid the Contras in their efforts to overthrow the Sandinista government in Nicaragua?
>
> Should state governments lower the drinking age to 19?
>
> Should the Federal Trade Commission (FTC) ban the use of celebrity endorsements in alcohol advertising?
>
> Should General Motors divest itself of holdings in South Africa until apartheid is eliminated?
>
> Should colleges and universities maintain separate dormitory facilities for athletes?
>
> Should both the U.S. House of Representatives and the Senate repeal authorization for televising their proceedings?

Questions of policy are frequently very complicated, requiring much varied information to answer. Questions of policy require not only an agreement on definition, but both factual information and value information. The following example illustrates this.

Should the FTC ban the use of celebrity endorsements in alcohol advertising? What are some of the kinds of information we would have to have to know what national policy should be on this matter? Or, put another way, what questions of fact and value would we have to answer before we could answer this question of policy? First, however, we need to agree on what we are studying, that is, on questions of definition: What is advertising? What constitutes a celebrity endorsement? And so forth.

At a minimum we would need to know the answers to value questions associated with several related concerns. (1) Regarding alcohol consumption—some people believe that no one should consume or be allowed to consume alcohol under any circumstances. (2) Regarding government regulation—some people believe that federal government regulation of any kind is wrong and that federal government has no role in public affairs, other than perhaps national defense. (3) Regarding censorship—some people believe that the government has no role to play in regulating communication of any kind, whether broadcast via the mass media or spoken on a streetcorner.

Furthermore, we would probably want to know the answers to questions of fact, such as (1) How widespread is the use of celebrities to endorse alcohol products? (2) What are the intended and actual audiences at which these advertisements are aimed—do young people see these ads? (3) What is the effect of these messages—for example, do people who see the former athletes like Bob Uecker in Miller Lite Beer ads drink more Miller Lite? Do they drink more beer in general? If we had clear-cut definitions and answers to all these questions, answers that were widely agreed upon, setting a policy would be relatively simple. As with most policy questions, however, we usually do not have definitive answers to either the value questions or the factual questions. So policy questions are open to debate, and ultimately answered through discussion, argument, and reason.

If you have taken or will take an argumentation class as part of your communication studies, or plan to be on the debate team or advertising team, much of your energies will be spent researching the answers to questions of fact and value as they relate, ultimately, to questions of policy. *Argument* is the use of reason and evidence to persuade someone that a policy is correct. And the evidence for correctness of a policy is usually information about answers to questions of fact and value based on accepted definitions.

So far we have been concerned with examples of a policy question about the course of action to be taken by a large structured organization. But policies, and questions about them, also exist in informal organizations such as families and dyadic relationships, for example:

> Should we buy what we want (e.g., a VCR, a computer, a new dress) on credit or should we operate strictly on a cash basis?
>
> Should Bob and Molly date other people over the summer vacation?
>
> Should you take turns with your roommates doing the dishes or let the person who dirtied them wash them?
>
> Should you persuade your best friend to loan you money?

Relevant factual and value information would also be important to have in deciding policy questions about these more mundane and informal situations. Although structured debates in government, industry, and academia are frequently the mechanisms by which questions of policy are answered, more informal discussions are usually the way policies in interpersonal and small group communication systems are decided. The important point is that regardless of the level of the policy question, whether it concerns the entire world or your relationship with your roommate, questions of policy require that answers to questions of fact and value be addressed first. These answers are then (or should be) applied with the use of cogent reasoning to the policy question.

Now that we have an introduction to the categories of questions people ask about human communication, we will turn to the question of where we might look to answer them. Specifically, we are going to turn to the general issue of how people came to believe the things they believe.

EPISTEMOLOGY

We began this chapter by noting some of the changes that have taken place in education in the past 30 years or so. These changes are especially apparent in fields such as computer science, but we feel they are equally important in communication. Thirty years ago speech students studied public speaking and maybe group discussion, while their journalism brothers and sisters studied news and editorial writing. Today we still study these topics, but also much more. Communication as a discipline has come to cover an enormous range of subject matter. Students take courses that present information about communication in relationships, both fleeting and long term; in social and work groups; in political campaigns and social movements; in courtrooms and churches. They study nonverbal communication and persuasion and cross-cultural communication. They study advertising and public relations and mass communication effects, and on and on.

From where does this information—the knowledge that constitutes the content of these courses and specializations—come? How do we know what message exchanges characterize the beginning and ending stages of a relationship? How do we know that one president uses more ethically appropriate message appeals than another? How do we know what role communication plays in a group's decision making? How do we know the effects of a political debate on voters' perceptions of the credibility of the candidates? How do we know what arguments will be most effective in convincing jurors that a defendant is guilty? How do we know if Martin Luther King's "I Have a Dream" speech was a better speech than John F. Kennedy's inaugural address or Abraham Lincoln's "Gettysburg Address"? How do we know the impact of an automobile commercial or a violent music video on adolescent viewers? The following discussion, in a general way, presents how our discipline, communication, comes to "know" the things that we teach.

Epistemology is the study of how we come to know things. It deals with how individuals and groups come to believe what they believe. Educational psychologist Fred N. Kerlinger has presented a widely cited category system for organizing the various ways we come to arrive at beliefs.[7] His treatment is useful for both understanding how *individuals* come to hold the beliefs they hold and how communication *researchers* reach conclusions about the answers to research questions. This treatment centers on four approaches: tenacity, authority, intuition, and science.

Tenacity

The first method discussed by Kerlinger is *tenacity.* Some things we believe simply because we have always believed them. We know these things to be true because, well, we know it. We have never even thought to consider the possibility that they might not be true. We take them for granted to the point that we will cling to these beliefs *tenaciously,* regardless of conflicting information. Centuries ago humans believed that the world was flat, and that heavenly bodies—the sun, moon, and the stars—revolved around the Earth, which was the center of the universe. To believe differently was heresy and there are examples of individuals, quite literally, being put to death if they failed to conform to the conventional wisdom, as was the case during the Spanish Inquisition of the 1500s.

These kinds of beliefs come from traditions we inherit from our culture or subcultures. A researcher who had occasion to observe a Ku Klux Klan (KKK) rally as part of a study of group communication rituals noted that the individuals in attendance expressed beliefs about black people and a whole host of other "out" groups that we know to be false. But frequent repetitions of "truths" seems to reinforce their veracity. These people grew up hearing these "facts" from the time they were small children. (And, in fact, there were small children at the rally.) One can imagine the number of times members of the KKK and their ilk repeat and reinforce their shared beliefs—beliefs that they have learned from their culture, or in this case, from their small, isolated subculture. Unfortunately, for the time being it appears that these people are clinging to their beliefs with great tenacity. We can only hope it will not take the centuries to change these beliefs that it took to convince people that the world is round.

This is not to say that to believe something our culture has ingrained in us is necessarily bad, or even that the belief is necessarily incorrect. Many such beliefs are probably quite proper, and especially in the area of fundamental human values, we probably should accept them. Take the belief that brushing your teeth is good for you. We accept this blindly. We know it is true. We will cling to it tenaciously. We are also as sure as anyone can be sure of anything that human life is sacred. So the problem with tenacity as a method of knowing is not that the beliefs are wrong. Sometimes they are and sometimes they are not. The problem is that if they *are* wrong, they may be difficult to change (the question of whether tenaciously held beliefs are especially difficult to change is itself an empirical question that has not been answered definitively). And if a belief is factually or morally wrong, desirable changes may be slow in coming.

Clearly, all of us, as human beings, believe some of what we believe because of tenacity. Does tenacity as a source of knowledge operate with communication researchers as well? Most assuredly. Many researchers train within research traditions that *emphasize* certain kinds of questions, and certain approaches to answering them, to the point of excluding other questions and other methods. In our field, considerable journal space and researcher energies have been devoted to stating in some form or another, "my way is best." Or worse, "my way is the only way." Communication researchers sometimes believe things because they have been told them over and over again by their "culture"—that is, their colleagues who subscribe to the same beliefs. Academicians sometimes cling to their beliefs as tenaciously as anyone. We discuss this in more detail in Chapter 2.

Thomas Kuhn, in his influential book, *The Structure of Scientific Revolutions*, writes of research paradigms.[8] To Kuhn, a *paradigm* is a dominant way of conceptualizing a phenomenon, of approaching it methodologically, and of looking for solutions to research problems. A paradigm may dominate for decades, even centuries, with its adherents defending it bitterly in the face of conflicting information, until, ultimately, a revolution occurs and a new paradigm takes over. The new paradigm offers radically new conceptualizations, research strategies and methods, and suggestions for solutions.[9] Again, the problem is not that the particular set of beliefs that constitute a paradigm are necessarily wrong, but that beliefs held because of tenacity may be extremely difficult to change.

Authority

A second method of knowing discussed by Kerlinger is *authority*, a source of some kind that has established knowledge and shares it with us: "The Bible says it, therefore it must be true." "Dr. Ruth said so on television; it must be so." "My research methods instructor disagrees with your view, so you clearly are mistaken." This method has also been called the *granny method*. One can imagine the oldest member of a family, the grandmother, sitting in a rocking chair on the front porch. When an important question needed answering, a family member would go up to the porch for an audience with Granny, sit at her feet, and let this wise old woman tell the truth.

Much of what we know, both as individuals and as students of communication, we know because some authority has told us. For many things that we know this is entirely sensible, especially if the authority is speaking within the realm of his or her expertise. If our dentist tells us that we need a cavity filled, we almost certainly do. She is knowledgable about teeth in general and about our teeth in particular. Further, she is trustworthy. She is not going to lie to us. Nevertheless, authorities can be wrong and second opinions should be obtained. Even the best people at times make mistakes; there is nothing wrong in getting a second opinion, in dentistry or communication.

The key to using an authority as a source of information is an accurate appraisal of the extent that he or she (or it, in the case of an inanimate object such as the Bible or the U.S. Constitution) really is an authority. A special problem exists when the authority steps outside his or her area of expertise. We see this commonly in advertisements. Former football player and Navy veteran Roger Staubauch is the spokesperson in ads for life insurance. Obviously, the company believes that he will be viewed as an authority by many people. But what does he know about life insurance? Evaluating the credibility of an authority is an important part of the research process, particularly when conducting historical, critical, and rhetorical research. People in academia, including communication researchers, sometimes espouse truths in areas outside their area of expertise. And some of them are right or wrong with equal confidence. How to evaluate sources of information, including authorities, is a major theme of Chapter 5.

Intuition

A third method of knowing discussed by Kerlinger is the a priori method, also called the method of *intuition*. Basically, this is the idea that the truth tends to be self-evident and that if reasonable people engage in open-minded discussion, the correct answers to problems will tend to surface. This is similar to one of the premises that democratic governments are based on—that other things being equal, open discussion inclines us toward the truth. Kerlinger is critical of this method as a way of knowing, stating, "The difficulty with this position lies in the expression 'agree with reason.' Whose reason?"[10] However, he is concerned primarily with answering questions of fact that are amenable to scientific inquiry. For questions of value and questions of policy, in particular, the a priori method of allowing reason to prevail is a good way to proceed.

There is nothing to preclude the open discussions in which reason prevails from including arguments that contain a variety of kinds of evidence, including statements from authorities and even relevant scientific findings. If, for example, a national policy is to be decided, this method has generally served our country well.

Science

For questions of fact that do lend themselves to empirical study, we agree with Kerlinger. The fourth method of knowing, *science*, is best. Communication researchers who take a scientific approach, like other scientists, model their methods after those used in the physical sciences and as articulated by philosophers such as John Locke, Karl Popper, Carl Hempel, and John Dewey. In brief, the scientist starts with a problem or obstacle, proposes a solution—a *theory*, predicts that if the proposed solution is correct certain events ought to occur under certain circumstances, creates those circumstances in a manner that allows for careful observations to determine if the prediction was correct, and uses the results of the observation to modify the theory.

Science has one advantage over other ways of knowing—and it is a big one. If an error has been made with the scientific method there are built-in checks explicitly designed to maximize the likelihood that the errors will be detected and corrected. The *ideal model of science* includes the following features. First, science is authority-free. Research is evaluated not by who did it, but by how it was done, whether proper procedures were followed, objective methods used, and so on. Thus, research papers submitted to journals for publication or for presentation at scientific gatherings are usually evaluated by reviewers who do not know who wrote the paper. It is not who you are that counts; rather, it is the quality of your research. As with most methods, however, practice sometimes does not meet the ideal; the fact is we do have authorities, not all journals use blind reviews, and some published research is invited, based on the reputation of the researcher.

Second, scientific knowledge is always *public* knowledge. The researcher describes not only his or her results but also the methods used to obtain those results. Furthermore, the methods are described with enough detail to allow other researchers to evaluate and reproduce them. Flaws in the method used are described openly. Honesty and openness characterize science in the ideal.

Third, because of the openness and detailed descriptions of procedures, other researchers are free to attempt to reproduce the results using the same or slightly modified procedures. If researcher A believes that researcher B has biased the results in some way, A is free to repeat B's observations with the alleged biasing elements eliminated. A is then free to present his or her observations and results for public scrutiny.

Like all research methods, science has its limitations and disadvantages. It does not address, directly at least, questions of value. (Although the results of scientific research might help an individual reach a decision about a value question.) Nonetheless, the methods of the scientist have become an essential set of tools for contemporary communication researchers.

SUMMARY

This chapter focused on the beginning of the research process. We examined what research is and how the way research is approached is, to large degree, dictated by the types of questions asked. We suggested that processing of information is more important than simple storage and that decisions made concerning research must be enlightened ones. Five common elements that bind researchers together, elements that lead to an understanding of the unknown, were discussed.

Inquiry, we noted, has at its core the asking of questions. In this regard we examined the four types of questions researchers ask: questions of definition, value, fact, and policy. We noted that all researchers work from questions that may lead to different answers; that the type of question posed will determine the research method. We then examined the concept of an epistemology, or a way of knowing what we know, using four basic ways of knowing: knowledge based on tenacity, authority, intuition, and science.

PROBES

1. Why *do* people conduct research? From your point of view, what is important about the research process? Based on what you have learned thus far in your communication courses, what has research provided that allows us to understand better how humans communicate?

2. All research begins with a question. What does this statement mean? How do we go about finding a good question to study?

3. There are three major questions posed by researchers (value, fact, and policy). Take an interest area and pose one question for each of the three types. Looking at these questions, do they suggest any particular *process* or *systematic* relationships between the concepts in this particular area? Take a concept from an earlier communication course and provide any reportive and stipulative definitions you can find. Are some better than others? Why?

4. The study of how we come to know things is called "epistemology." Looking through the literature in your area of interest, list examples you believe reflect knowledge through tenacity, authority, intuition, and science. Which do you believe is best? Why?

5. React to the argument that to understand research better the reader of research should become an educated consumer of information. In reacting to this, think about who uses information provided by researchers and how that information is both used and abused.

NOTES

1. Elliott Aronson, *The Social Animal* (San Francisco: W. H. Freeman, 1972), viii.

2. Gerald R. Miller and Henry Nicholson, *Communication Inquiry: A Perspective on a Process* (Reading, Mass.: Addison-Wesley, 1976). Our treatment of this distinction between types of questions is heavily influenced by Miller and Nicholson.

3. Dewit H. Parker, *Human Values* (New York: Harper, 1931), 20–21; however, we should note that while this is our position on the nature of value judgments, there is a contrasting view that values are objective and out there in the world to be discovered. Roman Catholic philosophy, for example, holds that goodness and beauty exist in their own right.

4. Michael D. McGuire, "Darkness on the Edge of Town: Bruce Springsteen's Rhetoric of Optimism and Despair," in Martin J. Medhurst and Thomas Benson, eds., *Rhetorical Dimensions in Media: A Critical Casebook* (Dubuque: Kendall-Hunt, 1984).

5. See Harold H. Titus, *Living Issues in Philosophy* (New York: American Book, 1964), 351–367 for a discussion. See also Miller and Nicholson, *Communication Inquiry.*

6. Some complex philosophical issues that are beyond the scope of this book are raised by this seemingly simple distinction. *Subjectivism* is a philosophical view that objects do not exist independent of our awareness of them, while *objectivism* is the view that there is a reality that exists independent of human perception. When dealing with questions of fact or value, an intermediate view between these two extremes is probably the most useful. See Harold H. Titus, *Living Issues in Philosophy,* 44–52, for a discussion.

7. Fred N. Kerlinger, *Foundations of Behavioral Research,* 3rd ed. (New York: Holt, Rinehart & Winston, 1986), 6–7.

8. Thomas Kuhn, *The Structure of Scientific Revolutions* (Chicago: University of Chicago Press, 1962).

9. Kuhn.

10. Kerlinger, 6.

The Role of Theory in Communication Research

*T*here are many ways to categorize the communication discipline—to make sense of the "buzzing, blooming confusion" that sometimes seems to characterize our field. A number of often ambiguous terms are used to describe the variety of research approaches used in communication studies. Rhetorical, historical, critical, humanistic, scientific, quantitative, and qualitative are the most commonly used labels, but there is by no means universal agreement about what each means, or about the nature of research conducted by someone who calls him- or herself by one of these labels. In this chapter we are going to build on the foundation laid in Chapter 1, specifically on the distinction between questions of fact and questions of value, and use this distinction to clarify terms. In the process we will provide an introduction to the role of theory in addressing both kinds of questions.

APPROACHES TO STUDYING COMMUNICATION

Gerald R. Miller argues that there are three primary purposes for studying communication. First, "in some situations, students of speech communication observe communication phenomena primarily for the purpose of making factual generalizations about similar phenomena not encompassed by the observations."[1] In other words, sometimes we are interested in observing events not because of the event itself, but because of what the event will tell us about communication in general. This is what the communication scientist is interested in—always. (As will be explained later, this is what the rhetorician is interested in much, if not most, of the time.) The scientist wants to make statements about the relationships between objects or concepts that, although observed in one setting, exist in others as well. This approach is similar to what Earl Babbie calls the *nomothetic* model of explanation.[2] The researcher is interested in a relatively few factors that provide explanations for a broad range of human behavior. The communication researcher in these instances is interested in questions of fact about the relationship between objects or concepts in the present and the future.

For example, imagine that a researcher is interested in the kinds of messages people exchange in initial encounters, specifically the depth of self-disclosure achieved during a one-hour encounter. She brings 40 strangers together in pairs to her laboratory and videotapes their initial interaction. Later, she observes these videotapes, and based on carefully stipulated definitions, categorizes the information exchanged in terms of "depth of self-disclosure" during the first 20 minutes, the middle 20 minutes, and the final 20 minutes of a one-hour meeting. The researcher is not interested in the specific information an individual pair exchange, per se, or even what all 20 pairs collectively say to one another. The researcher is interested in the *relationship* between two abstract variables—time and depth of disclosure—in general. She wants to make statements about the way these variables relate in this situation not as an end in itself, but as evidence about the way these variables relate in other situations.

Second, according to Miller, "[in other situations, students of communication] study and observe phenomena so they can draw factual conclusions about the observed phenomena themselves."[3] In other words, sometimes we are interested in observing the event as an end in itself. We may learn nothing about any other event; rather, this event is of such interest that learning about it is ample justification for its study. This approach is sometimes called an *ideographic* model of explanation.[4] The researcher is interested in identifying as many factors that contribute to a particular event as possible, even if these factors are unique to this event. If the event is in the present or future, the researcher can conduct a *case study*, which might involve direct observations of the event, interviews with participants before, during, or after it, and a host of other data-gathering techniques that will be discussed in detail in later chapters.

For example, a researcher might be interested in the depth of self-disclosure George Bush achieves when talking about his involvement in the sale of arms to Iran and the subsequent diversion of funds to rebels in Nicaragua. The researcher might videotape Bush's various speeches and news conferences on the topic and carefully categorize and describe when he reveals various information. The researcher is not interested in self-disclosure generally or even self-disclosure by United States presidents; he is interested in this specific president's disclosure on this specific issue. The issue is of such great importance that it is worthy of study as an end in itself.

Since, by definition, the events being studied are communication events, the researcher is focusing on the processes by which human beings exchange symbols and influence one another. The researcher is likely to use the methods of *rhetoric* to understand the event and to call him- or herself a *rhetorician.* The rhetorician in this case is addressing questions of *fact* about specific communication events. The study of the specific event, however, may suggest to the rhetorician general principles about how communication works in other situations. And, in fact, in most cases, this is a major purpose of a rhetorical study.

A rhetorical case study may suggest relationships between variables that apply in other situations. Some of these generalizations may lend themselves to carefully repeated, objective observation. To the extent that the rhetorician does this, he or she is behaving very much like a social scientist. It is also here that the rhetorician and scientist may be able to complement and supplement one another's research efforts. A rhetorical study of a specific communication event may suggest questions that a scientist could test. There are examples of principles or theories that were suggested in a case study later being tested in the controlled conditions of a laboratory.[5]

If the event was in the past, the researcher would use the methods of the historian to "observe" it indirectly. The methods of the historian include examining diaries, newspapers, and other documents, film clips, interviews, and a host of other techniques (see Chapter 5). If asked what he or she did for a living, the response might be, "I am an historian," or perhaps, "a rhetorical historian." In these situations the researcher is interested in questions of *fact* about *specific* communication events that have occurred in the past. Specific facts, in turn, may illuminate larger issues. The issue of whether historical/rhetorical research has as its purpose theory building, the explication of historical facts, or an examination of discourse as an end in itself, has been debated long and hard by rhetorical critics.[6] Suffice it to say that there is disagreement among rhetoricians on this issue.

Finally, Miller states that we "study communicative phenomena for the purpose of arriving at ethical or aesthetic judgments about the phenomena themselves, or about the event, or events, with which the phenomena are associated."[7] Here, Miller is talking about questions of value. Individuals who address questions of value do so using the methods of the critic. The critic often attempts to apply some established ethical or aesthetic principles to a situation in an effort to answer a question of *value.* If asked what he or she did for a living, the answer would likely be, "I am a rhetorical critic." We should note that there is also disagreement over whether rhetorical critics should make explicit value judgments as they conduct their research and write their criticism. Such criticism would seem to seek to change the world; that is, to make the world as it ought to be.[8]

The use of these labels becomes more complicated because frequently the nature of the inquiry is not clearly of one kind or another. Rather, there may be some overlap between these seemingly discrete categories of types of questions. For example, a researcher might be interested in both describing an event and in offering a critical evaluation of it. In fact, George Bush made several speeches in which he claimed that he was not involved in trading arms to Iran in exchange for the release of American hostages. A historian could examine the facts of this incident, come to conclusions about whether, in fact, Mr. Bush's claim was truthful or not, *and then* go on to offer criticism of the event, including judgments about Bush's integrity. This researcher would be addressing questions of fact and questions of value within the same overall research project. We would probably say that this person was conducting a historical (it happened in the past, or near past)—rhetorical (the focus is on a persuasive speech or speeches)—critical (value judgments are made, either explicitly or implicitly, concerning the events surrounding the speech[es] and the speech[es] themselves) study.

THEORETICAL ORIENTATIONS

Few words in the English language are used in more different ways than *humanism.* In the most general sense it is used to refer to an attitude or philosophy in which human beings are of paramount importance, that human interests and values are worthy of study as ends in themselves. When research questions focus on single events, as ends in themselves, or with the more qualitative—as contrasted with quantitative—approach to communication the label humanistic is often used. Thus rhetorical/historical/critical research, which often examines questions of value and the qualitative dimension of research, is frequently referred to as humanistic; we will use this definition to identify any method that focuses on specific events that have occurred in the past.

One final point should be made. Humanistic research is often contrasted with, or seen as the opposite of, social scientific research. This is unfortunate. Our view is that both kinds of research have the same general goal: *the improvement of the human condition.* The questions each is able to address are different, and the methods used to answer them are different, but, as noted earlier, both make an important contribution.

We are going to collapse Miller's distinction between the communication researcher who is interested in an event as an end in itself and the researcher who is concerned with questions of value. Although it may be an oversimplification, we believe this is a sensible approach because, in practice, the rhetorician, whether studying a present or past event as an end in itself, is also usually offering *critical analysis* of the event. In short, all rhetorical studies require description, but many rhetorical studies use rhetorical theory to evaluate and interpret the meaning of the event. We will distinguish between the two dominant methods used by communication researchers by using the term humanistic to refer to rhetorical/historical/critical research and use the term scientific to refer to social scientific research.

Humanism and science have some fundamental things in common as well as some fundamental differences. In this chapter we will describe these similarities and differences, particularly as they relate to the use of theory in the field. Again, we hope to show that the two approaches complement one another. First, we will take a look at science, its method in general, and specifically the role of theory.

SCIENTIFIC RESEARCH AND THEORY

As stated in Chapter 1, we believe that any collective human endeavor, including research of all kinds, must have as its ultimate goal the betterment of the human condition. Science contributes to this lofty goal through building theory. Fundamentally, the purpose of any science is to build theory about the phenomena that fall within the range of that scientific discipline. Communication theories provide explanations for, and predictions about, observed communication phenomena and their effects. In this section we are going to define theory formally, show how theory is built using the scientific method, and illustrate how theories are *useful* to researchers and practitioners alike.[9] Finally, we are going to take an example that demonstrates how science is self-correcting; that is, when mistakes are made, when theory is in error, the design of the methods of science detects the error and corrects the theory.

The term *theory* is used in many different ways. In everyday language we use the word as a synonym for a conjecture or a guess. For example, someone might say, ''I have a theory that he is lying,'' or ''my theory is the Democrats will pick a conservative candidate for president in 1992.'' People talk about something working in theory, but not in practice. They say that an idea is *merely* a theory.

In science, the word theory has a special use. Although scientists sometimes use the word in different ways, fundamentally, to a scientist theories are *statements about the relationships between abstract variables*. A simple theory might specify how only two or three variables are related. For example, a researcher who is interested in the effects of self-disclosure on relationship development might reason thusly:

> Self-disclosure by person A to person B results in B coming to the decision that A trusts B. It is rewarding to be trusted. People like to be trusted. It feels good. Therefore, people who indicate that they trust people are likely to be liked by other people. Thus, self-disclosure leads to increased liking. Person B will like person A as a result of A's self-disclosure to B.

This is a small theory, to be sure. It has only three variables: self-disclosure, perceived trust, and liking. Some might call this a *mini-theory* and reserve the word *theory* for more elaborate theories involving the relationships between many variables.

We are going to use Kerlinger's definition of scientific theory [10]:

> A theory is a set of interrelated constructs (concepts), definitions, and propositions that present a systematic view of phenomena by specifying relations among variables, with the purpose of explaining and predicting the phenomena.

It is often said that science has four purposes: description, explanation, prediction, and control. The following sections examine the key features of Kerlinger's
definition and observe how theory contributes to each of these purposes. Obviously, the kinds of research questions we ask are influenced by our purpose.

Description

A theory includes definitions of *variables*. But what is a variable? It is literally
anything we can think of that is changeable, that varies. Variables require definition. A good theory stipulates to what a variable, concept, or construct refers. Note
that Kerlinger speaks of concepts and constructs. The term *construct* is carefully
selected. Quite literally, the scientist builds or *constructs* the variables. They did
not exist before the scientist, working in the abstract world of symbols, created
them. And, since they are abstract creations, we need to know to what they refer.
The definitions constitute descriptions of categories of events. They are typologies,
conceptual schemes for organizing these events into manageable groups.

Explanation

A theory involves specifying the *relationships* between variables. If we know the
conditions under which events will occur, we can say that you have explained the
event. The specification of the relationships between independent and dependent
variables constitutes scientific explanation. An *independent variable* is the variable that is the cause of, or the antecedent to, or the predictor of, the dependent
variable. The *dependent variable* gets its name because it depends on the independent variable for its value.

   The concept of cause is controversial among philosophers and social scientists.
Some treatments of explanation emphasize the specification of causal relationships
as the ultimate goal to which science aspires.[11] Other writers, including Kerlinger,
feel that the notion of causality is not necessary for scientific understanding. Our
position is that causal thinking is such an integral part of human thinking that it
is difficult to conceive an orderly universe without it. Theories tell us which
independent variables cause which dependent variables to take on particular values.

   How do we know if the "relationship between variables" in Kerlinger's definition of theory is out there in the external world that we can see, feel, and hear?
In other words, how do we know that the explanation offered by the theory is
correct? The answer lies in the next level in which science operates: *prediction*.

Prediction

If we know the way that variables are related, it follows quite closely that knowledge of the value of an independent variable will allow us a good chance of
predicting the value of the dependent variable to which it is antecedent. If *X* occurs
and we know that *Y* follows, then we can predict: If *X*, then *Y*. If we know that
high source credibility results in more audience member attitude change than low

source credibility, we can predict that when there is high source credibility there will be more attitude change than when there is low source credibility among audience members. The test of a theory is whether the explanations it provides, that is, whether the relationship among the variables that are contained in its statements (frequently called *propositions*), allow for accurate predictions of observable events. Theories that allow accurate predictions are useful. We can think of them as correct. Theories that do not allow accurate predictions are not useful. We can think of them as incorrect. Accuracy, however, is a relative term. In most instances we use some type of inferential statistical test to determine whether the propositions are accurate or not. In this regard we test the hypothesis that, given some type of test, the relationships specified came about because of our knowledge and logic and not from chance.

Hypotheses   How do we know if a theory predicts accurately? We test it empirically. While the variables in a theory are abstract, when the time comes to test that theory, to make observations about whether the variables are related in the presumed ways, concrete definitions are necessary. These definitions *allow us to make hypotheses.* A *hypothesis*, like a theoretical proposition, is a statement of the relationship between variables. However, whereas theoretical propositions are abstract, hypotheses are more concrete statements. A *research hypothesis* predicts that changes in the dependent variable(s) will occur in specified ways due to the independent variable(s). Hypotheses, then, include variables that are less abstract and suggest implications for testing the prediction empirically.

Operational Definitions   To test theories the variables must be defined operationally. *Operational definitions* specify the procedures—literally the operations—the researcher engages in to observe the variable. Both the independent and dependent variables require operational definition. There are two general categories of operational definitions: manipulated and measured. We will discuss manipulated operational definitions first.

 If a researcher wanted to test the relationship between self-disclosure and liking, she might conduct an experiment in which a confederate—a person who appears to naive research participants to be another participant, but who in reality has been trained by the researcher—engaged in either a high or low degree of self-disclosure to the participant. The specific context that was created, the verbal and nonverbal messages emitted by the confederate in the two experimental conditions—high and low self-disclosure—would constitute the operationalization of the independent variable. The operational definition would be so specific as to include the actual message. For example:

> In the high self-disclosure conditions the confederate stated to the participants that (1) she had just taken an exam and failed it; (2) that she had caught her boyfriend on a date with another woman; and (3) that she was deathly afraid of catching herpes. In the low self-disclosure condition the confederate states that (1) she has just taken an exam and does not know how she has done; (2) she has a boyfriend; and (3) she was afraid of spiders.

Note that with this much detail other researchers have the potential to evaluate the research procedures and repeat the study.

The second kind of operational definition involves stating the procedures used to measure the concept. In the self-disclosure experiment, the researcher would need some way to assess the impact of high or low self-disclosure on the participants' degree of liking for the confederate. Most variables have many potential operational definitions and "liking" could be assessed in a variety of ways. The researcher might give a paper and pencil measure to the participants and ask them, "How much did you like the person you were paired with in this interaction?" The participant could be given scaled response options, such as: "I like them: A Great Deal, Somewhat, A Little, or Not at All. Or, the participant might be given an opportunity to sit next to the confederate on a sofa and the number of inches they sat apart could become the operationalization of "liking."

Independent variables can be manipulated *or* measured. Dependent variables are *always* measured. We shall have a good deal more to say about manipulated operational definitions in Chapter 9 and on measured operational definitions in Chapter 6.

Control

If we know that under certain conditions certain things will happen, we can sometimes control these conditions and achieve outcomes that are more favorable than they would have been otherwise. It is for purposes of *control* that the notion of causality becomes especially useful. If an independent variable is known to cause a dependent variable to take on a particular value, we have the potential to change the independent variable so that the dependent variable will take on the value *we want.* It is through the increased ability to control our social environments that communication theory offers the potential to contribute to a better world.

This basic idea is applicable at several levels. On the personal level, if we know that, under certain conditions, self-disclosure generally results in increased liking, we can self-disclose to someone under these conditions and increase the probability of their liking us. On a more global level, if we know that segregation leads to racism, we can make integration a national policy and reduce racism. Or, if we know that a particular message strategy used in public service advertisements will reduce the incidence of smoking among adolescent girls, we can use this strategy to achieve such an outcome. In short, theory creates the potential for controlling communication and its effects. And the better the theory, the better the control potential.

No doubt some are concerned that scientifically derived knowledge about human communication, that is, communication theory, has the potential to be put to evil ends—perhaps to control people for evil outcomes. (Hitler's use of propaganda is a commonly cited example.) There are several responses to this legitimate concern. First, remember that scientific knowledge is *public* knowledge; it is available to all scientists, and, in fact, quickly diffuses to the population as a whole. It shows up quickly in college and (later) high school textbooks, and it appears in such popular magazines as *The Atlantic, Harpers, The New Yorker, Psychology*

Today, and even *Woman's Day.* Just as knowledge of how to control people can be used to control them, the knowledge also can be used to prevent people from being controlled in undesirable ways. Second, everything turns out some way. Allowing "what will be to be" obviously results in a good many poor outcomes—loneliness, suicide, relational dissatisfaction, job unhappiness, poor group decisions, political fiascoes—and each such outcome shows that the world deviates from perfection. Knowledge gives us the potential to change these poor outcomes to more positive ones. Our view is that the potential benefits far outweigh the risks. [12]

The Utility of Scientific Theory

To the scientist, theories are both an end in themselves and the means to an end. Theory begets better theory, on and on. A theory tells a researcher what variables to look at and, by implication, what variables to ignore. If the theory is supported, that is, if observations reveal the variables to be related in the way stated by the propositions of the theory, then the scientist has increased confidence in it. He may refine it by adding new variables or expand its scope by making further observations to test it in other situations. If the theory is not supported by observation, the researcher must either modify the method of observation or modify the theory. Much like definitions of terms, theories are not true or false in any absolute sense. Rather, they are useful or not useful. To the extent that a theory provides explanations that allow accurate predictions, they are useful. To the extent they do not provide explanations that provide accurate predictions, they are not useful.

Theory tells the communication researcher what variables to study, what to observe. If you were interested in understanding the role that communication plays in relational satisfaction, you might start with a simple theory: Couples who talk a lot will be more satisfied than those who do not talk very much. Although the theory only has two variables—"amount of talk" and "relational satisfaction"—it nonetheless serves the important function of directing the researcher to look at certain variables and to ignore others. In this case, observations would be made about the amount of talk and about relational satisfaction. If the theory were more developed, it might make statements about the relationship between the kinds of information exchanged during the talk periods and relational satisfaction. You would then be able to look for the effect of the exchange of these types of information on satisfaction (either in general or examined as levels, such as high, moderate, and low satisfaction). As the theory was expanded, tested, modified, retested, refined, tested again, you would move closer and closer to a fuller understanding of communication and relationship satisfaction. The better the theory, the better able you will be to specify new variables to study.

Let us look at a concrete example of how theory is useful to the scientist. In January, 1986, a national tragedy occurred when the space shuttle *Challenger* exploded, killing all seven people on board, including school teacher Christa McAulliffe. Until this event, all 24 shuttle launches had been successful. Obviously, something was different on launch number 25. We can think of the shuttle "launch success" as a dependent variable. It is a variable because it can *vary,* that is, take on different values. The shuttle can be launched successfully or it can explode. The problem the various scientists and engineers faced immediately after the accident was to find out which of an almost limitless number of potential independent variables caused this launch to fail. For several days after the accident, there did not seem to be a clue as to what went wrong. The U.S. Navy and Coast Guard began collecting every bit of physical evidence they could find. Radio messages received from the shuttle were examined, as were vocal transmissions, and photographs. For several days, it looked pretty hopeless. There was even speculation that we might never find out why *Challenger* exploded.

Then NASA found a still photograph that appeared to show a plume of smoke emitted from one of the solid fuel booster rockets. Almost immediately, those investigating the accident focused on the booster rocket seals as a *possible* cause, that is, an independent variable. They now had a hunch, the beginnings of a theory. It told them what to look at and what to possibly ignore. Very quickly it was discovered that there had been trouble with and concern about the "O rings" that sealed the booster rockets sections. They now were to piece together the evidence and create their explanation as to why *Challenger* exploded. It was learned that cold affected "O ring integrity"; further photos showed a puff of white smoke from one of the seals at the moment of ignition of the rockets. Although government officials were cautious about making a hasty conclusion, and it was a full year before the O ring problem was officially proclaimed to have been the cause, it became very clear that this, in fact, was the key independent variable. As a result of this investigation, the booster rocket seals were redesigned.

This example also shows how theory is useful in controlling the environment. By identifying the independent variable, O ring integrity, that caused the particular effect on the dependent variable, shuttle launch success, the engineers and scientists were able to change the independent variables as a means of exerting control over the dependent variable. In this case a change in the way in which the O rings were used, or even eliminated from future booster rocket designs, affected the future shuttle launchings (environment). The ability to explain and predict provides the potential for control. And, as we now know, shuttle launches since the *Challenger* disaster have been controlled in a manner that has resulted in successful outcomes.

It may not be quite so obvious how theory is useful to the nonscientist. Imagine that you have just graduated from college and have taken a job as an organizational communication consultant. Your firm has been commissioned by a company to make recommendations about how to correct problems they are having at one of their manufacturing plants. Employee morale at the plant is at an all-time low. Absenteeism, turnover, tardiness, and poor work quality are all indications of the seriousness of the problem. Company management has no idea what is wrong, but, in desperation, they think it may have something to do with "communication." Thus your firm has been hired to make specific recommendations to correct the problem. And, they send you out to the plant to appraise the situation. Imagine, furthermore, two variations on the basic scenario: you arrive with no theory; or, you arrive with a whole briefcase full of theories.

Scenario 1: No Theory. What do you do? What do you look for? What could be the cause of these problems? What independent variables could be causing this dependent variable, employee morale, to take on such a low value? You have no idea. You are theoryless. Soon, you will also be jobless.

Scenario 2: Theory. What do you do? What do you look for? What could be the cause of these problems? What independent variables could be causing the problems? Your theories (those that you learned in your classes while in school as well as those you learn, refine, and test as a communication professional) will tell you exactly where to look, what to observe, whom to interview, what to study, and how to proceed.

You know, for example, that a well-supported theory indicates that employees who are allowed or encouraged to have input into decisions that affect their jobs are more likely to be committed to, and involved with, their jobs than are employees who have no such input. This theory is sometimes given as one of the reasons that Japanese managers, who typically use a more participatory form of management than their more autocratic American counterparts, have been so successful in producing high-quality goods. Armed with this knowledge, you examine the communication flow within the plant, specifically with an eye toward determining if employees are given the opportunity to have input into decisions that affect their jobs. If further investigation reveals that they have no such input opportunity, you have a good candidate for an independent variable that may provide a solution. If, on the other hand, your study reveals that the plant already has a well-run and thoroughly diffused quality circle program, a program specifically designed to provide such input, you will have to look in your briefcase again. Fortunately, it is full of theory, and will direct you what to look at next.

It has been said that, nothing is as practical as a good theory. What differentiates you, as a researcher in general and a communication researcher/scientist in particular, from those not trained in communication is the ability to identify the problems and those things that may be causing them. As philosopher Robert Dubin, writing on how science and theory can be applied to the work place, notes [13]:

> The scientist's and practitioner's views of what constitutes a 'problem' clearly differ. The practitioner operates with a finite world and continually grounds his decisions and predictions about how that finite world will be ordered. Problems occur when the predictions go wrong and decisions deriving from the predictions become inaccurate. . . . Absenteeism is a problem to a business executive because he would like to make decisions based on a prediction that would mean low absenteeism for his organization. For the scientist, the nature of an individual's attachment to an organization may be his analytical problem and he views absenteeism as a form of temporary disengagement, the reasons for which is one of his analytical tasks to discover.

Knowledge of theory allows both the practitioner and the scientist to solve their respective problems better.

Deductive Theory or Inductive Theory

As noted, the research process begins with a question about something that is unknown. There is a problem or obstacle that is not understood. The traditional approach to science would be to propose a solution, a theory. Then observations would be made about whether the proposed theory is correct. The model is basically *deductive;* the researcher *presumes* a relationship between particular variables ahead of time and then deduces a testable hypothesis. The theory precedes the research. It has to because the theory tells the researcher what variables to study.

Some philosophers of science have advocated an *inductive* approach to scientific theory building. Basically, an inductive approach would involve selecting a particular communication phenomenon and observing every identifiable variable that might conceivably be related to the phenomenon. The researcher would then sort through the data and look for patterns that may allow him or her to make a generalization. In short, the research precedes the theory.

This is essentially the approach that was used to study the space shuttle disaster. The engineers and scientists were looking at *everything.* However, they were in a unique situation of having virtually limitless resources and many extant measures of variables already available. Paul Reynolds is particularly critical of an inductive approach to theory building and we agree. [14] In the natural and social sciences, there are just too many *possible* variables to observe and too many ways that they might be related to expect patterns simply to "emerge." An inductive approach is, in general, terribly inefficient. Recall how slowly the space shuttle investigation proceeded *until* a theory was developed. We are proponents of the traditional deductive model of science: theory, then research, then better theory, then more research, and so on.

Self-Correctiveness

We asserted in Chapter 1 that science has a major advantage over other ways of answering questions, specifically, it is *self-correcting.* The rules of openness, of describing procedures in great detail, of tying claims about the nature of the world to systematic and reproducible observations, increase the chance that if mistakes are made, if claims about the relationship between variables are wrong, these procedural rules will help us identify and correct them. This is the ideal, the goal, but does it actually work? An examination of the risky-shift phenomenon shows one instance where it did.

The Risky-Shift Phenomenon: A Mistake Corrected   Group discussion and decision making has been written about and studied by communication researchers since the 1930s. How do groups reach decisions and how do these decisions compare to decisions made by individuals? In 1962, Michael Wallach and his colleagues reported an interesting finding in which groups of people were found to make decisions that were riskier than these same decisions made by individuals. [15] The finding was replicated among different populations and in a very short time became known as the *risky-shift phenomenon.* The finding quickly diffused into textbooks in group and interpersonal communication and in social psychology. The risky-shift phenomenon was now a "fact."

The methodology of the studies on this topic involved asking people how risky or conservative they would be in a variety of hypothetical "life dilemma" situations. Twelve such situations were described and the respondent was asked how great the chances of success would have to be before he or she would recommend that the riskier of two alternatives be selected. After they responded to all 12 situations individually, they were put into groups and asked to make group recommendations on the same 12 situations. As noted, the groups of people generally recommended increased risk taking, compared to their earlier individual responses. Virtually all of the earlier research on the risky-shift was conducted using the "life-dilemma" technique.

A number of years later, different researchers, using different measures of risk taking, failed to reproduce a group shift towards risk taking.[16] Other researchers subsequently went back to the early research and carefully examined the procedures that were used.[17] (Of course they were only able to do this because the procedures, including the operational definition of risk taking, were published in sufficient detail.) After careful consideration, the researchers felt the instructions might be conveying to respondents the idea that the original researchers wanted to find increased risk taking. Thus, they changed what they suspected were biased instructions and repeated Wallach, Kogan, and Bem's research. *Their results showed no risky-shift.* In fact, they found that if the instructions were changed so that participants were leaning toward a conservative direction prior to group discussion, the group decision would shift toward a more conservative position than had been the individual's prediscussion opinion.

To make a long story short, and many studies into a succinct point, we now know that under some circumstances groups will make systematically more *extreme* decisions than would be made by the individuals who constitute the group. This is referred to as a *group polarization phenomenon.* On any decision-making continuum, if the majority of the members of a group lean slightly in one direction or the other, they have a tendency to shift to a more extreme—a more polar— position as a result of group discussion.[18]

The important point is that a mistake was made about a question of fact. Carefully controlled, systematic observation of the world out there resulted in the mistake being identified and corrected. The methods of science, then, are designed to minimize human biases and fallibility as theory is tested and reevaluated.

HUMANISTIC RESEARCH AND THEORY

Inquiry into human communication is at least 2500 years old, probably older. The dialogues of Plato, and Aristotle's work, *Ars Rhetorica,* demonstrate that understanding the process by which we communicate is a fundamental area of human inquiry. These ancient Greeks, as well as the Romans such as Cicero and Longinus who followed them, were interested primarily in the "one-to-many" communication event, that is, public speaking. They focused on factors that made a public speech effective at influencing others such as the type of argument used and the ethos (credibility) of the speaker. These earliest of communication "theorists" wrote prescriptively; that is, they prescribed the ways to be persuasive when making a public speech. This knowledge about how to be an effective speaker was called *rhetoric*—the use of all available means of persuasion—and those who studied and described it were called *rhetoricians.*

Although this text emphasizes science, we are including a brief introduction to humanistic approaches to studying communication. Our view of humanistic research is that it usually has as its end the understanding of a particular event, person, or thing. This body of research in communication is typically labeled, historical, rhetorical, or critical method. The common thread running through each of these methods is their concern with the *uniqueness* and the *individualness* of the particular event, person, or thing; this uniqueness is sometimes studied as an end in itself, while at other times it is studied to shed light on a larger issue. As noted, the humanistic researcher's goals are similar to those of the scientist; that is, the humanistic researcher is striving to make the world a better place. The major differences, however, are the type of questions asked and the degree of subjectivity allowed in the methods used to obtain an answer. First, while the scientist is concerned with questions of fact, the humanistic researcher's questions usually deal with both questions of fact and questions of value, the world as it *ought* to be. How *was* something done and how *well* was that something done? Second, while the goal of science is objectivity and bias-free results, humanistic research tends to be more subjective and the answers to research questions more affected by the personal views of the researcher.[19]

Another difference between the humanistic method and the scientific method is found in *control* and *prediction.* Both methods strive to describe the phenomena they are studying. Both methods try to understand why what happened in the past happened the way it did. Science is more concerned with predicting the *relationships* between abstract variables. For the most part, the humanistic research emphasizes the study of past history, frequently focusing on how well the communicators operated. These major distinctions are the core of Chapter 5.

Before we continue, we should also note that other lengthy treatments of humanistic theory are available for both historical and rhetorical theories. It is important to understand the variety of other modes of analysis and perspectives on theory that exist. Although this book is oriented toward the social sciences, we feel that ignoring the contributions of humanism in communication theory—rhetorical theory, history, or rhetorical criticism—would produce a rather lopsided and short-sighted view of research and the process of research.

Indeed, as we noted in Chapter 1 and in the beginning of this chapter, theory is a way of looking at something. As you will find in the later chapters that emphasize scientific method, the theory formally stated tends to be *empirically* oriented and involve the relationship between abstract variables. The theory of the humanistic researcher tends to be more *qualitatively* or value-oriented. As Miller noted[20].

> Often students of speech communication study communicative phenomena for the purpose of arriving at ethical or aesthetic judgments about the phenomena themselves, or about the event, or events, with which the phenomena are associated. In short, they strive to articulate reasoned value judgments about a communicative act or acts.

Thus Miller argues that there are particular questions that can be better answered by methods other than science. These questions he suggests are those associated with specific events or people and questions dealing with whether the communication is good or bad, ethical or unethical, beautiful or ugly.

The traditional humanistic model presupposes a model emphasizing the particular over the general. This model suggests, rightly or wrongly, that an understanding of the practices will yield some general knowledge about human behavior.[21] This is not atheoretical, but presupposes that the communication act, behavior, or event will yield the theory. It is an inductive approach. As Michael C. Leff notes, "Theory [from the perspective of traditional humanistic critic] is the outcome of critical practice, not its starting point."[22] That is, beginning from the *act* is as valuable as observing that same act after establishing your theoretical perspective. Action, then, may, at a later time, yield theory.

Practice Versus Theory

As noted earlier, scientific method generally presupposes a deductive model; that theory comes before testing. In humanistic methods this, however, is not usually the case. Rather, the humanistic method is more concerned with the unique contributions of a particular person, event, or movement; that is, the norm is an in-depth understanding of a particular speech or related event; the focus is on the individual "act" or "event," not the wider ramifications of such communication. This approach is not universally accepted, however. Leff, for example, notes that[23]:

> [One] approach, which has dominated contemporary criticism, follows the model of conventional scientific and logical theories. It seeks to discover high order abstractions that inform or govern rhetorical practice, and these abstractions enjoy a privileged status whether the system works from general precepts to particular cases or from particular cases to general precepts. Thus, [traditional] theories eventuate in predicative generalizations or in extremely abstract models of the rhetorical transaction. Such theories provide an orderly direction for inquiry, and their proliferation has proved useful in breaking down the staid monism of earlier criticism.

In contrast, the traditional approach seems to suggest that theory is not paramount, except insofar as it illuminates and helps explain the unique contributions of the individual person, event, or thing.

What type of research would you conduct if you adopted the traditional approach? What if you were interested in the impact of former Alabama governor George Wallace's communication during the school desegregation years. What kinds of questions might you ask? Some interesting questions might include: Were Wallace's words his own or simply reflective of the sentiments of the specific time and constituents Wallace represented? Were Wallace's communications morally justified if they prevented violence and ultimately contributed to peaceful, albeit slower, desegregation? To answer these questions you would need to understand in great detail the goings on during the early 1960s in Alabama. You would have to know a lot about George Wallace, his background, and the situation as it existed at that time. Your answers would not generally be valid if compared to another politician, but would instead reflect your ability to get under his skin, or into his psyche. You would study his speeches, his stances, and look for central themes, you would look to see how he presented his messages, and you might center on one or two major themes as representative of his work.

On the other hand, you might address questions derived from a general rhetorical theory. In this use of theory, however, a real danger can be that the humanistic researcher will only see what he or she wants to see.[24] If we were interested in Wallace's political communication and our theory suggested that he only communicated from a "populist" perspective, then we would be looking for support for that theory. While you are working with an abstract theory, that theory may direct your "world view."

Which of the two views is correct and which incorrect? Probably neither. Both approach an understanding of a communication event, communicator, or communication object with the intent of asking questions that require value or valuelike responses. How well? Why? Answers to these questions do not always yield truthlike generalizations that can be applied to all communicators. Instead they tell us something about the aesthetic, ethical, and descriptive aspects of the communication. Their value lies in the uniqueness of the event, person, or object.

While the scientist strives to be an impartial observer, the humanistic researcher is sometimes a subjective participant in the communication event, whether that communication took place today, a hundred years ago, or a thousand years ago. The humanistic researcher becomes a critic looking at or for specific phenomena. Once these phenomena are found, he or she then examines how well certain principles were applied and with what effect. A distinct advantage comes from the fact that he or she already knows the outcome and can work out specifically what was "good" or "bad" about the communication.

The question of a methodological or theoretical "superiority" is not of concern here. The questions we ask will dictate the method we choose. If, as we have suggested, the type of question you seek to ask and the outcome you seek are amenable to one particular method, *adopt it*!

SUMMARY

This chapter suggests some theoretical foundations for conducting research in communication. It has extended the material in Chapter 1 by presenting two basic approaches to research: the scientific method and the humanistic method. In instances when you are interested in factual observations, empirical research, the method of science will be adopted. With this adoption you choose a method that begins with description, moves to explanation, and yields prediction. In order to use this method you must be prepared to take abstract concepts and create "concrete" variables. Ultimately, environmental control through theory building is the goal of scientific research.

The choice of science also provides the researcher with a self-correcting method. What we mean by this is that the method of achieving results is done in such a way (is reported through the literature) that others can seek to replicate or extend the research. In this regard other findings will either support or call into question the usefulness of the theory from which the research is derived.

Finally, we examined humanistic research. We noted that the humanistic approach examines the unique contributions of the communicator or communication. This approach usually seeks answers to questions of fact and value.

In the end, the method you adopt should parallel your research question. The quality of your research, then, is dependent upon the quality of your research question. A good question almost always suggests the methodological approach you should be taking.

PROBES

1. What relationships, if any, exist between research aimed at making generalizations and research aimed at making value statements? Should students of research be aware of the contributions from research models that take nomothetic, ideographic, and critical approaches to communication inquiry? Why or why not?

2. How does the scientist differ from the humanist? Or, is this a moot question since both are interested in understanding the human condition as it relates to communication?

3. What does *theory* provide the scientist? The nonscientist? Can both look at the same phenomenon? If they do, will they arrive at the same answers? Take a concept from your particular area of interest and examine it from first the scientist's point of view and then from the humanist's point of view.

4. If we were to assume that *all* communication researchers could be divided into either scientific or humanistic camps, into which would you fall? Why? What types of questions would you ask? What types of answers would you expect from your research approach?

5. Gerald R. Miller argues that communication researchers must *understand* both the scientific and humanistic approaches to research. Why? Is there a special *focus* in communication research that differs from other disciplines also interested in communication which may require both approaches be examined? Can you provide examples where this is true?

SUGGESTED READING

Dubin, R. (1969). *Theory building.* New York: The Free Press.

Lewin, K. (1951). *Field theory in social sciences.* New York: Harper.

Littlejohn, S. W. (1988). *Theories of human communication.* 3rd ed. Belmont, CA: Wadsworth.

Miller, G. R. (1975). Humanistic and scientific approaches to speech communication inquiry: Rivalry, redundancy, or rapprochement. *Western Journal of Speech Communication, 49,* 230–239.

Reynolds, P. D. (1971). *A primer in theory construction.* New York: Bobbs-Merrill.

Skinner, B. F. (1971). *Beyond freedom and dignity.* New York: Alfred A. Knopf.

NOTES

1. Gerald R. Miller, "Humanistic and Scientific Approaches to Speech Communication Inquiry: Rivalry, Redundancy, or Rapprochement," *Western Journal of Speech Communication* 49 (1975), 232.

2. Earl Babbie, *The Practice of Social Research,* 4th ed. (Belmont, Calif.: Wadsworth, 1986), 54–55.

3. Miller, 232.

4. Babbie, 54–55.

5. Many of the self-concept studies—and most that take their origins from symbolic interactionism, clinical psychology, and from instances where something has occurred with a particular speaker that is then generalized to other speakers—come from this tradition. In the area of organizational communication, because of its obvious closeness to management, many case studies produce findings that are then tested in the controlled conditions of the laboratory or in field experiments.

6. See Barnett Baskerville, "Must We All be Rhetorical Critics?" *Quarterly Journal of Speech,* 63 (1977), 107–116.

7. Miller, 235.

8. See Forbes Hill, "Conventional Wisdom—Traditional Form—The President's Message of November 3, 1969," *Quarterly Journal of Speech,* 58 (1972), 373–386; and Karlyn Kohrs Campbell, "Conventional Wisdom—Traditional Form: A Rejoinder," *Quarterly Journal of Speech,* 58 (1972), 451–454.

9. A thorough discussion of communication theory is beyond the scope of this book. For detailed treatments, see Don W. Stacks, Sidney R. Hill, and Mark Hickson, III, *An Introduction to Communication Theory* (Fort Worth: Holt, Rinehart & Winston, 1991); Sarah Trenholm, *Human Communication Theory* (Englewood Cliffs, N.J.: Prentice-Hall, 1986); and Stephen W. Littlejohn, *Theories of Human Communication,* 3rd ed. (Belmont, Calif.: Wadsworth, 1988).

10. Fred N. Kerlinger, *Foundations of Behavioral Research,* 3rd ed. (New York: Holt, Rinehart & Winston, 1986), 9.

11. See, for example, Hubert M. Blalock, Jr., *Theory Construction: From Verbal to Mathematical Formulations* (Englewood Cliffs, N.J.: Prentice-Hall, 1970).

12. See Buris F. Skinner, *Walden Two* (New York: Macmillan, 1948), and Buris F. Skinner, *Beyond Freedom and Dignity* (New York: Alfred A. Knopf, 1971) for a discussion of the issue of controlling human behavior through the knowledge gained through the methods of science.

13. Robert Dubin, "Theory Building in Applied Areas," in M. D. Dunnette, ed., *Handbook of Industrial and Organizational Psychology* (Chicago: Rand-McNally, 1976), 21.

14. Paul Davidson Reynolds, *A Primer in Theory Construction* (New York: Bobbs-Merrill, 1971).

15. Michael A. Wallach, Nathan Kogan, and Daryl J. Bem, "Group Influence on Individual Risk-Taking," *Journal of Abnormal and Social Psychology,* 65 (1962), 75–86. The finding was originally reported in P. Stoner, "A Comparison and Group Decisions Involving Risk," unpublished master's thesis, Massachusetts Institute of Technology.

16. See D. E. Clement and D. W. Sullivan, "No Risky Shift With Real Groups and Real Risks," *Psychonomic Science,* 18 (1970), 243–244.

17. R. D. Clark and S. E. P. Willems, "Where Is the Risky Shift: Dependence on Instructions," *Journal of Personality and Social Psychology,* 13 (1969), 215–221.

18. D. G. Myers and M. F. Kaplan, "Group Induced Polarization in Simulated Juries," *Personality and Social Psychology Bulletin,* 2 (1976), 63–66.

19. See Philip Wander and Steven Jenkins, "Rhetoric, Society, and the Critical Response," *Quarterly Journal of Speech,* 58 (1972), 441–450.

20. Miller, 235–236.

21. See, for example, Edwin Black, ''A Note on Theory and Practice in Rhetorical Criticism,'' *Western Journal of Speech Communication*, 44 (1980), 331–336.
22. Michael C. Leff, ''Interpretation and the Art of the Rhetorical Critic,'' *Western Journal of Speech Communication*, 44 (1980), 343.
23. Leff, 348.
24. Black.

Chapter 3

Considerations: Knowledge, Ethics, and Science

*E*thics deals with questions of value about whether something is right or wrong. Consciously and unconsciously we make ethical judgments every day. Based on these judgments we engage in daily behaviors. Ethical judgments are made in research situations just as they are made in social and business situations. Ethical questions include: Is it okay to cite an original source in a paper we are writing for a class even though we only read about what the original source said in another source; in other words, is it ethical to cite a secondary source? Does a political candidate's campaign commercial unfairly distort his opponent's record? Should we tell a friend that his girlfriend has been dating another man? Can we give a highly physically attractive member of the opposite sex "the benefit of a doubt at grade time'' because he or she came by the professor's office and was friendly several times during the term? Must we leave a note on the windshield of a car that we barely scratched in the parking lot? Should we allow our friend to cut in line to get good concert tickets even though the people behind us have waited all night for the same coveted tickets? Like most questions of value, the answers to these questions are not always simple or obvious.

Until recently, chapters on ethics did not appear in research methods books. There are probably several reasons for this neglect. First, ethics, by definition, concerns questions of value: What is right and wrong, what is good and bad. And, as we noted in Chapter 1, science cannot do much to answer such questions. Sometimes the results of empirical research can help us decide if something is right or wrong, but, ultimately, it is the individual who makes this decision. The locus of the answer to value questions lies within us.

Second, some ethical issues are so fundamental, so universally accepted, that they have been taken for granted. Here we are speaking of basic rules of scholarship, such as giving appropriate credit for ideas, reporting the results of research in an impartial and complete way, and describing openly and honestly any flaws or weaknesses in research procedures. Unfortunately, many of us have assumed that these kinds of basic rules of scholarship are so obvious that everyone, including our students, are explicitly aware of them. It is as if some things are known at birth—they never need mentioning.

An especially important area of ethics concerns how humans who participate in our research projects are treated. Yet even this area was scarcely mentioned until about 15 years ago. Most researchers, we believe, just assumed that they themselves treated their human participants (sometimes called ''subjects,'' a label we will explore later in this chapter) ethically, and so did their colleagues. To even raise the question of ethical treatment seemed to imply that they, or their colleagues, might be doing some things that were ''wrong,'' which, of course, they would not do. And, anyway, the researcher seemed to be saying: We are after *knowledge* here. If some people are damaged in the process that is just a necessary price to pay for the advancement of the common good. And finally, researchers could be secure in the knowledge that if their research procedures did harm the subjects, the *debriefing* would erase any negative effects. There is a general human tendency to place a high value on one's activities, including one's research projects. Many researchers seem to believe that the intrinsic value of their research offsets any harm that might accrue to participants.

We will spend some time addressing four ethical issues relevant to all research. (1) Are the basic rules of scholarship being followed? (2) Have the participants in the project been adequately informed of the procedures involved, including any potential risks that may be involved (physical and psychological), and with this knowledge, freely consented to participate? Is an adequate debriefing provided to the participants and do they have an opportunity to ask questions of the researcher after the study has been completed? (3) Is deception appropriate? (4) Is the topic being studied ethically appropriate? We begin our analysis of these issues with the one we feel is most basic to *all* research methods: rules of scholarship.

RULES OF SCHOLARSHIP

Recently, we had three experiences that brought into focus the importance of including an explicit discussion of some of the basic rules of scholarship. In the first case a student turned in a paper that reviewed the literature of a narrow subarea of communication. The student, a well-intentioned, bright, and hard-working individual, was attempting to summarize the results of several research articles and then offer some ideas of her own that would reconcile any inconsistency between several studies. Being somewhat of a neophyte at writing papers of this sort, the paper was awkwardly worded. Embedded within the paper were bits and pieces—a sentence here, a paragraph there—of professional social scientific writing. How could the student be so uneven in her style? An examination of the articles reviewed in the paper revealed the answer. A sentence here, a paragraph there—had been copied directly from the papers being reviewed. There is nothing wrong with doing this, *except*—and this is extremely important—there was no indication of the fact that this material was not original. The reader of the paper could not easily discern, except by writing ability in this case, which parts of the paper came from the student and which came from the articles being reviewed. Was the student behaving unethically? Not if ignorance of the law, of the rules of scholarship in this case, is an excuse. She did not know that what she had done was inappropriate. When the problems with her paper were discussed, she was embarrassed, upset, and apologetic. She was simply ignorant of how to *reference* sources appropriately.

A second experience was more serious. In one instance an upperclassman was required to write a review of a particular theoretical perspective in a persuasion course. The paper he turned in was excellent; it was well written, had all the catch words, and even began with an abstract. A close reading, however, found an opening quotation mark at the start of the title and a closing quotation mark at the end of the reference section. The student had copied, word for word, an article that reviewed this particular area. He had mistakenly assumed that since he enclosed it in quotation marks that he had fulfilled his ethical obligations.

The third case was more clear-cut. It dealt with the buying of a paper for a class. In this instance students were required to write short, five-to-ten-page papers for the course. A number of students in this class needed a passing grade in this course in order to graduate. When reading the papers it became apparent very quickly that several students had chosen the same topic and even the same sources to quote. After reading several papers it became clear that the papers *were* the same, only a few sentences here and there were modified to make the papers "different." When this was brought to the students' attention they, like others, were embarrassed, upset, and apologetic. However, they freely admitted to *buying* the papers. In their minds, while the purchase would be wrong and unethical if they had turned in the papers without revision, that revision made it ethical. The penalty for such practice—obviously unethical—was quite severe.

Scholarship Considerations

Unfortunately, these are not isolated cases. It happens every day on campuses all over the country. A survey conducted by Jerold Hale suggests that *most* college students have plagiarized written work for college classes.[1] And we believe the problem is not that students intentionally do unethical things, although, of course, some do. The problem is that there is no formal and systematic way to assure that everyone knows the rules of scholarship. Reviewing some of these rules might help to clear up the sometimes blurred distinction between ethical and unethical scholarship.

1. Give Appropriate Credit for One's Ideas   The most fundamental rule of all scholarship is to credit other people's ideas and statements, whether a direct quotation from a source or the paraphrasing of ideas. Furthermore, you must completely give credit, in terms of textual statements (through quotation marks or setting off the material if it is a long quote) and referencing. Different style manuals advocate different ways to give credit. We are not going to review those here, but you might want to purchase one or two and familiarize yourself with the requirements. Two of the most widely used are those of the American Psychological Association (APA) and the Modern Language Association (MLA).

2. Report Conflicting Evidence and All That You Find   Not all that you read or learn will support your own personal view of the world. In research you will almost always find results that differ from each other. It is your responsibility to report *all* that you find, refuting what you can, accepting as valid other views if they cannot be refuted. Remember, in many instances you will be more knowledgable in the area than your reader and you have a certain responsibility to make sure that he or she understands both sides of the issue or question being addressed.

There is a natural tendency to put our best foot forward. We all like to find what we set out to find, to support some hypothesis or refute some question. Unfortunately, many times we either fail to get results that support our thesis or only partially support it at best. In such cases it is easy to gloss over that which was *not* found in favor of the more favorable results. Part of doing research is to accept the responsibility for failure. In so doing you may actually help yourself or others later by a frank assessment of why you did not find what you expected. The reasons may be many, but perhaps you found new documents, a new way to analyze the facts you explored, or (in the scientific method) were unable to duplicate exactly the conditions of the study as you proposed. These problems must be emphasized, not deemphasized.

3. Describe the Flaws in Your Research   This follows from the previous requirement. What problems came up that may have invalidated your results?

What were the flaws? If your study dealt with physical attraction, for instance, were your manipulations of attraction too subtle? Not subtle enough? In a humanistic study, did you choose the most appropriate documentation? Did you have access to the *original* materials? By including your flaws you allow others to understand why your interpretations are as they are and provide information for new and perhaps better research.

4. Use Primary Sources Whenever Possible   A primary source is the research as presented by the author in whatever form it was originally distributed to the public. Careful citation requires more than the correct use of quotation marks and footnote systems. Be clear when you are paraphrasing: do not just provide the explanation, include phrases such as "the authors go on to explain." After doing an enormous amount of research you would probably like to be cited in someone else's work. It is a courtesy to reference others' work, but it is also a necessity and allows the reader to understand the theoretical background from which you are coming. In general, when not sure whether to reference or not, it is much better to include the reference.

Part of the method of research deals with understanding that all people perceive things differently. Whenever possible get to the original source. It is very tempting to rely on others, but your interpretation of the event fits your theory much more closely than even that of your best friend. As will be pointed out in Chapter 4 and Chapter 5, secondary and even tertiary evidence has its place in research, but only under certain conditions. If you do use secondary or tertiary sources, write "cited in . . . ." As a general rule, however, primary sources are usually the ones on which we depend.

5. Honesty and Integrity Go Hand in Hand   We assume that research and the reporting of that research is done in an honest manner. The integrity of the author (and, to a degree, the integrity of all those with whom you have studied or worked) is on the line. Most academic institutions have academic integrity codes. It is in your best interest to investigate your institution's integrity statement.

6. When Working in Groups Give Appropriate Credit for Work   When the end product is in final form (paper, article, book, film, tape, or in-house monograph) *all* associated with the project are assumed to share equally in responsibility and credit. If one person contributed more than others, that should be stated in a footnote (this is usually done when there are multiple authors and responsibility is shared by all). In classroom projects, for example, failure to include a coauthor's name could result in that person failing the assignment. Similarly, it is frequently a good idea to include footnotes thanking others who helped significantly during the design and analysis stages.

7. All Research Is Conducted Under a General Ethical Code   Major professional associations have specific codes of ethics. These codes provide the basic rules for scholarship in a given field. You should be familiar with how each field views scholarship. Ignorance is no excuse for unethical scholarship.

All these rules are enforced most rigorously in an academic environment. But they are rules that should be used in other environments as well. Consider the following example: An associate of ours worked as a city planner. It was routine when putting together zoning reports in the planning office to pull entire paragraphs from other zoning reports, even from textbooks on how to write zoning reports. There is nothing wrong with this, per se, *if* appropriate credit is given. Certainly those individuals whose lives are being affected by the zoning decisions have the right to know from where the specific wording and justification for the decisions that are made are coming.

In business and politics, do the same principles apply? Recently there has been a general questioning of the ethics of people in general and certain groups—lawyers, stockbrokers—in particular. A related issue concerns the use of ghostwriters to produce political speeches. Political leaders are frequently judged by the quality of their speeches. However, many of these speeches are written by someone other than the speaker. For example, former President Ronald Reagan's speeches were so good that he was sometimes described as "the great communicator." George Bush's acceptance speech at the 1988 Republican National Convention was generally judged to be outstanding, and to have contributed significantly to his successful fall campaign. As it turns out, many of Mr. Reagan's speeches and Mr. Bush's acceptance speech were written by one of their employees, Peggy Noonan. This same ethical issue exists in business: corporate executives often have their speeches ghostwritten. If we may offer a value judgment, the basic rules of scholarship should apply here as well. (See Box 3.1.) Part of a liberal education should be to reinforce such fundamental values as truth and honesty, the basis of the rules of scholarship.

TREATMENT OF HUMAN SUBJECTS (PEOPLE)

Imagine that you have been given an assignment in an introductory communication class to participate in a research project being conducted in the department that is offering your class. Furthermore, imagine this is your first term and you have been having a rough time of it so far. You have not made too many friends. Your self-concept, never as high as you would like, is at an all-time low. You have even considered quitting school and returning to mom's home-cooking. But if you do, your parents, who have taken second jobs to help send you here, will be disappointed.

Well, at least you are in an *interpersonal* communication course. No speeches. A poll you once read showed that public speaking is Americans' biggest fear, ranking even ahead of death. No wonder—you do not have to make any speeches when you are dead.

So you show up at the designated time and place to participate in a research project to complete the course assignment. A distinguished, authoritative, and important-looking man comes into the waiting room, introduces himself as Dr. Smith, the project director, and goes on to explain that the research involves studying how effective people can be when they make speeches on various topics,

Box 3.1 # Turning Some Light On '1,000 Points'
Mike Royko

Let's have a brief literary quiz. Please, don't run away, it won't be heavy stuff.

I will give you a phrase, and you name the author. If you miss it the first time, don't worry. You get three guesses.

The phrase is: "A thousand points of light."

See? I told you it wouldn't be hard. You said George Bush. You may even know when and where he used it.

The first time was at the Republican convention, when he accepted his party's nomination in a finely crafted speech.

He said: "This is America . . . a brilliant diversity spread like stars, like a thousand points of light in a broad and peaceful sky."

And he used it again in his inaugural address when he said: "I have spoken of 'a thousand points of light' of all the community organizations that are spread like stars throughout the nation, doing good."

So if you identified the author of that phrase as George Bush, uh, sorry, but you're wrong.

But you have two more guesses, so try again.

If you are a student of politics, a Washington insider, or a political journalist, I know what you're saying. You probably had it as your first guess.

Peggy Noonan, right? Ms. Noonan is an outstanding political speech writer, and it's generally acknowledged that she wrote Bush's acceptance speech.

The White House press office won't come right out and say that she wrote the "thousand points of light" phrase. But a White House source says, yes, she did.

So if you guessed that Ms. Noonan authored the "thousand points of light" phrase, sorry, you're wrong, too.

But don't feel bad. I would have flunked my own quiz. My first guess would have been Ms. Noonan, since I knew she wrote the speech.

I knew it couldn't have originated with President Bush, because he would have been more likely to say: "I want to tell you about this points of lights thing. We have about one thousand of them. They represent this goodness thing."

So you have one more guess. Take your time. You have three seconds.

Give up?

The answer was provided for me by an irate and sharp-eyed man named Ray Riley, who lives in Seekonk, Mass.

Mr. Riley says: "I would like to suggest that George Bush's main campaign theme was borrowed unlawfully, in other words plagiarized.

"The definition of plagiarism is to steal and pass off the ideas or words of others as one's own; use without crediting the source; to commit literary theft; present as new and original an idea or product derived from an existing work."

And what is this existing work? Actually, there are two. Both are books written by novelist Thomas Wolfe, who died in 1938.

In "You Can't Go Home Again," Wolfe describes America this way: (the italics are mine.)

"It's your pasture now, and it's not so big—only three thousand miles from east to west, only two thousand miles from north to south—but all between, where ten thousand points of light prick out the cities, towns and villages, there, seeker, you will find us burning in the night."

OK, I concede that Wolfe saw 10,000 points of light, while Bush-Noonan saw only 1,000 points of light.

But wait. We then have Wolfe writing in "The Web and The Rock" about a character's longing to be back in his home.

Wolfe wrote: "And instantly he would see the town below now, coiling in a thousand fumes of homely smoke, now winking into a thousand points of friendly light . . ." Because of this, the irate Mr. Riley said:

"The political right has heaped praise on Bush for his points of light theme, calling it brilliant and visionary. There is nothing brilliant, nothing visionary, nothing even remotely admirable about stealing."

Oh, I don't know.

Assuming that Bush-Noonan did pilfer the thousand points of light from Thomas Wolfe, they should at least be credited with having good taste. Wolfe isn't easy to read, but he's generally accepted as something of a literary genius.

So in that regard, Bush has already moved beyond Ronald Reagan, who plucked many of his lines and anecdotes from old B-movies.

Reprinted by permission: Tribune Media Services.

and, that you are going to be required to make a speech to a group of visiting high school students. Dr. Smith escorts you to another room and explains your topic: You are going to have to try and convince the students that marijuana should be legalized. This is something that you definitely do not agree with and you wonder how on earth you are going to make the speech. Dr. Smith gives you a sheet of paper with the outline of a few arguments that he tells you to use in your speech. You will have 15 minutes to prepare. You start to shake. You are panic-stricken. There is no way you can make any speech, let alone one advocating the legalization of marijuana.

Gamely, you do your best to prepare, you jot down some notes and in 15 minutes Dr. Smith returns and escorts you to a room full of videotape equipment. He explains that a nearby room is full of high school students who are anxious to hear you speak. They will be watching you on television. Your heart is pounding, your palms are sweating, your knees are literally knocking, you start to talk into the camera, but you are so nervous you can barely speak. All you can think of is how embarrassing this is, how everyone watching can tell how nervous and inarticulate you are. Near the end of the speech, which lasts for 5 minutes but seems like 30, you nearly break down and start to cry.

A few minutes later, Dr. Smith enters the room and walks with you down a very long corridor to still another room. As you walk along he is looking through some sheets of paper and casually mentions that these are evaluations of your speech that were just filled out by the students who watched you on television. He gives them to you, explaining that he is sure you will be interested to see how you did. As you read the evaluation forms your worst feelings are confirmed. You did make a fool of yourself. The student comments indicate that you are stupid, nervous, tongue-tied, crazy for wanting to legalize marijuana, and worse. You have never felt lower. After arriving at the last waiting room, you are given a questionnaire to fill out. It asks, among other things, how you feel about the legalization of marijuana.

Finally, you are taken into still another room where another researcher asks you what your understanding is of the purpose of this research project. You explain, as best you can, that it was a study of how effective people can be in making speeches. The researcher then proceeds to debrief you. He explains that the real purpose of the research was to see if people who advocated a position that was different from what they believed would change their beliefs to be more consistent with what they stated in the speech. Furthermore the researchers wanted to see how the speaker's beliefs about the success of their speech affected any change in their opinion about the topic of the speech. There were, in fact, no high school students watching your speech. The forms you saw were filled out ahead of time and half the subjects in this experiment were shown forms that indicated that their speeches were well received.

In other words, you have been lied to, repeatedly and convincingly. You not only bought the lie but you just went through one of the most miserable experiences of your life. How do you feel?

This example is real, and the experience of designing and participating in this study served at least one very important function: It made the researchers realize the importance of ethical treatment of human participants. This sensitivity is important because there have been many abuses of human subjects in the past. For many years, there was no formal code of ethics regarding the treatment of human subjects. However, as examples of abuses came to light, in the early 1970s, the American Psychological Association, an organization representing over 35,000 psychologists as well as a good many communication researchers, appointed a committee to develop standards for ethical conduct. Because of the importance and almost universal acceptance of these standards, we believe that you should be both familiar with and understand what they say and mean. Box 3.2 lists the ten "principles" of ethical behavior the researcher should follow.[2]

From your reading of these principles you should identify six major themes. First, the researcher must accept ethical responsibility for the research project. This responsibility goes beyond simply saying "I am responsible for the research." It includes a clearly thought out research plan tied closely to the research question or hypotheses (theory) under test. The researcher must also ensure that those who are working with him or her understand the implications of the research and must take responsibility for the actions of these assistants, as well as ensure that all involved are treated fairly and equitably.

Suppose for a moment that you are interested in conducting a research project that will examine the effect of distraction on persuasion. In carrying out this study you must carefully weigh the possible benefits with potential risks. Will your research cause harm? Will psychological damage occur? Will the strength of the message without their knowledge, cause message recipients to change their attitudes in a way to which they object?

The question is then, is a topic such as the legalization of heroin, ethically appropriate? Several studies have used a message on this topic in persuasive research.[3] While preparing the stimulus messages much thought was given to this, especially the ethical ramifications of whether or not the message created problems for the *research itself*. These questions are concerned with value; hence, the researcher shoulders the ethical responsibility.

The second theme you should observe in the principles concerns *informed consent*. First, you must tell your participants *basically* what they will be doing. This is not to say that you must tell them exactly what your purpose is, as that could cause problems with the study, but you must inform them of the procedures and any possible risk. Second, you must allow your participants to decline participation. You must allow those who do not wish to participate, for whatever the reason, the ability to withdraw *at any point in the study*. This should be made clear in the Participant's Informed Consent Form (see Box 3.3). Use of such a form protects both the participant and the researcher. On this form you will tell the prospective "subject" approximately what you are doing and how it will be done (more on this follows). The general procedures the participant will follow should be outlined and any potential risk identified. Both researcher and volunteer sign the form.

Consider the speech research project described earlier. If you had been informed in advance that you had the right to withdraw from the project, would you have? If the project was for class credit, then you would have to have an opportunity to earn those credits in some other way, perhaps by submitting an additional paper. Had the researcher carefully laid out in general the procedures, the student may not have felt as negatively as he or she did about the research.

The third theme follows from this discussion. At times the researcher must engage in *deception* to get genuine reactions or behaviors. Such practice must be justified and immediately after participation the "subject" must be told of such deception and have the reason for it explained. Much social science research engages in some form of deception. Imagine what the results of your study might be if you told your participants exactly what you were trying to find. Would they behave normally, or would they try to "help" you get the results for which you are looking? Obviously, many would try to help.[4]

The practice of deception also may be necessary with your helpers, people we call confederates. A confederate is someone helping with the research. We must be careful that the confederate does not try to "help" get results. In most instances it is best if the confederate knows only as much as is needed to do his or her job. After the research has been completed, you have an ethical responsibility to debrief all confederates and other helpers as to the "real" procedures of the research.

The fourth theme concerns the risk you put participants to in the study. In

Box 3.2 **APA Code of Research Ethics**

The decision to undertake research rests upon a considered judgment by the individual psychologist about how best to contribute to psychological science and human welfare. Having made the decision to conduct research, the psychologist considers alternative directions in which research energies and resources might be invested. On the basis of this consideration, the psychologist carries out the investigation with respect and concern for the dignity and welfare of the people who participate and with cognizance of federal and state regulations and professional standards governing the conduct of research with human participants.

A. In planning a study, the investigator has the responsibility to make a careful evaluation of its ethical acceptability. To the extent that the weighing of scientific and human values suggests a compromise of any principle, the investigator incurs a correspondingly serious obligation to seek ethical advice and to observe stringent safeguards to protect the rights of human participants.

B. Considering whether a participant in a planned study will be a "subject at risk" or a "subject at minimal risk," according to recognized standards, is of primary ethical concern to the investigator.

C. The investigator always retains the responsibility for ensuring ethical practice in research. The investigator is also responsible for the ethical treatment of research participants by collaborators, assistants, students, and employees, all of whom, however, incur similar obligations.

D. Except in minimal-risk research, the investigator establishes a clear and fair agreement with research participants, prior to their participation, that clarifies the obligations and responsibilities of each. The investigator has the obligation to honor all promises and commitments included in that agreement. The investigator informs the participants of all aspects of the research that might reasonably be expected to influence willingness to participate and explains all other aspects of the research about which the participants inquire. Failure to make full disclosure prior to obtaining informed consent requires additional safeguards to protect the welfare and dignity of the research participants. Research with children or with participants who have impairments that would limit understanding and/or communication requires special safeguarding procedures.

E. Methodological requirements of a study may make the use of concealment or deception necessary. Before conducting such a study, the investigator has a special responsibility to (1) determine whether the use of such techniques is justified by the study's prospective scientific, educational, or applied value; (2) determine whether alternative procedures are available that do not use concealment or deception; and (3) ensure that the participants are provided with sufficient explanation as soon as possible.

F. The investigator respects the individual's freedom to decline to participate in or to withdraw from the research at any time. The obligation to protect this freedom requires careful thought and consideration when the investigator is in a position of authority or influence over the participant. Such positions of authority include, but are not limited to, situations in which research participation is required as part of employment or in which the participant is a student, client, or employee of the investigator.

G. The investigator protects the participant from physical and mental discomfort, harm, and danger that may arise from research procedures. If risks of such consequences exist, the investigator informs the participant of that fact. Research procedures likely to cause serious or lasting harm to a participant are not used unless the failure to use these procedures might expose the participant to risk of greater harm or unless the research has great potential benefit and fully informed and voluntary consent is obtained from each participant. The participant should be informed of procedures for contacting the investigator within a reasonable time period following participation should stress, potential harm, or related questions or concerns arise.

H. After the data are collected, the investigator provides the participant with information about the nature of the study and attempts to remove any misconceptions that may have arisen. Where scientific or humane values justify delaying or withholding this information, the investigator incurs a special responsibility to monitor the research and ensure that there are no damaging consequences for the participant.

I. Where research procedures result in undesirable consequences for the individual participant, the investigator has the responsibility to detect and remove or correct these consequences for the participant.

J. Information obtained about a research participant during the course of an investigation is confidential unless otherwise agreed upon in advance. When the possibility exists that others may obtain access to such information, this possibility, together with the plans for protecting confidentiality, is explained to the participant as part of the procedure for obtaining informed consent.

some studies psychological damage can occur. Imagine if you were engaged in a study of negotiation and, although you were told that nothing would actually happen to your "hostage" or "workers," your negotiation caused those people "harm." Such a study might entail you creating messages to another party and getting back bogus messages that attack your negotiating skills. What *potential* damage might this cause to your psyche at a later time and place, perhaps when you actually began negotiating for a pay raise? The researcher must keep this in mind. Part of accounting for risk concerns the debriefing the participant will receive after completing the project.

Most communication research has minimal risk attached to it. But, for example, some of the research into message processing is beginning to use physiological measures. In accessing physiological data the researcher must "hook" the participant to electrical equipment. The risk involved here is minimal, but the participant must be informed that he or she will be hooked to a machine with electrodes. In

Box 3.3 **Participant's Informed Consent Form**

Project Director:

Project Title: Analysis of Behavior in Problem-Solving Groups

The purpose of this research project is to examine how people operate in problem-solving groups. Students are being asked to view a segment of a group interaction that was conducted for an advanced course in group processes. After viewing the group in operation each student will be asked to complete a series of scales and respond to a number of questions about their perceptions of the group.

By signing this form you agree to view the videotaped group segment and evaluate the group via the scales and questions provided. No attempt will be made to identify you through your responses to the questions and scales; please do not make any identifying marks on your response packet.

Signing this form also acknowledges that you have been given the opportunity to withdraw from participation in this project without penalty.

_____   _____

Student's Signature   Date

_____

Project Director

studies of deception the researcher may use an electrocardiograph to assess heart rate as the participant is asked questions. Although there is very little risk here, the participant must know the procedures involved and feel confident that the researcher can use the equipment competently.

When using procedures that may constitute high risk, the researcher must accept any future responsibility to correct for any long-term consequences. No waiver of responsibility actually reduces the ethical responsibility of the researcher here. As noted, however, very few communication research projects will deal with actual physical harm. However, the question of psychological damage is always a possibility and should be considered when designing the study.

Fifth, the researcher must ensure anonymity or confidentiality of the data collected. *Anonymity* means that no one, including the researcher, knows who gave which responses. *Confidentiality* means that only the researcher knows who gave the responses. This means that once the participant has completed the study, his or her responses are maintained in such a way that only the researcher actually knows who responded in what way. In cases where participants must be identified later to assess if time factors in the study, confidentiality may become a problem, but can be dealt with by assigning numbers to participants or using special codes. Ethically, however, the researcher must protect the confidentiality of the participant. Obviously, if he or she must know who is who, then the data must be guarded carefully.

Sixth, the researcher is responsible for debriefing the participant. Because the debriefing process is so very important, and because it is controversial, we will treat this aspect of research in detail. In fact, the quality of the debriefing may determine whether or not the entire project is ethical.

DEBRIEFING

Debriefing refers to the postexperimental explanation that is provided to research participants at the conclusion of participation. There are at least four important purposes to be served by debriefing. First, a debriefing should erase any negative effects that may have resulted from participation. Second, debriefing should establish or maintain a favorable relationship between participants and researchers. Third, debriefing should make having participated in the research educational for participants by explaining thoroughly what has been done, how, and why. Finally, competent debriefing procedures provide researchers with feedback relevant to the efficacy of the research procedures. Unfortunately, the topic has seldom been mentioned in research methods textbooks. The intent of the following discussion is to emphasize the importance of the debriefing.

Eliminating Harmful Effects

Many kinds of communication research have potentially harmful consequences for participants. In the "counterattitudinal advocacy" study that was described earlier in this chapter first-year college students were presented with a situation in which they were required to give a short speech in front of a television camera. They were told falsely that an audience in another room was watching their presentation. The situation was carefully controlled to ensure that even though participants were nominally told they could decline to make the speech, few of them would exercise this option. Some of them were extremely anxious in this situation and, as described in the example, some were visibly shaken by the experience. At least one experienced such a high degree of anxiety that she could not finish the speech. It is highly probable that participating in this research was harmful to the self-concepts of at least some participants.

If research procedures do result in harm of any kind, the debriefing must eliminate this harm. The effectiveness of debriefing thus becomes a crucial determinant of whether or not the research project is ethical. Unfortunately, little is known about the effectiveness of debriefing in such situations. The one empirical study that has addressed this question explicitly provides results that are so important and illuminating that we will describe it in some detail.

Elaine Walster and her colleagues conducted an experiment designed to see if a careful debriefing eliminated any lingering negative effects resulting from participation in an experiment even after participants were thoroughly and carefully debriefed.[5] Participants were told that the study dealt with how socially skilled individuals were. They were required to respond to a questionnaire that was purported to measure their social skills. Half of the participants, selected at random, were falsely told that they had scored at the eighteenth percentile, meaning that fully 82 percent of the people who took the test were more skilled socially than they were. Furthermore, they were given a written profile stating that "they were reluctant to become involved with others, they could not express their real feelings to others, and that they lacked self-insight to the point of being largely unaware of these shortcomings." The participants then were given time to read and think about this highly critical feedback. The other half were given positive feedback about their social skills. They were told that they scored at the ninetieth percentile, meaning that only 10 percent of those taking the test were more skilled. They also received highly favorable written evaluations.

All participants were given a thorough, individual debriefing that took a minimum of 20 minutes. They were told that the questionnaire they had filled out had no validity whatsoever, that the feedback they received was completely false, and that they had been assigned to the positive and negative feedback conditions randomly. They were shown the version of the feedback material that the participants in the other conditions received. The debriefing was terminated only after it was clear that the participants understood that the feedback reports had nothing to do with their actual degree of social skills. Finally, they were asked to provide self-report measures of their perception of their own level of social skills.

The critical finding was this: Participants who were given unfavorable feedback about their social skills now rated themselves as less socially skilled than did those who received the favorable feedback. In other words, the debriefing was not entirely successful in eliminating a very obvious negative effect that resulted from participation in a research project. Whether a different debriefing strategy would have been more effective is unknown. Perhaps participants, given time during the experiment to think about their critical feedback evaluations, recalled and reinterpreted events in their lives in a manner that was consistent with this new evaluation. Whatever the explanation, it was obvious that their self-concepts were altered more profoundly than even a careful debriefing could erase. The important point is that we cannot immediately assume that a debriefing erases negative effects, and, in fact, the only available evidence suggests that the debriefing may *not* undo negative effects. We believe that if there is likely to be harm to participants resulting from research participation, serious ethical questions about the research itself are raised, regardless of the care given to debriefing participants. We will now turn to the other important reasons for conducting debriefing.

The Research Experience

For both ethical and practical reasons, participation in a communication research project should be a positive experience. Ethically we believe that it is simply wrong to take from people without providing something in return. It would be impossible to conduct social research without research participants. The participant provides time and energy to the researcher and makes it possible for the researcher to further his or her own career as well as make a contribution to knowledge about communication. It is reasonable for the participant to gain from the research experience, and he or she should gain more than whatever minimal grade or monetary incentive may have been used to induce participation. What the researcher can offer in return is a positive educational experience and the debriefing provides the opportunity to do this. (See Box 3.4 and Box 3.5 for sample debriefings.)

The second reason to make participation in experiments a positive experience is practical. College students do not frequently come into contact with social scientists. A large component of the impression that participants and others have of social science is probably a result of whatever personal contact they may have

---

Box 3.4 Debriefing Statement

The study you have just participated in examined perceptions of small group behavior and communication. Because participation in research of this kind should be part of all students' education, both as consumers of research in life and as critical readers of research, this sheet provides you the initial data you need to better understand why the study was undertaken. Please read the following paragraph and then sign this sheet to indicate (1) that you have been debriefed and been able to ask questions concerning the research by either the investigator or his representative and (2) (because the project will run over several days) that you will refrain from discussing the research project until the date specified has passed.

This study sought to examine the impact of touch and topic involvement on perceptions of the group. Specifically, students viewed a videotape in which the issue was "involving" or "not involving" and in which the confederates engaged in the discussion were either touching each other frequently or not. Additionally, some students simply read transcripts of the interaction. The two conditions (touch and topic) were the manipulations and we were interested in how they interacted to produce different perceptions of the observed group's credibility, attraction, cohesiveness, involvement and satisfaction, and how you felt about joining the group you observed in a future interaction. Your responses will be treated confidentially, in no way will your responses be made public. The results of the research should be available by next Fall Semester, please feel free to drop by the Department of Communication Arts and read them.

By signing this form you indicate that you have read the debriefing statement and have been given a chance to have any questions answered. Your signature also indicates that you agree not to disclose what you have seen or the scales you completed until after _____.

I have read and agree to abide by the wishes of the research director.

_____   _____
Volunteer's Signature   Date

Box 3.5 # Debriefing Letter

Dear _____:

Your participation in this research project is very important for a variety of reasons. First, when the data you provided are analyzed fully and written up for publication, our knowledge of the behavioral basis for accurate judgments of lying will have been advanced. This individual study, by itself, makes only a small contribution to our understanding of human behavior and its effects. However, other researchers interested in this same area will be able to examine our procedures and results and be able to extend and refine the knowledge gained. In this way, as more studies are completed, the accumulation of knowledge grows steadily and systematically.

Second, there are practical applications of this study. It was paid for by a National Science Foundation grant which is looking at the effects of using videotape during court proceedings. If, in the future, trials are recorded on videotape and shown to juries on television monitors, it will be important to know under what conditions jurors would have the best chance to detect lying by witnesses.

Third, the researchers have benefited from your participation in this research. It is necessary to conduct major research projects to complete graduate studies in all social science disciplines, including Communication. Your participation has been important to us personally for this reason.

Finally, you personally may have benefited from this experience. By participating in this experiment, by listening to the description of the research which was provided during the class period in which you participated, and by reading this letter, you may have learned a little bit about how Social Science research is conducted. Hopefully this project has been an educational experience for you. Also, much of the content of courses comes from research projects like this one. Thus, future communication students may benefit from your participation just as you have likely benefited from the contributions of past participants.

In short, your participation in this experiment was extremely valuable. We sincerely appreciate your help and would like to thank you very much.

had with social scientists. Any time a communication researcher comes into contact with a participant, he or she is, in a sense, representing both the communication discipline and social research in general. This is also true of the "student" researcher. This is an important responsibility, one that should be taken seriously.

The primary mechanism for assuring that research participation is a positive, educational experience is the debriefing session. This is the researcher's chance to communicate with the participant in a manner from which everyone involved—the researcher, the communication discipline, social researchers in general, and especially, of course, the participant—will benefit. If participants leave a research project with bad feelings about their participation, bad feelings about the researcher, or bad feelings about social science, then ethical questions about the researcher's behavior should be raised. Thus a major, and often overlooked, purpose of the debriefing is to make participation in the research a positive educational experience for the participant and, in the process, create or maintain a favorable relationship between the researcher (and all that he or she represents) and the participant.

Earlier we mentioned that the label *subject* has a negative connotation.[6] Because of this we have consciously avoided the term wherever possible because it tends to dehumanize the process of research. In some fields the subject may not be human; indeed, it may not even be an animal. We prefer to think of our participants as people who think, feel, and react to stimuli. One thing that communication researchers should always remember is that they deal with people and any process that dehumanizes those helping in research is likely to contribute to negative feelings toward future participation. Some academic journals, for example, now require that the term *subjects* be changed to refer to *respondents* or *participants*, hence humanizing the research.

The attitude of many subjects toward social research is captured in this hypothetical letter from a subject to a researcher written by psychologist Sidney M. Jourard[7]:

> My name is S. You don't know me. I have another name my friends call me by, but I drop it and become number 27 as soon as I take part in your research. I serve in your surveys and experiments. I answer your questions, fill out questionnaires . . . . I have started to wonder why I do these things for you. What's in it for me . . . ? I feel myself being pressured, bulldozed, tricked, manipulated everywhere I turn. You really seem to be studying me in order to learn how to influence my actions without my realizing it. I resent this . . . . I feel used, and I don't like it. But I protect myself by not showing you my whole self, or lying. Did you ever stop to think that your articles, and the textbooks you write, the theories you spin—all based on your data (my disclosures to you)—may actually be a tissue of lies and half-truths (my lies and half-truths) or a joke I've played on you because I don't like or trust you? That should give you some concern.

Indeed it should. Examining questionnaires that have been filled out at random or observing these attitudes being manifested in other ways happens all too frequently.

Suspicions and mistrust regarding the ethics of social researchers are not limited to research subjects. Even today, almost 30 years after David Berlo wrote *The Process of Communication*,[8] a book that contributed greatly to the diffusion of empirical approaches to studying human communication, there are some communication professionals who vocally denounce scientific research, or at least suggest that such inquiry leads to mistreatment of subjects. A recent attempt in a large Communication Studies Department at a major university to systematize procedures for obtaining student research participants was met by opposition from faculty whose orientation was "humanistic." According to a document circulated by an opponent, "the overriding reason has to do with treating people as instruments for professional ends."[9] We believe that such sentiments exist because many researchers have, in fact, shown a callous disregard for assuring that the research participants do, in fact, gain something from participation. As Herbert Kelman notes, "[the participant] should in some positive way be enriched by the [research] experience, that is he [or she] should come away from it with the feeling that he has learned something, understood something, or grown in some way." [10]

Does the impression that people form of a specific study as a result of their participation in it affect their attitudes toward social science in general? One experiment involved purposely putting participants through experiences designed to suggest to them that research was either interesting and important or dull and a waste of time. Those people in the positive experience condition subsequently felt more favorably toward research in general, and performed more conscientiously during a later study than did those in the negative previous experience condition. [11]

The quality of the debriefing influences participants' judgments of the value of a specific project and of social science research in general. [12] One study examined the detection of deceptive communications. The participants observed videotapes of 16 people who were either lying or telling the truth, and were asked to attempt to determine which was which. A third of the participants received no debriefing, a third received a minimal debriefing, and a third received a detailed and thorough debriefing that described the purpose of the study, how the results would fit into a larger framework, the practical and theoretical value of the research, and the potential benefits that could result for all involved, including the researchers, future communication students, mankind, and the participants themselves. In short, the detailed debriefing attempted to make sure that participation was a positive educational experience for participants and that there was a positive relationship between the researcher and participants. Several weeks later all subjects filled out a purportedly unrelated questionnaire that asked how valuable communication research was, how concerned researchers in general were for the "welfare of their participants," and how reasonable a use of class time research participation was. The people who received the detailed debriefing indicated more favorable views of research and researchers than did those who received no debriefing; those who received minimal debriefing fell in the middle. [13]

Debriefing Children Is it important to debrief children? Obviously, the nature of the debriefing, like all communication messages, needs to be adapted to the audience and the situation, but children have great potential to benefit from a debriefing. In a study examining adolescent drinking patterns, the youngest group in the sample was made up of seventh-graders, all about 12 years old. [14] Their participation involved observing some alcohol advertisements and filling out a lengthy questionnaire. The debriefing, which lasted over an hour, resulted in a stimulating class discussion about not only the specific research project and social science research in general, but also the effects of alcohol advertising and advertising in general, the propriety of alcohol use in a variety of situations, and the pros and cons of alcohol use in general. The teacher later reported that the students had learned a great deal about an important topic as a result of their participation in the research, especially from the debriefing.

Can the debriefing affect children's attitudes about social research? An experiment by Carol Weissbrod and Thomas Mangran suggests that the answer is yes.[15] Fifth grade boys and girls were deceived as part of an altruism experiment. Debriefed children subsequently indicated that they believed the research to be more "worthwhile" than children who were not debriefed. The authors conclude "that the debriefing may give children information that adds to their positive perception of the value and potential of experimental studies."[16]

Debriefing Procedures   How does one go about debriefing in such a way that participants will "in some positive way be enriched by the experience, that is he [or she] should come away from it with the feeling that he has learned something, understood something, or grown in some way."[17] First, let participants know that you appreciate their participation. Thank them for helping you. Second, be as open and honest as you can be at that particular time. (See, for example, the sample debriefing statement presented in Box 3.4.) Debriefing statements also frequently ask, in the name of the research, that the participant not divulge to other potential participants the purposes and procedures of the research.

Third, describe for the participants what you were attempting to do, the hypotheses or questions you asked, and your procedures. This not only educates them, but also provides feedback at times when your procedures are not working the way you thought they would. In this way the debriefing serves a corrective function. Fourth, if you are not conducting the debriefing yourself (as is the case with field experiments conducted by several confederates or helpers in the field), provide the participants with an address and telephone number through which they can contact you. Finally, attempt to contact them after the fact. If you used a class, go to a meeting of that class and present your results. If the participants came from a number of classes, either provide the instructors with a summary of what you found or send participants a letter thanking them for helping and giving them your major findings. This extra step almost always ensures the participant an educational experience and usually leaves him or her with a positive feeling about the research.

ETHICAL APPROPRIATENESS

Are there certain topics for research that may not be appropriate to study? The question of ethically appropriate topics is especially troublesome for researchers of communication.

The decision regarding what to study and how to study it is an individual choice and the individual must live with that choice. It is a value judgment tempered by an understanding of possible risk. In general, we believe that researchers should be given maximum freedom to study whatever they want and to go wherever their theory and findings lead them. Nonetheless, there are some points of concern. For example: Is it ethical to try to determine if a particular racial group has different characteristics, such as communicative competencies? Such questions may be debated as to whether they are ethically appropriate for study under current ethical standards.

A PARTING NOTE

We will finish our discussion of research ethics by concluding Sidney Jourard's letter. Read carefully what he is saying and see if you agree [18].

> If you'll trust me, I'll trust you, if you're trustworthy. I'd like you to take the time and trouble to get acquainted with me as a person, before we go through your experimental procedures. And I'd like to get to know you and what you are up to, to see if I would like to expose myself to you. Sometimes, you remind me of physicians. They look at me as the unimportant envelope that conceals the disease they are really interested in. You have looked at me as the unimportant package that contains "responses," and this is all I am for you. Let me tell you that when I feel this, I get back at you. I give you responses, all right; but you will never know what I meant by them. You know, I can speak, not just in words, but with my action. And when you have thought I was responding to a "stimulus" in your lab, my response was really directed at *you;* and what I meant by it was, "Take this, you unpleasant so-and-so." Does that surprise you? It shouldn't.
>
> . . . I'll make a bargain with you. You show me that you are doing your researches *for me*—to help me become freer, more self-understanding, better able to control *myself*—and I'll make myself available to you in any way you ask. And I won't play jokes and tricks on you. I don't want to *be controlled*, not by you or anyone else. And I don't want to control other people. I don't want you to help other people to understand how I can be "controlled," that they can then control me. Show me that you are for me, and I will show *myself* to you.

Jourard wrote this letter after serving as an unknowing subject in another researcher's project. Obviously, had he known he was going to be a participant, had the chance to withdraw from the project, and was fully debriefed afterward, he may have felt differently. Ethically, you need to treat your participants as feeling, thinking, and emoting people. In other words, treat them as you yourself would like to be treated.

SUMMARY

This chapter has examined a topic that is central to conducting quality research. We began with a general discussion of ethics, with an emphasis on the rules of scholarship in particular. All methods of research must adhere to the rules of scholarship. We then examined the ethics of choosing a topic; again, an ethical decision that transcends method and encompasses *all* types of research. We then moved to examine problems associated with the scientific method, specifically, the treatment of human beings as participants in research. We noted that the term "subject" connotes something subhuman and urged you to avoid thinking of your participants as subjects, or worse yet, victims.

We believe that this chapter serves as a sort of social etiquette for conducting research. According to that etiquette you treat those you work with as if you were treating yourself. Although the focus was on the scientific, it may be appropriate for the humanistically oriented researcher to substitute the word documents for people, participant, or individual. In the end the researcher must justify not only to others but to him- or herself the ethics of the research.

PROBES

1. What is ethics? When attempting to define this concept, what do you think is ethical research? To meet your definition, what are the minimal considerations the researcher must consider before saying that his or her research is ethical?

2. We have made a point in labeling the people involved in a research project as participants rather than subjects—or worse yet, victims. What does each label mean to you? Which would you rather be, assuming that you were involved as a student in another student's research? Why?

3. When we talk about the "rules of scholarship" we are talking about giving consideration to others. How much of a research report is *actually* the researcher's? Where do you draw the line between others' work and your interpretation of others' work as original? When do you cite their work? In research is it possible to really have a truly unique idea?

4. Suppose you are placed in the following situation. You have worked hard to prepare a research proposal for class, one that can be turned in either under single authorship or in conjunction with a classmate. The day before it is due your best friend comes to you and asks you to "return a favor" for something she helped you with earlier. That return favor is to be named as coauthor of the proposal. How would you handle the situation? Do you think a similar situation might occur to others? Why?

5. Discuss the balance between deception and debriefing. How would you handle conducting an advertising study in which the message advocated the public listing of AIDS carriers? What ethical considerations would you have to weigh in conducting this research project? Which are most important? Which are least important? Why?

SUGGESTED READING

Holmes, D. S., and Applebaum, A. S. (1970). Nature of prior experimental experience as a determinant of performance in subsequent experiments. *Journal of Personality and Social Psychology, 14,* 195–202.

Jourard, S. M. (1968). *Man disclosing to himself.* New York: D. Van Nostrand Company.

Kelman, H. (1967). Human use of human subjects: The problem of deception in social psychological experiments. *Psychological Bulletin, 67,* 1–11.

Walster, E., et al. (1967). Effectiveness of debriefing following deception experiments. *Journal of Personality and Social Psychology, 14,* 371–380.

Weissbrod, C. S., & Mangran, T. (1978). Children's attitudes about experimental participation: The effect of deception and debriefing. *Journal of Social Psychology, 106,* 59–72.

NOTES

1. Jerold L. Hale, "Plagiarism in Classroom Settings," *Communication Research Reports,* 4 (1987): 66–70.
2. American Psychological Association, 1983.
3. Michael Burgoon, Marshall Cohen, Michael D. Miller, and Charles L. Montgomery, "An Empirical Test of a Model of Resistance to Persuasion," *Human Communication Research,* 5 (1978), 27–39; Michael D. Miller and Michael Burgoon, "The Relationship Between Violations of Expectations and the Induction of Resistance to Persuasion," *Human Communication Research,* 6 (1979), 300–313; Don W. Stacks and Judee K. Burgoon, "The Role of Nonverbal Behaviors as Distractors in Resistance to Persuasion in Interpersonal Contexts," *Central States Speech Journal,* 32 (1981), 61–73; and Don W. Stacks and Daniel E. Sellers, "Toward a Holistic Approach to Communication: The Effect of 'Pure' Hemispheric Reception on Message Acceptance," *Communication Quarterly,* 34 (1986): 266–285.
4. See, for example, the Hawthorne studies, in which people changed their behavior because they *thought* they were being observed.
5. Elaine Walster et al., "Effectiveness of Debriefing Following Deception Experiments," *Journal of Personality and Social Psychology,* 14 (1967): 371–380.
6. Equally negative is the label "victim," which many beginning student social researchers use, either consciously or unconsciously, to refer to the people on whom they test their ideas.
7. Sidney M. Jourard, *Disclosing Man to Himself* (New York: D. Van Nostrand, 1968), pp. 9–12. Also cited in Arthur G. Miller, ed., *The Social Psychology of Psychological Research* (New York: Free Press, 1970).
8. David K. Berlo, *The Process of Communication* (New York: Holt, Rinehart & Winston, 1960).
9. Personal communication, 1981.
10. Herbert Kelman, "Human Use of Human Subjects: The Problem of Deception in Social Psychological Experiments," *Psychological Bulletin,* 67 (1967): 1.
11. David S. Holmes and Alan S. Applebaum, "Nature of Prior Experimental Experience as a Determinant of Performance in Subsequent Experiments," *Journal of Personality and Social Psychology,* 14 (1970): 195–202.
12. John E. Hocking, Joyce Bauchner, Edmund P. Kaminski, and Gerald R. Miller, "Detecting Deceptive Communication from Verbal, Visual, and Paralinguistic Cues," *Human Communication Research,* 6 (1979): 33–46.
13. The participants in the minimal and no debriefing conditions then were given the thorough debriefing.
14. Charles Atkin, John Hocking, and Martin Block, "Teenage Drinking: Does Advertising Make a Difference?" *Journal of Communication,* 34 (1984): 157–167.
15. Carol S. Weissbrod and Thomas Mangran, "Children's Attitudes About Experimental Participation: The Effect of Deception and Debriefing," *Journal of Social Psychology,* 106 (1978): 72.
16. Weissbrod and Mangran, 72.
17. Kelman, 1.
18. Jourard, 11–12.

PART TWO

Methods of Communication Research

Now that the bases of theory and research, and the relationship between them have been covered, we can move into the realm of research *methodologies*. Understanding the various available research methodologies is a necessary step in consuming and conducting research.

The foundation laid in Part One emphasized the types of questions different methodologies are best at answering. In this section we discuss those questions specifically asked by researchers attempting to build a knowledge base. Based on the foundation of theory and science/humanism, method provides the blueprints from which we will build our research projects.[1]

---

[1]The analogy of building blocks is similar to that suggested by Don W. Stacks, Sidney R. Hill, and Mark L. Hickson in *An Introduction to Communication Theory* (New York: Holt, Rinehart & Winston,

Before you can begin to create a blueprint, however, you must first understand the materials with which you build. These are typically found in the *literature* appropriate to the area(s) you are studying. The literature you review creates the foundation from which questions and/or hypotheses are drawn. Regardless of the research method chosen, all researchers begin by reviewing previous studies and existing theory. In the case of the historical method, the library becomes the major research source and analysis is rooted in those sources found in depositories of knowledge: academic libraries, personal libraries, archives, and so on. In other methods the library serves as the starting point.

Chapter 4 addresses the problems and resources involved in conducting library research. We begin by establishing what a document is and how to select appropriate documentation for particular research needs. We then move toward the literature review, or the formal analysis of the documents obtained in the search. The aim of this chapter is to provide the knowledge necessary to (1) decide what documents are necessary, (2) locate where they may be found in the library, (3) determine what resources may be available that make the search process easier, and (4) establish systematic procedures for putting research together.

Chapter 5 examines the historical/critical method from two perspectives: social science and humanism. The questions best addressed by historical methods are presented as an introduction to the methods themselves. Finally, as a special branch of historical method, critical method is addressed. Critical method is defined as research involving value judgments about communication, with emphasis given to oral communication, such as that found in rhetorical analysis and speech criticism.

Chapter 6 sets the stage for three methods that constitute the social scientific method by discussing how we *measure* the various cognitive and behavioral variables of interest to communication researchers. This chapter discusses reliability and validity and introduces the reader to commonly used scales and other measurement techniques.

Chapters 7 through 10 present the three major social scientific methods: participant observation, the survey, and the experiment. Remember, the purpose of science is to build theory—systematic statements of relationships between variables. Thus, each of these methods has as its goal the identification or confirmation of relationships between variables. Each method differs with regard to the degree of confidence the researcher can place in findings about whether variables are related and the degree of artificiality used to study the relationships between variables. On the one hand, the participant observer studies behavior from a qualitative/descriptive model that takes advantage of communication in naturally occurring contexts, but statements about whether the variables under observation are related to each other must be carefully qualified. The importance here is placed on *naturally occurring behavior.* Rigor is

---

1991). In their metaphor theory is perceived as the foundation for understanding. In our metaphor theory is viewed as the foundation upon which method is built, the type of question helps to establish particular method. The frame, therefore, is method and method rests upon a theoretical foundation.

sacrificed in favor of realism. The survey represents a quantitative/descriptive model that allows increased confidence in the results, but at some expense of realism. Finally, the experiment can provide great rigor and allows high degrees of confidence to be placed in statements concerning the relationships between variables, but often at the expense of realism. Thus, as we shall see, each method has its advantages and limitations.

Chapter 7 examines the first social scientific research method: participant-observation. This method is the most subjective of the social science approaches and provides a way of observing how people communicate in their environments under real-world conditions. Usually no effort is made to predict or to generalize the findings of the research to a larger population, instead participant-observation is addressed from a purely descriptive viewpoint.

Chapter 8 presents a more rigorous method of research: Survey research seeks to generalize findings to a larger population based on a subpopulation of people "selected" for study. This method examines the concepts of *surveying* a population by selecting a representative sample and asking that sample questions relevant to the variables under study. Sample selection techniques and survey design are discussed, as well as data collection techniques.

Chapters 9 and 10 examine the experiment. These chapters present experimental and quasi-experimental designs, focusing on features of designs that may invalidate the research, and how the researcher "creates" his variables through operational definitions. Finally, Part Two ends with an examination of content analysis, a methodology with both descriptive and predictive applications.

Part Two, then, builds upon the theoretical foundation laid in Part One. An understanding of the various methods provides the knowledge necessary to make intelligent decisions about which method best answers which research questions. It also provides a strategy for collecting and accessing the type of data needed before addressing the research question or hypothesis.

Chapter 4

Getting Started: Library Research

*P*erhaps the hardest part of conducting research is getting started. After you get an idea—or perhaps have a topic assigned to you—you must begin *systematically* to search available sources of information, make decisions, prepare arguments, and develop answerable questions or testable hypotheses. This search, which may begin by simply thinking about what you already know about a topic, usually takes you to a repository of information. The repository you usually check first is the library. However, there are other sources for the information, such as computerized data banks, or authorities, people who have expertise in a given area. This chapter will prepare you for your first step in research: collecting the relevant information from which to make choices.

Before we get to the nuts and bolts of conducting a library search, two philosophical comments are in order. Any time you begin to conduct a research project, even in conducting a literature review, you must have a *plan of action.* Such a plan allows you to make the best use of a commodity of which there is far too little: time. By carefully considering just what is needed, how you will attack the task of finding what you need, and what criteria you will use in deciding what to save and what to discard, you have taken your first step toward establishing your research methodology. This step is important in that it establishes the *parameters*—the limits or boundaries—of what you consider relevant to your topic. Establishing parameters, however, does not mean that you have irrevocably limited yourself. As more and more information is garnered the process of research often produces changes.

A second philosophical consideration deals with the type of analysis involved in a library search. Library research establishes the first *critical* analysis of sources and resources.[1] This means that while you are establishing how you will conduct the library search, you are also making decisions as to what is important and unimportant. This analysis is formalized in Chapter 5.

It is important to note here that the type of research you conduct will determine how often you use the library. Although *all* research methods require the use of documents and the library, some require more than others. For instance, if you were to take the social scientific method as your major approach to research, you would use the library to document past research in building your theoretical position and maintain your current state of knowledge through books and journal articles. If, however, you were more concerned with humanistic method, you would spend much more time in the library and your documents would probably be your primary source of data, the equivalent of the scientist's human participants. This chapter will serve as your first methodological tool whether you conduct scientific or humanistic research.

Finally, there are different types of library research. Just as different types of research produce different answers, different types of library research produce different outcomes. There are at least three types of library research.[2] The first is that which seeks to organize existing knowledge. The purpose is to take some of the randomness out of your search. Here you decide the whats and whens of the searches; you establish cutoff dates for sources, establish descriptors that will serve to guide your search (and help you create and maintain your data base of references), and generally establish the limits of the search.

Second, a search may establish relationships between the topics or concepts of interest. In so doing, you should be able to specify the strengths of the research base, the weaknesses, and areas in which further research is needed. This type of library research is based on a knowledge of existing sources and is the first step toward establishing a theoretical perspective. At this time you are ready to prepare a formal review of the literature.

The literature review represents the third type of library research. In the literature review you present the *relevant* literature pertaining to your topic. As Paul Leedy notes, the literature review's function is "to 'look again' (*re+view*) at the 'literature' (the reports of what others have done) in a *related* area: an area not necessarily identical with, but collateral to, your own area of study."[3] This third type of research, then, establishes *your* perspective of the relevant literature. Note, also, that the review of literature should bring together material from *related* areas of research.

In most instances the literature review becomes a formal written document and may be in the form of an article, chapter, or paper. These articles can be extremely important in a library search; reviews of the literature can provide you with the necessary sources and reviews of previous research. Care should be taken, however, not to rely solely on such reviews. As with all research, the author's theoretical perspective will influence how he or she interprets the information presented. The good researcher relies on his or her own library research, but the literature review can provide a starting point for creating your data base.

It is important to note that *all* research, regardless of the approach taken, requires a literature review, although a formal written document need not be the final outcome. Most published research *begins with a literature review*, a review that sets the author's rationale, his or her theoretical perspective, and presents the context, the previous research, he or she feels lead up to the research questions or hypotheses addressed.

ESTABLISHING THE PARAMETERS OF STUDY

In establishing the first phase of the library research the researcher must decide just what he or she will examine. In part this decision is cast in terms of the research question(s) being asked. Hence, if we were interested in a study of nonverbal communication that examined the impact of personal space on the persuasiveness of a source, our questions might include: How is personal spacing perceived in persuasive settings? What is the impact of differing personal spacings between a source and her receiver? What variables must be taken into consideration when a spatial "norm" is established? Our questions deal with definition (personal space, persuasion) and fact (what is the *relationship* between personal space, persuasion, and other variables such as race, sex, age, culture; what is the *function* of personal space on persuasion; and, in turn, what variables change perceptions of personal spacing norms or expectations). In asking these questions we begin to establish the parameters of study—we have delineated the study via research questions into areas of study amenable to research.

But from where will your sources come? For the established researcher, one who has been working on his research questions for some time, a base of knowledge has already been amassed. For the researcher seeking to break new ground, however, the keys to establishing the parameters of study come from two forms of knowledge: tradition and authority.[4] *Tradition,* in some ways similar to what Kerlinger calls tenacity (see Chapter 1), is that which our culture presents to us. Tradition is what we are brought up to believe and generally accept without testing. Earl Babbie suggests that tradition provides a cumulative body of knowledge that allows us to begin our research with a data base of sorts.[5] Tradition, however, provides a biased and often unscientific base of knowledge. As a point of departure, however, tradition provides us with the necessary information to begin the library research.

In our nonverbal example, for instance, we might begin by examining basic works, such as textbooks and other reviews of the literature, to see what others have summarized about personal space and persuasion (as we will note later, these are *secondary* sources, compilations of original sources). We would then begin to define the area of study by what we felt was important in terms of the relationships we see forming between the variables under study: What variables are important in establishing a spatial expectation or norm and how do they interrelate with persuasion?

Sometimes tradition also provides us with counterideas and new thoughts. These thoughts reject the knowledge based on time and culture and suggest new vistas of knowledge. In rejecting tradition, however, you must be prepared to advance solid arguments and provide evidence that supports or will support your position. In such an instance, you will be relying on *authority.* Authority is steeped in the credibility of the source.[6] Within all fields of study are people we consider to be experts. An expert is one who has thoroughly researched the literature in his or her area and who usually has made important additions. Often what is said by an expert is accepted simply on the authority of the statement or the source. Many times we accept as authority the statements of those with whom we study, accepting blindly that with which we are presented. If you remember that all research is biased to a degree by the perspective taken, then you see one problem associated with authority. All too often in accepting one position we reject another, even though that position may have merit.

Tradition *and* authority, then, provide the basis from which we can begin our research. Knowing who the authorities are also will provide an edge in your library search; by using authorities as the first line of sources you can effectively reduce the amount of time necessary to get your initial grasp of an area. Also, by identifying authorities you can use their bibliographies as a basis for future searches.

THE ROLE OF DOCUMENTS

For the most part, the nature of library research is found in *documentation.* Documents can be of a variety of forms. The most familiar form of documentation is the book, followed closely by the periodical, including professional journals, and the newspaper. Other sources are available, however, and, as will be noted later in this chapter, are extremely important. These sources include microfilmed materials other than books, magazines, or newspapers, and audiovisual materials such as speeches or documentaries.

Books

The importance of understanding documents and documentation comes from the very nature of the material. Perhaps the most significant feature of a document is that it is out-of-date before it is released to the public. This is especially true of books, which must go through a publication cycle of anywhere between six months and several years. A book can present an in-depth analysis of the topic it covers, and provide a rich historical perspective along with a more clearly developed theoretical perspective. A book, however, takes longer to read and analyze. Reliance on books, especially when deadlines are short, can present a hazard to the researcher, unless he or she learns to skim textual materials for important or relevant information.

Books usually fall into one of two general classes. First we have books for the general public or beginning student. These documents are written at a level sometimes significantly lower than what you might want. An advantage with such a treatment, however, is that it provides the reader with a simplified (layperson) version of the topic. When beginning a new area of study these books provide a valuable knowledge base from which to work. The second class are those that are written for the advanced reader. These books are sometimes referred to as "academic" and take a more detailed and in-depth look at the topic under study. They are good for generating new sources of information and, in some instances, provide overviews of significant areas of study. Of importance in these type of books are the handbooks, yearbooks, and books in a series, which present reviews of major topics or concerns. As with all books, however, these are usually dated before they even get to the library.

Periodicals

The second type of documentation comes in the form of periodicals. Again, there are a number of different types of periodicals. Most of us are familiar with the magazines we purchase at the local newsstand: *Life, Newsweek, Time, People, Psychology Today,* and so forth. These magazines are designed for the general public and provide topical information in an interesting format and at a level most people can comprehend. Their value as research documents is disputed, but depending of course on the researcher's question, they can provide some good ideas and quotations. Remember, however, that they do not usually provide thoroughly tested and reviewed sources of information, but do provide timely opinion and data and generally reflect the world in the way the culture perceives it.

A second type of periodical is the *journal.* A journal is usually produced by a professional organization and reflects the ideas and interests of that organization. The journal typically presents more technical and theoretical information and may be more abstract than publications intended for a general audience. Journals typically have review boards that serve to select the material (articles) to be published. This review process tends to slow down the publication process and, as with the book, many articles are already dated by the time they are published. The journal, however, does provide a *scholarly* source of information about the concept or topic under study.

Journals of interest to communication researchers include national/international journals such as *Human Communication Research, Communication Monographs, Journal of Communication, Communication Education, Quarterly Journal of Speech, Critical Studies in Mass Communication, Journalism Quarterly, Communication Research, Public Opinion Quarterly, Journal of Advertising Research,* and *Journal of Broadcasting and Electronic Media.* Four regional speech journals also present reviewed articles or theme issues: *Communication Quarterly, Southern Communication Journal, Western Journal of Speech Communication, Central States Speech Journal.* Additionally, there are various special interest journals and journals published by state associations. Box 4.1 presents a representative list of communication and communication-related journals.

A fourth type of periodical is the *newsletter.* Newsletters, produced by special interest groups to present ideas and events, often provide information that the more formal sources cannot. Here you might follow a controversy or find new sources of information. Most divisions of such national or international associations as the Speech Communication Association, Association for Education in Journalism and Mass Communication, and the International Communication Association publish newsletters. The major limitation to such material is, of course, their availability—or, more accurately, their lack of availability. You may need to consult the private library of a department or a faculty member to gain access to such documents.

The third type of document is the *newspaper.* Like the general audience magazine, the newpaper presents information from less technical and theoretical perspectives but provides an extremely timely source of information. If you are interested in following something over a period of time, then you would go through the relevant newspapers of the day. Newspapers are extremely important in conducting historical research, providing in many instances the text of major speeches of the day.

Nonprint Resources

The final type of documentation includes nonpublished resources stored on *microfilm* and *computer disks.* More and more libraries are going to microfilm and computer-based retrieval systems. More about these will follow in later sections, but it is important to note that some nonpublished documents can be obtained through such microfilm services as ERIC (Educational Resources Information Center). Included in ERIC are previously unpublished convention papers, literature reviews, and other materials that might be of interest.

Documentation also takes the form of audiovisual materials. Some libraries have special collections of film, videotape, and audiotape. For instance, Vanderbilt University serves as the repository for the "CBS Evening News" tapes. And, Purdue University has tapes of all programs appearing on C-SPAN. Interviews with visiting scholars or dignitaries sometimes find their way into such special collections or are found in individual collections. Documents, then, may be more than simply the written word. A good researcher will use all the documents available.

Documents, then, serve as sources of information on which we base our research. The relevance of the information, however, is in the eye of the researcher. What might be considered an important source by one researcher may be ignored by another. What the document does is present information. What information is used and how it is used is left to the researcher. In general, you should provide evidence for *both* sides of an argument, showing the strengths and weaknesses of each side and then building your future arguments on this logic.

Box 4.1 **Pertinent Journals with Articles Relating to Communication**

Academy of Management Journal

Acta Psychologica

Acta Sociologica

Administrative Science Quarterly

American Anthropologist

American Behavioral Scientist

American Educational Research Journal

American Journal of Political Science

American Journal of Psychology

American Journal of Sociology

American Philosophical Quarterly

American Political Science Review

American Psychologist

American Sociological Review

American Sociologist

Archives of Psychology

Audio-Visual Communication Review

Basic and Applied Social Psychology

Behavioral Science

Behaviour

British Journal of Psychology

British Journal of Social and Clinical Psychology

British Journal of Sociology

Broadcast Monographs

Canadian Journal of Behavioural Science

Canadian Journal of Political Science

Central States Speech Journal

Child Development

Cognitive Psychology

Columbia Journalism Review

Communication Education

Communication Monographs

Communication Quarterly

Communication Research

Communication Research Reports

Comparative Political Studies

Critical Studies in Mass Communication

Current Anthropology

Developmental Psychology

Editor and Publisher

Editorial Research Reports

ETC: A Review of General Semantics

Ethics

European Journal of Political Research

European Journal of Social Psychology

Family Process

Feedback

Human Communication Research

Human Factors

Human Organization

Human Relations

Inquiry

Intermedia

International Journal of Aging and Human Development

International Journal of Psychology

International Organization

International Political Science Review

International Social Science Journal

Journal of Abnormal and Social Psychology

Journal of Advertising Research

Journal of Advertising

Journal of Anthropological Research

Journal of Applied Behavior Analysis

Journal of Applied Communication Research

Journal of Applied Psychology

Journal of Black Studies

Journal of Broadcasting and Electronic Media

Journal of Business

Journal of Business Research

Journal of Clinical Psychology

Journal of Communication

Journal of Communication Therapy

Journal of Conflict Resolution

Journal of Consulting and Clinical Psychology

Journal of Consumer Research

Journal of Creative Behavior

Journal of Cross-Cultural Psychology

Journal of Education

Journal of Educational Psychology

Journal of Experimental Psychology (General)

Journal of Experimental Psychology (Human Perception & Performance)

Journal of Experimental Social Psychology

Journal of General Psychology

Journal of Humanistic Psychology

Journal of Intergroup Relations

Journal of Marketing

Journal of Marketing Research

Journal of Marriage and the Family

Journal of Nonverbal Behavior

Journal of Personality

Journal of Personality Assessment

Journal of Personality and Social Psychology

Journal of Philosophy

Journal of Popular Culture

Journal of Popular Film and Television

Journal of Psycholinguistic Research

Journal of Psychology

Journal of Research in Personality

Journal of Sex Research

Journal of Social Issues

Journal of Social Psychology

Journal of Social, Political, and Economic Studies

Journal of Speech and Hearing Research

Journal of the American Forensic Association

Journal of Verbal Learning and Verbal Behavior

Journal of Written Communication

Journalism Educator

Journalism Monographs

Journalism Quarterly

Language and Speech

Language in Society

Learning and Motivation

Management Science

Mass Communication Review

Media, Culture, and Society

Memory and Cognition

Newspaper Research Journal

Organizational Behavior and Human Performance

Parliamentarian

Parliamentary Affairs

Perceptual and Motor Skills

Personality and Social Psychology Bulletin

Personnel Psychology

Philosophical Review

Philosophy and Rhetoric

Philosophy of Science

Political Behavior

Political Communication Review

Political Quarterly

Political Science Quarterly

Political Studies

Politics and Society

Presidential Studies Quarterly

Progress in Communication Science

Psychiatry

Psychological Bulletin

Psychological Record

Psychological Reports

Psychological Review

Psychology of Women Quarterly

Public Administration Review

Public Opinion Quarterly

Public Policy

Public Relations Journal

Public Relations Quarterly

Public Relations Review

Quarterly Journal of Speech

Science

Semiotica

Sex Roles: A Journal of Research

Signs: Journal of Women in Culture and Society

Small Group Behavior

Social Forces

Social Policy

Social Problems

Social Research

Social Science Quarterly

Social Science Research

Social Service Quarterly

Sociological Inquiry

Sociological Methods and Research

Sociological Quarterly

Sociology: Journal of the British Sociological Association

Sociometry: Social Psychology Quarterly

Southern Communication Journal

Television Quarterly

Vital Speeches of the Day	*Women's Studies*
Washington Journalism Review	*Women's Studies in Communication*
Western Journal of Speech Communication	*Women's Studies International Quarterly*
tion	*World Communication*

PRIMARY VERSUS SECONDARY SOURCES

As noted earlier, there are at least two types of source material available. Researchers would like to use as much *primary* material as possible. Primary material comes from original sources. It is the actual study, text, or data; it may be an experiment, a film, or a journal article. The main point here is that *it is what was reported or conducted;* with it you have the author's own reporting. *Secondary* sources, on the other hand, are compilations of others' work. In using secondary sources you must rely on the authors' interpretation of what was presented. While it is permissible to use secondary sources, you should always try and obtain the primary source (see Chapter 5). Sometimes, however, secondary sources are the only sources available. Sometimes, too, we use secondary sources as a beginning point in research, allowing the work of others to point us to questions or holes in the current theoretical thinking or data base.

USING THE LIBRARY

The most basic requirement of any library research is to learn your way around the library. Think of the library as a tool, one that with practice allows you to reduce the amount of time spent in it. Most libraries have handbooks, maps, and personnel to help you find your way around. Of importance is finding the card catalogue, or the computer terminals that serve the same purpose, the bibliographic room(s), and the location of journals and books. These sites should be clearly marked somewhere in the lobby of the library; if not, ask for directions.

Getting Started

Any library research plan should be systematic. You should have an idea of where you want to begin and then how you will use the information you found to move on to the next phase. Figure 4.1 presents a programmed approach to getting started. Note that you can begin with either books or articles. If you do not know where to begin, the card catalogue may provide a starting point.

The card catalogue provides information concerning authors, topics, and titles. Figure 4.2 shows a sample card. Note that the card provides a great deal of information, including author's name, the location of the document (including any special library or holding area), the call number, the title of the book, and the subject

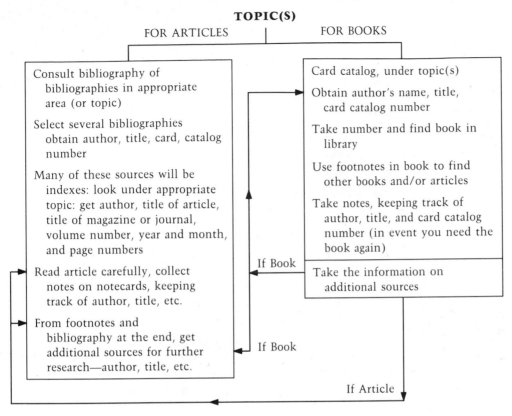

TOPIC(S)

FOR ARTICLES

FOR BOOKS

Consult bibliography of
  bibliographies in appropriate
  area (or topic)

Select several bibliographies
  obtain author, title, card, catalog
  number

Many of these sources will be
  indexes: look under appropriate
  topic: get author, title of article,
  title of magazine or journal,
  volume number, year and month,
  and page numbers

Read article carefully, collect
  notes on notecards, keeping
  track of author, title, etc.

From footnotes and
  bibliography at the end, get
  additional sources for further
  research—author, title, etc.

Card catalog, under topic(s)

Obtain author's name, title,
  card catalog number

Take number and find book in
  library

Use footnotes in book to find
  other books and/or articles

Take notes, keeping track of
  author, title, and card catalog
  number (in event you need the
  book again)

Take the information on
  additional sources

If Book

If Book

If Article

Figure 4.1 Programmed approach to the literature review. (*Source:* Don W. Stacks and Mark Hickson, III, "Research: A Programmed Approach," *Florida Speech Communication Journal*, 2 [1974], 22.)

heading. Of importance at this stage of the research are the author's name, the title, subject headings, and call number. With this information you can begin your search.

Most libraries are complex entities. Libraries will include collections of materials which, without some systematic way of classifying them, can overwhelm the novice researcher. Most college and university libraries classify their holdings according to the *Library of Congress Classification System,* which determines how documents are shelved and described. The classification system is based on a series of letters, each representing a major category (see Box 4.2). Subcategories are listed as further breakdowns of the major category. As you will note, communication is found under the call letters, PN. The P represents the major category, Language and Literature, and the N the subcategory, Drama, Oratory, and Journalism. Because a number of disciplines are concerned with communication, you may have to cross-reference to other call numbers, such as BF (psychology) or HM (sociology and social psychology).

The Library of Congress Classification System is found in most major research

```
                        ¹Organizational Communication

²HM          ³Organizational Communication: traditional themes
131               and new directions
.066695          ⁴/Robert D. McPhee and Phillip K. Tompkins,
1985              editors. - Beverly Hills: Sage Publications,
                  ⁵c.1985
                  ⁶296 p.; ⁷23 cm. - (Sage Annual Reviews of Communication Research;
                     v.13)
                  ⁸Bibliography: p. 259-293.
                  ISBN 0-8039-2186-1

                  ⁹1. Communication in Organizations
             I. McPhee, Robert. II. Tompkins,
             Phillip K. III. Series
```

¹Classification of book by subject matter
²Library of Congress Call Number
³Title and subtitle of book
⁴Author(s) name
⁵Copyright date
⁶Page numbers of book
⁷Book height
⁸Description of bibliography
⁹Categories under which the book is cataloged.

Figure 4.2 Reading the library catalogue card. (*Source:* Adapted from Paul D. Leedy, Practical Research Planning and Design [New York: Macmillan, 1985].)

libraries. Typically, the call letters will be found grouped on floors (or levels) within the library. If you need a hardbound journal (a journal that has been placed permanently in the stacks) or book and know the call number you will be directed to the particular location and then be able to track down the appropriate location in the stacks.

Periodical Indexes   Sometimes it is best to begin with a periodical index. There are a number of general periodical indexes, but the one best known is the *Reader's Guide to Periodical Literature* (see Figure 4.3). This index will provide information concerning popular periodicals broken down by general subjects. Additionally, there are other, more specialized indexes available (see Box 4.3).

Bibliographic Indexes   A number of bibliographic indexes exist to help you find information. The most general index is the *Bibliographic Index: A Cumulative Bibliography of Bibliographies,* which provides information about more specific indexes. Use it to gain mastery of the various indexes available. Some of the more specific indexes include *Index to Journals in Communication Studies Through 1985.* This work indexes 14 journals pertaining to communication from their first issue to 1985. *Current Index to Journals in Education* (CIJE) and

Box 4.2   **Library of Congress Classification System**

- A   General Works
- B   Philosophy, Psychology, Religion
  - B-BD Philosophy
  - BF Psychology
  - BL-BX Religion
- C   History-Auxiliary Sciences
- D   History (except America)
- E-F   History (American)
- G   Geography-Anthropology
- H   Social Sciences
  - HB-HJ Economics and Business
  - HM-HX Sociology
- J   Political Science
- K   Law
- L   Education
- M   Music
- N   Fine Arts
- P   Language and Literature
  - PN   Drama, Oratory, Journalism
- Q   Science
- R   Medicine
- S   Agriculture-Plant and Animal Industry
- T   Technology
- TR   Photography
- U   Military Science
- V   Naval Science
- Z   Bibliographic and Library Science

Resources in Education (RIJ) index ERIC materials and provide an outlet for unpublished materials. Finally, *The Times Index* and *The New York Times Index* provide comprehensive indexes to the *New York Times* and a number of other newspapers (see Figure 4.4).

Social Sciences Citation Index   The *Social Sciences Citation Index* provides citations for specified key word entries and may be cross-referenced for specific searches. The SSCI is computer-based and you may have to pay a fee for its services.

Government Documents   One final index to note is the U.S. government documents catalogue. Many libraries hold large collections of U.S. government

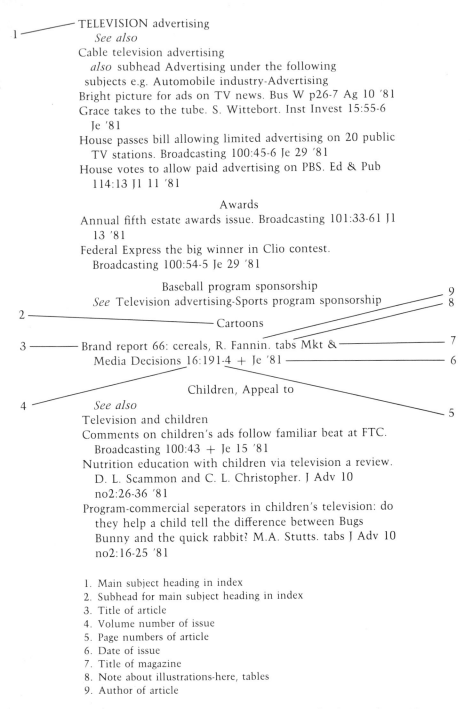

TELEVISION advertising
See also
Cable television advertising
also subhead Advertising under the following
subjects e.g. Automobile industry-Advertising
Bright picture for ads on TV news. Bus W p26-7 Ag 10 '81
Grace takes to the tube. S. Wittebort. Inst Invest 15:55-6
Je '81
House passes bill allowing limited advertising on 20 public
TV stations. Broadcasting 100:45-6 Je 29 '81
House votes to allow paid advertising on PBS. Ed & Pub
114:13 Jl 11 '81

Awards
Annual fifth estate awards issue. Broadcasting 101:33-61 Jl
13 '81
Federal Express the big winner in Clio contest.
Broadcasting 100:54-5 Je 29 '81

Baseball program sponsorship
See Television advertising-Sports program sponsorship
Cartoons
Brand report 66: cereals, R. Fannin. tabs Mkt &
Media Decisions 16:191-4 + Je '81

Children, Appeal to
See also
Television and children
Comments on children's ads follow familiar beat at FTC.
Broadcasting 100:43 + Je 15 '81
Nutrition education with children via television a review.
D. L. Scammon and C. L. Christopher. J Adv 10
no2:26-36 '81
Program-commercial seperators in children's television: do
they help a child tell the difference between Bugs
Bunny and the quick rabbit? M.A. Stutts. tabs J Adv 10
no2:16-25 '81

1. Main subject heading in index
2. Subhead for main subject heading in index
3. Title of article
4. Volume number of issue
5. Page numbers of article
6. Date of issue
7. Title of magazine
8. Note about illustrations-here, tables
9. Author of article

Figure 4.3 Sample entry from *Reader's Guide to Periodical Literature.* (*Source:* H.W. Wilson Company. Material reproduced by permission of publisher.)

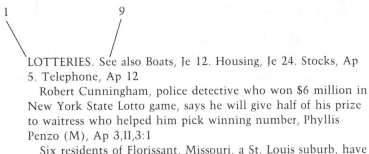

LOTTERIES. See also Boats, Je 12. Housing, Je 24. Stocks, Ap 5. Telephone, Ap 12

Robert Cunningham, police detective who won $6 million in New York State Lotto game, says he will give half of his prize to waitress who helped him pick winning number, Phyllis Penzo (M), Ap 3,II,3:1

Six residents of Florissant, Missouri, a St. Louis suburb, have been big winners in five weekly drawings of Illinois lottery; town, with population of 55,000, has scored more often than city of Chicago, with population of six million (M), Ap 8.I.25:1

George M. Early article on Connecticut lottery, notes large amount of money that must be paid in taxes to IRS; holds lotteries are run for benefit of state, not players; drawing (M), Ap 8, XXIII, 32;3

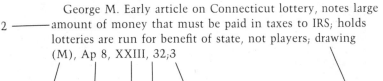

1. Subject heading in index
2. Short summary of article
3. Note about article length-here, "medium"
4. Date of article
5. Section of newspaper in which article appeared
6. Page number
7. Column number
8. Note about visuals-here, "drawing"
9. "See also" reference to related subject headings

Figure 4.4 Sample entry from the *New York Times Index.* (*Source:* The New York Times Company. Reprinted with permission.)

documents that may yield important information. To use the government documents system you must first access the *Monthly Catalog,* the primary index to U.S. government documents. The *Monthly Catalog* document contains both indexes and entries broken into 12 monthly issues (or yearly volumes). The *Monthly Catalog* has several indexes that include author, title, title key word, subject, and series statement or report number. You can use one or all to cross-index your search.

Abstracts   A number of sources available to you are found as abstracts. At least four abstract publications should be of value to you. *Communication Abstracts* provides coverage of about 200 journals in advertising, broadcasting, public relations, and speech communication indexed by author and subject. *Psychological Abstracts* and *Sociological Abstracts* provide summaries of research in journals

Box 4.3 **Selected Indexes**

Alternative Press Index

Agricultural Index

Applied Science and Technology Index

Bibliographic Index: A Cumulative Bibliography of Bibliographies

Biography Index

Book Review Index

British Humanities Index

Business Periodicals Index

Canadian Periodical Index

CBS News Index

Comprehensive Dissertation Index

Current Index to Journals in Education

Education Index

Humanities Index

Index to Journals in Communication Studies Through 1985

Index to Legal Periodicals

Index of Publications of Bureaus of Business and Economic Research

Index to Selected Periodicals

International Index to Periodical Literature in the Social Sciences and Humanities

National Union Catalog of Manuscript Collections

Newsbank

Newspaper Index

New York Times Index

New York Times Films Reviews

Obituary Index to the New York Times

Pool's Index to Periodical Literature, 1902–1989

Public Affairs Information Service Bulletin

Reader's Guide to Periodical Literature

Serial Bibliographies in the Humanities and Social Sciences

Social Sciences Citation Index

Social Sciences Index

Special Issues and Indexes of Periodicals

*Speech Index: An Index to Collections of World Famous Orations and Speeches
for Various Occasions*

Summary of World Broadcasts by the British Broadcasting Corporation

Television News Index and Abstracts

Topicator

United Nations Documents Index

Wall Street Journal Index

and papers published all over the world indexed according to major area by subject and author (see Figure 4.5). The fourth abstract publication, *Dissertation Abstracts,* provides abstracts of doctoral dissertations. You use *Dissertation Abstracts* by first going to the *Index of American Doctoral Dissertations,* which is indexed by author and subject area. Other abstracts that may be of interest are listed in Box 4.4.

Computer-Based Searches   An increasingly large number of computer-assisted data banks are becoming available. Some of these data banks are *on-line,* directly accessible via computer, telephone, and modem. Most data banks charge a fee for their service. Some are being bought by libraries on CD ROMs (computer disks with huge read-only memory storage) and stored at the site. Box 4.5 lists some of the data bases of interest to communication researchers. Many of the abstract services mentioned earlier (e.g., *Psychological Abstracts*) are now available on-line or via CD ROM.

Because you will most likely have to pay a fee for use (including possible telephone charges), you need to think out ahead of time just what you want to find. A computer-assisted data search can be costly if, for example, you ask the computer to search and report all it has in its data banks for communication and leave the dates of search open. Typical charges for data base searches of up to 50 citations (including short abstracts) may run between $5 and $30. Therefore you should try to define specifically how you want the computer to search for documents and what time frame you wish to cover.

Before the computer-assisted search identify any *key words* you think will help to specify the needed information. (Key words are terms that describe some topic

[1]13849. [2]**Dillard, James P.; Hunter, John E. & Burgoon, Michael.** [3](U Wisconsin, Madison) [4]**Sequential-request persuasive strategies: Meta-analysis of foot-in-the-door and door-in-the-face.** [5]*Human Communication Research*, 1984(Sum), Vol. 10(4), 461-488. [6]Applied recently developed methods of meta-analysis to the literatures on the foot-in-the-door (FITD) and door-in-the-face (DITF) message strategies to enable an estimate of the effects of statistical artifacts and to assess the impact of moderator variables. The FITD strategy refers to the situation in which a small, 1st request is made before a larger, target request is made. The DIFT strategy refers to the situation in which an initial, large request is followed by a more moderate request. Results of this study, based on 46 research reports, show both effects to be small, even under optimal conditions. Both require a prosocial topic in order to work. The amount of time between the 1st and 2nd requests plays a different role in the operation of each of the 2 strategies. DITF was effective only when the delay between requests was brief. Effectiveness of FITD was unrelated to delay but did depend on whether or not an incentive was provided with the 1st request. The positive relationship between effort and FITD predicted by self-perception theory was not found. Self-perception theory and reciprocal concessions theory, the theoretical perspectives usually applied to FITD and DITF, respectively, are examined in light of the findings, and it is concluded that both are flawed. [7] [8,9](53 ref)—[10]*Journal Abstract*.

[1]Record Number.
[2]Author(s) or editor(s). Multiple authorship is followed by first author and "et al."
[3]Affiliation of first-named author/editor.
[4]Article title, including subtitles. Language of original is indicated by parentheses, if applicable.
[5]Publication title and bibliographic data.
[6]Text of abstract.
[7]References to other PA abstracts may be included in the abstract body.
[8,9]Summaries included in original document are listed here if appropriate and the number of references displayed.
[10]Abstract source.

Figure 4.5 Sample entry from *Psychological Abstracts*. (*Source:* American Psychological Association, *Psychological Abstracts*. Reprinted with permission.)

addressed by the article.) Some journals now require authors to list up to nine key words appropriate to their work. You might want to specify the key words, nonverbal communication, proxemics, and violations of expectations. This combination would provide a listing of *all* documents within the data base that dealt with nonverbal communication, proxemics, and violations of expectations. By specifying a beginning date, say five years ago, you limit the search to that period of time. Or, you may ask for the latest 15 entries matching that combination of key words. The computer will output a full citation, a short abstract, and other key words for future use (see Figure 4.6).

A note of caution must be interjected here. Just because a source is listed in a data base does not necessarily mean it is good or even relevant. All too often

---

Box 4.4 **Selected Abstract Services**

Child Development Abstracts

Communication Abstracts

Criminal Justice Abstracts

Dissertation Abstracts

Historical Abstracts, 1775–1945

International Political Science Abstracts

Language and Language Behavior Abstracts

Psychological Abstracts

Public Administration Abstracts

Race Relations Abstracts

Sage Public Relations Abstracts

Sage Urban Studies Abstracts

Sociological Abstracts

Urban Affairs Abstracts

Women Studies Abstracts

---

articles or papers may be omitted, may slip through the acquisition process, or the source needed may not be tied into the particular data base. Much of what you receive may be inapplicable; a good researcher will use the abstract as a filter for selecting documents for further analysis.

Establishing the Notation System

How do we go about reducing the volumes of material found? There are several options. First, we can duplicate all documents, or portions of documents, found. Obviously, this is expensive and creates a storage problem. There are times, however, when duplication of the materials is both appropriate and necessary. When you feel a document will be cited or used many times, it may be economically feasible to reproduce it. If the document is important, copy it.

Second, we can create a bibliographic note system. This system should consist of note cards (4 × 6 inch note cards seem best). The card should contain all important information: *complete* citation, including page numbers, issue number or month issued, and a short one- or two-line annotation of what the

Box 4.5   **Selected Data Bases**

AB/INFORM (Business data base)

ADTRACK (Advertising data base)

AP NEWS (Newspaper data base)

BRS (Bibliographic Retrieval Services)

CENDATA (Demographic data base)

CIS (Data base of U.S. Congress reports)

COMPUSERVE (General data base)

DONNELLEY DEMOGRAPHICS (Demographic data base)

DIALOG (General service access to over 200 data bases)

DOW JONES NEWS/RETRIEVAL (Business data base)

ENCYCLOPEDIA OF ASSOCIATIONS (Association data base)

ERIC (Educational Resources Informational Center)

GPO MONTHLY CATALOG (Government Printing Office)

INFOSERVE (General data base)

LLBA (Language and Language Behavior Abstracts)

MAGAZINE INDEX

MARQUIS WHO'S WHO (Biographical data base)

MEDLINE (Biomedical data base)

NEXIS (Newspaper data base)

document contained. Additionally, you should mark the card with a list of key words you can later cross-reference (see Figure 4.7). Obviously, this system will not provide complete recall of the material, but it will provide the first listing of information.

The third strategy is to *abstract* the document. The abstract card provides the same information as the bibliographic note card—a complete bibliographic citation—but expands upon the annotation to include a complete abstract of the document. For an abstract card, 5 × 8 inch note cards work best. Under the complete citation (and any key words you may want to include) you should *briefly* abstract the major concepts, the hypotheses, questions, or theoretical statements

STACKS-DON W., ROSENFELD-LAWRENCE, HICKSON-MARK L.[1]
UNIVERSITY OF ALABAMA, UNIVERSITY OF NORTH CAROLINA AT CHAPEL
HILL, UNIVERSITY OF ALABAMA AT BIRMINGHAM[2]
PERCEPTIONS OF REGIONAL SPEECH COMMUNICATION ASSOCIATIONS[3]
COMMUNICATION EDUCATION. 1989. APRIL VOL 38(4) 144-150[4]
EN[5]
89[6]

SOCIOLOGY OF KNOWLEDGE. ASSOCIATION SURVEY. PROFESSIONAL
ASSOCIATIONS. REGIONAL COMMUNICATION ASSOCIATIONS. PERCEPTIONS
OF PROFESSIONAL JOURNAL.[7]
GIVEN THE RELEVANCE OF REGIONAL ASSOCIATIONS, THEIR CONVENTIONS
AND JOURNALS, IN THE PROCESS OF RESEARCH AND INFORMATION
DISSEMINATION, A SURVEY OF REGIONAL COMMUNICATION ASSOCIATION
MEMBERS WAS UNDERTAKEN TO ASSESS PERCEPTIONS OF THE SOUTHERN
STATES COMMUNICATION ASSOCIATION, PRIMARILY, AND THE OTHER
REGIONAL ASSOCIATIONS SECONDARILY. RESULTS INDICATED THE
EXISTENCE OF A CONSISTENT IMAGE OR STEREOTYPE, BOTH WITHIN AND
OUTSIDE THE MEMBERSHIP OF THE REGIONAL ASSOCIATIONS. IMPACT OF
THESE FINDINGS WERE DISCUSSED FROM A FACULTY MEMBER'S PERSPECTIVE.[8]
STEREOTYPES OF ASSOCIATIONS, JOURNAL AND ASSOCIATION RANKINGS,
SOUTHERN STATES COMMUNICATION ASSOCIATION.[9]

[1]Author
[2]Author's institution
[3]Title
[4]Source/citation
[5]Language printed in
[6]Year Published
[7]Key words
[8]Abstract
[9]Identifiers

Figure 4.6 Sample data base citation. (*Source:* Reprinted with permission of the Speech Communication Association.)

made, the design of the study (the method used to collect whatever data was obtained: historical/critical, descriptive, experimental), the results, the conclusions, and your evaluation of the study (excellent, good, average, poor, terrible) and why (see Figure 4.8). In using an abstract system you must learn to be concise yet accurate. Any quotations should be placed on the back of the note card—in quotation marks—along with the page location of the quotation. When writing the card be sure that you are both accurate and complete.

When working in the library, make sure that your notes are legible. It is a good idea to copy the cards later, typing the information for greater legibility if necessary. If you have access to a personal computer and either a data base program or a word processor you can create your own computer data base and call up "cards" of information by key words.

Stacks, Don W., and Sellers. Daniel E. "Toward a holistic approach to communication: The effect of 'pure' hemispheric perception on message acceptance. COMMUNICATION QUARTERLY 34 (Summer, 1986), 266–285.

Key Concepts: message processing, hemispheric style, language intensity, persuasion information processing, neurocommunication, auditory processing

Notes: behavioral measures ONLY.

Figure 4.7 Sample note card.

John E. Hocking, "Sports and Spectators: Intra-Audience Effects," *Journal of Communication* 32, 1 (1982), 100–108.

"Intra-audience effects" refers to the impact of audience members overt responses to any stimulus on other members of an audience. This descriptive study, supplemented with reviews of relevant literature, examined how crowd behavior and spectator's reactions can contribute to the entertainment value and involvement that result from watching sports in a live context. Specifically, Hocking argues that crowd response contributes to the degree of arousal, excitement, and enjoyment experienced by crowd members.

Four theoretical perspectives, each of which postulates different social influence processes, were proposed as being useful for understanding intra-audience effects at sports events: contagion theory, convergence theory, emergent norm theory, and information theory. Each perspective is described.

Future research directions and methods for conveying the "stadium event" through the broadcast media are suggested.

Figure 4.8 Sample abstract card.

CONDUCTING THE LIBRARY SEARCH

This section is the nuts and bolts material needed to find and use documents effectively. As with most endeavors, actual use of the library, that is, practice, will enhance performance. Different libraries have different procedures and policies; to be effective you must understand how *your* library works. At many colleges and universities there are courses on the use of the library. If your school offers one, you might consider enrolling. If not, then most library personnel are more than happy to introduce you to their realm. One final note: when in doubt about anything in the library, *ask for assistance;* librarians are there to help you and, when asked the appropriate question, usually can answer it, or, if you are not sure of the question, they can help you formulate it.

APPRAISING THE DOCUMENT

At this stage your plan of attack should include the basic criteria by which you will select a document for possible inclusion at a later stage. Although there probably are as many different criteria as there are different research questions and researchers, several rules of thumb may be applied to any document you encounter in your search. Use these as your initial screening criteria.

Content

The first criterion applied to any document deals with its content. To what degree does the document deal with your research questions? Is it central to your topic, on the periphery, or irrelevant? Does it report the findings of a particular research project or is it a summary of existing research? A literature review? A critical analysis of your area of interest? Does the article add anything *new*? These questions can be answered in part by reading the abstract that accompanies most scholarly articles.

Authority

The second rule of thumb deals with authority: Is the document from a reputable source? This appraisal would be based on knowledge concerning the type of document (book, journal, etc.), the authors of the document, and their backgrounds. In appraising the document you might consider whether it was subjected to a peer review or was invited by the editor. The publisher also should be considered. Is the publisher (in the case of a book) large and well respected in the particular area you are researching? Is the publisher a major association (in the case of a journal) and what type of circulation (international, national, regional, local) does it have?

This is not to suggest that smaller circulation works or presses should be evaluated as less important. In many cases a small journal in a particular area may be the *only* outlet for research and theory. In many instances the "academic" presses (i.e., *University of . . . Press*) fall into this category, as do some journals (i.e., *Journal of Communication Therapy*). Do not overlook these documents in your search.

Critical Standards

A third selection criteria is more subjective and deals with your ability to evaluate critically the content of the documents that make it through the selection process to this point, that is, are in print. This appraisal takes the form of a critical analysis of document content. According to Mona McCormick, critical standards are something that can be learned as a skill. As you go through the literature in your area you should become relatively skilled at answering the following questions[7]:

1. Are the main issues or points clearly identified? Does the author(s) clearly explain and define the issues and assumptions being made? Is the theoretical perspective of the author(s) addressed? These concerns are usually identified through the use of *sidebars* (journals) or chapters (books) or *headers* (both) within the document.

2. Are the underlying assumptions of the arguments advanced by the author(s) generally acceptable? Are the questions asked or hypotheses advanced testable or have the potential to be tested? In applying this criteria you must obviously have some background in the area of study. At first some literature will have to be analyzed later, but going with a "gut level" feeling about a document is not a bad idea. It is usually harder to find it again later, once you realize you may need it.

3. Is the evidence presented adequate, evaluated clearly, and does it support the conclusions drawn?

4. Is there any bias and is that bias addressed by the author(s)? Does the author(s) admit to a particular bias and address that bias? Sometimes we may come to a different conclusion simply based on the bias we bring into the research; be prepared for this, it may yield alternative solutions to your problem.

5. How well is the document written? Are concepts clearly defined? Are they operationalized (made testable) in ways that allow for testing? Is the language concise, clear, and concrete? Often the best writing is concise, to the point, and streamlined. This is most often found in the academic journals and professional books. Be prepared for it.

Obviously, not all documents will meet these criteria all the time, but those that come closest will probably be more important to you than those that do not. As will be noted in the last half of this chapter, the process of appraisal should begin as soon as the document is *first* obtained and some type of systematic analysis employed that tells you the importance of the document to your topic or area of interest.

THE LITERATURE REVIEW

The literature review represents a way to interpret formally the documents you have reviewed. In preparing the literature review you put those documents together in a way (1) that provides a clear rationale and history of the area of study, (2) prepares the reader for your theoretical perspective, and (3) serves to establish your hypotheses or research questions. For the novice, the literature review offers a plan of library study that should reduce the time and effort spent in the library. Without a plan you may end up with a lot of "good" documents whose value is questionable.

It is important to note that the literature review is necessary for *all* methods of research.

Statement of the Problem

A good literature review begins with the statement of *the problem.* Basically, to say that there is "a problem" means that there is something that is not known, but that should be known, and the fact that it is *not* known is "the problem." The problem should be stated in such a way that it is restricted in scope. In stating the problem, then, the topic should be limited to something "doable." The problem may be a reaction to something you have read or it may be something you have been thinking about for a long time. The problem statement should accurately reflect the essence of what you will be examining. It may evolve as a result of the library search. The researcher might find that his or her initial question has been answered, but a related one has not.

Historical Review

The historical review section is where the documents are reported. Although there are any number of organizing patterns to the review, most reviews are constructed around one of the following patterns:

1. *Chronological* patterns report the topic in a time sequence. You might begin at a particular time and trace your topic through its development. For instance, you might examine propaganda from 1900 to date.
2. *Cause-effect* patterns begin with a problem and review the various solutions. You might examine the reduction of communication apprehension as the product of speech rehearsal.
3. *Inductive-deductive* patterns begin with a general concept or problem and deduce to more specific concepts and problems (deduction) or begin with a specific idea or problem and build to a larger problem or idea (induction). You might consider how brainstorming affects group behavior in general (inductive) or how personal space violations influence attitudes depending on the type of violator (deductive).
4. *Topical* patterns break the topic into subtopics and examine each individually. This pattern sometimes includes the other three within it. For example, you might be interested in source credibility and break it into topical areas such as expertise, attraction, or dynamism. You would then present the research addressing each topic separately.

Critical Analysis

The next stage is a critical analysis of what has preceded it. This analysis is sometimes done in the historical review, but should be undertaken here even if done earlier. It is at this stage that you critically review the research with an eye toward establishing patterns, relationships, strengths, weaknesses, and future research needs. The critical analysis establishes *your* theoretical perspective as it relates to those of others who have researched similar areas. The critical analysis, then, serves as your contribution to study in the area.

A second form of critical analysis is more specific and called *meta-analysis*. [8] In its simplest form a meta-analysis is an analysis of previous literature in an area that has been studied *quantitatively*. A meta-analysis provides information on the comparative effectiveness of a number of variables that may influence a given area. For example, a recent meta-analytic study by Mike Allen, John E. Hunter, and William A. Donahue examined the impact of public speaking anxiety as self-reported data on communication apprehension reduction programs. [9] The meta-analysis they conducted provided information on which treatment techniques, if any, were preferred, and the relative effectiveness of each or combinations of each.

Meta-analysis, although a statistical analysis, seeks to establish a communality among the studies by converting the reported results to a common metric. Conducting a meta-analysis requires that you first identify and define the variables of interest. In Allen, Hunter, and Donahue's study these variables included communication apprehension treatment type (systematic desensitization, cognitive modification, and skills training) and over 20 different measurement instruments. Next, boundaries on the type of studies included in the analysis are established. In this example they included: one or more treatments on one or more measured variables; each study had to have a pretest and a posttest measurement; the study had to be available (the authors had to be able to review the *actual* study, not a summary of the study); and there had to be enough *reported* results (in terms of descriptive statistics). Once the variables have been identified and defined and the boundary conditions specified, an exhaustive literature review is conducted. The studies are then statistically analyzed and the results critically evaluated. What Allen, Hunter, and Donahue found was that of the seven possible treatment combinations, all were effective, but several were more effective than others (based on the size of the correlations obtained between the studies).

Meta-analysis provides a way to evaluate topic areas more quantitatively, and some would argue, more objectively. In the end, however, the analyses must still be critically analyzed and subjective conclusions drawn. The advantage of the meta-analysis is that the studies reviewed have been "standardized." The results of different studies on different populations and samples can be compared and some form of comparative judgments made. Many times such analyses will identify variables that in isolation—in individual studies—seem important, but when compared with others in the larger picture may not be as important. An important feature of this type of analysis is the identification of moderator variables (variables that intervene in a study to change the results of the expected relationship). Based on such a study, new research questions may be posed and new approaches to the research undertaken.

Generation of Questions and/or Hypotheses

After the critical analysis you might consider asking questions or stating hypotheses. This stage of the literature review allows you to question past research (Will it [the problem or solution] still hold true today? Given this new information does the same relationship still hold?) in such a way that you propose new research projects. You may ask value questions (How well did President John F. Kennedy manipulate the media? What were the rhetorical principles of Nazi Germany?). You may see new relationships emerging from your review and formally state them as hypotheses (Given direct eye contact to an audience, perceptions of source credibility will increase. Emotional information received by the brain's right hemisphere will be interpreted faster than emotional information received by the brain's left hemisphere.). Not all literature reviews generate research questions or hypotheses, instead they may point out areas where more research is needed before such statements can be made or questions asked.

Closing Section

Like all formal papers, all literature reviews should end with a summary or conclusion section. This section should summarize the problem, the areas of the historical review, the essence of the critical analysis, and point to the future.

Bibliography

A literature review should contain a bibliography. The bibliography is more than just the references listed throughout the paper, it is a listing of all the sources you found that relate in some way to your topic. Some bibliographies are annotated; that is, they contain a statement describing the entry. A good bibliography will serve you in later years, you will find yourself coming back to it.

Summary

What does the literature review do? Leedy suggests seven benefits of a literature review [10]:

1. It can reveal investigations similar to your own, and it can show you how the collateral researcher handled these situations.
2. It can suggest a method or a technique of dealing with a problematic situation which may also suggest avenues of approach to the solution of similar difficulties you may be facing.
3. It can reveal to you sources of data which you may not have known existed.
4. It can introduce you to significant research personalities [authorities] of whose research efforts and collateral writings you may have had no knowledge.
5. It can help you to see your own study in historical and associational perspective and in relation to earlier and more primitive attacks on the same problem.
6. It can provide you with new ideas and approaches which may not have occurred to you.

7. It can assist you in evaluating your own research efforts by comparing them with related efforts done by others.

In preparing to enter the library, the literature review, in its outline form, provides a plan of attack. In short, the literature review, whether it is actually written or not, provides the basic strategies necessary to conduct a library research project effectively.

CREATING THE END PRODUCT

Once a library search has been completed, what do you do with the material? This depends, of course, on the nature of the research you plan on doing. If, for instance, you did the library search for a specific paper, you would then gather your information together and use it to write the paper, the literature review section of the study, or whatever. If you are writing a comprehensive overview on your topic (sometimes called an *area paper*) then you need to go over the Literature Review material presented earlier. However, there are other things that can be produced from a library search.

It is important to remember that the method you choose may dictate how your end product is written. If you are preparing to conduct social science research your paper may examine, for example, the effects that a series of variables have on other variables—you may conduct your own meta-analysis of the relevant research. If you are dealing with a project focusing on the more value-oriented or humanistic dimensions of research, such as those found in historical analysis or in the critical analysis of a particular speech event or movement, your search will center on the more qualitative dimensions of interpretation of past events. As was noted in Chapter 2, there are significant differences in each method's approach to research and these are usually borne out in the end product, as discussed in Chapter 5.

Finally, one important step is left: the creation of a *bibliography*. The bibliography provides a listing of all the sources you found in your library search. The bibliography simply lists—usually in alphabetical order—the citations you have on your cards or in your data base. The bibliography, however, could be broken into sections relating to the key words you used in your search. Again, the listings would usually be in alphabetical order, but possibly in some other order as well (chronological or topical, for instance).

Another type of bibliography is the *annotated* bibliography, which is similar to the straight bibliography or topical breakdown bibliography, but also includes brief synopses—descriptions—of each source. This bibliography can be important if you plan on using the sources in a programmed series of projects.

There are several advantages to the bibliography. One is being able to locate all your sources in one document. A second is being able to carry the bibliography around without worrying about spilling all your cards. Finally, the bibliography allows you to put your materials together in such a way as to create some form of perspective on your topic or area. Even after creating the bibliography (in whatever form) you should keep your cards—they are invaluable.

LIMITATIONS OF LIBRARY RESEARCH

Like any method of research, there are limitations to the library-documentary form of research. First, there is the problem of availability of documents. For a number of reasons, many documents you need may not be available. The library may not have the particular document you need—the book may be checked out, lost, stolen, or being rebound. The journal needed may not be among the library's holdings, may be at the bindery, lost within the library itself, or, after finding it, you discover someone has torn or ripped the article out. This behavior, by the way, is absolutely despicable; about on par with stealing food from a starving family.

In these instances you might turn to the *interlibrary loan* office of your library. Often, for a small fee, they are able to locate the particular book or article you need at another library and obtain it for you. However, you may have to travel to other libraries or depositories of special collections. Be prepared to use all available library sources, including contacting the author(s) for reprints or copies of their works.

Finally, at some point you have to stop the library research and move on to other stages of your project, although you should never assume that you have all there is to get. Be aware, however, that the assumption of closure after an exhaustive search can limit your effectiveness. Get into the habit of going to the library and updating your files as periodicals and new books are received. It may be to your benefit to join a professional organization; students typically pay reduced dues and receive journals at a discount. The good researcher keeps up to date with developments in his or her areas of interest.

SUMMARY

This chapter has introduced the first tool all researchers must use and master: the library. We examined search strategies and methods of gathering information. Sources and methods have been described that should enhance your ability to gather information for whatever type of research you conduct. Taken together these strategies become skills that you can use to utilize your time better and produce better products.

We began by looking at the library research as the first critical analysis made by the researcher. We noted that from this base you can move to the particular methodology necessary to probe deeper into the area of interest. We worked through several stages of research, including using the library itself, the identification of sources, ways of appraising what was found, and systems for producing the literature review or bibliography. We also examined certain limitations to library research and potential ways of overcoming those limitations. Finally, we noted that library research is an ongoing and continuous process. The good researcher keeps abreast of findings in his or her areas of interest and those that may be related from other areas.

Before you move on to the specific methodological chapters and available tools, we feel it necessary to remind you that *all* research methods require library research. For humanistic methods—those of the historian, rhetorician, and critic—the library may serve as the primary source of information. Good humanistic research is facilitated by a fondness for library research and, perhaps, a reverence for documents. The scientific method utilizes the library, but not to the same degree. The scientist's library tools are located more in the area of current periodicals and journals (and perhaps a few books); the historian/rhetorician/critic's tools are bound to the raison d'être of the library: documents of all types.

PROBES

1. Why is library research important? Why should a researcher be concerned with spending hours in the library? What does the library research process establish for you?

2. How does library research establish parameters of study? Assume that you have been asked to research in the area of message credibility, how would you attempt to begin this research? From what perspective?

3. What is the role of the document in library research? How does a researcher go about appraising the document? What critical standards must be assessed and why? Assuming that you have used documents before, which have met all five criteria? Which have failed? With what effect?

4. All research begins with a literature review. What does that statement mean to you? What does the literature review do? Can you think of any reasons for making the literature review the major thrust of your research? Why or why not?

5. What features of the library have you used in the past? Based on your reading of this chapter, which would you now use? What aspects of the library search are new to you? What features did you already know? What features do you think will become important in the future?

SUGGESTED READING

Anderson, P. J. (1974). *Research guide in journalism.* Morristown, NJ: General Learning Press.

Ball, J. E. (1971). *A guide to library research in psychology.* Dubuque, IA: William C. Brown.

Daniels, L. M. (1976). *Business information sources.* Berkeley, CA: University of California Press.

Friedes, T. (1973). *Literature and bibliography of the social sciences.* Los Angeles, CA: Melville.

Rubin, R. B., Rubin, A. M., and Piele, L. J. (1986). *Communication research: strategies and sources.* Belmont, CA: Wadsworth.

Todd, A. (1979). *Finding facts fast: How to find out what you want and need to know,* 2nd ed. Berkeley, CA: Ten Speed Press.

NOTES

1. Mark Hickson and Don W. Stacks, *NVC: Nonverbal Communication, Studies and Applications*, 2nd ed. (Dubuque: William C. Brown, 1989), chap. 2.
2. Raymond K. Tucker, Richard L. Weaver, and Cynthia Berryman-Fink, *Research in Speech Communication* (Englewood Cliffs, N.J.: Prentice-Hall, 1981), 45–51.
3. Paul D. Leedy, *Practical Research Planning and Design*, 3rd ed. (New York: Macmillan, 1985), 69.
4. Earl Babbie, *The Understanding of Social Research*, 4th ed. (Belmont, Calif.: Wadsworth, 1986), 7–9.
5. Babbie, 7–8.
6. Babbie, 8.
7. Mona McCormick, *The New York Times Guide to Reference Materials*, rev. ed. (New York: Times Books, 1985), 186.
8. For more information, see John Hunter, F. Schmidt, and G. Jackson, *Meta-Analysis* (Beverly Hills, Calif.: Sage, 1982); R. Rosenthal, *Meta-Analytic Procedures for Social Research* (Beverly Hills, Calif.: Sage, 1984).
9. Mike Allen, John E. Hunter, and William A. Donahue, "Meta-Analysis of Self-Report Data on the Effectiveness of Public Speaking Anxiety Treatment Techniques," *Communication Education*, 38 (1989), 54–76. For another example, see David B. Buller, "Distraction During Persuasive Communication: A Meta-Analytic Review," *Communication Monographs*, 53 (1986), 91–114.
10. Leedy, 69.

Chapter 5

Evaluating Sources: Historical/Critical Methodology

*T*here are three traditional classifications of research methods: historical, descriptive, and experimental. These three classifications can be further divided into two groups: humanistic (historical and critical) and scientific (descriptive and experimental). Although this book reflects more of the scientific approach, we would be remiss if we did not provide a brief introduction to the humanistic method. The purpose of this chapter is to examine the humanistic methodology associated with history, rhetoric, and criticism.

Some research questions are more appropriately addressed by humanistic methodology. For the purposes of the communication researcher, then, there exists a *qualitative* dimension of methodology. As an extension of the previous material (Chapter 2 and Chapter 4), the logical progression of research methodology is from the building of the bibliography and literature review to the scrutiny of the obtained materials. While this process is found in *all* types of research, those mastering the historical method do so in much finer detail, and move from a simple *description* to a critical analysis and interpretation of the event or person of interest.

We look first at the logic associated with historical method, including some philosophical assumptions associated with qualitative and quantitative historical methods. We then turn to the historical method as a general way of studying communication. Then, because many people (for instance, journalists as "rhetorical critics") are turning to a *critical analysis* of some event, speech, play or movie, person, or institution, we will differentiate between historical and critical methods. Finally, we will examine some of the advantages and problems associated with the historical/critical methodology.

Before moving into the realm of humanistic methodology, remember that *all* methodology, whether humanistic or scientific, can make an important contribution to the study of communication. In choosing this type of research question and thus one method over others, the researcher indicates a philosophical stance toward the phenomenon studied. This choice most likely originates from those with whom you study. If, for instance, your background is rhetoric, public address, or in the history of institutions or social movements, you will probably opt for the historical/critical, humanistic approach. If, on the other hand, you are more interested in questions of fact about the relationship between variables, descriptive analyses of larger groups of people, or more natural science-like research then you will gravitate toward the scientific.

When you choose a methodology you also choose a degree of generality from which you can then explain your results and apply them to a larger population. In choosing the historical/critical methodology you generally choose to study the concept, event, or person in great detail. This detail places limitations on the extent to which you can generalize your findings to other people or events. When you use the survey or experimental methodology, your ability to generalize may be expanded and your ability to establish or test scientific *theory* is expanded.

How do you decide which methodology is appropriate? Regardless of your preference, the *research question* should provide the answer. At some stage, all researchers use historical methods. Literature reviews are one kind of historical research. Later the *type* of question you ask may dictate that surveys or experiments are most appropriate, or that a quantitative approach to historical methodology provides the best way to answer your question (or test your hypothesis).

By choosing the historical/critical methodology as the way to approach your research you lean toward an understanding of particulars over processes. Humanistic research is interested in establishing the unique contributions of a person, event, or institution to communication. In *most* cases the historical/critical researcher is not interested in groups of people—normative actions or reactions to some stimuli or average attitude toward some topic or person—but in how the specific thing or individual acted, reacted, or emoted. In some instances, the thing may be a social movement or culture, such as the women's movement. This is not to say that all historical research embraces the humanistic approach. There have been many contributions made by historical researchers who embrace a more quantitative, social science orientation, as might be found by skimming an issue of the *Quarterly Journal of Speech, Communication Monographis, Journalism Quarterly,* or similar journals. Although the focus of this chapter is on the humanistic orientation to historical research, an understanding of the social science methodology should enhance your understanding both of how and why historical researchers yield the interpretations they do.

PHILOSOPHICAL ORIENTATIONS

Any person who studies the past could be said to embrace the historical methodology. Additionally, we are concerned with a special case of the historical approach to research: the critical approach. The critical approach is frequently combined with the historical approach and the bulk of this chapter will treat the critical approach as a special tool for the historian.

When we turn to the historical approach we are not simply studying the past, as many would define it. The historical researcher utilizes a methodology that embraces both what has been labeled as *humanistic* and *social scientific.* At the most basic level we need to consider what makes up the study of history. Or, what general orientation to the study of past events, people, or institutions the researcher takes. Many historians, and most of those who take an orientation that is "humanistic," are interested in unique events and seek an in-depth understanding of that event as it relates to its own special outcome in terms of specific time and space. By taking this philosophical orientation the historian understands the focus of his or her study extremely well, but is restricted in the degree of generalization that can be made of the results of the study.

Other historians, some of whom embrace the social sciences, seek to understand the event, person, or institution as part of a larger process. The social science approach seeks to generate generalizations in the form of theory, which can be used to explain events or institutions that affect specific people without regard to time and space.[1] This approach may deal with the *quantification* of records and information in an attempt to understand the past better and predict the future on the basis of some social theory. This historian may rely on statistical methods, formal sampling procedures, and computer analyses.[2] If this approach to history best answers the research questions or hypotheses in which you are interested, you will want to spend considerable time focusing on the quantitative chapters of this text.

If, on the other hand, you are more interested in the description and explanation of past events as end in themselves, then you would focus more on a humanistic approach. Your approach to history would parallel that of Lawrence Stone, who notes, "It [history] deals with a *particular* problem and a *particular* set of actors at a *particular* time in a *particular* place."[3] Some historians, then, are concerned with relating history as it has occurred with an emphasis on the *uniqueness* of history. Others study history to derive or confirm theories—theories that may be useful in understanding the present and predicting the future.

In reality, today's historical communication researcher will probably have to learn both approaches. Given the increase in the amount of information we can access, deciding on which sources to examine and deciding on how to limit research will almost certainly require some understanding of sampling. From a humanistic perspective, historical methodology is characterized in a number of ways: emphasis on the unique, the specific, and the personal nature of the research.

One characteristic of the humanistic approach is the ability to "get close" to the person or event under study. While the social scientific approach emphasizes the contributions of groups of people (aggregates of individuals), the humanistic approach emphasizes the unique and particular.[4] The historian may make sense out of the complex past by understanding how one particular person influenced (or was influenced by) a particular time period. The historian, then, is interested more in an in-depth understanding of one particular person or thing than in how many people or things operated. The thing might be very big and involve many people and groups—World War I, literary or newspaper guilds, for example.

A second characteristic is the ability to focus on a specific and concrete event or person. Much like the psychologist who conducts a case study of a patient, the historian's method produces a case with which he or she is extremely familiar, knows in great detail, and of which, in some way, may even feel a part. This may allow for an insightful analysis of what happened and why.

A third characteristic, closely related to the second, is the way in which the historian may report his or her findings. The historian is in a sense a teller of stories, stories of the past that describe and attempt to explain what happened in the spirit of the particular time. The story may be embellished, something Louis Mink suggests may be a "sequential explanation," or an understanding based on knowledge of events prior to and after the event.[5] Historical method, then, may allow the researcher and the reader to enter into "close contact with events and persons long past and dead."[6]

The stress on the unique and individual contribution makes the humanistic approach to history a rich and detailed research method. The historical researcher must enjoy digging, analyzing, and understanding specific people and events. This research allows for an in-depth understanding of an event or person placed in a specific time and space. The stress on this form of research is description and understanding; generalizing to other people and periods is limited.

As a way of overcoming this limitation of generalization and in an attempt to build "theory," some historians have embraced the social scientific approach. In taking this approach they give up specific and individual knowledge in favor of a better understanding of how that history evolved. As such, the social scientific orientation examines the advent of groups of people and how they, as a group, lived. The advantage to this approach is found in an increased potential to generalize to other time periods and to predict to today or tomorrow.

In the end we would agree with Charles Beard when he says that historical method is "scientific."[7] How the researcher perceives the data he or she collects, however, will determine which approach is appropriate. For the humanistic historian, facts and order in history may be more subjective. For the social scientist, facts and order are less subjective. Again, which approach you take should be determined by your research question, which is influenced in turn by the theoretical perspective you take. If you are trying to gain an understanding of broad social forces or movements across time or trying to understand better the unique contributions of others at specific points in time and space, then the historical methodology is the appropriate method of research.

AN OVERVIEW OF HISTORICAL RESEARCH

Historical research requires following systematic rules and procedures rigorously. According to William Lucey, historical methodology employs a rigorous set of standards aimed at ordering knowledge in such a way as to pass several tests of critical analysis.[8] These tests are what the historian utilizes in his or her quest for knowledge, knowledge that is both "correct" and "appropriate." In examining the past the historian attempts to build upon known "facts" and "evidence" in such a way as to understand better the quality of what happened and how certain events may have contributed to that event.

Raymond K. Tucker, Richard L. Weaver, and Cynthia Berryman-Fink suggest that the historical methodology can be used to study several general areas of investigation. Historical research can be used to "ascertain the meaning and reliability of past facts."[9] It can evaluate past "facts." It can examine how and why events happened as they did and make comparisons and contrasts of major figures or movements. Historical study can also examine how an individual contributed to change within a particular strand of society or social structure. And, historical research can help us to understand better how we arrived at where we are today and even provide insight into the future.

Understanding the Meaning of History

Paul Leedy suggests that history "is the means by which the researcher deals with the latent *meaning* of history."[10] To do this the researcher must get as close to the original sources of information about the *original event* as possible. We can do this by looking at history either as a *chronology of events* or as a reflection of an event occurring in *time and space*. In studying history as chronology the researcher merely traces the events as they occurred in some time pattern. Although this provides insight into cause-effect relationships, it does not help us to understand *what* happened; instead it serves as a road map that simply chronicles events as they happened over time. To understand what happened better the researcher needs to go beyond the chronology (use it as a stepping off point) and examine what happened during this period (for instance, during the Middle Ages, did rhetoric develop or stagnate? What was the impact of Darwin on the study of communication? How did the Hellenistic rhetoric differ from later Greek rhetoric?). This is the *first* step in analysis.

Once the concept of time has been established, the researcher needs to examine the spatial dimension of history. The events had to occur *somewhere*. How did the geographical location affect the events or people? For example, is there a difference between Asian rhetoric and Western rhetoric? Does the geographic location influence our communication patterns? How does location reflect itself in terms of the institutions of communication? By taking location into account the historical researcher is better able to key in on the unique contributions of the person, event, or institutions and make his or her analysis.

Areas of Potential Historical Research

An appraisal of research conducted by the communication historian suggests that historical study falls into seven areas:[11]

1. *Biographical or biographical/critical studies.* Research concentrates on the life of a particular person, such as Abraham Lincoln, Ronald Reagan, Adolf Hitler, Randolph Hearst, or Walter Cronkite.
2. *Movement or idea studies.* These studies center on the development of social movements (political, social, economic) such as ERA, anti-war protest, the Grey Panthers, and Black rhetoric and freedom of press and speech movements.
3. *Regional studies.* Regional studies examine the impact of geographical location, such as a city, state, or nation. Research areas might include American journalism, British oratory, or German film criticism. Crossing region with time also produces areas of research, for instance, American journalism since Watergate, First Amendment attacks by the Reagan presidency, Nazi rhetoric, and French film, 1920–1930.
4. *Institutional Studies.* Institutional studies center on the history of particular institutions, such as IBM, the *New York Times*, CBS, or particular schools of thought (i.e., the Chicago School of Symbolic Interactionism). As with regional studies, they may be located in time and space, yielding specific histories of specific institutions at specific times.
5. *Case histories.* Case histories center on specific events or persons at a specific point in time. Case histories could be conducted on institutions or people. One could research the impact of Watergate on Nixon's rhetoric, or a particular event, such as the incident at Kent State in 1970.
6. *Selective studies.* Selective studies examine one particular aspect of a complex process, for example, the rhetoric of Abbie Hoffman during the Vietnam War period or the impact of "happy talk" in television news, 1970–1979. Selective studies may examine particular aspects of one person's or institution's communication.
7. *Editorial studies.* This area of research focuses on translation of texts or discovery of new texts. Much of this research focuses on the *meaning* of particular statements and their translation to English.

J. Jeffery Auer suggests two other potential areas of study.[12] Auer suggests that *bibliographic* study is an alternative historical research area. Bibliographic study focuses on documentary research and the creation of information bases (see Chapter 4). A second area is the *study of sources,* that is, a study of those with whom the person studied (teacher, mentor) or someone acknowledged as influential in the subject's life. Hence, you might note who influenced the communication style of John F. Kennedy or the political style of Lyndon B. Johnson, the type of reporting of a specific journalist, or the speeches of a particular speaker.

Completing a good historical research project requires a lot of access to information, perseverance, and a little luck. The historical researcher must be willing to spend time gathering and reading primary sources of information: documents (which may include books, photographs, audiotapes, videotapes, etc.). Once the documents have been read (or heard or viewed), categorized, and scrutinized, the researcher can begin to make the interconnections between the "facts" as seen by the particular source and those that he or she can verify.

Advantages and Disadvantages

Historical research has both advantages and disadvantages. Advantages include the ability to know already part of the outcome (e.g., the impact of a particular speech on foreign policy, or the popularity of a particular singer); hence, while obtaining sources the researcher can ascertain whether or not the source agrees or disagrees with history *as it happened.* As the researcher works through the documents certain patterns that may help to explain why others saw or reported the event or person differently may become evident. Finally, as the historian adds to the corpus of knowledge about the topic, he or she gains an insight into how that entity may have acted or thought.

There are also significant disadvantages facing the historical researcher. First and foremost is the problem of *accuracy.* Although we will cover this in detail later, it should suffice here to note that the historian is faced with a major hurdle in determining accuracy. Records are incomplete; often the one piece of the puzzle that would make sense out of a document is lost. Some records are simply inaccurate, reflecting some bias. Mistakes are made by other historians both in terms of data collection (such as premature closure in the document search, note mix-ups, accidental destruction of documents) and in writing the results of the study for publication. Once the research has been written, publishers may make subtle changes that alter the editorial tone. Often space considerations make it necessary to leave out portions of the text originally scheduled for publication. Historical accuracy may then be a relative term.

A second disadvantage is the result of the *new sources of data acquisition and retrieval* available. Today a researcher can use a computer and modem to access data bases and documents in a way never imagined in the past (see Chapter 4 and Chapter 14). This availability produces two major problems. First, rather than reading all the documents identified, we may rely instead on the services of others, hence our access may actually take us further from the sources we need (these become, as we will discuss, secondary sources). Second, the information explosion may cause us to wait forever to reach closure. If we keep both problems in mind, treating the data we have as a continual process of gaining knowledge, we can draw conclusions as accurate as the information we have and feel fairly confident in what we report.

HISTORICAL METHODOLOGY [13]

Historical research reflects the careful and systematic assembling of all the authentic "facts" that may have a bearing on the target of study. The historian's methodology is tied to how he or she gathers information. In some cases the interview may yield the information necessary to make conclusions. However, more commonly this information takes the form of extant documents and records (visual, written, or auditory).

Historical Facts

In examining these sources the research is seeking the "facts" as they might have been known at that time. These "facts" may be different from those we believe or know today. For instance, at one time or another it was believed to be a "fact" that the earth was flat and that the sun revolved around the earth. A fact, in terms of history, is not simple. Facts are created through human perception, perceptions that may change as times or locations change. Therefore, the historical fact is something the researcher sees and uses to make a particular event clear. Facts are usually derived either directly or indirectly from historical documents and verified by others. Hence, the historical fact is dependent upon verification, even if that "fact" is different from what we know today.

Historical Documents

The historical fact arises from documentation. Historical documents may be defined as any evidence the researcher uses to establish or help explain the event or person under study. In most instances a document is any original written, auditory, or visual record, official or unofficial. It may take the form of a report, newspaper article, editorial, transcript of a speech, tape (audio or video) of a speech, diary, letter, correspondence, or, even garbage. A document, then, is something the researcher seeks that may add to his or her knowledge of the period, person, event, or institution.

Historical Research

The historical method blends the data (or facts) obtained from various sources into a lucid and flowing narrative. The major goal is to explicate some event from the past in a manner that illuminates the communication and its effects. To do so the researcher collects *surviving objects*—the printed, written, and oral materials that may be of relevance and can be authenticated. After this he or she then extracts the material that he or she believes is (and tests out as) credible. Finally, he or she organizes that material into a reliable narrative or exposition.

One of the major functions of historical research, then, is to (1) set out to find all available information, (2) scrutinize that information in terms of accuracy, and

(3) get the "story" (or narrative) out. (Gathering information is discussed in Chapter 4.) We now need to examine more closely the sources of information we gather and how we can test for authenticity.

Sources, Information, and the Test of Evidence   Broadly speaking, there are two sources of information. We actively seek *primary evidence,* that is, evidence from the source itself. Primary evidence consists of testimony, documents, and evidence that comes from those actually engaged in the activities of the period. At times, however, we are forced to deal with *secondary evidence,* that is, evidence from those of the time period who may have observed but did not actually engage in the activities in question. Secondary evidence also represents sources whose credibility or testimony you cannot personally verify through access to primary sources. Sometimes we are forced to begin our research with *tertiary evidence,* or evidence based on the accounts of accounts of the primary source.[14] Obviously, tertiary evidence must be approached with even greater caution, but it may yield important clues to securing secondary or primary evidence.

In general it is best to use evidence from primary sources. When we cannot get to the primary source, secondary evidence should be carefully cross-checked for accuracy. In establishing criteria for secondary and tertiary evidence, the researcher must establish both the context of the source and the accuracy of the researcher. If the context can be established and the source is reputable, secondary evidence may be accepted. Tertiary evidence, however, is accepted less frequently and must be viewed skeptically.

Testing for *external evidence* concerns the following questions: Is the information the real thing? Is it genuine? Is it authentic? There are certain physical tests that can establish authenticity. Authenticity could be established through scientific tests on the documents found. Such tests include examination of handwriting, paper and ink used, and whether the language reflects the period under study. Additionally, you have to ask yourself whether or not, based on the reporter's abilities, the materials you are working with are accurate. At least eight questions should be asked in establishing textual authenticity[15]:

1. Was the person in a position to perceive the event clearly? With little distraction?
2. Was the source *physically* able to observe the communication (was he or she blind? deaf?)?
3. Was the person *intellectually* able to perceive the event?
   a. Was the testimony or material presented in a clear, concise and intelligible fashion?
   b. Did the reporter present the material in a clear, concise, and intelligible fashion?
4. Was the person able to *morally* report what occurred? (Did the event run against current religious or social norms? What pressures may have been on the witness or reporter?)
5. Was the person aware of the significance of his or her reporting? (Was the person accurately reporting the event or how it should be for posterity?)
6. Was the person reluctant to report what was reported? (The reluctant

reporter is generally perceived more credible. Did the person have an ''axe'' to grind?)
7. Did the person have a personal interest in the event or the way in which the evidence was presented? (Knowledge of potential bias? Was any such bias made clear in the document?)
8. Is the person supported by other sources and evidence?

Additionally, you might consider the source's training as an observer and establish the source's relationship to the event, person, or institution. You might consider how long it was between the event and the writing about the event. Obviously, the longer the time period between event and document, the less reliable it is likely to be. Make certain, especially in the case of speeches, that the text you work with is the one actually presented. In the case of speeches before Congress, make certain that the indicated speaker actually delivered the speech. Also, ascertain whether you are working with the speaker's own words. Finding two or more forms of the same material is not uncommon. Check variant forms against each other for verification.

Testing for *internal evidence* follows external testing. Now that the authenticity of the material has been established to some degree of satisfaction, the researcher begins to evaluate the statements made within the material. The criteria we examine at this stage of research concern the source's *meaning.* Here we are asking: What is the person trying to say? What is behind the statements made, and the way they are made? The focus is on the meaning of the words or symbols used in communication.

Internal testing focuses on the credibility of the document. When testing the internal criteria we focus on the *literal meaning* of the document. What does any given statement really say? Are there technical, foreign, archaic, or unfamiliar terms? If so, the researcher must delve into the symbols and slang of the period to gain an understanding of what the source was trying to say. Finding the meaning the source intended is difficult. Rarely, for instance, do two people agree on what someone else has said. The researcher must take into account ambiguity and the use of figurative language in the original source's words. Also, because most of the documents will be in written form, sarcasm and humor may be difficult to spot, let alone analyze. The researcher must also watch for statements taken out of context. A statement taken in context provides a wealth of information; a statement taken out of context is next to worthless, unless, of course, the researcher is interested in how original communications are used out of context by others.

Ultimately, the researcher must decide whether or not the statements reviewed and analyzed are believable. Much like external evidence, a statement's believability is based upon confirmation. Confirmation in this case, however, may deal with the internal consistency of the document or statement, the ability to verify that this was indeed communicated in the way it was and in the correct context. Finally, the researcher must decide if the statement made reflects the person or institution he or she has been studying all along.

Skepticism The acceptance or rejection of a document or the testimony of a source must be approached with skepticism. In attempting to arrive at truth, the historical researcher must wade through streams of manuscripts, notes, and other relics that may help or hinder the quest. In the end, the historical researcher must be prepared for conflicting testimony and information. In many instances what was true was repressed or rewritten by the powers that be. Only a careful analysis of all sources of information allows the researcher to arrive at a decision regarding the *degree* of truth to be found in any one document or statement.

Analytical Strategies   Historical research is both inductive and deductive. In some cases the historian relies on the deductive approach, reasoning from an idea or thesis, looking for evidence to support the thesis, then leading to new ideas or thesis statements. In other cases the historian relies on a keen sense of induction. Sometimes a particular piece of evidence will derive theses or ideas concerning relationships or events.

Some argue, however, that historical research is *adductive*, that the process of inquiry is neither deductive nor inductive. Rather, inquiry takes the form of "adducing answers to specific questions, so that a satisfactory explanatory 'fit' is obtained."[16] That is, it follows a *general systems* approach to the event being studied.[17] This approach suggests that communication (or other phenomona) are best *described* when *all* possible causes are examined for their impact on some event. As such, the historical researcher would examine the *interactive* impact of all possible causes, rather than singling out one or two for specific attention.

According to MaryAnn Smith, then, "Adduction permits the historian to respond to a research question with multiple measures."[18] Hence, the historian takes a "holistic" approach to research, taking all the information and extrapolating meaning based on a viewing of the whole corpus of data without the dictum of some form of reasoning (deductive or inductive). This is what Edward DeBono calls *lateral think*[19]—rather than digging a deeper hole based on the analytical techniques of induction or deduction, the historian may widen the hole as he or she digs deeper into the research. In this way a "new" depth and breadth of understanding may be reached.

There are times when the historian must borrow from social scientific colleagues. At times there may be too much data to comprehend or there may be large gaps in the data. In such cases statistical methods can be brought to bear on the problem, sampling frames designed, and reliability and validity ascertained. The historian may also wish to conduct a content analysis described in detail in Chapter 11, in which a category system that allows for an objective and systematic classification of communication content is created.

Thus, when the research question suggests it is appropriate to do so, the historian can turn from a humanistic, qualitative approach to a more quantitative, social scientific, behavioral approach. This requires that the historian understand quantitative methodology. Later chapters in this text will help provide that understanding. There are times, however, when objective methods do not answer the research question. It may be that the researcher must make artistic (aesthetic or ethical) decisions based on a *communicative performance* that has occurred at some time (either historically or in the immediate past). In times like these the researcher must become a *critic.* The next section examines historical/critical research.

CRITICAL METHODOLOGY

The application of critical analysis to a communication event or communication performer is increasingly finding its way into applied communication research and reporting, that is, the media. Hardly a day passes without news reporters delivering critical commentaries about some speech or communication. While the reporter may be trained in traditional journalism, seldom does he or she understand critical methodology. Critical method is part of the humanistic approach to historical research. We also view it as an extension of the tests of internal evidence or criticism the researcher uses when examining the question of how well the act was accomplished. This section examines how to use critical methodology.

Critical research requires that the criteria or standards appropriate to the communication be chosen and analyzed.[20] In conducting a critical study the researcher should examine at least four aspects of the communication: the results, the artistic standards, the basis of the ideas, and the motives and ethics behind the communication. In examining the results of the communication, the researcher attempts to answer the questions, What was the purpose of the communication? What was the *true* purpose of the communication? And, what connection can be found between the communication and the results?

Artistic standards refer to the use of appropriate rhetorical methods and principles to examine how well the communication was accomplished. There are many sets of artistic standards. For example, there are the five traditional canons of rhetoric—invention, arrangement, style, delivery, and memory—although such classical models of proof themselves have been criticized, by which the critic examines how the communication was put together, the language used, the units of "proof" employed, and how it was delivered.[21]

A second critical method often employed is that of critical discourse. Thomas Farrell has identified three "models" of performance of discourse, each slightly different in its approach to the communication event or person.[22] The first model, *symptom criticism,* approaches the communication event or person as a symptom of some larger social concern. This approach tends to be more sociological in nature, examining the social features or themes underlying the culture of the communication. For instance, suppose you were interested in addressing the question of culture and alienation in a modern media presentation, such as the film *Taxi Driver.* You might examine how the artifacts of alienation (which you define) are exhibited by the particular culture and are identified by themes within the film and its impact on that culture. You might do the same by looking at the ways in which film portrays the "Vietnam experience," through both the rhetoric of *Rambo* and, later, *Platoon.*

Farrell's second model is more traditional. The critic using this model follows the notion that the study of the event or person is the model. Farrell calls this *didactic criticism.*[23] Here the critic is interested in the particular communicator and how he or she uses communication as a tool. For instance, we might be interested in the use of metaphor as a rhetorical tool in the lyrics of a particular composer. We might want to know the particular *themes* that are found in the communications of a particular person, the personal meanings associated with the communication.

Finally, Farrell suggests a third model, one he labels *thematic criticism*. [24] Here the critic is interested in how the communication is constructed. A particular model is constructed and the messages of the communicators are examined in light of that particular model. Bruce E. Gronbeck's assessment of thematic critical method is found in Figure 5.1. [25] This model suggests that we can analyze communication based on the communicators' (actors as performers and actors as audience) meanings and actions (verbal and nonverbal communications) as they interact with and within particular social and cultural contexts. Hence, the theme becomes a way of analyzing the mental constructs that created the communication.

One particular thematic method that has enjoyed particular attention by communication researchers is that of Kenneth Burke. [26] Burke's approach is to examine the language as if it were used "on stage." In Burke's method the language employed is examined in terms of action rather than information. Burke's analysis has been labeled the Pentad and examines the interrelationships between symbol use and the *act* (communicative message), *scene* (the situation or background against which the act is performed), *agent* (the source of the communicative message), *agency* (the means or instruments used to communicate, or how the agent went about carrying out the act), and the *purpose* (the aim or goal of the message act). An example of this method might be Burke's analysis of *Mein Kampf* as a critical event: Adolph Hitler (agent) delivering a propagandistic message (act) at mass rallies (agency) with the setting of post–World War I economic and political turmoil (scene) with the goal (purpose) of uniting Germany and securing political

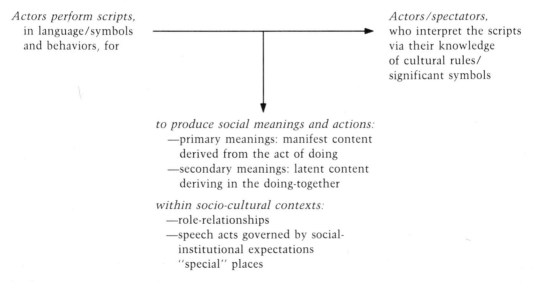

Figure 5.1 Dramaturgical models of communication in society. (*Source:* Bruce E. Gronbeck, "Dramaturgical Theory and Criticism: The State of the Art [or Science]?" *Western Journal of Speech Communication,* 44 [1980], 317.)

power. Each element of the Pentad may be analyzed for results and artistic standards or all may be analyzed.

The basis of ideas concerns what was actually communicated. Here the critic is interested in establishing whether or not what was said was worthy of being said. Analysis centers on the integrity of ideas presented in the communication. The motives and ethics concern the unstated reasons for the communication. By specifying the motives and ethics the critic gets a better understanding of the psychological being of the speaker. Finally, the critic examines how each of the four categories relate to one another.

Conducting a Critical Examination of Communication

In conducting a historical/critical study the researcher begins by describing what has happened. This sets the stage so to speak. In this analysis the researcher focuses on two sets of factors: those that are extrinsic to the communication and those that are intrinsic to the communication.

Extrinsic Factors   In describing the event the researcher seeks to: (1) describe and analyze the period in which the communication occurred. As with Burke's analysis of *Mein Kampf*, the time in which the communication occurred is extremely important, it sets the stage against which other communication could be compared or contrasted. (2) The researcher describes the audience, both in terms of the intended and the real audience. What audience was the speech, for instance, written for and which audience actually received it? (3) The occasion for the speech is then described and analyzed. In the case of Lincoln's "Gettysburg Address," for instance, what was the occasion? Was the occasion used for a particular effect? (4) The researcher describes and analyzes the speaker (or organization), giving attention to the speaker's background and training. And, (5) the communication itself is described and analyzed.

Intrinsic Factors   This leads to the analysis of the communication itself and the evidence with which it was constructed. Here attention is placed on the interpretation and evaluation of the ideas and supporting logic presented. Analysis is focused on how the logic fits with the period in which the communication was presented. Next, the analysis and description turns on the speaker and his or her ability. What sort of speaker was he or she? What were his or her strengths and weaknesses? How well were verbal and nonverbal skills incorporated? Hence, the intrinsic features stress the individual's skills at creating and presenting the communication.[27]

LIMITATIONS AND HAZARDS IN HISTORICAL RESEARCH

Just as with all methods, the historical method has certain limitations and hazards. In historical research the researcher must be prepared for fragmentary and incomplete records. In many cases you will not be able to find all the available data. A second limitation concerns the facts with which you work. Facts change as language and meaning change. As these facts change, any attempt at fixing cause and effect becomes problematic. Finally, there are certain limitations on the researcher him- or herself. These limitations include personal bias, selective perception of what is "right" and what is not, and faulty interpretation.

SUMMARY

This chapter has examined a methodology that almost all researchers must learn to some degree: historical research. By conducting historical research we learn something of our past. From this past we can then better understand contemporary actions and feelings. For some, the historical methodology serves as the appropriate methodology for the particular research question. It may be that the type of research you are interested in stresses the unique and particular; and through historical research you may gain greater understanding of the complexities of the past.

In conducting historical research several difficulties were examined. Then the concept of the historical document and fact were discussed. Finally, historical methodology was pursued as a base for conducting research and critical methodology was examined as a special tool for examining *communication* events on a qualitative level. It was noted, however, that the historical researcher may borrow quantitative and statistical tools from the social sciences. In many ways, the good historical researcher must know a little about several methods and choose the most appropriate method or tools within the method.

PROBES

1. What differentiates the historical/critical method from other methods? Practically, what can historical/critical do that scientific method cannot?

2. Assume for the moment that you have an assignment that requires that you get to know a particular speaker or editor. How would the historical/critical method help you gain a better understanding of this person? What research questions might you ask when approaching the research?

3. What is the "latent meaning of history"? How does this approach to historical research differ from a chronological or time and space analysis of some event or person?

4. How does the historical researcher go about testing his or her data? What limitations are you faced with when you take the historical method and apply it to communication? Using the Vietnam War as your event, what type of research could you conduct from this perspective?

5. How does critical method differ from historical method? What does critical method provide that historical does not? Taking the Vietnam War as your concern, what research questions might you ask about that era? How would you analyze the communication(s)?

SUGGESTED READING

Auer, J. J. (1959). *An introduction to research in speech.* New York: Harper & Row.

Black, E. (1965). *Rhetorical criticism: A study in method.* New York: Macmillan.

Carter, E. S., & Fife, I. (1961). The critical approach. In C. W. Dow (ed.), *An introduction to graduate study in speech and theatre.* East Lansing: Michigan State University Press.

Fisher, D. H. (1970). *Historians' fallacies.* New York: Harper & Row.

Mishler, E. G. (1986). *Research interviewing: Context and narrative.* Cambridge, MA: Harvard University Press.

Nord, D. P., & Nelson, H. L. (1981) "The logic of historical research," in G. H. Stempel, III & B. H. Westley (Eds.), *Research methods in mass communication.* Englewood Cliffs, NJ: Prentice-Hall.

Phifer, G. (1961). The historical approach. In C. W. Dow (Ed.), *An introduction to graduate study in speech and theatre.* East Lansing: Michigan State University Press.

Thonssen, L., Baird, A. C., & Braden, W. W. (1970). *Speech criticism* (2nd ed.). New York: Ronald Press.

NOTES

1. David P. Nord and Harold L. Nelson, "The Logic of Historical Research," in Guido H. Stempel, III, and Bruce H. Westley, *Research Methods in Mass Communication* (Englewood Cliffs, N.J.: Prentice-Hall, 1981), 282–283.
2. Nord and Nelson, 298.
3. Lawrence Stone, "History and the Social Sciences in the Twentieth Century," in Charles F. Delzell, ed., *The Future of History* (Nashville: Vanderbilt University Press, 1977), 28.
4. Nord and Nelson, 285.
5. Louis O. Mink, "The Autonomy of Historical Understanding," in William H. Drey, ed., *Philosophical Analysis and History* (New York: Harper & Row, 1961), 172.
6. Nord and Nelson, 289.
7. Charles A. Beard, "Written History as an Act of Faith," *American Historical Review* 39 (1934), 219–231.
8. William J. Lucey, *History: Methods and Interpretation* (Chicago: Loyola University Press, 1958), 22.
9. Raymond K. Tucker, Richard L. Weaver, III, and Cynthia Berryman-Fink, *Research in Speech Communication* (Englewood Cliffs, N.J.: Prentice-Hall, 1981), 68.
10. Paul D. Leedy, *Practical Research: Planning and Design,* 3rd ed. (New York: Macmillan, 1985), 119.
11. Gregg Phifer, "The Historical Approach," in Clyde Dow, ed., *An Introduction to Graduate Study in Speech and Theatre* (East Lansing: Michigan State University Press, 1961), 52–80.
12. J. Jeffery Auer, *An Introduction to Research in Speech* (New York: Harper & Brothers, 1959), 120–122.
13. This material in this section has been gathered from two basic sources: J. Jeffery Auer's

An Introduction to Research in Speech and Gregg Phifer's "The Historical Approach." Additional sources include MaryAnn Y. Smith, "The Method of History," in Guido H. Stempel, III, and Bruce H. Westley, eds., *Research Methods in Mass Communication* (Englewood Cliffs, N.J.: Prentice-Hall, 1981), 305–319; and Leedy.

14. Phifer, 59.
15. Henry L. Ewbank and J. Jeffery Auer, *Discussion and Debate,* 2nd ed. (New York: Appleton-Century-Crofts, 1951), 108–109.
16. David H. Fisher, *Historians' Fallacies* (New York: Harper & Row, 1970), 1.
17. See Don W. Stacks, Sidney R. Hill, and Mark Hickson, *An Introduction to Communication Theory* (Fort Worth: Holt, Rinehart and Winston, 1991). Stacks, Hill, and Hickson examine systems theory as a way to approach inquiry that differs from deductive and inductive methods; some define this as "adductive."
18. Smith, 315.
19. Edward DeBono, *New Think* (New York: Avon, 1968).
20. This material in this section was drawn primarily from Elton S. Carter and Iline Fife, "The Critical Approach," in Clyde Dow, ed., *An Introduction to Graduate Study in Speech and Theatre* (East Lansing: Michigan State University Press, 1961), 81–103 and Lester Thonssen, A. Craig Baird, and Waldo W. Braden, *Speech Criticism,* 2nd ed. (New York: Ronald Press, 1970).
21. See Edwin Black, *Rhetorical Criticism: A Study in Method* (New York: Macmillan, 1965).
22. See Thomas B. Farrell, "Critical Models in the Analysis of Discourse," *Western Journal of Speech Communication* 44 (1980): 300–314, for an excellent overview of the rhetorical critical methods in general and Bruce E. Gronbeck, "Dramaturgical Theory and Criticism: The State of the Art (or Science?)," *Western Journal of Speech Communication* 44 (1980): 315–330 for the dramaturgical.
23. Farrell, 307–311.
24. Farrell, 311–313.
25. Gronbeck, 316–320.
26. See Kenneth Burke, *A Grammar of Motives* (New York: Meridian, 1965); and Kenneth Burke, *A Rhetoric of Motives* (New York: Meridian, 1965).
27. For more information about conducting a critical analysis, see Carter and Fife; Thonssen, Baird, and Braden.

Chapter
6

Measurement

*I*n Chapter 2 we introduced the notion of the operational definition, the social scientist's bridge between the abstract world of theories about the relationships between variables and the observable world in which the variables either are or are not related as stated in the theory. Operational definitions specify the procedures for observing: They state how we will know a particular variable when we see it, and the values the particular variable takes on. Operational definitions, then, constitute the rules that spell out how to assess the existence of a variable. Earlier we described two kinds of operational definitions, manipulated and measured, and noted that an independent variable may be manipulated, as in an experiment, *or* measured, as in a survey. Dependent variables are always measured. Measurement is a crucial part of any research project that addresses a question of fact. Measurement is an integral part of doing scientific or social scientific research.

WHAT IS MEASUREMENT?

Any observation can be thought of as a measurement. When we look out the window and see trees we are involved in measurement. We have a sense of what a tree is, we know when we see one, and we know when we do not. Thus, when we look out the window and see trees we are observing the amount of "treeness" in what we see. Like all measurements, our observation of trees involves a *comparison.* We compare what we see with what we have seen at other times and in other settings. We can see trees because we know that at other times we have seen no trees. To be sure, these sorts of measurements are casual and imprecise, and we are generally unconscious of the process, but they are measurements nonetheless. If you arrived home one evening and the trees were not there, you would know it.

In fact, whenever we process incoming data through any of our five senses, we are involved in measurement. When you touch your pet, smell the coffee brewing, hear a mail truck, taste a doughnut, see a computer, you are making observations—measurements, comparisons—regarding your immediate environment. The difference between the measurements that all of us spend most of our waking hours making and the measurements made by scientists revolves around the care and precision with which they are made. We measure casually, without much thought. However, when we take on a social scientist role, we measure variables with great care and give them a great deal of thought.

Suppose that someone tells you that it is raining right now. You would know this because you have seen rain previously and you also know what "not raining" is and can compare the two. The variable "amount of rain," however, can take on many different values, as many as our language can describe. It is presently "sprinkling lightly." Later, it might rain harder. It might "pour," or "rain cats and dogs." It could even develop into a "torrential downpour," or possibly into a real "gully washer," or even a "toad choker." Each of these labels is an attempt to *quantify* the variable, "amount of rainfall." Unfortunately, our language can be terribly imprecise. A meteorologist attempting to develop theories that would allow her to explain and predict the amount of rainfall would be severely handicapped if she had to assess her dependent variable, "amount of rainfall," with terms such as "toad choker." Instead, she uses mathematics. And, to a greater or lesser extent, all scientists do the same thing. Using precisely described rules, we assign numbers to our observations. In fact, measurement is commonly defined as the process of assigning numbers to observations according to specified rules.[1]

In measuring rainfall, the notion that 1 inch of rain is half as much as 2 inches is taken for granted. It is obvious. Likewise, the difference between $\frac{1}{4}$ inch of rain and $\frac{1}{2}$ inch is the same as the difference between 3 inches and $3\frac{1}{4}$ inches. It might seem tempting to conclude that all measures that associate numbers with observations of variables allow similar conclusions. However, depending on the "level" at which a variable is measured, these conclusions may or may not be justified.

Levels of Measurement

What is the "appropriate" level of measurement? The answer is found in the particular research question you ask. There are four levels of measurement: nominal, ordinal, interval, and ratio.

Nominal Measurement   "The nominal scale represents the most unrestricted assignment of numerals."[2] Nominal measurement involves assigning numbers to categories that have *qualitative* rather than quantitative differences. For example, the numbers on uniforms worn by athletes serve this function. Football players are differentiated by the numbers they wear. Yet a player who wears number 34 does not have more of something than a player who wears number 17, let alone twice as much of it. The numbers only serve as substitutes for the names of the players. They allow the spectators to tell which player is which and sometimes what position they play.

Variables of interest to the communication researcher, which are generally measured at the nominal level, include sex, race, political party affiliation, and communication media (face-to-face, telephone, mediated). The advantage of labeling a variable 1, 2, or 3 instead of Democrat, Republican, or Independent, is that variables with numeric category labels can be summarized and related to one another using special statistical techniques designed for nominal variables.

Ordinal Measurement   Most variables of interest to communication researchers are measured at least at the next level of measurement precision, the ordinal level. Ordinal measures involve being able to say that something or someone has more or less of whatever is being measured than someone else. A person could be asked to list the message strategy that he or she would be most likely to use to end a relationship, then to indicate the next most likely strategy, then the third most likely strategy, and so on. The researcher would assign a 1 to the individual's most favored strategy, a 2 to the next strategy, a 3 to the third listed strategy, and so on.

Note that nothing about the *size* of the differences between the various strategies is known. The difference between the most favored strategy and the second favored strategy might be small or large, and it might or might not be the same as the difference between the second and third preferred strategies. Further, nothing is known about the absolute *magnitude* of the individual's favorableness toward any of the strategies. The person might be highly favorable toward all three strategies, or may not like any of them at all and merely have viewed the "ranking ordering" as choosing the lesser of several evils.

Any time values for a variable are *rank ordered*, the ordinal level of measurement is being used. Mass media researchers have asked people to list their most important sources of news information. For about the past 20 years, television has ranked first, with newspapers holding down second. Unless follow-up questions are asked, all we know is that people believe television to be a more important source of information than newspapers. We do not know if the difference between television and newspapers is large or small. We merely know the order of magnitude of the two news sources.

Interval Measurement   Interval measures meet the criteria of ordinal measures, but importantly, the *distance* between adjacent scores are assumed to be of equal intervals at all points along the measure. Thus, the difference between a score of 4 and 5 is assumed to be the same as the difference between 5 and 6. Further, the difference between a score of 22 and 31—8 units—is assumed to be the same as the *difference* between any two scores that are 8 units apart. Although the issue is somewhat controversial, most measurement scales, including those described later in this chapter, are treated as if they provide interval data.

Ratio Measurement   The fourth level of measurement is ratio measurement. Ratio measures meet all the criteria of interval measures, but also have *a meaningful, absolute zero point.* This zero point allows statements about the ratios of numbers to be made. Thus, one person can have a score that is twice or three times as high as someone else's. Time is a commonly used ratio variable. For example, someone can be in a relationship for any length of time, from zero to many years. A couple who have been involved in a relationship for two months have been involved for twice as long as a couple who have been involved for one month (ratio—2:1) and two-thirds (also a ratio) as long as a couple who have been involved for three months.

Precision and Power   Interval and ratio measures are more precise than nominal and ordinal measures. It follows logically that if two variables that are predicted by some theory to be related, are, in fact, actually related, the more precise the measures of these variables, the greater the probability of the researcher detecting this relationship empirically. For instance, assume that self-disclosure and interpersonal attraction are, in reality, positively related. If a researcher has a theory that predicts that these variables are related, he or she wants to have every opportunity to observe this relationship. Accurate and precise measures of self-disclosure and interpersonal attraction are much more likely to provide confirmation of the theory than less accurate, less precise measures.

Contributing further to the advantage of interval and ratio measures at detecting existing relationships between variables are the statistical techniques for analyzing data derived from these measures. Variables that are measured at the nominal and ordinal levels must be analyzed with *nonparametric* statistics. In contrast, interval and ratio data can be legitimately analyzed using *parametric* statistics. Parametric statistics are more "powerful," in that they provide a greater likelihood of detecting whether two or more variables are related. Thus, the more precise the measures and the more powerful the statistical techniques, the better the chance the researcher has of showing that two related variables are, in fact, related. (This point will become clearer in Chapter 11 and Chapter 12, when we discuss nonpara-metric and parametric statistical techniques and tests.)

RELIABILITY

Regardless of the level of measurement, variables must meet certain criteria regarding their usefulness. These criteria fall into two areas: reliability and validity.

Reliability refers to the extent to which measurement yields numbers—data—that are consistent, stable, and dependable. Social scientists use the term reliability in association with measurement much the same way that it is used in everyday parlance. A reliable student, for example, is one who is dependable and predictable. He will perform in class pretty much the same way today, tomorrow, next week, and next term. An unreliable student is not so stable, dependable, or predictable. He may do well today, but may not do so well tomorrow or next week. Next term he may not even be in school.

A completely unreliable measure would not be measuring anything at all. Imagine a researcher who is trying to assess an individual's level of communication apprehension. Suppose we have a measure that revealed a particular individual's level to be 27 on a possible 100-point scale. Then suppose we tested that same measure again and the same individual scored 74, then 11, then 59, then 48, then 65, then 22, then 82. In other words, the measure yielded *random* results. This measure quite literally would not be measuring anything at all, let alone communi-cation apprehension. Data from such a measure could be worse than no data at all; time spent gathering and analyzing it would be completely wasted. A completely unreliable measure of a variable could never be demonstrated to be related to another variable. Randomness is, by definition, related to nothing.

On the other hand, to the extent that a measure yielded very similar answers each time it was applied to the same person or group of people, to the extent that all the scores were consistent, stable, predictable, and dependable, it would be a reliable measure. If the measure of communication apprehension was administered to the same person again, and this time the score was 28, then 25, then 24, then 29, then 26, then 27, it would be a reliable measure. It would be measuring *something*, even if it was not communication apprehension.

To aid in understanding measurement reliability it may be useful to think of any measure as being composed of two separate components. One component is *systematic*—here repeated applications yield identical responses. The other com-ponent is *randomness*, and is not a measure of anything. Perhaps a question was worded ambiguously or the person was distracted as she placed a pencil mark on a scale or missed the intended mark. Whatever the reason, all measures are to some extent affected by randomness. This nonsystematic random fluctuation is measurement unreliability. The more a measure reflects systematic factors, the more reliable it is—the more it reflects randomness the more *un*reliable the mea-sure.

Factors Influencing Reliability

All measures suffer from some degree of unreliability. And, while several factors can be identified as contributing to this, perhaps the most important reason lies in asking people to make extremely fine or difficult judgments. The more difficult the judgmental task or the more ambiguous the rules for assigning numbers to persons, objects, or events, the more a measure will tend to be unreliable. For example, researchers attempted to train two observers (called "coders") of nonverbal behavior to observe videotapes and rate the degree of inconsistency between verbal and nonverbal messages. It could not be done, at least not by those particular researchers. Two coders, even after considerable training, consistently came up with different judgments of the degree of inconsistency between, for example, eye contact and gestures. On the other hand, the researchers had no trouble training the same coders to reliably count the number of verbal nonfluencies, the amount of eye contact, and a whole host of other variables. The more subtle the nonverbal cues the researchers attempted to measure, the more difficult it was to train the coders to agree in their judgments.

Similarly, if you were asked how much you liked the president of the United States, on a 100-point scale, with 0 representing Strongly Dislike and 100 representing Strongly Like, you will be likely to give slightly different responses every time the question is asked. You may say 85 one day, 82 the next day, 79 the next, 88 the next, and so forth. A 10-point random variation would not be uncommon on this scale. To decide exactly where one stands on a 100-point scale is a fairly tough judgment to make. On the other hand, if you were asked the same question on a 10-point scale, with 10 representing Strongly Like, you would be much more likely to respond consistently day after day. This is because it is much easier to pinpoint a rating on a 10-point scale than it is on a 100-point scale.

What factors serve to detract from a measure's reliability? Because measurement is the process of assigning numbers to observations according to specified rules, to the extent that the assignment rules are unclear or ambiguous, the measures are likely to be unreliable. Thus, whether the measure is a questionnaire being filled out by a respondent, or the researcher studying videotapes to examine interview behavior, the rules about how to answer the questions, or the rules about how to assign the numbers, need to be as explicit as possible.

Establishing Reliability

Reliability is always established by showing that two or more measures of the same variable are in agreement. This simple idea transcends the type of measurement employed. With these fundamental ideas in mind, we will examine ways of increasing and establishing reliability in four common research measurement settings.

Self-Administered Questionnaires   A very common data-gathering technique used by communication researchers is the self-administered questionnaire. Whether the researcher is conducting an experiment or a survey, part of the research procedures may involve the distribution of a paper and pencil test or response sheet on which participants indicate their responses to the researcher's questions. Several factors may reduce the reliability of this kind of self-report measure. First, unclear or ambiguous instructions, which may be interpreted in alternative, random ways, detract from reliability. Thus, researchers attempt to write instructions and questions as clearly and unambiguously as possible. It is common to "pilot test" a questionnaire on a small group of people similar to those who will participate in the actual study as a means of identifying, rewriting, or eliminating poorly worded items and/or instructions.

Reliability can be improved by increasing the number of specific measures of the same variable. As noted earlier, at least two such measures, items, or subscales are required to establish any degree of reliability at all. Also, as the number of items measuring the variable increase, the randomness component of a person's answers to individual questions becomes less influential in determining the overall score assigned to the variable. As the number of items measuring the variable increases, the random fluctuations on particular items tend to cancel one another out. Additionally, as the number of measures of the same variable increases, reliability increases in generally systematic and predictable degrees.

Another factor that increases reliability concerns the circumstances under which the questionnaires are administered. Many researchers have experienced the frustration of examining questionnaires that have been filled out at random. Respondents who have been motivated to participate in a research project in a serious, conscientious manner are not likely to provide such useless data. For this and for some of the ethical reasons discussed in Chapter 3, participants should feel free to choose to not participate in the research.

Questionnaires should be administered under standardized and well-controlled circumstances. Reliability decreases as the number of ways in which a questionnaire is administered increases. So, for example, the instructions—including the written ones accompanying the questionnaire and the verbal statements made by the researcher or confederates during the actual administration of the questionnaire—about how to fill out a questionnaire from administration to administration should vary as little as possible.

For many communication variables studied repeatedly, there exist standard measures for which reliability has been established. For example, there are generally accepted self-report measures of such variables as communication apprehension, perceptions of source credibility, and attitudes toward a variety of objects and topics.[3] If extant measures adequately operationalize the variables under study, their selection may facilitate measurement reliability, as well as allow for more direct comparisons between the results of the current study with those of other studies using the same measures. When no such measures are available, the researcher must design his or her own questions or response scales. In either case, an effort is usually made to assess the reliability of the measures used. There are two general ways of establishing reliability. The first is the *test-retest* method, designed to assess reliability *over time.* Test-retest reliability is assessed by administering the same measures, for example a self-report questionnaire, to the same respondents under as nearly the same conditions as possible at different points in time. To the extent that each respondent's second score agreed with his or her first score, the measure is reliable. The degree of reliability is formally assessed by computing the correlation between the two sets of scores. The correlation coefficient, usually the *Pearson r* if the measures are at the interval or ratio level, is commonly treated as a good statistical assessment of the degree of reliability.[4] This coefficient can range from 1.0, perfect reliability, to 0, no reliability.

A second way to establish reliability is to assess the *internal consistency* of a measure. This is done by examining the extent to which several different measures that appear on the same questionnaire, *and* are designed to measure the same variable, are in agreement. For example, if the researcher were measuring public speaking apprehension, a respondent might be asked at one point on the questionnaire to state his or her degree of agreement or disagreement with the statement, "I look forward with pleasure to opportunities to speak to large groups of people." Later, the respondent might be asked to respond to a similar statement, such as: "I enjoy making presentations in front of large audiences." To the extent that a specific respondent provided similar or identical responses to each of these statements, the overall measure would have internal consistency; it would be reliable. The formal statistical assessment of the reliability of the measure is generally included in the research report to give the reader additional information to aid in evaluating the research and interpreting the results.

There are a variety of techniques for measuring the internal consistency of a measure. Two techniques are found consistently in the communication literature. The *Kuder-Richardson KR-20* test measures the reliability of nominal and ordinal measures.[5] *Cronbach's Coefficient-Alpha* tests a measure's reliability when interval or ratio level data are used.[6] These are *statistical* tests that yield what is commonly called a *reliability coefficient*, which, like the Pearson *r*, ranges from 0, completely unreliable, to 1.0, perfectly reliable. Regardless of the specific statistical indication of reliability used, they are all examining the same fundamental thing: the extent to which multiple measures of the same variable agree. To the extent that they do agree, the measure is reliable, to the extent that they do not, the measure is unreliable.

It has become somewhat of a *convention* within communication journals for scaled responses to have to achieve reliability coefficients of .70 or better to be considered "acceptable." As with other conventions in the social sciences, however, this figure is somewhat arbitrary. The underlying concern that makes having highly reliable measures desirable is this: The more reliable the measure, the more probable it is that systematic relationships that exist between variables, and are predicted by theory, will be found empirically. Unreliable measures decrease the chances of obtaining research results that support or refute the theory.

Note, however, the arbitrary nature of a .70 "required" reliability figure. If a variable was particularly difficult to measure, perhaps being measured reliably at .50 or less, and was still found to be related to another variable, this would be an indication that the relationship between the two variables might be quite powerful since this systematic relationship was detected *in spite of* considerable randomness in the measurement process. It also might be your purpose to *create* a measure.

Because this type of research could be considered exploratory, you might set your acceptable reliability standards slightly lower, hoping that refinements in the measure will later yield higher reliability coefficients. Either way, the decision to accept a particular reliability coefficient is up to the researcher.

Not all researchers would agree. There are those who would dismiss the value of a study on the grounds that one or more measures failed to achieve reliability figures at a certain level. These people may have lost sight of why we do research: to construct and test theory. Instead of looking at what was measured and to what other variables the measure was found to relate, many people rely on accepted levels of reliability as a fiat, instead of evaluating the research by reason. There are times when any of a number of factors can reduce reliability. It is important to understand that measurement is a relative phenomenon and that reliability lower than .70, or some other arbitrary target figure, will sometimes be unavoidable.

Interviews   Interviews are conducted either face-to-face or, more frequently, over the telephone. Most of the same guidelines that apply to the self-administered questionnaire also are useful for increasing the reliability of interview responses. There are two key differences, however. (1) Questions used in the interview must be written even more simply and clearly since they will be heard and not read. There is a difference between how a question "sounds" and how it "reads," the researcher should be aware of such differences. (2) The interviewers must be trained with meticulous care. Poorly trained interviewers reduce measurement reliability in a number of ways. Interviewing training procedures are discussed at length in Chapter 8, but here it will suffice to note that all interviewers must behave in the same way in each interview, which is why training is so important. Questions must be asked—and answers recorded—*in the same way each time, over and over.* To the extent that there are variations, either within the same interviewer, or from one interview to the next, or between interviewers, reliability is reduced.

Reliability of measures used in interview situations can be assessed in the same ways as measures on self-report questionnaires. Either the same questions can be asked of the same respondents at a later time (test-retest reliability), or multiple questions, each designed to measure the same variable, can be asked during the same interview (internal consistency). Additionally, as a check on *interviewer* performance, which directly affects measurement reliability, different interviewers may be required to interview the same respondent independently. This person could be a confederate of the researcher, a person trained to give identical responses over and over to each interviewer. An examination of the recorded responses for each interviewer provides an opportunity to assess the extent to which each interviewer is providing reliable and accurate data. In this manner, interviewers who are not behaving in a professional or conscientious manner, or who have been inadequately trained, can be identified.

Trained Observers   Here we are referring broadly to individuals who have been trained to observe and assign numbers to any variable of interest to a researcher. Observers are sometimes called *coders,* because they replace observations with numeric codes. The material being observed might be written text, such as a transcript of an interaction or newspaper editorials, which were being analyzed for their content. Or the focus of observation might be individuals, either live or on videotape, who were making speeches or engaged in group discussions. The material being observed might be radio or television broadcasts. In all cases the observers have been trained to assign numbers to what they observe according to carefully specified rules. To the extent that they are able to do this in a consistent, dependable, and stable manner, reliable measures of the variables being observed will result.

Again, the key to having reliable measures is careful training of the observers. They should be given clear, concise, definitions of what they are looking for, shown examples of material that falls within the various categories, given the opportunity to practice their observation tasks, given feedback about how they have done, have errors pointed out to them, and given an opportunity to practice again. Only when an observer has demonstrated his or her ability to assign the same numbers to the same observations consistently should he or she be allowed to proceed.

Reliability can be established in one of two ways. Two or more observers are trained to observe and code the same material independently. The extent to which they agree on the assignment of numbers to their observations is a measure of their reliability, usually reported as a correlation of *interrater* or *intercoder* agreement. As with other measurement procedures, the more difficult the judgmental task, the more difficult it is to develop reliable measures. For example, it will be more difficult to train observers who are analyzing the latent meaning of poetry than it would be to train them to count the number of times a specific word appears in that same poetry. As with other measures, the key to establishing reliability is showing that there is *agreement.* Thus, two or more observers must be shown to code the same material using the same category system with the same outcome.

Several procedures are available for estimating interobserver reliability. As with other statistical techniques, the specific method selected depends on the level at which the observers are measuring the variables. *Cohen's Kappa* provides an assessment of the reliability of two observers who are assigning observations to *nominal* categories.[7] Cohen's Kappa provides a statistical assessment of the degree of agreement between the observers, allowing for the level of agreement that would be expected by chance. Other procedures are available for higher levels of measurement.[8]

Alternatively, the same observer might observe the same material at different times and, purposely avoiding knowledge of how he or she coded it the first time, code it again a second time. An example of this would be a teacher grading essays and assigning a number of points to each essay. To assure reliable grading, a good habit is to grade a few of the essays independently a second time, of course taking care to remain ignorant of the grade given the first time. If the same grade is given both times, reliability has been established.

Participant-Observation   Chapter 7 deals with the problems associated with establishing reliability in participant-observation research. It is extremely difficult to have observational rules that are detailed enough to specify clearly how all the many nuances of behavior are to be coded in the natural setting. While it may not be possible to achieve the high level of reliability achievable on a self-report questionnaire, there are ways of increasing reliability in qualitative research. Again, the key is to establish agreement or consistency. Thus, two participant observers might make at least some of the same observations and compare results. Unfortunately, participant-observation research frequently involves only one observer, making reliability extremely difficult to establish. However, if the researcher is careful, the consistency by which he or she observes the same behaviors over time will produce a form of reliability. However, as discussed in Chapter 7, reliability is a major problem with the method. We must point out, however, that participant-observation is less concerned with reliability than with an introspective and subjective perception of the communication event *as it happens in its natural setting.* However, as will be noted when we discuss the relationship between reliability and validity, some minimal level of reliability is needed before a measure has any validity.

VALIDITY

Validity is commonly viewed as the issue of whether a measurement technique, such as a questionnaire or the use of trained observers, provides measures of what its user thinks it is measuring. To the extent that scales or questions do measure what they are thought to measure, they are valid. To the extent that the scales or questions measure something else, or nothing at all, they are not valid. While this is the most common conception of measurement validity, there are several more specialized uses of the term, for example criterion-related validity, content validity, and construct validity. It should be emphasized that a measure is valid only in the context in which it is being used. A measure of a variable that is valid for one purpose may not be valid for another.

Criterion-Related Validity

Criterion-related validity focuses on the notion that a measure is valid to the extent that it enables the researcher to predict a score on some other measure or to predict a particular behavior of interest. The concern is not with what is being measured but whether the measure predicts relevant behaviors and responses on a second measure. For example, if the goal of a study is the practical concern of predicting voter turnout, a measure yielding responses that allows you to do this accurately is valid, regardless of what it is measuring. The interest is more in the *criterion* itself—the variable the research wants to predict (voter turnout)—than in the *relationship* between what is being measured and the criterion. Thus, a measure labeled Voter Turnout Instrument might ask questions about past voting behavior, campaign interest, attention to campaign advertising, and educational level. Although this measure would seem to be measuring several different things, it would have criterion-related validity if the responses could be combined or weighted in such a way that voting could be accurately predicted. (This assumes, of course, that the criterion is measured validly.) This type of validity is often more useful in applied research than in theoretical research.

An example of criterion-related validity is found in the Scholastic Aptitude Test (SAT). Most users of the SAT are solely interested in its criterion-related validity. To the extent that it predicts student performance in college, the SAT is viewed as valid. Controversy about *what* is being measured surfaces periodically. SAT critics claim, among other things, that it is *really* measuring socioeconomic status (SES) and the concomitant degree of understanding of white, upper-middle class American culture.[9] This controversy seems to miss the point. The purpose of the SAT is to *predict* college performance; this it does, albeit imperfectly. The test survives not because it *really* measures aptitude or, for that matter, because it *really* measures anything at all. It survives because students who score 1400 tend to do better in college than those who score 1100, who, in turn tend to do better than those who score 800, and so on. It has criterion-related validity.

Content Validity/Face Validity

The second kind of measurement validity is content validity, and, its very close cousin, face validity. Content validity refers to whether a measure captures the content or the meaning of the variable being measured. You might, for instance, be interested in measuring someone's level of communication apprehension in general and writing apprehension in particular. It would be possible to write scores of relevant statements (called *items*) about this concept and ask respondents to state their agreement or disagreement with each statement. You cannot, however, ask respondents to answer several hundred questions. Instead, you select a sample of items, that is, a smaller subset of items from your pool of questions, ones that seem to be both indicators of apprehension and fit your particular conception of what apprehension is. To the extent that the sample is representative of the large list of relevant items, the measure will have content validity.

Whether a measure has content validity is somewhat of a subjective judgment. The relevance and representativeness of specific items would need to be judged by the researcher. An item that stated "Writing is fun" probably would be relevant to the content of the writing apprehension variable. The statement, "I use the dictionary a lot" probably would not be relevant to the same concept.

Content validity and face validity are virtually indistinguishable. Face validity is achieved if a measure appears, on the face of it, to be valid. Content validity has been achieved if a measure is judged to capture the content of whatever is being measured. Both types of validity require the use of common sense and logic to form a judgment about whether the variable is being validly measured. Put another way, a decision is made about whether the operational definition is consistent with the conceptual definition of the variable. Is this operationalization "capturing" the meaning of the conceptual definition? The key point is that both types of validity require a *judgment* to be made by someone—usually the researcher, but perhaps by experts on the specific topic about which the measures were asking.

For example, on a measure of writing apprehension for mass communication students, researchers began with over 100 items or statements about feelings and attitudes concerning writing. Some of these items reflected behavioral implications of writing, while others reflected attitudinal implications. From the item pool about 75 items were selected as representing the various dimensions of writing apprehension the researchers felt the literature supported. These questions were then submitted to a panel of professional educators, journalists, and public relations practitioners. Each read the list and commented on the items. Based on their comments the researchers revised several items, dropped others, and added even more. This process helped to establish the validity of the measure's content (and face) validity.

Construct Validity

While criterion-related and content/face validity are fairly straightforward, construct validity is both complex and controversial. *Construct validity,* Kerlinger writes, "bores into the essence of science . . . it is concerned with the nature of reality and the nature of properties being measured."[10] In brief, construct validity is concerned with *what* is being measured.

The "known-group" method is a commonly described way to establish construct validity.[11] Let us suppose that as the researcher you are interested in a valid measure of extroversion-introversion. You develop a paper and pencil measure designed to assess this variable, which includes statements such as: "I am very talkative around other people." "In some group situations I speak up more than the average person." And, "I enjoy interacting with strangers." To the extent that people agree with these and related statements, they will be considered extroverted. To the extent they disagree, they will be categorized as introverts. But is the instrument valid? The known-group technique involves identifying groups of people known to exhibit whatever variable or concept you are interested in analyzing. Perhaps you have access to a group of students who live in a particular dorm. You could ask each to identify the five most introverted and the five most extroverted residents of the dorm. Residents who showed up on at least five of the students' lists might be labeled, accordingly, "highly extroverted" or "highly introverted." Then you could administer your instrument to the two groups. To the extent that the two groups differed on the measure as anticipated, the measure could be said to have construct validity.

Another way to establish construct validity involves showing that the variables being measured behave in theoretically expected ways in relation to other variables. For example, you might hypothesize that trust of another person leads to increased levels of negative self-disclosure (bad things stated about oneself). Trust is an elusive concept and one that is difficult to measure. One way to provide evidence for the construct validity of your measure of trust would be to show that, as predicted by the theory, trust was related to negative self-disclosure. There also might be theoretical reasons for expecting trust not to be related to other variables. By demonstrating that these variables were not related to trust would provide evidence for the construct validity of the trust measure. In short, a pattern of findings that shows that relationships that are predicted by a theory are found, while other, not-predicted relationships are not found, would be evidence for the construct validity of the measure.

THE RELATIONSHIP BETWEEN RELIABILITY AND VALIDITY

A good measure is both reliable and valid. However, reliability must be present or validity is impossible. Recall that a completely unreliable measure would not be measuring anything at all, so it obviously could not be measuring validly. Reliability is a necessary, although not sufficient condition for validity.

If you were interested in assessing people's attitudes toward a topic about which they had just received a persuasive appeal—airline deregulation, for example—and you asked your respondents how many siblings they had, the result would likely be reliable, but invalid data. Someone who said he had two siblings would very likely give the same dependable, stable, consistent answer again and again, as would someone else who had none and someone else who had six siblings. But these numbers would not be indications of the respondents' views on airline deregulation. To summarize, without measurement reliability, the researcher has measured nothing. But reliability by itself is equally useless unless, within the context of the purpose of a study, the measure is also valid.

Figure 6.1 suggests an analogy between the accuracy of a marksman firing a rifle at a target and the relationship between measurement reliability and validity. [12] A measure is valid to the extent that it consistently hits the target. In the case of target (a), the marksman shoots a random pattern of shots and therefore necessarily misses the target with most shots. He is not firing reliably, so his shooting is inaccurate, that is, not valid. In (b), his firing is reliable, the shots are grouped closely together, but he is missing the target, thus validity is absent. Finally, in (c), he is both firing consistently and hitting the target. This is analogous to a measure that is both reliable and valid.

By now you should realize that measurement is a complex process. We establish an instrument by which to measure objects (concrete or abstract) through the specification of some form of rules. We create our instrument with different types of data; it can be ordinal or nominal or it can be interval or ratio. These instruments can be assessed for their reliability and their validity. We now turn to creating the measuring instruments used in research. These instruments, in turn, are composed of *scales*.

MEASUREMENT SCALES

Ultimately, social scientists in general, and communication researchers in particular, are interested in explaining and predicting human *behavior*. That is why they are sometimes called *behavioral scientists*. Behavior is overt. It can be observed directly. However, while this is true in principle, in practice many behaviors are extremely difficult to observe. Consider the following questions:

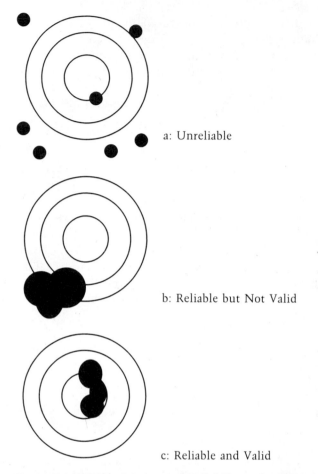

a: Unreliable

b: Reliable but Not Valid

c: Reliable and Valid

Figure 6.1 Relationship between reliability and validity.

Does exposure to pornography increase spousal abuse?

Are speeches that use fear appeal messages more likely to affect teenage sexual practices than ones that do not?

Do presidential debates contribute to voting decisions?

Is a particular compliance-gaining strategy more effective than another?

Is one relationship-disengagement strategy more effective at minimizing depression and suicide of the partner than another?

All of these are important research questions about the effects of communication. The independent variable implied in each of the examples is exposure to some type of message. The dependent variable (the thing the researcher believes to be affected by the independent variable) is, in each case, the receivers' *behavior.* Unfortunately, the affected behaviors may be very difficult to observe. Spouse abuse, voting, sexual practices, compliance with requests, suicides, and many other important variables occur in private, or, if they do occur in public, you are not likely to be there to observe them. This difficulty in assessing the effect of various messages on behaviors is alleviated by constructing *intervening variables* to account for internal psychological processes that, in turn, account for overt (observable) behaviors.

Attitudes as Examples of Intervening Variables An *attitude* is a common example of intervening variables. An attitude is a "relatively enduring predisposition to respond favorably or unfavorably to an attitude object."[13] As predispositions, attitudes exist in people's minds and cannot be observed directly. Their existence must be inferred, usually from responses to *attitude scales.* Thus, a researcher constructs the variable attitude to intervene between a stimulus—exposure to a message of some type or form—and a response—sexual behavior, spouse abuse, voting, suicide, compliance, and so on. As the researcher you presume that the message does not have a direct effect on these behaviors, but rather it influences receiver attitudes (or some other internal state) which, in turn, influences behavior.

The most common way intervening variables such as attitudes are measured in communication research is through the use of *measurement scales.* Scales are generally used on questionnaires, which respondents complete either as part of a survey or after receiving some type of experimental stimulus. Scales also can be used in face-to-face interviews and, with more difficulty, in telephone interviews. Measuring a variable via a scale technique involves the placing of a mark somewhere along a linear continuum. Numbers are then assigned systematically (according to rules) to points along the line that composes the scale. Responses to such scales are assumed to be indications of the internal psychological states of the participant. Such scales are assumed to provide interval- or ratio-level data; they assume that distances between assigned numbers are equidistant and some even establish an arbitrary ($+3$, $+2$, $+1$, 0, -1, -2, -3) or absolute zero point.

The scales described here are frequently constructed according to detailed procedures and pilot-tested, that is, tried out, prior to use in the actual research. A *pilot test* is a preliminary data-gathering effort whose purpose is to examine the research procedures, including the measures used, in order to correct any problems before the full study is conducted. If confusing scale items are present, the pilot test allows them to be identified and changed before investing time in flawed data-gathering procedures. When conducting pilot tests, whether testing the efficacy of an experimental manipulation or the clarity of the measurement procedures, participants and circumstances under which the test is conducted should be as similar as possible to those that will exist during the actual research. If, for example, the people who participate in the actual research will do so in a classroom setting, the individuals who participate in the pilot test should also be in a classroom setting, the same room, if possible.

All the scales described here, if constructed carefully and used properly, can be reliable and valid measures of variables in communication research. We turn now to four popular types of measurement scales.

Types of Measurement Scales

Semantic Differential   The *semantic differential scale* is a general scaling technique for measuring the meaning that an "object" has for an individual. The "object" could be almost anything—a physical object, a social practice, another person, an ethnic or national group, an abstract concept, even, the respondent him- or herself. Developed by Charles Osgood and associates, the semantic differential has been widely used in communication research. [14] Osgood's technique is based on the notion of *semantic space*, the idea that people evaluate objects along spatial continua. Using the technique involves placing the name of the object at the top of a series of 7-point scales anchored by bipolar adjectives. The respondent then places a check at the point along each scale that reflects his or her judgment about the object. For example, the following scales might be used to measure your view of your instructor.

My Instructor

Informed	__:__ :__ :__ :__ :__ :__	Uninformed
Unfair	__:__ :__ :__ :__ :__ :__	Fair
Well Prepared	__:__ :__ :__ :__ :__ :__	Poorly Prepared

Using a statistical technique (*factor analysis*) designed to determine if responses to a relatively large number of different scales (usually 10 or more) will result in a smaller number of underlying *dimensions* or *factors*, Osgood concluded that people evaluate objects along three general dimensions of meaning—activity, potency, and evaluation (see Figure 6.2).

The evaluation dimension has proved especially useful to communication researchers as it generally measures attitudes—predispositions to *behave* favorably or unfavorably toward attitude objects. Since assessing the *effects* of communication is one of the major goals of communication research, a means is needed to assess these effects empirically. As noted, assessing the effects of various messages on behaviors is difficult, sometimes impossible. Thus, assessing the effects of measures of attitudes is an important technique. The evaluation scales are anchored by items such as Valuable-Worthless, Honest-Dishonest, and Good-Bad. Typically, several items are used to measure the meaning that an object holds for an individual. If the scales are all measuring the same underlying dimension, as already noted, multiple measures increase the reliability with which it is measured. The scale items are usually scored by assigning a 1 if the respondent marks the line next to the negative side of the scale, a 2 if the next line over is marked, and so on, up to 7, if the space next to the positive side of the scale is marked, as in the example:

My Instructor

Good **X** : : : : : : _____ Bad

Worthless _____ : : : : : **X** : _____ Valuable

Honest _____ : : **X** : : : : _____ Dishonest

These items would be scored 7, 6, 5, (good, valuable, honest) or total score 18, or 6.0 (18 ÷ 3 items) out of 7. Note that the items have been reversed so that a *response set*, a pattern the respondent might get into based on simply marking down one side or the middle, is less likely to be induced. The reversal of items also provides an indication when people simply "fill out" the scales rather than thinking about how each item relates to the object.

One of the most widely cited uses of the semantic differential is that of David Berlo and associates.[15] These researchers administered hundreds of semantic differential scales to people and asked them to evaluate the credibility of message sources. Berlo et al. found three independent subcomponents of source credibility: trustworthiness (sometimes called character), expertise (also called authority), and dynamism.[16] Trustworthiness is measured by scale items anchored by such adjectives as Honest-Dishonest and Trustworthy-Untrustworthy. Expertise is measured with scales items anchored by adjectives such as Wise-Foolish and Knowledgeable-Not knowledgeable, while dynamism is measured by scale items such as Interesting-Dull and Active-Passive. Each of these dimensions of source credibility is *independent.* That is, a source evaluated as being high on one dimension could be low on another or high on one and high on another.

Evaluation:

Good _____ : : : : : : _____ Bad
Beautiful _____ : : : : : : _____ Ugly
Clean _____ : : : : : : _____ Dirty

Potency:

Large _____ : : : : : : _____ Small
Heavy _____ : : : : : : _____ Light
Strong _____ : : : : : : _____ Weak

Activity:

Active _____ : : : : : : _____ Passive
Sharp _____ : : : : : : _____ Dull
Fast _____ : : : : : : _____ Slow

Figure 6.2 Semantic differential scales.

For example, suppose that you were interested in the concept of presidential credibility. You might use Berlo's semantic differential scales and, depending on your research question, measure presidential credibility in general or the credibility of certain specific presidents. Imagine, for example, that you are interested in the credibility of Ronald Reagan and Richard Nixon. You administer your measure to a group of people, compute the various "scores" and find that Reagan was viewed as highly trustworthy—he was viewed as an honest man who would not knowingly lie—but low on expertise—he is not knowledgeable about as many areas as he should be. Nixon, on the other hand, was perceived by your participants as high in expertise—he is a smart man who knows a lot—but low in trustworthiness—he might very well lie to you. Hence, the independence of the scales allows for multiple interpretations.

When measures are added to form a composite score, as we just did, it is extremely important that they be measures of the same thing. Thus, only measures of the expertise dimension of source credibility should be added together. If the scales measuring trustworthiness, for example, were added to the expertise scales, to the extent that individual respondents had different evaluations of the expertise and trustworthiness of the president as a source, reliability and validity would be reduced. For this reason a statistical technique, factor analysis, is frequently performed on the responses to scales before any substantive analysis is performed. (Basically, factor analysis clumps the scales together in semantic space. Those scales that "hang together," that is, those to which individuals responded to in the same way, correlate highly with one another. These scales form factors or dimensions that can be safely added to form a composite score.) Thus, those scales that are measuring the same underlying dimensions can be added together to increase measurement reliability.

Likert-type Scales   Likert-type scales are another commonly used measurement technique. Named for their developer, Rensis Likert, they are also called *summated rating* scales.[17] Likert-type items are statements that yield responses that range from favorable to unfavorable toward an object (as with the semantic differential, the object could be anything—a person, a rock 'n' roll band, an abstract concept, a public policy, etc.). The respondent is presented with a series of these statements and indicates his or her degree of agreement or disagreement with each. It is important to note that a *neutral* point must be provided, usually termed Uncertain, Undecided, or Neither Agree nor Disagree.

Creating a Likert-type scale involves three stages. First, you generate a large number of favorable and unfavorable statements about the object of interest. Second, you pilot test these items on people who are asked to indicate their degree of agreement or disagreement with each statement along a 5- (or sometimes 7-) point continuum. For favorable statements about the object in question, a Strongly Disagree might be scored 1; Disagree, 2; Neither Agree nor Disagree, 3; Agree, 4; and Strongly Agree, 5. The scoring is reversed for unfavorable statements (i.e., 5=1, 4=2, 3=3, 2=4, 1=5). Each of the respondent's answers are summed to produce a composite score. Third, you select a smaller number of items as being representative of the measure for administration; these are the responses that tend

It is all right to kiss on the first date.

Strongly Disagree	Disagree	Neither Agree nor Disagree	Agree	Strongly Agree

Girls should be allowed to ask boys for dates.

Strongly Disagree	Disagree	Neither Agree nor Disagree	Agree	Strongly Agree

It is all right for dating partners to talk about sex.

Strongly Disagree	Disagree	Neither Agree nor Disagree	Agree	Strongly Agree

Dating couples between 18 and 20 should be allowed to stay out as long as they wish.

Strongly Disagree	Disagree	Neither Agree nor	Agree	Strongly Agree

It is *not* all right for a girl to invite a boy to her home when no one is there.

Strongly Disagree	Disagree	Neither Agree nor Disagree	Agree	Strongly Agree

Young people should make love as much as they wish on a date.

Strongly Disagree	Disagree	Neither Agree nor Disagree	Agree	Strongly Agree

(a)

Figure 6.3 Two displays of Likert-type scales. (a) Attitudes toward dating.

to agree with an individual respondent's overall score. (Factor analysis could again be used to obtain "dimensions" of agreement.) Thus, if your overall score indicates that you are unfavorable toward the object, items would be selected that also indicated this unfavorable attitude. Figure 6.3(a) provides examples of Likert-type items designed to measure attitudes toward dating.[18] Figure 6.3(b) presents an alternative way to present the same scales. Both are assumed to be equally reliable and valid.

SD = Strongly Disagree
D = Disagree
N = Neither Agree nor Disagree
A = Agree
SA = Strongly Agree

Place a check opposite each of the following statements to indicate your degree of agreement or disagreement.

	SA	A	N	D	SD
It is all right to kiss on the first date.	[ ]	[ ]	[ ]	[ ]	[ ]
Girls should be allowed to ask boys for dates.	[ ]	[ ]	[ ]	[ ]	[ ]
It is all right for dating partners to talk about sex.	[ ]	[ ]	[ ]	[ ]	[ ]
Dating couples between 18 and 20 should be allowed to stay out as long as they wish	[ ]	[ ]	[ ]	[ ]	[ ]
It is *not* all right for a girl to invite a boy to her home when no one is there.	[ ]	[ ]	[ ]	[ ]	[ ]
Young people should make love as much as they wish on a date.	[ ]	[ ]	[ ]	[ ]	[ ]

(b)

Figure 6.3 (b) An alternate presentation.

Thurstone Scales   It would be hard to overemphasize the contributions of Louis Leon Thurstone to the development of measurement theory in general, and attitude measurement in particular. The main technique associated with Thurstone is also called the *equal appearing interval* scale.[19] Unlike the semantic differential or Likert-type scale, the Thurstone scale has predefined values associated with each statement. As might be expected, these scales are a little more difficult to construct.

Constructing Thurstone scales involves five steps. First, you create a large number (around 100) of positive and negative statements about the object to be evaluated. Second, you have the statements, frequently called items, sorted by a number of judges (usually 20 to 30 people) into 11 piles, which represent categories of similar items that appear to your judges to be equally distinct from one another. The categories are assigned numbers from 1, Very Unfavorable, to 11, Very Favorable. For each statement an average is calculated based on the categories to which the judges have assigned it. So, for example, a statement that was assigned to category 8 by all the judges would have a value of 8. One that was assigned exclusively to category 11 would have a score of 11. One that was assigned by half of the judges to category 1 and by the other half to category 2 would be assigned a 1.5, and so on. Third, you calculate the degree to which the judges are in agreement with their category assignment. Items about which the judges agree are desirable. It would make little sense to choose an item that some judges placed in category 1 or 2, while other judges thought it was moderately favorable and placed it in category 6 or 7. Finally, you choose a small number of items, usually around 20, for the final measure. The items that have high judge agreement (judgments correlated highly with one another) and that represent all points—unfavorable to favorable—along the 11-point continuum are selected.

Examples of Thurstone items appear in Box 6.1. You would ask each respondent to indicate with which statements he or she agreed. The scale in Box 6.1 was designed to measure attitudes toward any school subject.[20] We have taken writer's license and substituted a communication research methods course as the subject being evaluated. (Note, the scale values for each item, which are shown in parentheses, would not appear on the actual scale.) Your participants would be instructed to select the items with which he or she agrees. Each person's score is the average of the scale values with which he or she agrees. If, for example, one person agreed with items 1, 4, and 8, her score would be 6.4, or approximately midpoint in the 11-point scale. As can be seen, each participant should only agree with a small number of scales, all of which have similar values. This serves as a way to assess possible response sets: If a person responds favorably to all the statements he or she probably did not read the items carefully, if at all; you would be suspicious of this person's responses.

Thurstone scales are time-consuming to construct and for this reason they are

---

Box 6.1   **Thurstone Scales**

1. The very existence of humanity depends upon this communication research methods course. (10.3)

2. Communication research methods is one subject that all Americans should know. (9.4)

3. All of our great men (and women) studied communication research methods. (8.4).

4. Communication research methods is not receiving its due in public schools. (7.6)

5. Communication research methods might be worthwhile if it were taught right. (6.0)

6. Communication research methods is all right, but I would not take any more of it. (4.7)

7. Communication research methods reminds me of Shakespeare's play, *Much Ado About Nothing.* (2.6)

8. Communication research methods is more like a plague than a study. (1.3)

9. Words cannot express my antagonism for communication research methods. (0.7)

used much less frequently than semantic differential or Likert-type scales. However, there are many extant scales that have already been constructed and validated.[21]

Multidimensional Scaling   *Multidimensional scaling* (MDS) is a relatively new communication research technique. Its usefulness has been demonstrated in the communication discipline primarily by Joseph Woelfel and Edward L. Fink.[22] The basic assumption of this technique is that we can draw an analogy between a *physical* space and distances and a similar space and distances in our *minds.* In this way the technique is similar to Osgood's notion of semantic space. However, unlike semantic space, which is limited to seven units of length, objects in the "multidimensional space" of our minds can be *any* distance apart—from zero to any number. Just as we know that it is about 2500 miles from Chicago to Los Angeles, we also might know that it is about 188 mental units from new wave rock music to country and western music.

   MDS uses information about how similar or how different certain objects are perceived to be; it then places the objects in a spatial relationship to one another. Respondents are given a list of objects and asked to make judgments about how different or similar they are. In making this request, the researcher provides respondents with an arbitrary psychological yardstick to apply in making their judgments about the distance between the objects. The yardstick is of the form: If Object A and Object B are X units apart, how far apart are Object C and Object D? So, for example, a researcher who was studying an election might assess perceptions of the distance between the following five objects: (1) personal voting intentions; (2) a political candidate; (3) arms control; (4) the federal deficit; and (5) inflation. To do so, the researcher might provide the following yardstick for respondents:

   If George Bush and Ted Kennedy are 100 political inches apart, how far apart
      are:

Then, as shown in Figure 6.4, each respondent would be asked to compare each of the objects with each of the others. For instance:

   Inflation and George Bush   36

   The federal deficit and George Bush   166

   Arms control and the federal deficit   54

   Arms control and George Bush   44

   Inflation and the federal deficit   101

   Arms control and inflation   86

   George Bush and my vote   39

   Arms control and my vote   5

   Inflation and my vote   200

   The Federal deficit and my vote   452

If George Bush and Ted Kennedy are 100 "political inches" apart,
how far apart are:

Inflation and George Bush _____

The federal deficit and George Bush _____

Arms control and federal deficit _____

Arms control and George Bush _____

Inflation and the federal deficit _____

Arms control and inflation _____

George Bush and my vote _____

Arms control and my vote _____

Inflation and my vote _____

The federal deficit and my vote _____

Figure 6.4 Hypothetical multidimensional scale.

To compare each of the objects with all other objects, the respondent is required to make $[n(n-1)] \div 2$ different judgments, where n is the number of objects being judged. In our example there are five objects, thus ten $[5(5-1) \div 2 = 10]$ judgments are required. Ten objects would require 45 judgments.

Using special statistical techniques developed specifically for this type of scaling technique, respondents' perceptions of the objects' distances from one another can be "plotted" in hypothetical space. The procedure is designed so that the distance between any two objects approximates the average distance between the two objects indicated by the entire group of respondents. Thus, the plot results in an approximation of the *relationship* of each of the objects to every other object in hypothetical multidimensional space for the group as a whole.

The value of the technique lies in its potential for assessing cognitive *changes* that result from receiving messages. By administering the MDS questions before *and* after messages are received, for instance, changes between spatial relationships between the objects can be plotted.

In the example, "my vote" is presumed to represent voting intention and the closer a candidate is to "my vote," the more likely the candidate will be to receive the respondent's vote. Similarly, the closer the candidate is to issues that are also close to the concept, "my vote," the more favorable the voter is presumed to be toward the candidate. Conversely, if the candidate is perceived to be close to issues that the respondents collectively view as a great distance from their vote, the candidate would be well advised to generate messages that would move him or her away from that issue and toward "my vote."

Table 6.1 shows data resulting from an hypothetical administration of the MDS questionnaire shown in Figure 6.4. Respondents might collectively indicate

Table 6.1 MULTIDIMENSIONAL SCALING DISTANCE MATRICES

	1	2	3	4	5
1. Arms control	—				
2. Inflation	55	—			
3. George Bush	37	16	—		
4. My vote	07	189	46	—	
5. Federal deficit	29	64	132	426	—

that "arms control" was an average of 7 "political inches" from their vote, while the federal deficit was 426 inches from their vote. These responses would be interpreted as meaning that this particular group was much more favorable to the concept "arms control" than they were to the "federal deficit." The candidate, George Bush in this case, would be well advised to generate messages that would move him toward identification with arms control and away from the federal deficit. In fact, MDS has been used to advise political candidates about the nature of campaign messages to generate to move the candidate closer to "my vote."[23] Changes following the receipt of messages could be assessed by administering the MDS questionnaire a second time and comparing the results.

MDS has several disadvantages associated with its use. Large groups of people, usually of at least 100 people and frequently many more, may be required to ensure that the results will be reliable. Additionally, as the number of objects being compared increases, the number of comparisons required of respondents increases dramatically. Thus MDS questionnaires are typically tedious and time-consuming to fill out; hence, respondent motivation is often difficult to maintain. Nonetheless, MDS has been shown to be a viable measurement technique that in some research applications can be superior to more traditional scaling techniques. Its use will likely increase in the future.

OTHER MEASUREMENT TECHNIQUES

There are other measurement techniques that we may use in collecting data. These techniques, however, are often more ambiguous than those discussed earlier and the researcher must be concerned with the reliability and validity of each.

Open-Ended Questions

Scales provide respondents with a set of categories from which to select a response. Open-ended questions differ in that no such predetermined response options are provided. Rather, the respondent is free to provide whatever responses he or she chooses. Open-ended questions may be used in either face-to-face or telephone interviews (discussed in detail in Chapter 8), or on self-administered questionnaires. Examples of open-ended questions include, How do you feel about the job the President is doing these days? and In what way have the revelations about Jimmy Swaggart affected your perceptions of television ministries?

Open-ended questions can be extremely useful. They allow the researcher the potential to identify respondent views that may not have been anticipated when the questionnaire was designed. They also offer the opportunity for more in-depth responses. Thus, open-ended questions are especially useful in providing qualitative data that may supplement that provided by participant observation, telephone or mail surveys, or face-to-face interviews. Open-ended questions are the staple of "focus group" sessions. A focus group is a group "interview" in which the researcher uses open-ended questions and follow-up questions (*probes*) to stimulate a controlled discussion among a small group of respondents. Focus groups are frequently used as a preliminary research step from which qualitative information is gathered to help design a subsequent quantitative study.

During interviews or on self-administered questionnaires, a few open-ended questions also can help increase rapport with the respondent, who may feel frustrated by having to answer a long series of closed-ended scaled responses that do not always fit what he or she wants to say.

Open-ended questions, however, have several disadvantages and should be used sparingly in most research projects. First, they are time-consuming to gather and to interpret. Long irrelevant answers are not uncommon. Second, it is often difficult to reliably code (assign numbers to) the answers. In effect, open-ended responses frequently need to be content analyzed, a measurement discussed in detail in Chapter 11. Further, as with other self-report measurement techniques, there is always the danger of a respondent telling you what you think you want to hear, or what he or she thinks is a desirable answer. For this reason, we will conclude our introduction to measurement with a discussion of a class of techniques that eliminate this danger: unobtrusive measures.

Unobtrusive Measures

Research participants are almost always aware that they are being studied. Sometimes this awareness becomes manifest in an effort to help the researcher—to behave in ways you believe the researcher wants you to behave, to answer questions in ways you believe the researcher wants them to be answered. The phrase *demand cues*, has been coined to describe the sometimes subtle, unconscious cues that the researcher may emit to let the participant know what the researcher wants to find. These cues "demand" of the participant certain behaviors, certain responses. [24] Merely knowing that research is taking place has been shown to affect respondent behavior. The term *Hawthorne effect* refers to this well-known phenomenon. [25] In a series of research studies at Western Electric in the 1920s, researchers were looking for ways to increase productivity. They increased plant lighting and production went up. They piped in music and production went up. In fact, for everything they did, production increased. So they reduced lighting to its previous level; production went up again! The workers were responding to the fact that they were part of a research project. Apparently they were stimulated by this knowledge and worked harder and harder, but the variable that explained this was not lighting, or music, it was researcher presence. Thus, the novelty of being studied has the potential to change behavior in and of itself.

In their highly influential book on unobtrusive measures, Eugene Webb, Donald Campbell, Richard Schwartz, and Lee Sechrest argue for the use of measurement techniques that do not require respondent awareness of the fact they are being measured.[26] They suggest that unobtrusive measures should not replace the interview or questionnaire but should "supplement and cross-validate it [the interview or questionnaire] with measures that do not themselves contaminate the response."[27] They describe three general types of such measures: physical traces, archives, and observations.

Physical Traces   Physical traces include "erosion measures, where the degree of selective wear on some material yields the measure" and "accretion measures, where the research evidence is some deposit of materials."[28] An example of an erosion measure with a nonverbal application might be an assessment of traffic patterns and, hence, the popularity of exhibits in a museum. Such a study examined the frequency with which floor tiles around various exhibits had to be replaced.[29] Tiles around a chicken-hatching exhibit had to be replaced every six months, while tiles around other exhibits lasted years, thus demonstrating an environmental trafficking effect. An accretion measure might include assessing the readership levels of advertisements by counting the number of fingerprints on the pages of selected magazines in public places.

Archives   Archives include *running records*, the ongoing, continuing public records of a society, such as the *Congressional Record*, or actuarial records, such as birth and marriage records. For example, library records have been used to study the effects of introducing television into a community. Withdrawals of fiction titles were found to have dropped, while withdrawals of nonfiction titles did not. A second type of archival records are defined as *episodic* and *private* records, such as sales records, institutional records, and personal documents. (Archival records stored in libraries are discussed in detail in Chapter 5.) However, many archival records are not available in libraries. Here we will simply note several unusual examples provided by Webb et al. Several researchers attempted to measure airline passenger anxiety after major air crashes by assessing sales of airline tickets, trip life insurance policies, and airport bar liquor sales.[30] Sales of wholesale food orders were examined to assess the effects of subliminal persuasion. No effect was found.[31]

Observation   The final type of unobtrusive measure presented by Webb et al. is *observation*. For example, racial attitudes in two colleges were compared by observing the groupings of whites and blacks in classrooms. The degree of fear created by ghost stories has been measured by observing the shrinking diameter of a circle of children.[32] Measurement through the observation of behavior is the subject of Chapter 7 on participant-observation, wherein several different types of observation are discussed.

SUMMARY

This chapter began by defining measurement as the process of assigning numbers to objects according to rules. We noted that there are four levels of measurement available to the communication researcher: nominal, ordinal, interval, and ratio. Nominal and ordinal refer to the grouping or ranking of objects. Interval and ratio refer to the scaling of responses to some object via a fairly precise and powerful mode of measurement. Discussion then centered on the dual concepts of reliability and validity. Finally, different types of measurement scales were discussed, examples provided, and advantages and disadvantages pointed out.

PROBES

1. Is measurement important to research? Why or why not? In answering this probe, take a variable of interest to you and create a measurement scheme that represents each of the four levels of measurement.

2. What is the tension between reliability and validity? Can you think of a measure that is valid but not reliable? One that is reliable but not valid? Look at ways a variable from your area of interest is measured and examine available evidence concerning its criterion-related validity, its content/face validity, and its construct validity. Are there any problems with this measure?

3. What is a measurement scale? Assume that we are interested in assessing interest in an event on campus, what things would you have to consider in creating a scale to measure this event? Which of these considerations is most important? Least important? Why?

4. We are interested in tapping attitudes about AIDS on your campus. How would you go about measuring this topic using semantic differential scales? Using Likert-type scales? Using Thurstone scales? Using multidimensional scaling? Try to create several items for each of the scales.

5. Why might a researcher have to employ techniques other than scaling to answer a research question? What research question would be best answered using open-ended questions as your measurement technique? Using unobtrusive measures? Compared to scaling techniques, what do you gain and what do you lose by adopting each?

SUGGESTED READING

Guilford, J. P. (1954). *Psychometric methods.* New York: McGraw-Hill.

Kerlinger, F. N. (1986). *Foundations of behavioral research* (3rd ed.). New York: Holt, Rinehart, and Winston.

Likert, R. (1932). A technique for the measurement of attitudes. *Archives of Psychology,* *40*, 1–55.

Nunnally, J. (1978). *Psychometric theory.* New York: McGraw-Hill.

Osgood, C., Suci, G. J., & Tannenbaum, P. (1957). *The measurement of meaning.* Urbana: University of Illinois Press.

Shaw, M. E., & Wright, J. M. (1967). *Scales for the measurement of attitudes.* New York: McGraw-Hill.

Thurstone, L. L., & Chave, E. J. (1929). *The measurement of attitude.* Chicago: University of Chicago Press.

Torgerson, W. (1958). *Theory and methods of scaling.* New York: Wiley.

Webb, E., Campbell, D. T., Schwartz, R. D., & Sechrest, L. (1966). *Unobtrusive measures: Nonreactive research in the social sciences.* Chicago: Rand-McNally.

Woelfel, J., & Fink, E. L. (1980). *The measurement of communication processes: Galileo theory and method.* New York: Academic Press.

NOTES

1. Stanley Smith Stevens, "Mathematics, Measurement, and Psychophysics," in S. Stevens, ed., *Handbook of Experimental Psychology* (New York, 1951). See W. Torgerson, *Theory and Methods of Scaling* (New York: Wiley, 1958), 13–14, for a discussion of definitions of measurement.
2. Stevens, 25.
3. For examples of these measures, see James C. McCroskey, "Scales for the Measurement of Ethos," *Speech Monographs,* 33 (1966): 65–72; David Berlo, James B. Lemert, and Robert J. Mertz, "Dimensions for Evaluating the Acceptability of Message Sources," *Public Opinion Quarterly,* 33 (1967): 563–577.
4. The Pearson *r* is discussed more thoroughly in Chapter 12.
5. G. F. Kuder and M. W. Richardson, "The Theory of Estimation Test Reliability," *Psychometrika,* 2 (1937): 151–160.
6. L. J. Cronbach, "Coefficient Alpha and the Internal Structure of Tests," *Psychometrika,* 16 (1951): 297–334.
7. J. Cohen, "A Coefficient for Nominal Scales," *Educational and Psychological Measurement,* 20 (1960): 37–46.
8. See Klaus Krippendorff, *Content Analysis: An Introduction to its Methodology* (Beverly Hills, Calif.: Sage, 1980).
9. Roy D. Goldman and Mel H. Widawski, "An Analysis of Types of Errors in the Selection of Minority College Students," *Journal of Education Measurement,* 13 (1976), 185–200; Christopher Jencks and James Crouse, "Should We Relabel the SAT . . . or Replace It?" in W. Schrader, ed., *New Directions for Testing and Measurement: Measurement, Guidance, and Program Improvement* (San Francisco: Jossey-Bass, 1982), 33–49; T. Anne Cleary, Lloyd G. Humphreys, S. A. Kendrick, and Alexander Wesman, "Educational Uses of Tests with Disadvantaged Students," *American Psychologist,* 30 (1975): 15–41.
10. Fred N. Kerlinger, *Foundations of Behavioral Research,* 2nd ed. (New York: Holt, Rinehart & Winston, 1973), 473.
11. Marvin E. Shaw and Jack M. Wright, *Scales for the Measurement of Attitudes* (New York: McGraw-Hill, 1967), 19.
12. This analogy is suggested by Kerlinger, 405–406.
13. Herbert W. Simons, *Persuasion: Understanding, Practice, and Analysis* (Reading, Mass.: Addison-Wesley, 1976), 80.
14. Charles Osgood, George J. Suci, and Percy Tannenbaum, *The Measurement of Meaning* (Urbana: University of Illinois Press, 1957).

15. Berlo, Lemert, and Mertz; McCroskey.

16. Gary Cronkhite and Jo Liska, "A Critique of Factor Analytic Approaches to the Study of Credibility," *Communication Monographs,* 43 (1976): 91–107.

17. Rensis Likert, "A Technique for the Measurement of Attitudes," *Archives of Psychology,* 140 (1932): 1–55.

18. P. D. Bardis, "A Dating Scale: A Technique for the Quantitative Measurement of Liberalism Concerning Selected Aspects of Dating," *Social Science,* 37 (1962): 44–47, cited in Shaw and Wright.

19. L. L. Thurstone and E. J. Chave, *The Measurement of Attitude* (Chicago: University of Chicago Press, 1929).

20. E. B. Silance and H. H. Remmers, "An Experimental Generalized Master Scale: A Scale to Measure Attitudes Toward Any School Subject," *Purdue University Studies in Higher Education,* 35 (1934): 84–88, cited in Shaw and Wright, 295–297.

21. Shaw and Wright contains 175 attitude scales that can be used by communication researchers, many of which are in a Thurstone format.

22. See Joseph Woelfel and Edward L. Fink, *The Measurement of Communication Processes: Galileo Theory and Method* (New York: Academic Press, 1980); J. Saltiel and J. Woelfel, "Inertia in Cognitive Process: The Role of Accumulated Information In Attitude Change," *Human Communication Research,* 1 (1975): 333–344; and Edward L. Fink, John P. Robinson, and Sue Dowden, "The Structure of Music Preference and Attendance," *Communication Research,* 12 (1985): 301–318.

23. George A. Barnett, Kim B. Serota, and James A. Taylor, "Campaign Communication and Attitude Change: A Multidimensional Analysis," *Human Communication Research,* 2 (1976): 227–244.

24. Robert Rosenthal and Ralph L. Rosnow, *Artifact in Behavioral Research.* (New York: Academic Press, 1969).

25. For a discussion of the Hawthorne effect, see Gerald Goldhaber, *Organizational Communication,* 4th ed. (Dubuque: William C. Brown, 1986), 86.

26. Eugene Webb, Donald T. Campbell, Richard D. Schwartz, and Lee Sechrest, *Unobtrusive Measures: Nonreactive Research in the Social Sciences* (Chicago: Rand-McNally, 1966).

27. Webb et al., 2.

28. Webb et al., 36.

29. Webb et al.

30. Webb et al., 90–91.

31. Webb et al., 97.

32. Webb et al.

Chapter 7

Qualitative/Descriptive (Participant-Observation) Methodology

Mark Hickson, III
University of Alabama at Birmingham

Qualitative/descriptive research employs primarily nonquantitative observation techniques. Usually the purpose of such qualitative research is to employ procedures for "counting to one."[1] The qualitative researcher often attempts to "discover" a variable and to define it. A number of research techniques may be used by the qualitative researcher, including, but not limited to, open-ended interviews, representational maps, and participant-observation. Additionally, the qualitative method often employs two or more qualitative techniques along with one or more quantitative techniques for the purpose of verifying data; this is sometimes referred to as *triangulation.*[2] In this chapter we focus on how qualitative research methods have developed in the social sciences and how they have been adapted for use in the field of communication. Because qualitative research is so different from so many of the other more quantitatively oriented techniques, we will begin with an example of why we might use one of these techniques—participant-observation.

WHY PARTICIPANT-OBSERVATION?

Why would communication researchers be interested in participant-observation? In some ways the methods already discussed point us to participant-observation: One major flaw with historical and critical study is the inability to understand how the participants viewed the communication, the scene, the act. The historical/critical researcher most often examines the event after it has occurred and, even with much empathy, cannot understand the events as they occurred to the participants. Participant-observation, on the other hand, allows the researcher to record the actual messages presented in the situation in which they were presented. At the same time, it allows the researcher to *understand and feel* how the participants felt as they were involved in an ongoing event; that is, participant-observation deals with *real behavior as it occurs in a naturally occurring setting*. As we will see with other, more quantitative methods, the ability to study the behavior in the actual setting is reduced in favor of being able to establish *control* over the research.

If real-world behavior is the major concern of the researcher, then participant-observation is an appropriate methodology. But, in choosing this method, he or she also assumes some liabilities. The major liability is that participant-observation is more subjective than objective; the researcher lives the event, participates as do others, and then steps back and attempts to rationalize what happened and how it fit with what was expected; that is, reliability may be reduced in favor of validity. In reality, this is a trade-off, one that the researcher is willing to make in order to *understand* better how the particular variables he or she is interested in operate unconstrained by the control that typifies other research methods.

In making this "fit" between theory (what was expected) and observation (what was participated in) the researcher does not reduce the theoretical base. As will be seen, participant-observation relies heavily on theory—on what the participant *expects* will occur in the situation. What, then, does the researcher observe? Obviously, there are messages to observe and record. Here we might examine what is presented verbally and how it was delivered nonverbally. Reading or viewing a copy of an emotional speech is one thing, but actually being there, being affected by the feelings of others, is another. Participant-observation allows for this addition to the situation, but it does so within the constraints of systematic observation and relies on an understanding of communication roles, rules, and routines as they relate to the verbal and nonverbal messages present.

Consider, for example, a research project during which you had a chance to observe the communication occurring at a secret meeting of some sect or society. You could conduct an historical study—read the accounts of participants and try to understand the type of messages that *might* occur in such situations. However, you might also engage in a participant-observation study of the behavior. To do so you would have to (1) study carefully the group you want to enter, (2) establish a model of the behaviors (to include the types of verbal and nonverbal messages) expected of members (this might include special greetings, clothing or robes, or gestures), (3) establish the roles different members might assume (which may be vastly different than in other situations), and (4) establish how the group would communicate according to their particular norm or routine. You would then attempt to join the group, participate in one of their meetings; you would carefully note those behaviors and messages that conformed to your model and those that did not. To do a good job you would attend several meetings and observe over time who spoke to whom, with what effect, and through what channels. Finally, you would go over your notes and write up your report, noting where this group met expectations and where it did not. But, because you were there and experienced what they experienced, you now can *interpret* the event as they might have— noting which messages were communicated in what ways, for instance.

Participant-observation allows the researcher to get close to the research. This advantage reduces the reliability of the study since we can never be totally certain that research did not change the way in which the researcher *observed* what occurred. The results are still valid, they are exactly as the researcher observed, but they might differ from other observers. With this in mind, we now turn to a detailed examination of participant-observation as a method of research.

HISTORY OF PARTICIPANT-OBSERVATION

The discipline of communication has undergone a number of changes in its approximate 2500-year history. Some of the changes have been directed toward theoretical development; others have been concerned with more practical, particularly pedagogical, factors; probably among the most dramatic, however, have been the changes in the realm of methodology. Early writers were concerned with presenting descriptive and prescriptive methods for delivering speeches in public places. Public speaking continued to be a dominant force in the discipline even with the development of quantitative studies. According to Wayne N. Thompson, "Aristotle produced a comprehensive system that in its Whatelian modification still is dominant, and the rhetorical history of the intervening twenty-three centuries can be written in terms of Aristotle's imitators, his modifiers, and his dissenters."[3]

With that introduction, Thompson continued to study the use of quantitative methods in the field of communication. With some notable improvements, research using this "psychological motif" has continued to the point where today a number of major journals in communication are dedicated almost exclusively to studies using a laboratory, experimental approach.

Another methodology with a different historical background, however, is beginning to be seen more frequently in communication journals; this method is known by the general term *field research.* Its origins can be traced to the historical writings of Herodotus in the fifth century B.C., and the historical-observation technique has been continued by such notables as Tacitus in Western culture and Fa-hsien in the East.[4]

In the intervening years, there have been numerous other observers of human behavior, but extensive use of a *scientific* observation technique did not begin until the late eighteenth century. From 1771 to 1793, Arthur Young published his accounts of agricultural practices in Great Britain.[5] These forerunners of our own agricultural communication studies eventually developed into the work of organizational communication. By the middle of the nineteenth century observational research was undertaken by researchers using social Darwinism as their theoretical base. In the 1880s, however, the observation technique was being used less frequently by academic scholars but more often for *reform-oriented research*, the precursor to *applied research.*[6]

Especially in Germany, professors of economics and philosophers used fieldwork to understand the underprivileged classes better. In 1890, "Paul Gohre, a student of theology, undertook what may have been the first systematic attempt at participant observation."[7] Gohre pretended to be a factory apprentice; each night he recorded his observations. After reading some of Gohre's publications, German sociologist Max Weber became interested in field research and collaborated with Gohre on a study of agricultural workers.

German sociologists, and later British anthropologists, rekindled the interest in field research. Franz Boas was the leader among the British anthropologists; he advocated that researchers eliminate their "Western culture" bias to understand other groups. But it was Bronislaw Malinowski who was given credit for first "pitching his tent in a native village." One of Malinowski's students, Hortense Powdermaker, was one of the first to view a U.S. community in her 1932 study of black families in small-town Mississippi.[8]

The German sociological viewpoint was continued in the United States at the University of Chicago. More contemporary "Chicagoans" began referring to their research as *participant-observation.* Among the contemporary researchers of this ilk are Howard Becker, Anselm Strauss, Erving Goffman, and Eliot Liebow. Participant-observation has since been expanded to include *phenomenological sociology* (an understanding of human behavior from the individual's perspective) and *ethnomethodology* (the way that people make sense out of the situations in which they find themselves).[9]

Early qualitative research in communication was devoted to longitudinal studies of a few people, primarily in speech therapy sessions where clients were assisted in improving their vocal expression, cross-cultural communication, applications in business, theatre, broadcasting, and speech education.[10] More recently participant-observation studies have focused on social and political problems. These studies include research on academic protest, bilingual education of migrant children, and political campaign speeches.[11]

In the initial article of the *Journal of Applied Communications Research*, Mark Hickson called for more in situ research in the communication discipline. Among the participant-observation studies appearing in that journal since that time have been research on case studies on such topics as winning a school bond election, phenomenological investigation of femininity, organizational climate, leadership development, and the effects of apparel on waitress perceptions.[12] Notice the wide variety of *messages* studied: from verbal to nonverbal, from sex role expectations to the unconscious impact of "culture."

Other expansive studies include Gerry Phillipsen's work on labor organization, the work of Hickson on communication among commuter travelers, the study of the communication of a social class group (southern rednecks) by Julian B. Roebuck and Hickson, and John Daniel Goldsmith's study of initial attorney/client consultation.[13] Knowing something about the history of this research technique brings us to a number of questions. First, exactly what is participant-observation? Second, when and how should this method be used? Third, what are the advantages and limitations of using such a method? And, finally, what is the future of this research method?

WHAT IS PARTICIPANT-OBSERVATION?

To understand a research method it is important to discover where it falls within the realm of other possibilities. Like many research techniques, participant-observation attempts to answer a question and explain how we know the answer simultaneously; that is, when we use a more conventional quantitative approach, we explain what the answer to the hypothesis was, try to analyze the answer, and provide some statistical justification of how we know that is indeed the answer.

For our purposes, we will look at four different kinds of methods typically available to communication researchers in answering their research questions. First, there is the laboratory experiment. Through the use of an extended review of the literature we discover the questions that need to be answered. This information provides us with a *rationale* for asking our own question(s). In the laboratory experiment, the questions are usually formed as hypotheses. We then select some method of researching such hypotheses. These methods usually involve gathering a specific group of people into a specified place so that the experimenter can control as many conditions as necessary to limit the focus of the study. The laboratory experimenter cannot control what goes through the minds of the participants, but can control what kinds of external factors are available that might distract peoples' attention from the objects of the experiment. Statistical procedures are usually used to check the results of the study. Good laboratory experiments include severe restrictions on the immediate environment, a structured means for selecting the participants, the development and testing of one's tools for measurement, limited generalizations of results, and a focus upon what may be the next step in studying the phenomenon under investigation. While the experimenter may have direct, face-to-face interaction with participants, this is not always necessary—or even desirable.

The second method usually used is the survey/questionnaire method. Again, the researcher seeks out questions through the use of an extended review of the available literature and a theoretical perspective. Questions that may be asked of the respondents via telephone, person-to-person interaction (interview), or through the mail are devised. Again, respondents are carefully selected so that they will be legitimate samples of the entire population for the ultimate purpose of generalization. Results are indicated and the researcher proposes the answers to questions as well as his or her epistemological verification, usually by way of statistical techniques and methods of drawing the sample. In most cases, many more respondents are used in a survey than in a laboratory experiment.

The third research approach involves the field experiment. (Here we use the term "experiment" in a more nontechnical way. The field experiment attempts to combine the best of two worlds; first, the researcher is interested in *some* control over the variables under study and, second, testing those variables in more real-world situations than would be found in a laboratory.) Again, the researcher is responsible for determining the question(s) to be answered. Theoretical approach and an extensive review of the literature allow for the appropriate questions to be posed. Next, the researcher seeks to limit the number of variables being studied. As a simplistic example, you might walk down a city street, speak to each and every person who walks toward you. The question might involve what percentage of people speak back. You take much time deciding how you will dress, and ensuring that you speak the same way each time, and so forth, however, you have *no* control over the selection of participants. Thus, while the study is conducted in a *naturalistic setting,* unlike the laboratory setting, you do not know who will be part of such a setting.

The fourth method is the field study. Here the researcher "pitches his or her tent in the native village." The researcher becomes a living part of the study. As the researcher, you may or may not know who the participants will be. While an extensive review of the literature is important, a well-developed theoretical perspective might inhibit the field researcher, for it may close out some possibilities that may be important to the conclusions of the study. There is no attempt to limit the variables because the variables are to come from the participants *themselves.* The epistemological verification must be a constant concern for the field researcher because only through verifying that the perspectives offered are those of the participants, not the researcher, can the study come across as believable.

A fifth mode is that taken by the novelist. In such a case, the writer uses his or her own intuitions and judgments about the characters he or she creates. The "subjects" do not have a chance to verify the results. While the novel may be believable, it is only believable because the readers' notions of how the "subjects" act is similar to those offered by the author.

Thus, we have five modes of studying people. Each one has its positive and negative aspects. If we look at each of these from the standpoint of *subjectivity* versus *objectivity,* however, we find some differences that may at first appear inaccurate. (Remember, participant-observation allows the researcher to *feel* how the events occurred, whereas other methods only allow for indications of the behaviors under study—survey and experimental research, for instance.) Obviously, the most objective way to get the behavior of a person recorded is to view the act from the viewpoint of the *actor,* to be a part of the occurring behavior as it exists in the natural world. The least satisfactory is to view the act from the intuitive judgment of an outside, omniscient forecaster (an author). (See Table 7.1.) What are the other possibilities? More on the objective side are video recordings of the act, followed by audio recordings, and written, paper recordings of the act. This is followed by participant-observation, during which elaborate and extensive procedures are used to ensure that the information being recorded is exactly what happened. To this point, we have discussed acts, recordings, and fiction. How do we categorize experimental laboratory studies, surveys, and experimental field studies?

These last three categories are parts of synthesis and interpretation. Self-re-

Table 7.1   LEVELS OF SOCIAL RESEARCH

	Person	Nature	Method
More "Objective"	1st	Act Recording	Act VTR Audio Recording Paper Recording Participant-Observation • as participant • as participant-observer • as observer-participant • as observer
	2nd	Synthesis	Self-Report (and interpretation by subject[s]) Historical Report and interpretation—from primary source
	3rd		Historical Report and interpretation—from secondary source • Self-Report • Historical Report Interpretation • Self-Report with stimulus (lab) • Historical Report with stimulus
More "Subjective"	Omniscient narrator	Fiction Contrived	

Source: M. Hickson, III, J.B. Roebuck, and K.S. Murty, "Creative Triangulation: Toward a Methodology for Studying Social Types," in N. K. Denzin, ed., *Studies in Symbolic Interaction,* vol. 2 (Greenwich, CT: JAI Press, 1990), p. 121.

ports, on which participants record their ideas and interpret them, are in the middle range of objectivity-subjectivity. Historical reports have a third-person nature to them. In these cases, the researcher is taking for granted some objectivity on the part of the person who initially wrote the report. Most experimental studies are based on "average" self-reports and/or "average" historical reports; that is, if you have enough people the average (usually "mean") report is indicative of the group. This assumption, however, is significantly related to how many people there are and how the participants were chosen. Thus, when a person gives as complete an account of his or her actions as is possible (preferably during the act) we have a first-person report. When observation is used, we have a second-person report. But when statistics are used, based on averages, we have a third-person report.

Participant-observation is, then, *a combination of a first-person and a second-person account, which takes place in a naturalistic setting, of the actions and behaviors of a specific group of people.* There is no "average." The sample is your population. There is only a development of what may be considered to be *typical behavior* and *atypical behavior.* If in any way this sense of norms may be quantified, typical refers to those who behave in accordance with a mean, median-oriented rule. Atypical is behavior that occurs when one is distant from the mean or median.

Participant-observation in communication research allows us to examine many different types of communication *messages* as they occur naturally. For instance, we can examine how people *speak,* the language they use in the workplace or at home, without interjecting an outside presence, which may change the way the speaking naturally occurs. Or, we can examine the *behaviors* (verbal and nonverbal) people exhibit in particular situations (at rallies, sports events, on the job, during family arguments). Finally, we can observe how people adopt and employ different *roles* in the real world and how these roles change verbal and nonverbal messages. The focus of participant-observation, then, is on a variety of messages in naturally occurring situations. Additionally, participant-observation may be the first step in a program of research that seeks to first identify and explain normal behaviors in the field before manipulating those behaviors in the laboratory. Hence, participant-observation provides some form of explanation that may later allow us to predict how others might act in similar situations.

WHEN AND WHERE SHOULD PARTICIPANT-OBSERVATION BE USED?

There are three basic types of questions that can be asked using the participant-observation method. First, does the social grouping *exist*—one that is communicatively different from others? Second, what is the *normative* behavior of such formal and informal groups—how do the people who compose these groups use verbal and nonverbal communication? Third, how does communication *function* in these groups? In this section, we will first discuss how one determines the existence of a social group.

Participant-observation, as a research method, should be used primarily to develop useful, beneficial research questions. For example, in the Roebuck and Hickson study, the researchers entered the community of the southern redneck primarily to discover whether such a social group as a construct—redneck—actually existed as well as to study the norms and characteristics of such a social group if, indeed, it did exist. [14] To investigate this community, the researchers found it necessary to do historical search first to determine what had been found previously. The researchers found that in the past 100 years such a group seemed to be associated with "poor whites" in the southern part of the United States. Following a detailed historical account of the group, the researchers entered their community. The purpose of the second phase was to provide an account of the *social norms* of such a group as well as determine how the group described itself.

The second phase was undertaken by visiting all aspects of the social world of the redneck. These aspects included honky-tonks, the homes of rednecks, the places where they worked, and the places where they transacted business. The conclusions indicated that the redneck considered himself somewhat of a social rebel, choosing to place himself against other groups rather than holding a specific identity for himself.

Such an investigation would have been extremely difficult if not impossible to undertake using traditional methods. For example, rednecks would not be open to entering a laboratory situation because they do not like academia nor academicians, and therefore would not be willing participants. For similar reasons, it would be difficult to entice rednecks to answer questions honestly using a traditional survey approach. Especially because they consider themselves social rebels, rednecks do not wish to participate in any study or anything that might be considered part of mainstream society. They do not like to talk to strangers. While a field experiment would have been within the realm of possibility, such a study would provide answers to very limited and specific questions about the social behavior of rednecks.

Novels, however, may be useful in the sense that they can provide basic data about such groups and their group norms. *Tobacco Road* is an example of such a novel. The problem with the novel, novella, or short story, however, is that sometimes the information is based on data and at other times it is not. Liebow, for example, found that while streetcorner blacks in Washington, D.C., held their own set of norms, those norms were not typical of society as a whole. [15] In writing fiction, the author might be tempted to discover similarities in the behavior of the characters without exploring the differences. On the other hand, the author might exaggerate the differences at the expense of the similarities.

Thus, it may be "dangerous" to use traditional methods of study, as in the case of Liebow's study. Assume that you are interested in studying prison behavior. Traditional methods will not give you the insight you need to explain the channels of communication, for instance, between prisoners and guards. Prisons have their own codes of behavior, which may or may not be consistent with mainstream society. Assuming a white, middle-class mentality may be both physically dangerous and theoretically unjustified. Participant-observation is an effective method to use to study whether a group exists in the sense of having its own system of normative behavior.

Another example of participant-observation occurs when the participants themselves are unaware of their own behavior. Hickson's 1977 study of people who rode commuter buses found that normative behavior changed over time. [16] Had the participants been surveyed about their normative behavior, they probably would not have recognized that such changes had taken place. Thus, at certain times, in such an investigation, it is necessary to "test" the normative behavior of the group by violating what the researcher believes are the norms. [17] As a member of the "group," the participant-observer is only one step removed from the behavior; the method provides the ability to examine differences over time because they have been noted *as they occurred.* The group members (the *actors*), because they are involved with everyday activity, caught up in their daily life, are more likely to ignore such changes—unless, of course, the violations are so dramatic as to stimulate discussion.

Such violations involving *ethnomethodology* (how people make sense out of the situations in which they find themselves) not only provide answers as to what constitutes the norms but also what kinds of sanctions the group assesses for violations. Again, as a researcher, you must take care to watch for your own physical well being as well as assuring the accuracy of your data. In a sense, the Hawthorne effect can take place in a participant observation study just as easily as in a field experiment or laboratory experiment (see Chapter 6). What if the people are acting in such a way *because* a researcher is present?

Hickson has dealt with this particular problem in a study of the communication patterns in a community action agency in Illinois.[18] Hickson has made three recommendations regarding studying an organization: (1) The researcher must be able to communicate with personnel on all levels, (2) it is probably better if the researcher is assigned a volunteer job in a low-status position, and (3) the researcher should attempt to balance the roles of participant and observer.

When studying the communication of organizations, it is important to remember that the low status workers' communication patterns are as important, if not more so, than the communication of the higher-status staff. In such a hierarchical organization, the bottom part of the pyramid holds many more people than does the top. With the larger number of people, the lower status group has much more of an opportunity to affect the relationships with individuals outside the organization. In addition, they tend to establish the norms for external communication behavior. For this reason, when you engage in participant-observation, you need to be accepted as an insider in the group of low-status workers. You must use language and dress the part of the low-status worker. To engage in the research you should be a volunteer; entering the organization as a paid worker may yield perceptions of threat to other low-status workers. As a researcher, it is important that you make it clear that you are not interested in having a long-term, paid position in the organization and that you do not associate with the value system of upper-level management.

To produce such an atmosphere, a researcher must stay in the organization for a long period of time (probably at least six months) but must also have a deadline for a final exit from the group. The roles of participant and observer must be remembered at all times. If a researcher becomes too much the participant, he or she will lose objectivity and become too sensitized to the needs and desires of the group. If a researcher becomes too much the observer, the workers will lose trust and will withhold information.

Participant-observation, then, is used in organizations to determine the answers to a number of *general* questions concerning different levels of communication. It is important that a researcher remain objective and sensitive at the same time, realizing that it is as possible to be fooled by management as by the workers.

Other more traditional research methods can be used when there is a specific question or questions to be answered, or when the group is more open to answering questions, when the group does not fear repercussions for answering questions honestly, or when a researcher is seeking to generalize the results of the study. It is important to remember, however, that perhaps the *generalizability of findings* is not as important as we may want to think. For example, if we are studying community action agencies, it may be more important to understand the unique personalities that work in such an organization than it is to generalize such personalities across other, similar, agencies. This understanding is more critical, for example, than the general principles of organizations that may have been derived from corporate communications.

HOW DOES ONE UNDERTAKE A PARTICIPANT-OBSERVATION STUDY?

There are seven basic steps to undertaking a participant-observation study:

1. Establish the general research questions.
2. Review the literature on the subject group.
3. Develop a *theoretical model* based on the literature, which provides an understanding of what *should* be observed given this particular group of people, organization, or event.
4. Collect the data.
5. Analyze the data.
6. Develop an *empirical model.*
7. Compare and contrast the theoretical model with the empirical model to determine the conclusions and implications of your research.

Research Questions

The participant-observer must be aware that establishing explicit, hypothesis-like research questions is not in his or her best interests. For example, you must be aware that new questions may be derived in the process of investigation. Participation-observation requires a flexible, adaptive researcher and research technique. The following questions are appropriate for participant-observation:

Is there such a phenomenon as the southern redneck?

Do black streetcorner people have a set of communicative norms? If so, what are the nonverbal ways they communicate (the nonverbal norms)? What are the verbal norms (do they employ slang, street English, obscenities?)

To what extent do these communication norms change as a result of changes in the environment?

What communicative behaviors are associated with a newsroom? Are there special nonverbal behaviors employed? Is there a special layout that provides clues as to status or power? Are there special vocabularies?

What types of verbal and nonverbal communication occur in families undergoing marital stress?

In Mark Hickson's *Communication Quarterly* study of commuters in Washington, D.C., there was rarely a problem with any of the commuters finding a seat on the bus until the energy crisis of 1973. The arrival of the crisis caused a number of people to take the bus who had never taken it before. Because of the increase in the number of commuters certain nonverbal norms changed. One change in norm and role was identified when the riders began lining up to get a seat in the bus. Such lining up was not a result of intentional changes in normative behavior as much as it was pragmatics. As the researcher, you could not have predicted such a change in norms, but you still must be open to whatever changes take place in the environment as well as the changes in the norms of the participant pool. In more traditional research, it is the job of the researcher to keep such intervening variables out of the study. When the study is undertaken in a naturalistic environment, however, such controls do not exist (the researcher could not alleviate the energy crisis).

The second example is the study of the community action agency discussed earlier. Data were collected in 1970. This was the second full year of Richard Nixon's first presidential term. While the community action agency was the brainchild of Lyndon Johnson, Nixon's views on such social programs were far less supportive. Therefore, such programs were criticized more acutely than they had been in the past. The particular Illinois agency under observation was given two different opportunities to make internal (communication) changes during the period of investigation. Again, as the researcher, you could not have predicted that you might be studying an organization in the process of its own demise. However, that is precisely what occurred in this particular study.

Review of the Literature

While a literature review may be undertaken using the traditional library search of books and articles, various subject groups for qualitative studies require the use of nontraditional methods of understanding the subject "pool" as well. For example, it may be necessary to read newspaper articles about organizations as diverse as the National Socialist Party, the Black Panthers, or even the Kiwanis. Such a review of articles could provide you with information on what is going on in the organization as well as the media's views of the importance of that organization's activities. A thorough review of the subject pool should enable you to discriminate the differences between the First Presbyterian Church in Terre Haute, Indiana, and the First Presbyterian Church in Savannah, Georgia.

A review of the literature about the group should provide certain demographic data (age, sex, race), the level of formality of the group (amount of policies and procedures in written form), the identity of leadership of the group (names, demographics, biographical data). In addition, the review should provide a historical account of the group. The review should provide data about how you could go about being assimilated into the group; the group's systems of rewards and sanctions should be available.

A review of a prison system, for example, would provide information concerning how safe you might be in the environment. Records from the warden's office might prove beneficial. Prison fights, however, would probably *not* be reported in the local newspapers unless guards or innocent victims were killed or taken hostage. [19] As a researcher, however, you must be suspicious even of "official records" such as those in the warden's office, because various underlying motives might prevent the warden's maintenance of accurate records. While a review of books or articles in the library might provide information about what "artifacts" (or weapons) are available to inmates, guards at the prison might show you some of the *actual* weapons found in that particular prison. Such a demonstration by the guards would be helpful toward understanding what is happening in the prison under study prior to beginning the investigation. All available sources should be tapped before you move to the next step—developing a theoretical model.

Developing a Theoretical Model

From an extensive review of the literature, undertaken prior to entry into the naturalistic setting as a participant-observer, the researcher should have a number of clues about: (1) why the group is unique, (2) why the event is unusual, (3) how similar organizations function from an idealistic perspective, and/or (4) why most people would consider the behavior and communication processes deviant in comparison with a norm. Thus, the *theoretical model* is an outline of what the researcher *presumes* will be the case, taken from the context of the review of literature and his or her knowledge of the communication event itself.

An example can be taken from a study of the communication that occurs at a communication convention. The research question you would consider might be, What type of communicative behaviors occur at conventions of people engaged in the study of communication? The specific questions would center on what particular convention(s) you were interested in examining. Suppose, for reasons of access, expense, and interest, you are interested in how people at regional communication conventions communicate. Suppose also that you are located in the southeastern portion of the United States.

Assuming that you are going to undertake the study of a number of such conventions over a period of years, you can determine from a general review of literature what goes on at conventions in general, what goes on at academic conventions in general, and what goes on at academic conventions of communication faculty members in particular. Such a review would encompass a library search, particularly in the fields of sociology and education. In addition, you would visit the archives of the associations you wish to study. In this instance you would find that the archives of the Southern States Communication Association were located at the University of Florida. A review of the records there would provide the information about what programs have been presented, what individuals have been part of the programs over the years, what individuals have been officers over the years, where the conventions have been held, and what other nonacademic events take place during conventions.

Data concerning the demographic composition of conventioneers would also be found in the official records of the organization. However, this information might have to come from the office of the executive secretary instead of the archives. With this review of the literature, you should be able to make the following kinds of determinations about the "ideal"—typical, normative—convention.

Establishing Typicality   The following are typical examples of occurrences a researcher interested in convention communication might expect to find; that is, the research question is concerned with how the role of conventioneer alters both communication role *and* the resultant communication norms—both verbal and nonverbal messages. First, there is a registration for both the convention hotel and the convention itself. Second, there is a placement service available for employers and potential employees to meet, greet, and talk with one another. Third, there are a large number of presentations and seminars. Fourth, there are a number of events that call for the participation of all persons gathered at the convention (cocktail parties, association business meetings, association social events, addresses to the association, etc.). Given these factors, you might begin by asking questions about which members would attend which of these events.

It might be expected that all members would be registered at the hotel and at the convention. Thus, this is a gathering place at the beginning of the convention, a place where each person can get a notion of who is there and who is not there. If the convention has an association cocktail hour late on the first day of registration, you might determine that this would be a second place for people to find out who is there.

In establishing this *typicality mode,* a researcher must first visualize the physical areas of interaction (see Figure 7.1). There are individual rooms for the members, registration area, large convocation rooms for cocktail parties and major addresses, smaller rooms for the presentation of papers and seminars, restrooms off the lobby area, and the lobby area itself. Since we know that there is a need for eating meals at such conventions, the researcher should be aware that there may be one or more restaurants in a hotel, one or more bars at a hotel, and bars and restaurants near the hotel at which individuals can meet and interact with one another.

Second, you must anticipate *expected* behavior. A researcher might expect, for instance, that the convention attendees would register early to get a name tag so that others would recognize them by name. When people see one another once a year or less, it is easy to remember the face but not the name.

You might expect that employers and potential employees would look for the placement service space very early upon arrival. In other words, a researcher should expect that each person involved in the event under study has a *role.* In this instance the roles might include potential employer and potential employee, paper presenter, seminar leader, or simply observer; that is, each person has a pragmatic reason for attending the convention and this reason—or role—will influence the messages he or she produces. Additionally, you would expect that people attending for a particular reason would also have *rules.* Rules are unwritten behaviors dictated by the norms present as established by the group. For example, it might be that the potential employer feels at ease going to a bar in the hotel and having a few drinks. Such behavior may be against the rules for the potential employees, lest

Lobby Level

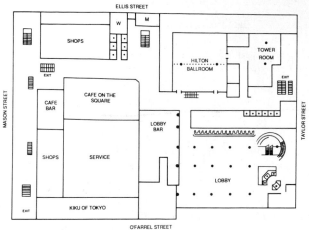

Ballroom Level

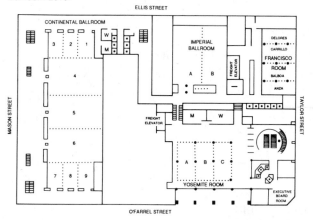

Sixth Floor

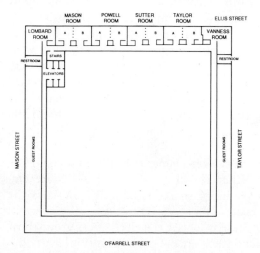

Fourth Floor

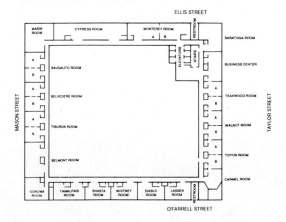

Figure 7.1 Floor plan: convention layout.

161

they run into one of the potential employers in the "wrong" place. It also may be a rule violation for the potential employer to be seen "interviewing"—even if that person is just talking to a potential job seeker—at an inappropriate time and place.

Finally, you might expect that a person would get into a *routine;* that is, employers and employees might go back and forth to check the job and interview possibilities at the placement service periodically. Individuals who are not seeking a job might never go to the placement service. Thus, through this review of literature and commonsensical evaluation, we have developed a theoretical model. The communication—at communication conventions, as our example indicates— should encompass roles, rules, and routines. [20] Hence, our theoretical model must define the general roles, rules, and routines we *expect* to be typical of the event and the group. Based on these definitions, we create expectations of what communicative messages (both verbal and nonverbal) we would *expect* to observe, given the circumstances. Obviously, each may change as either the group *or* the event changes, something over which the researcher has *no control.*

Creating Roles   For the theoretical model to be helpful, however, the researcher should be more specific; that is, what verbal and nonverbal communication roles seem to go with what verbal and nonverbal rules and the resultant routines (the *application* of the roles and rules)? It would appear feasible first to outline all of the possible roles. Given our example of convention behavior, the following are some possibilities:

1. *The job seeker:* What communication strategies does the person seeking a job adopt? Are there any particular rules that he or she employs communicating with others, both potential employers and competitors?
2. *The politician* (the person holding or seeking office at the convention for the particular group [the office-seeker may be seeking an organization-wide office or may be seeking an office in a smaller division of the organization, and this should be taken into account as the expectations might change according to the role's role]): What communication strategies does this person use? Here we might note the particular types of language employed; where (the nonverbal aspects) this person communicates with others; and whether or not a particular routine is followed by each politico.
3. *The information-seeker* (the person there to learn, to be trained, to compare different ideas): How does this person communicate? Where does he or she sit in meetings? In what type of verbal questioning does he or she engage? With whom does he or she normally spend her time? Is there a common purpose in the group?
4. *The presenter* (the person there to deliver a paper or lead a seminar): How does he or she communicate? What verbal or nonverbal skills are employed? By what set of "rules" is he or she constrained? How does the presenter approach his or her task?
5. *The conventioneer* (the person present to "see the city"): As a group, how do these people act? Do they spend their time at the convention? Individu-

ally, does he or she establish a minimal time to be spent in meetings? Does he or she dress differently?

6. *The socialite* (the person there to "see old friends"): What distinguishes this person from the politician? What verbal behaviors are observable that would establish a "rule" that there should be only social talk? Does this person use different nonverbal codes or systems to indicate the communication norm is social and not business?

7. *The playboy/playgirl* (the person there to flirt with others and, perhaps, seeking intimate encounters): In what verbal *schticks* does this person engage? What "quasi-courtship" behaviors are displayed? Where does this person spend his or her time? With whom?

Understanding that these roles are not mutually exclusive, the researcher can then go about determining which communicative roles are attached to which communication rules and the resultant routines. Following through on this process, you, as the researcher, will have developed a *theoretical model*. You will test this model against the actual data you observe; the next stage in your research will be the collection of data.

Data Collection

The participant-observer must be cautious about using the theoretical model as an hypothesis-testing device. For the participant-observer, the theoretical model is simply a preliminary stage for establishing a sense of what is being studied. In no way should the researcher feel impelled to support, defend, or reject the model. It merely serves to prepare you for what you *might* observe; in this regard the theoretical model helps establish data collection by creating possible roles, rules, and routines against which you measure the actual behavior(s).

Note-Taking   The researcher should make certain that careful notes are taken. We recommend that two different types of notes be taken when conducting research using participant-observation: immediate records and delayed, reflective log observations. You might call the former field notes, and the latter refined notes. One drawback of participant observation is found in taking notes. In places where you are surreptitiously recording behavior, the taking of notes may be too overt, it may create behaviors in the population under study not normally found in either the group or the situation. Therefore, a researcher should try to limit the number of notes taken if he or she feels that in the process of note-taking he or she is observing behaviors created because of his or her presence. This, of course, leaves much to memory. As a participant-observer you would need to find an isolated spot to record your observations.

If you are in a position to observe without it being obvious to the group, then you might consider taking more complete notes. In the example of convention behaviors, you might sit in the lobby area and note the behaviors occurring around you without raising suspicion. One way to do so might be by pretending to complete a crossword puzzle; take time to look around, write something in the book or paper, look around, and so forth. The actual act of observation and note taking becomes "typical" for the area. While Hickson was observing commuter behavior among bus riders, he pretended to read a book.[21]

Obviously, it would be easier if we could audio- or videotape the interactions. Tape recordings are not recommended, except in those cases where a person could be *publicly* overheard talking with another person. There is a fine line between participant-observation and violating another person's right of privacy. Remember, in many instances your observations are going on without the participant's knowledge or, as in the case of working as a volunteer within an organization, your participants may "forget" that you are there as a researcher and treat you as "one of the guys." Therefore, as a participant-observer, you should carefully take notes, either in the immediate environment (if possible) or as soon as possible in an isolated environment.

Immediate records should be as factual as possible. In general, you should record your observations as carefully and completely as possible. Use the margins around your notes to review and elaborate behaviors that might have gone unnoticed at first but, when reviewed, come to mind. When doing such a review, you should be careful to avoid interpreting what you observed; the immediate notes should reflect the actual behaviors *as they occurred and without interpretation or analysis.*

The delayed, reflective log of observations, however, should incorporate the feelings of the researcher. The reflective log contains the interpretation of the facts observed in the field/immediate notes. As a participant-observer, it is important that you get into the habit of writing the reflective log at the end of each day. In writing this log, you use the immediate observations as a guide to reconstructing what you observed, trying both to describe and interpret the behaviors and situations. What was typical and atypical might be noted as well how the participants in your study reacted on that given day. Among other items, the reflective log should tell the reader how the observer was influenced by the observations and to what extent he or she may have influenced the behaviors of the subjects.

Our example of roles, rules, and routines is only one way of approaching participant-observation. It appears to be a good method *for this particular study* (convention behavior). In reflecting on this study, the researcher should note his or her experience with such conventions; that is, is this the first time the researcher has ever been to such a convention? If not, certain biases may exist. In previous conventioneering the researcher may have decided that people from certain areas act in certain ways or that some rules or roles are appropriate or inappropriate. These biases should be reported in the reflective log as a way of interpreting the factual data garnered from observation. Remember, a limitation to this method of research is the perspective of the observer. The researcher must be careful not to be drawn into taking sides or joining a particular clique or group. At all times the participant-observer is a researcher first and a participant second. At times this distinction is hard to maintain and reflecting on problems or things that makes the distinction hard to maintain provides much insight when trying to write up the final product.

Change and Adaptability   The methods for collecting data may change in the process of actual observation. As the researcher, you may decide that open-ended interviews are needed to gain additional information from some of the participants. The observations may call for the researcher to mail a questionnaire to the participants *after the event,* the convention in our example. The important thing for the participant-observer to remember is that he or she should be open to such changes throughout the investigation. Consider the following questions:

1. Given the communication roles suggested in the theoretical model, do they hold up?
2. What *combinations* of communication roles seem to occur?
3. What communication roles tended to show up that were not considered in the theoretical model?
4. What communication roles suggested by the theoretical model did not show up?

Answers to these questions may require further investigation or indicate that changes in method are necessary *in this naturalistic setting.* Participant-observation, as a method, must adapt to changes in both the group and the setting. A major strength of such change is the interpretation you would make on why changes were necessary in your later analysis and reporting.

Objectivity in Data Collection   Once the data collection has begun, the objectivity of the researcher is paramount; that is, a person should not attempt to observe an organization or people to whom he or she is very familiar, nor should he or she try to observe organizations or people with whom he or she shares a close ideological agreement or has a major disagreement. The participant-observer is above all a researcher, a person trying to make objective, rational explanations for people's behavior. Attempting to infiltrate an organization or group that you either agree or disagree with will probably yield biased observations from the beginning, and this should be avoided at all times. Where you are interested in such groups or situations, you should consider working with others who do not share your feelings. Or, you might consider employing another person to observe the same group and setting simultaneously. Careful comparison of both field notes and reflective logs might point out potential biases and aid in interpretation later.

The data collected should be as complete and specific as possible. You should collect the data in a form as if you were conducting the research for a novel. In the end, the final product of participant-observation should sound as real as a good novel. It should be as specific as a novel in describing the characteristics of the participants, the actions taken by the participants, and so forth, that are relevant to the investigation. The data should contain the *typical* and the *atypical* information.

Validity and Reliability   One final comment is necessary regarding data collection. Validity of observation is not a major concern with participant-observation. Because you are actually observing behavior in the context of normally occurring communication, what you observe is as valid as the perceptions that you as the researcher have of the behavior; that is, to the degree to which you can observe what has happened, the language used, the norms established, you have at least face and content validity. Because there are no intervening variables, you are interested in the behaviors associated with the various communication roles, rules, and routines. Reliability, however, becomes problematic. Reliability is limited in at least two ways. First, there are potential biases associated with observing others. The degree to which you cannot identify your biases, your reliability in observing and reporting is diminished. Second, participant-observation is a very personal experience and your interpretation is *your* interpretation. The decisions you make are based on your understanding of what should and did happen. To the degree that one or the other is off the theoretical or observational mark, reliability is reduced. However, what you observe reflects the actual behaviors, both verbal and nonverbal, that occurred in the context of actual communication.

How can the problems of reliability be overcome? One way would be to employ more than one *trained* observer. To the degree that the two or more observers agreed on what they observed, reliability could be enhanced. This is no different than intercoder reliability, which was discussed in earlier chapters. In interpreting participant observation you should remember that the method provides insight into actual day-to-day communication activity. The results cannot usually generalize to other situations, although previous research may help establish a theoretical model. When reading such research, it may be best to add the comment: This is what the observer saw and it tells me as much about him or her as it does about what he or she actually reported.

Data Analysis

Once the observations have been collected and compressed into a form of data, the participant-observer begins a new role, that of telling a story to the reader. Here the researcher is trying to provide an account of the everyday happenings under investigation. In the example of the communication convention, you try to present your findings in an account that is so real that the reader feels he or she is actually present in the situation. In conducting this phase of participant-observation the researcher should take care neither to underestimate nor to exaggerate the findings. In selecting the information out of the notes, the researcher should include information about similarities and dissimilarities among the participants, the actions taken by the participants, and the researcher's own feelings—his or her own personal reactions to the observations collected—as an introspective analysis. In particular instances the researcher might excise certain interpretations and place them in explanatory footnotes attached to the report. Whether the analysis is in the text or in footnote form, it will be reporting what the *researcher* observed, hence it is based on the researcher's observations of what he or she observed as it occurred. One of the characteristics of the qualitative researcher that is not present in the work of the quantitative researcher is the reporting of the researcher's biases. This characteristic lends a particular uniqueness to both the method and the style of reporting.

Development of an Empirical Model

After the data have been collected and analyzed, the participant should develop an empirical model. The empirical model is simply a summary of the observations and the findings of the analyzed data. In its most simplistic form the empirical model presents what was observed in the naturalistic setting. The empirical model reflects data that are similar to that of other methods. The empirical model represents the world as it was when the observations were collected.

Model Comparison and Contrast

The final aspect of the participant-observation process is the reporting of similarities and differences between what was expected (theoretical model) and what was observed (empirical model). Guiding this stage of analysis are a number of general questions that are adapted to the specific questions asked in the study, for instance, How did the original review of the literature and subsequent theoretical model compare with the empirical model developed out of the data collection and analysis? That is, how similar or dissimilar are the two models? Where were the differences observed? Why? Where were similarities observed? Did the similarities hold up across time? Other questions guiding this analysis include:

1. What communication roles were observed?
2. What communication rules were observed?
3. What communication routines were observed?
4. What were the norms for communication, given this particular group, institution, or event? How did roles, rules, and routines interact to create norms?
5. Under what circumstances were the rules and routines that made up the norms violated?
6. Why were norms violated? In what ways were the norms violated?
7. Which norms were upheld? Why?

The ultimate purpose of this final comparison-contrast model is that it should act as the theoretical model for the next investigator. In this way, the next researcher can be ahead of the game in beginning research on a similar event or organization. It also allows other researchers to compare how this particular study differs from other studies of the same or similar events or organizations.

ADVANTAGES AND LIMITATIONS

As with any method, there are certain advantages and limitations to research conducted by participant-observation. As with all the methods discussed in this book, however, the participant-observation method best answers certain kinds of questions. If the research question requires a qualitative but social scientific method, then participant-observation may be best suited to find the *appropriate* answers.

Advantages

First, the researcher is directly involved in the communication process; that is, the data are first- and second-person data taken in the context of the communication situation. Second, the longitudinal nature of participant-observation allows the researcher to see patterns of behavior rather than isolated instances (videotapes as opposed to snapshots); that is, the researcher can observe the changes of the participants over time, in differing contexts, and so forth. Third, the researcher can see both the typical situations and the exceptions, whereas most quantitative methods allow only for typicalities. Fourth, the researcher, through actual participation, reports findings that are highly valid; they represent that which occurred as it occurred. Participant-observation focuses on the behaviors that occur rather than the description of a behavior via some measuring instrument.

Limitations

First, good participant-observation research usually takes a long time. It may take a year or longer to complete; most researchers who use this method take a number of years to collect their data. This is not a method for researchers who are in a hurry. Second, participant-observation studies are usually not generalizable. They cannot be generalized to time nor to other similar groups. The results, while valid for the particular group observed, may not be reliable when compared to other, similar studies. The participant-observation method yields a *case study*. You understand in great detail what happened in this given instance at this given point in time. In conducting research via this method you are more interested in understanding what occurs than being able to predict that behavior again or to generalize to other groups. A third limiting factor is found in the realization that not all researchers can undertake studies using this method. Some people cannot set aside their biases; because there is no external source for accounting for biases (such as statistics or sampling procedures), many beginning participant-observers simply give up on this method.

THE FUTURE OF PARTICIPANT-OBSERVATION RESEARCH IN COMMUNICATION

As we mentioned early in this chapter, most early participant-observation research was developed in the areas of speech correction and education. In recent years, however, much study has been devoted to using the participant-observation approach in organizational communication. With items such as communication audits (highly quantitative accounts of how information flows in an organization), it becomes even more important that qualitative techniques be used to triangulate findings into meaningful analysis. The study of organizations almost requires that the researcher(s) be there. We believe that the future of organizational communication may be in the hands of those undertaking research using this qualitative method as one way of ensuring that true communication phenomena are studied and reported.

Additionally, those studying politicians have recently begun studying contemporary examples. In order to understand fully what is going on in political communication, the researcher should be present. Textual accounts, for instance, do not provide for audience response. Nor do videotapes of speeches. Only when the researcher is present can a realistic account of political or religious speeches be made.

Most interpersonal communication situations are too unique for such field studies. The amount of time, energy, and money needed to fund research on interpersonal communication using field methods would be enormous. Even then, the accounts would be usable only for those particular situations. Clinical accounts by psychologists might fall into this category, but we seriously doubt that communication researchers would use this expensive method for studying interpersonal communication.

SUMMARY

In this chapter we have attempted to introduce the ideas behind participant-observation research. We have outlined a history of the method, provided information about what participant-observation is and is not, demonstrated when and where it should be used, provided the advantages and limitations of the method, and suggested areas of communication in which participant-observation may be used in the future. Much can be learned about how others communicate simply by listening and observing them communicate verbally and nonverbally.

PROBES

1. Why participant-observation? What does this method offer you that other methods do not? Can you think of a research question based thus far on your academic training in communication that would be best handled by participant-observation? Why?

2. Assuming that you are going to conduct a participant-observation study of communication research methods courses, what would your research question(s) be? What would this method provide you that other (library, historical/critical, survey, experimental, content analysis) methods do not? Why?

3. In conducting a participant-observation study you must develop a theoretical model. How is this done? What is typicality in the model? Why is the establishment of typicality important? How does typicality relate to the concept of *role* in this method?

4. Assume that you are going to conduct a participant-observation study at a fraternity or sorority rush party. Assume also that you have established your theoretical model (use your experiences here). How will you conduct the study? What methods of data collec-

tion will you employ? How will you assess reliability and validity (and are they important)?

5. Take your answers to Probe 4 one step further. How will you analyze your data? Against what will you compare the obtained data? What questions should you answer in assessing the data at this stage of the study? What will your end product tell us about the specific event you studied? Where will it point us to in your program of research?

SUGGESTED READING

Bogdan, R., & Taylor, S. J. (1975). *Introduction to qualitative research methods: A phenomenological approach to the social sciences.* New York: John Wiley.

Hickson, M. (1973). Applied communications research: A beginning point for social relevance. *Journal of Applied Communications Research, 1,* 1–5.

Hickson, M., III. (1974). Participant-observation technique in organizational research. *Journal of Business Communication, 11,* 37–42, 54.

Phillipsen, G. (1975). Speaking "like a man" in Teamsterville: Culture patterns of role enactment in an urban neighborhood. *Quarterly Journal of Speech, 61,* 13–22.

Roebuck, J. B., & Hickson, M., III. (1982). *The southern redneck: A phenomenological class study.* New York: Praeger.

Spradley, J. P. (1980). *Participant observation.* New York: Holt, Rinehart and Winston.

Van Maanen, J., Manning, P. K., & Miller, M. L. (eds). (1986). *Sage qualitative research methods series.* Beverly Hills, CA: Sage Publications.

Wax, R. H. (1971). *Doing fieldwork: Warnings and advice.* Chicago: University of Chicago Press.

Webb, E. J., Campbell, D. T., Schwartz, R. D., & Sechrest, L. (1970). *Unobtrusive measures: Nonreactive research in the social sciences.* Chicago: Rand McNally.

NOTES

1. J. Van Maanen, P. K. Manning, and M. L. Miller eds., *Sage Qualitative Research Methods Series, Vols. 1–4* (Beverly Hills, Calif.: Sage, 1986), 5.
2. E. J. Webb, D. T. Campbell, R. D. Schwartz, and L. Sechrest, *Unobtrusive Measures: Nonreactive Research in the Social Sciences* (Chicago: Rand McNally, 1970).
3. Wayne N. Thompson, *Quantitative Research in Public Address and Communication* (New York: Random House, 1967), 3.
4. E. O. Reischauer and J. K. Fairbank, *East Asia: The Great Tradition,* Vol 1 (Boston: Houghton Mifflin, 1958).
5. R. H. Wax, *Doing Fieldwork: Warnings and Advice* (Chicago: University of Chicago Press, 1971), 24.
6. Wax, p. 25.
7. Wax, p. 27.
8. Hortense Powdermaker, *Stranger and Friend: The Way of an Anthropologist* (New York: Norton, 1966).
9. J. L. Heap and P. A. Roth, "On Phenomenological Sociology," *American Journal of Sociology,* 38 (1973): 354–367.

10. See J. J. O'Neill, "The Practice of Group Speech Therapy," *Central States Speech Journal*, 5 (1954): 12–14; D. Rasmussen, "High School Students Can Take Phonetics—and Like it," *Central States Speech Journal*, 7 (1955): 17–19; W. Schrier, "A Goodwill Visit to Six German Universities," *Central States Speech Journal*, 13 (1961): 35–42; M. Morris, "Indian Oratory," *Southern Speech Communication Journal*, 10 (1944): 29–36; L. L. Hale, "Program and Methods of Teaching English to Latin American Students at the University of Florida," *Southern Speech Communication Journal*, 11 (1945): 1–5; T. J. McLaughlin, "An Industrial Communications Training Program," *Central States Speech Journal*, 8 (1957): 43; A. B. Womack, "Rehearsal Problems," *Southern Speech Communication Journal*, 13 (1948): 128–129; G. L. Arms, "Formal Education Through Television: Report from KUHT at the University of Houston," *Southern Speech Communication Journal*, 20 (1955) 262–269; and G. Patrick, "Training of the Voice and Diction of a Southerner for Moving Pictures," *Southern Speech Bulletin*, 1 (1935): 24–25.

11. See H. H. Martin, "The Rhetoric of Academic Protest," *Central States Speech Journal*, 17 (1966): 244–250; P. G. Friedman, "Special Reports: Closing the Cultural Gap: Awareness Groups for Migrant Children," *Central States Speech Journal*, 28 (1977): 134–139; and William D. Brooks, "A Field Study of the Johnson and Goldwater Campaign Speeches in Pittsburgh," *Southern Speech Communication Journal*, 32 (1967): 261–272.

12. See *Journal of Applied Communications Research:* Mark Hickson, "Applied Communications Research: A Beginning Point for Social Relevance," 1 (1973): 1–5; Bonita L. Perry, "Winning an Election: A Communication Case Study," 1 (1973): 61–71; Sandra L. Fish, "A Phenomenological Examination of Femininity," 4 (1976): 43–53; Stanley Deetz, "Social Well-Being and the Development of an Appropriate Organizational Response to the De-institutionalization and Legitimation Crises," 7 (1979): 45–54; Sanford B. Weinberg and Susan H. Rovinski, "A Longitudinal Study of Leadership Development," 7 (1979): 125–133; and JerriJayne W. Stillman and Wayne C. Hensley, "She Wore a Flower in Her Hair: The Effect of Ornamentation on Nonverbal Communication," 8 (1980): 31–39.

13. Gerry Phillipsen, "Speaking 'Like a Man' in Teamsterville: Culture Patterns of Role Enactment in an Urban Neighborhood," *Quarterly Journal of Speech*, 61 (1975): 13–22; Mark Hickson, III, "Communication in Natural Settings: Research Tool for Undergraduates," *Communication Quarterly*, 25 (1977): 23–28; Julian B. Roebuck and Mark Hickson, III, *The Southern Redneck: A Phenomenological Case Study* (New York: Praeger, 1982); and John Daniel Goldsmith, "The Initial Attorney/Client Consultation: A Case Study," *Southern Speech Communication Journal*, 45 (1980): 394–407. See also Mark Hickson, III, Julian B. Roebuck, and Komanduri S. Murty, "Creative Triangulation: Toward a Methodology for Studying Social Types," in Norman K. Denzin, ed., *Studies in Symbolic Interaction* vol. 2 (Greenwich, CT: JAI Press, 1990): 103–127.

14. J. B. Roebuck and M. Hickson, III.

15. E. Liebow, *Tally's Corner: A Study of Negro Streetcorner Men* (Boston: Little, Brown, 1967).

16. Hickson, "Communication in Natural Settings."

17. For more on this, see J. D. Douglas, ed., *Understanding Everyday Life* (Chicago: Aldine Press, 1970); and H. Garfinkel, *Studies in Ethnomethodology* (Englewood Cliffs, N.J.: Prentice-Hall, 1967).

18. Mark Hickson, III, "Participant-Observation Technique in Organizational Research," *Journal of Business Communication*, 11 (1974): 37–42; 54.

19. For more information, see: H. J. Gans, *Deciding What's News: A Study of CBS Evening News, NBC Nightly News, Newsweek and Time* (New York: Vintage, 1979).

20. Mark Hickson, III, and Sidney R. Hill, Jr., "Communicating at Conventions: Roles, Rules, and Routines," paper presented at the convention of the Southern Speech Communication Association, Biloxi, Miss., April, 1979.

21. Hickson, "Communication in Natural Settings."

Chapter 8

Quantitative/Descriptive (Survey) Research

Steven T. McDermott
California Polytechnic State University, San Luis Obispo

*I*f someone were to ask you political questions over the telephone, mail you a questionnaire about nuclear power plants, approach you at the local mall with a clipboard full of questions about what you do in your leisure time, or stop you in the grocery store and ask you questions about ice cream or frozen pizza, you would be the subject of descriptive research. If you read that a researcher has concluded that the amount of violence depicted on television is up this year, you probably have read a descriptive study. In each instance a researcher has gathered information in such a way that he or she can paint a picture of what people think or do. He or she is using a questionnaire or some form of systematic observation to present a realistic representation of a topic by describing people's attitudes, beliefs, behaviors, or intentions at one level and the content of those same people's communication—whether it be via interpersonal communication or through the mass media.

The results of these efforts will be used to form the basis for determining whether what he or she *thinks* about reality (his or her theory or theoretical conceptualizations) is *isomorphic* (relates to the behaviors under study) with what *is* reality. If the outcomes of the observations are the same as what he or she expects reality to "look like," then the description is isomorphic. For instance, suppose a researcher thinks that MTV portrays women as sex-starved. In fact, the researcher may hypothesize that young boys who watch excessive MTV programming believe older girls to be like those they see on MTV: sex-starved. For the researcher to conclude such a relationship, he or she must first determine if what he or she thinks is on MTV is isomorphic with what is on MTV and what he or she thinks young boys believe about older girls is what young boys *really* believe about older girls.

To draw any conclusions about MTV and perceptions of sex, the researcher must conduct a descriptive research project. This project must do three things. First, it must determine the actual content (programming) of MTV. Second, it must accurately measure attitudes toward that programming. Third, it must reflect a sample large enough to say reliably that some relationship between viewing and attitude exists. This, obviously, is a project that asks questions of fact and definition and is amenable to scientific method. However, there may be times when descriptive research, as discussed in this chapter, is useful to the humanistic researcher, when, for instance, the researcher must "sample" from many communications or time periods.

This chapter introduces a *systematic* set of methods designed to help you have confidence that your theoretical thinking is isomorphic with actual attitudes or behaviors. If you apply the principles of descriptive research well, your study will provide an accurate and reliable picture of how your respondents think or act.

TYPES OF DESCRIPTIVE RESEARCH

Although there are many different types of descriptive research, this chapter will concentrate on one method: *the survey.* This coverage is designed to familiarize you with how to conduct descriptive research with an emphasis on gathering the data. Hence, the *methodology* of descriptive research is emphasized. Appropriate analytical procedures (how you would analyze the data collected) are covered in Part Three. Additionally, for those of you who will be conducting participant-observation or historical/critical research and need to select speeches, articles, editorials, or parts of a message in a manner that reduces researcher bias, the techniques of sample selection should prove very interesting.

The bias in this chapter is scientific. The term *descriptive* was chosen because the method involves describing a subset of a population of people in such a way as to present accurate descriptions of how the total population would act or react. In general, there are two types of descriptive research, each requiring a different set of procedures. The observational method was covered in Chapter 7. Extending the observational method from the qualitative dimension to a more objective, quantitative dimension, is accomplished through specific rules of observation. Thus, much of what is covered in this chapter can be extended to that research as well. The survey method, however, requires that the researcher remove him- or herself from the research as much as possible and in such a way as to reduce potential bias. Because of this, the descriptive methodology requires that specific procedures be followed as well as the use of a set of measures for obtaining data.

THE SURVEY AS DESCRIPTIVE METHODOLOGY

When we speak about surveying people, we are talking about questioning individuals about their attitudes, emotions, beliefs, intentions, and behaviors. These questions are usually asked either orally—a *personal interview survey*—or through written questions, a *questionnaire survey.* Some of the questions (Q) and hypotheses (H) that can be answered by surveys include:

Q: How do people perceive decision-making style and satisfaction within an organization?

H: Extensive exposure to television shows with a great deal of violence/crime brings about fears of being an actual victim of crime.

H: Exposure to presidential debates leads to the perception that the U.S. system of elections is orderly.

Q: What is the relationship between cognitive style and self-reported use of certain compliance-gaining strategies?

Q: How is a child's understanding of commercial disclaimers related to his or her requests for products?

Q: What is the relationship between exposure to alcohol advertising and drinking while driving among teenagers?

H: People who read editorial opinions will be more in favor of the person or event if the editorial is positive.

A second type of survey examines behavior. The *observational* research methods examined also fall under the descriptive method. Here, the researcher is interested in the messages people use:

Q: What is the incidence of sexist language in national newspaper reports?

Q: How many references to war and peace do presidential candidates make during debates?

H: There are more references to sex in country & western songs than in rock n' roll songs (in the top 100 songs played in the United States).

H: Television reporting on Iran-gate was biased against President Reagan during the first three months of 1987.

These questions and hypotheses also require that elements of either a population of people or events be sampled. Often we cannot pick *all* people or events to study; we must choose, in some orderly and rigorous fashion, subelements that will, within a certain degree of confidence, possess those traits. This is a major advantage of survey research: We are able to construct a sample of people that will represent all those within the population we seek to describe.

Where do we begin? As with any type of research, questions or hypotheses are proposed and appropriate measures are chosen. Descriptive research using survey methods provides the researcher with a systematic way of measuring, including who, when, where, and how to measure the variables under study. The *who* involves sampling. The *when* is part of sampling, too, but refers to the measurement time frame. The place you collect the data is the *where*. *How* you structure the observation (treated in this chapter as the interview, either face-to-face or via telephone or the mail) constitutes the last consideration. Our discussion of descriptive methodology begins with the *who*, the concept of sampling.

Sampling

To make accurate descriptions that apply to all members of a population you can do two basic things: You may question every member of a population or you can question only part of the population and infer from that part of the population to the entire population. If you question every member of the population, you have conducted a *census*. In many cases a census is practical, but more often than not it is quite impractical. If, for instance, you wanted to find out the opinions of the tenants of your apartment complex about a recent raise in rent, it may be practical to question all the residents. However, if you wanted to find out how the people of your state feel about putting warning labels on records, you would have a difficult time trying to question all of the people. In this example we see the impracticality of questioning all of the people. In this case you would have to *sample* some of the people and hope to make the best educated guess you could about how all the people would feel about warning labels.

Sampling, then, is the practical selection of people from some population in such a way as to ensure that they will meet whatever criteria you specify. As indicated in Figure 8.1, the sample is simply a representative group of people similar to the population and, although these group members may differ from that population, they will not differ much.

In constructing your sample you will follow a set of fairly rigorous procedures. These procedures help ensure that the people you sample are representative of the target population. Generally, there are two categories of sampling: probability sampling and nonprobability sampling. In probability sampling we select our respondents as randomly as possible; that is, every person in the population should have an equal chance of being chosen. In nonprobability (purposive) sampling we take certain subpopulations and work from these peoples' responses. Because not all possible respondents are represented in the sample, the amount of confidence we can place in their representativeness is less than that of people selected at random. Which method of sampling you use will depend on your specific research purpose as stated in your research question or hypothesis.

Nonprobability Sampling   When we use a nonprobability sample we do so for a specific purpose. Generally, there are two reasons for using the nonprobability sample: *convenience sampling*, and ensuring that a particular number of people meet certain criteria, or *quota sampling*. Use of nonprobability sampling should be approached with caution; researchers using this form of sampling usually tend

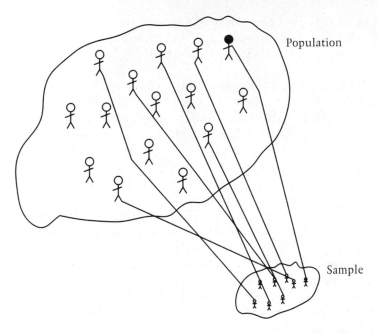

Figure 8.1 Sampling.

to be very careful when interpreting their findings because the sampling procedure does not reflect the *entire* population, but only selected segments.

Convenience sampling means that the researcher questions the people that are convenient to him or her. Convenience sampling may be necessary due to a limited amount of time or a limited access to people with whom to work.

A descriptive study on the effect of exposure to television family dramas that had black characters in them and childrens' attitudes toward black and white people in real life points out why nonprobability sampling is employed. [1] This research project required that children be used as the population. One of the problems associated with using children in research is difficulty in obtaining access to them. In this study it would have been impossible to question all children about their television viewing habits, and it would have been difficult to get anything more than a convenience sample. To get their sample the researchers approached 12 different schools and asked permission to enter classrooms and hand out questionnaires. Out of these schools, only one allowed access to their students, thus a convenience sample was the only option. The only children who could participate in the study were those to whom access was given, and, because parental permission was not obtained from all parents, the representativeness of the sample was further reduced.

What can we conclude about children in general from a sample of convenient children? Obviously, the children who participated in this study do *not* generalize to the total population of children who watch family dramas on television. Other problems are associated with convenience sampling. For example, what if this particular school was located near a large state university? Would this make the children different from those located in either rural or urban areas? Are there differences in the way the children are raised? What about access to television or to particular stations?

To use convenience sampling we must carefully and cautiously interpret the findings. We might try to find some other variables with which we could later see how well the children generalize to some other population. Questions concerning parental income, occupation, length of time they have been in the community, whether or not the parents owned or rented the place in which they lived, number of brothers and sisters, and so forth, help to identify the sample as compared to other samples from other descriptive research projects. To the degree that other samples might match on these demographic variables, some degree of generalization might be possible. However, *convenience sampling should only be used after all other attempts have been made to get a probability sample.*

Quota Sampling   Quota, or purposive, sampling is another nonprobability technique. It is similar to convenience sampling in that it also involves questioning people to whom the researcher has access, but it differs in that the characteristics of the population are identified and used to guide the selection of respondents. For example, suppose you are a consultant to a local politician who wants to run for city commissioner. She needs a rough idea of the issues that are on the voters' minds so that she can begin to address them in campaign speeches and advertisements, but, the budget is limited and you have very little time to conduct your survey.

After careful consideration you decide that the best thing to do is to go to the local mall and get people to participate in your survey of issues, but you realize that during the day, more women are shopping than are men and that while very few college students are at the mall, there are a lot of people over 50 years of age there. If you just started asking people who walked by, you would end up with a convenience sample, but with a disproportionate number of women, older people, and nonworking people. You need to decide how many men and women, how many people from each age group, and of certain working status to select. This can be done by obtaining the latest census data, which will tell you the proportions of males and females, age groupings, and occupational differences for your city, county, state, and region. You would then select your sample of respondents by using the proportion of each group in the population.

For instance, suppose that the general population in your area is 56 percent female and 44 percent male. The percent of voting age people aged 18 to 30 was 35 percent, of people aged 31 to 40 was 25 percent, and of people aged 50 or more was 40 percent. Finally, you found that 33 percent of your population were unemployed (including students and housewives), 33 percent were employed in blue-collar jobs, and 33 percent were employed in white-collar jobs. Assume that for reasons of limited time and money, you decided you only needed 100 total respondents. Your quota for your sample would then break down as being 56 females and 44 males. Your age quotas would run approximately 35 people under 30, 25 people between 30 and 50, and 40 people over 50. Finally, your quota would require that

33 people be unemployed, 33 be engaged in blue-collar occupations, and 33 be engaged in white-collar occupations. Obviously, the closer you try to match, the more complicated the quota sample technique becomes.

Quota sampling allows you to make certain that you have not excluded certain people from your sample. Although quota sampling helps with representativeness, it is still basically a convenience sample within groups; that is, you are still sampling whomever you can get, but now making sure that certain groups of people are represented via some quota system. Like the convenience sample, this technique should be used only after other probability sampling methods are deemed impractical.

Probability Sampling

A probability sample insures that *the chance for selecting a member of a population is known.* This means that no one person will be excluded due to researcher biases, accessibility of the respondent, or by questionnaire administration. Probability sampling generates the most *representative* sample that can be acquired, although it does not guarantee perfect population representativeness. Additionally, this technique allows the researcher to estimate the probability that the sample represents the population through the use of *probability theory.*

Random Selection   The central requirement of probability sampling is the *random selection* of members of a population for inclusion in the sample. Random selection means that since each person has an equal chance of being chosen, factors other than chance that might bias the sample will not influence the selection. For example, suppose that there are 10,000 marbles in a jar. Of these marbles, 8,000 are red and 2,000 are blue. As part of its marketing campaign, a local store is giving away a new car to the person who correctly guesses how many marbles are of each color. The catch is that you cannot count all the marbles, but, in the spirit of fairness, you are allowed to select 10 marbles before making your guess.

What is the likelihood that the first marble you pick out will be red (assume that you have been blindfolded and that someone has thoroughly mixed the marbles)? Eight out of 10, or 8,000 out of 10,000! But by chance you *may* pick out a blue marble. What is the chance of this happening again? Is it still 8 out of 10? No, since you have one marble already in your hand, there are only 9,999 marbles left from which to choose. So, the probability is now less than 8 out of 10. The point is that unless you replaced the marble each time you made a new selection, your estimate of the population (of marbles) would be distorted. By the tenth pick you would be down to having only 9,991 marbles from which to pick.

Although the number of marbles left is still quite large, you change the characteristics of the population with each choice. Therefore, to estimate the population characteristics (called *parameters*) accurately, you would need to select a marble, note its color, replace it in the jar, mix the marbles up, and select again. If you follow this procedure you should be confident that your sample, within a certain degree of confidence (you may make an error somewhere), is likely to be represent-ative to the extent that chance prevented you from selecting a sample that accurately reflected the color parameters of the population of marbles in the jar. Still, however, chance will influence your selections. By chance alone, you *could* pick blue marbles on all 10 tries. Probability theory, however, helps in determining how much *confidence* you can have that your sample is selected due to representativeness rather than chance.

There is a limitation to our example. How representative a sample will 10 marbles be of 10,000? If you had selected 5,000 marbles, would your sample be more representative? In answering this question we begin to examine the related questions of accuracy and confidence. *Accuracy* depends upon three factors: (1) the parameters you set out to represent, (2) the size of your sample, and (3) the amount of error you are willing to tolerate in making your selection (the *standard error* of the measurement).

Because sampling is based on probability theory, a subarea of mathematics, there are ways of estimating the accuracy with which a sample represents the population parameters. One way is to calculate the standard error we will have before selection. There are many ways to calculate this error, depending on the type of sample you select. Below is an example formula for a simple random sample. This simple formula takes into account the population parameters and the sample size in estimating the error in measurement (selection):

$$s = \sqrt{\frac{P(1-P)}{n}}$$

where
s = standard error
n = number of cases
P = population parameters

To calculate the standard error you need to know the population parameters of interest (P) and the sample size you plan on using or are using (n). The calculated standard error is s. Going back to the marble example, P is .80, representing that 80 percent of the marbles are red; $1-P$ is .20, representing that 20 percent of the marbles are blue. If our sample size is $10 (n=10)$, then the standard error is the square root of $(.8 \times .2)/10$, which is .126 or 12.6 percent. If the sample size were 100, the standard error would be .04 or 4 percent.

The standard error tells us the extent to which our sample will be like the population. Generally, 68 percent of the samples we might choose will fall within one deviation away from the true parameter value; that is, we know that as we choose our sample, the amount of error in our selection will approximate a *normal curve* (see Figure 8.2). As indicated in Figure 8.3, a normal curve skews from the mean (the center of the curve) in a predictable way. As the size of the sample increases, the more normally distributed is the curve. Hence, standard error is a function of both sample size and knowledge of population parameters.

The standard error, then, tells us the extent to which our samples will be like the population from which they are drawn. Sixty-eight percent of samples we might choose will fall within one standard error of the true parameter value. Thus, with a sample size of 10, we know that 68 percent of the samples we could choose could be off by up to 12.6 percent on the population parameters. On the other

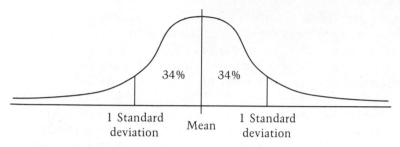

Figure 8.2 The normal distribution.

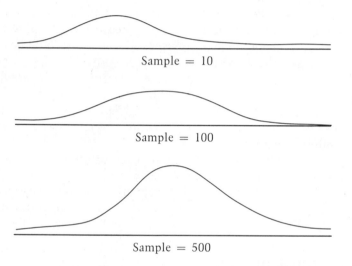

Figure 8.3 Possible distributions with increased sample size.

hand, we could know that we would be off only 4 percent each way with 68 percent of the total population if we increased the sample size to 100.

We also know from probability theory that 95 percent of our samples will fall within one or two standard errors (deviations) from the true population value. So, we know that in 95 percent of our sample (with a sample size of 100), our selections should fall 8 percent each way around our parameter value—between 72 percent and 88 percent of red marbles.

What does all this tell us? Basically, we know with a certain assurance that the people we select will reflect the population parameters we establish. From probability theory we also know that by increasing sample size we can reduce the error in sample selection. But we can also figure one more thing: confidence in the way in which people respond to the questions we ask.

A second way of looking at sampling error deals with the degree of confidence we can place in the responses people give us. Just as we can measure the amount of error in drawing the sample, we can also estimate the error in responses. Assume, for example, that you have been asked to survey people about their intent to vote in the next election. You choose your sample carefully, ensuring that respondents are of voting age and voted in the last election. The question you are concerned with most, however, is a simple yes/no response to the question: "Are you planning to vote in the upcoming election?" How many respondents do you need to be certain that their responses are accurate? What degree of accuracy (or, put another way, how much error) will we tolerate in their responses?

Convention assumes that we want to be within a 95 percent confidence level, or two standard errors in measurement for any response.[2] You could, if you so desired, move to a 99 percent confidence level. Here you know that your sample is within three standard errors of the true value, hence, you increase your accuracy. But, what is the cost of increasing our confidence level? Table 8.1 presents the number of people you would need to achieve both a 95 percent and a 99 percent confidence limit with varying degrees of tolerated error. Note that for the 95 percent confidence level and a 5 percent error tolerance you would have to include 384 people in your sample. Why so many? Table 8.1 provides a shortcut to selecting sample size and standard error. The population *size* the samples are drawn from, however, is assumed to be above 500,000. This means, for example, that a random survey of people in the state of New York would need only 384 respondents to ensure with a 95 percent confidence level that their responses would be off no more than plus or minus 5 percent.

Suppose, for example, that you did a statewide survey of voting intent in New York. The 384 people selected would have to come from all parts of the state (represent the entire population). You would analyze the results based on the total sample (not breaking down by sex, or age, or whatever—that would increase your tolerated error), and all people who meet your population parameters would have

Table 8.1   SIMPLE RANDOM SAMPLE
SIZE AT 95 AND 99 PERCENT
CONFIDENCE WITH
TOLERATED ERROR

	Confidence	
Error	95%	99%
1%	9,604	16,587
2%	2,401	4,147
3%	1,067	1,843
4%	600	1,037
5%	384	663
6%	267	461
7%	196	339

Assumes that the population proportion is .50.

Source: Charles H. Backstrom and Gerald Hursh-Cesar, *Survey Research,* 2nd ed. (New York: Macmillan, 1981). Reprinted by permission of Macmillan Publishing Company. Copyright © 1981 by Macmillan Publishing Company.

an equal chance of being selected. Should you desire ahead of time to see how males and females responded, to break your sample by sex, you would need 384 males and 384 females (doubling your sample size) to be 95 percent confident that your error would be no more than 5 percent on any response. So, by sampling 384 people in general, you might find that 63 percent said they were planning to vote and 37 percent were not. Your actual deviation from these responses would be between 68 percent and 58 percent voting and 42 and 32 percent not voting.

Your error of measurement, then, tells us how certain we can be that a response is accurate. In most *national* surveys (such as those reported on ABC, CBS, NBC, and CNN networks) the tolerated error is reduced to 3 percent, but at a confidence level of 95 percent. The sample size, drawn from throughout the country is *1067* people. And, we can be 95 percent certain that these 1000+ people represent our views and feelings! The cost of being 99 percent certain that we have the true value of our population almost doubles the number of people we must contact: At a 5 percent error rate we would need 663 people rather than 384; at a 1 percent error rate we would need 1843 people rather than 1067. If it takes 30 minutes to interview each person, you can see how increased accuracy will cost you in both time and money.

What size should your sample be? That depends on how confident you need to be about sample representativeness and the degree of error you will tolerate. The larger the sample, the more representative the sample will be of the population and the smaller your error will be. The decision, then, is a personal one based on the confidence you have in your ability to ask good questions.

Up to now we have been dealing with extremely large populations. What about smaller populations? Philip Meyer has worked out the different sample sizes you would need at the 95 percent confidence level for the following populations[3]:

Population Size	Sample Size
Infinity	384
500,000	384
100,000	383
50,000	381
10,000	370
5,000	357
3,000	341
2,000	322
1,000	278

Notice the difference between 50,000 and infinity. These are the populations most of us sample. Generally, we will need about 384 people to be confident that we have sampled a representative group of people! If you have fewer than 1000 people in your population, you should consider working out the error formula provided earlier or conducting a census of that population.

Before we provide several examples of sample selection, you might want to consider the information presented in Table 8.2. Table 8.2 provides you with the error in response (again, at the 95 percent confidence level—a 20:1 safety factor) at differing sample sizes *and* responses. The far right column, the one labeled 50 percent, is the most conservative response we could hope for with a simple yes/no response: 50 percent of the respondents said, yes, and 50 percent said no. Notice that the 5 percent error tolerance is found for a sample of 400 (the numbers have been rounded off for ease of use). To be within 5 percent of the response at the most conservative response you need 400 respondents. But, if your response is 25 percent yes and 75 percent no, your error rate drops to 4.3 percent; at 90 percent yes, the error is now 3 percent. Hence, you can determine your error not only from the sample size but also the response rates you receive.

This information is useful if, for instance, you believe that your respondents are fairly decided in their attitudes and opinions. You could conceivably reduce the number of respondents and maintain a tolerated error rate. You can also establish how much error you have if some reason—time, money, or help restrictions—dictates a smaller sample. Suppose, for example, that you are doing an image study for a small town, population of 50,000 or more in the town and surrounding area. You have enough money and help to contact only 200 respondents. Your error rate at worst will be 7.1 percent. If you can live with that error rate then you only need 200 respondents.

However, in spite of the principles of probability sampling, we often are unable to stick to the procedures in the same way we have tried to do with the marble example at the beginning of this section.

Sample Selection

An example from a study conducted by Steven McDermott and Bradley Greenberg points out some of the problems faced when the research moves from the sample size question to the question of who to sample and how to construct the sample.[4] This research project required a sample from every member of the population of the city of Detroit, Michigan. Detroit is a rather large city and presented several selection strategies. The researchers approached the task of selecting the sample in the following way. First, they needed to get a list of all the residents of the city (to insure that every member of the population had an equal chance of being chosen). Ideally, this would guarantee everyone an equal chance. But where could one find such a list? Here the actuality of conducting research interacts with the more abstract theory of research. Such a list is next to impossible to get. Therefore, the researchers had to decide on a method that would locate as many people as possible that met the parameters of the study. Several solutions were possible. The first possibility was to go door-to-door and interview respondents, but that still does not guarantee that all people could be contacted. Second, a telephone interview could be conducted using names and telephone numbers found in the city telephone directories. That still would not guarantee that the person would be home. And what if not everyone had a telephone? In the end the telephone interview was decided upon, as is the case with much of today's descriptive research. But how

Table 8.2 PROBABLE DEVIATION (PLUS OR MINUS) OF RESULTS DUE TO SIZE OF SAMPLE ONLY
Safety Factor of 20:1

Survey Result	1% or 99%	5% or 95%	10% or 90%	15% or 85%	20% or 80%	25% or 75%	30% or 70%	35% or 65%	40% or 60%	45% or 55%	50%
Sample of: 25	4.0	8.7	12.0	14.3	16.0	17.3	18.3	19.1	19.6	19.8	20.0
50	2.8	6.2	8.5	10.1	11.4	12.3	13.0	13.5	13.9	14.1	14.2
75	2.3	5.0	6.9	8.2	9.2	10.0	10.5	11.0	11.3	11.4	11.5
100	2.0	4.4	6.0	7.1	8.0	8.7	9.2	9.5	9.8	9.9	10.0
150	1.6	3.6	4.9	5.9	6.6	7.1	7.5	7.8	8.0	8.1	8.2
200	1.4	3.1	4.3	5.1	5.7	6.1	6.5	6.8	7.0	7.0	7.1
250	1.2	2.7	3.8	4.5	5.0	5.5	5.8	6.0	6.2	6.2	6.3
300	1.1	2.5	3.5	4.1	4.6	5.0	5.3	5.5	5.7	5.8	5.8
400	.99	2.2	3.0	3.6	4.0	4.3	4.6	4.8	4.9	5.0	5.0
500	.89	2.0	2.7	3.2	3.6	3.9	4.1	4.3	4.4	4.5	4.5
600	.81	1.8	2.5	2.9	3.3	3.6	3.8	3.9	4.0	4.1	4.1
800	.69	1.5	2.1	2.5	2.8	3.0	3.2	3.3	3.4	3.5	3.5
1,000	.63	1.4	1.9	2.3	2.6	2.8	2.9	3.1	3.1	3.2	3.2
2,000	.44	.96	1.3	1.6	1.8	1.9	2.0	2.1	2.2	2.2	2.2
5,000	.28	.62	.85	1.0	1.1	1.2	1.3	1.4	1.4	1.4	1.4	.40

Example: When size of sample is 500 and survey result comes out 25%, you may be reasonably sure (odds 20 to 1) that this result is no more than 3.9 off, plus or minus. Doubling this margin to 1,000 reduces this margin to 2.4-X.X.

Source: *A Broadcast Research Primer.* Washington, D.C.: National Association of Broadcasters, 1976, p. 19. Reprinted by permission.

do you actually pick a sample that gives each listing in the phone book an equal chance of being selected? And, is this a representative sampling of *all* people with telephones?

Researchers do at least three things to select a sample randomly. The first, yet most difficult and costly, is to have a computer select from actual telephone numbers in the phone book. The second is to consult a table of random numbers that will instruct which numbers, say the 38th, 79th, 1,004th, 1012th. . .to select from the telephone book. This is relatively inexpensive, but very time-consuming; you have to count down from the beginning to all the numbers in the telephone book—a task that would be difficult with a sample of about 400. If selected, the first step is to use a table of random numbers to tell you which telephone numbers to choose from each page of the directory. Then take the total sample size, divided by the number of pages in the telephone book, and pick as many random numbers needed (between 0001 and the total possible on a given page) so you could sample from each page.

A third way to select the sample would be through the use of the telephone exchanges (the three digit numbers that begin all telephone numbers in the United States). By listing each exchange and the approximate population for the exchanges the sample could drawn by simple random selection. A survey conducted by Don W. Stacks and Ricky T. Gordon did just this.[5] They took the number of exchanges, found out how many people were in each exchange area and *weighted* the number of people from each exchange to the sample. For example, one exchange represented 45 percent of the population. Of the 384 respondents, 45 percent—173 people—were drawn from that exchange. Similar proportions were drawn for other exchanges. A table of random numbers provided the four digit extensions.

The use of microcomputers and random number generation programs simplifies this technique even more. Suppose that you need 100 numbers selected at random from all possible numbers for a given exchange. Your population for that subsample will be somewhere between 1 and 9,999. (The telephone company does not assign telephone numbers to exchanges sequentially, but does so randomly; you must include all 10,000 numbers as possible numbers.) You then ask for 100 numbers to be selected at random from between 0 and 9,999. The numbers you get will be random, just as with a random number table, but it is much easier to get than the time-consuming methods used previously.

The use of telephone interviews to contact respondents poses two problems. First, if you use a telephone book are you assured that the numbers are current and that someone might answer the phone? Are you also assured that you are reaching a residence and not a store or hospital? There are also a large number of *unlisted* telephone numbers that you have excluded. To be representative you should include unlisted numbers. How do you get them? One possible way is to reverse the last two digits of the telephone numbers drawn. A second, often used method is called random digit dialing. Here the computerized random number generation program comes into play. You simply use the four-digit numbers drawn from the computer and assign them to one of your telephone exchanges. There is no guarantee, however, that you will hit upon any unlisted numbers. The only way you will know you are reaching unlisted numbers is if your respondents begin to ask how you got their unlisted number.

The second problem is ensuring that the person you are speaking with meets the parameters of the study. It is useless to interview a 14-year-old on voting behaviors, but finding out how old that person is something usually done last. In the same way, there may be times when you will have to ask for the "man of the house"; in most households the telephone is answered by the wife, hence you may have to ask for one or the other sex to balance out your sample.

Sometimes simple random selection is insufficient to guarantee that certain groups within the population will be sampled. For instance, suppose you hypothesize that attitudes toward nuclear power plants vary with age. Specifically, you predict that people over the age of 50 and people under 30 are in favor of nuclear power plants, but people between 30 and 50 are generally opposed to them. If you left your sampling to random chance, you may not get representative samples of each age group. Thus, to insure that each age group is adequately sampled, you need to conduct a *stratified random sample.* You determine the number of people you need in each age group, then randomly select from within each of the three age groups. This particular type of sampling is used by political opinion pollsters who need to stratify by demographic characteristics (e.g., sex, age, race) so their candidates know what issues affect each set of voters.

Stratified sampling allows the pollster to anticipate accurately the results of elections in which many millions of people vote from a sample of about 1200 voters. A stratum is a subgroup of the population whose members are *known* by the researcher to be more homogeneous, that is, more similar to one another, in terms of what is being measured than is the population as a whole. The more homogeneous a group, the fewer group members it takes in a sample to determine how the entire group feels. To take the most extreme example of this point, assume that you knew that all members of a group—say, Republicans from Indiana—agree completely on an issue, say capital punishment. How many of these Indiana Republicans would you have to survey to determine how the group felt about this issue? Only one! Since everyone in the group agrees, whomever is sampled at random can provide all the information you need to know about how the entire group feels. If this one person states that he is in favor of capital punishment, you know that the entire group feels this way.

In reality, groups are seldom completely homogeneous in ways relevant to the questions being asked. And even if they were, the researcher would not be likely to know this. But many groups are *more* homogeneous on a relevant variable being measured than the larger population of which the group is a part. To the extent the researcher is aware of this homogeneity, the overall sample can be designed to sample systematically within various strata as a means of reducing sampling error or as a means of reducing the sample size necessary to achieve "acceptable" error goals. (It is important to note that *within* the stratum the sample must be selected using probability procedures, i.e., at random.) If groups that are homogeneous with regard to the variables being measured cannot be identified, stratified sampling is impossible and the researcher must rely on simple random sampling.

Pollsters such as George Gallup and Louis Harris have been studying voting patterns among various groups (strata) for years. They use their knowledge of how individuals within particular strata vote to design a sampling plan that results in generally accurate estimates of voting outcomes.

A second way to conduct random sampling is again with a telephone book or some other directory or listing of people. When you do this, however, you are conducting a *systematic random sample.* This technique requires three things: (1) you start at some randomly chosen point in the directory, (2) that everyone has an equal chance of being chosen, and (3) that you choose a *skip interval.* The random start can be done with a random number table or computer-generated random number. Suppose that you are going to contact 200 recruiters for top Fortune 500 companies. To get your sample you could go to a directory of directors for these companies, and choose a random page number to begin (say, page 32 out of 100 pages). If the names are listed in one column per page you then choose a second random number (say, 17) and count down 17 people. This is your first person. To get your skip interval you would divide the total number of names and addresses in the directory by your sample size (assuming that there are 23 names per page, 100 pages, you would have 23 times 100 divided by 200 as your skip interval, or 11.5—which we would round to 12). You would then choose every twelfth person from the one with whom you started.

One advantage of this method is that you approximate stratification of your sample at the same time.[6] Because most names are listed in alphabetical order your systematic sampling procedure will select from various nationalities, assuming, of course, that certain names are representative of certain ethnic backgrounds. Obviously, this method is not as precise as if you actually weighed your sample, but it does help with representedness as to ethnic origin.

Designs

Once you have determined the most efficient way of getting a sample, you need to consider how you will measure them. The type of hypothesis or questions you ask will determine the type of design you select. There are many variations of design, but survey designs typically follow two forms: cross-sectional and longitudinal design.

Cross-sectional Design   The cross-sectional design takes a cross section of a population to study *at a given time.* For example, suppose that you are interested in how the students at your institution perceive themselves. Are they liberal or conservative in their political attitudes? Are they supportive of causes or movements? To answer these questions you would develop a questionnaire that taps these questions, ask demographic questions to see how your sample might differ according to say, student classification (Do freshmen differ from seniors?), and select a stratified random sample of college students. In this case, you would be conducting a cross-sectional study. You would draw your conclusions about the group of people you selected at that time and only about that group.

Notice, however, that you have not really measured or observed *changes* in people. You infer change on the basis of differences between demographic variables (if you found differences between demographic variables, such as student classification, sex, age, race, major, etc.). In fact, there could be other reasons for the differences. What you can infer from your sample only reflects that sample at that given time. You cannot, for example, really compare your findings to those of other times.

Similarly, a cross-sectional design might be used to examine the relationship between the number of hours a third-grader watches television programs and his or her reading ability. Your questionnaire would include measures of each variable. Assuming that you found a relationship between the two variables, that the children who watched a lot of television were poorer readers than those who did not watch a lot of television, could you conclude that watching television brought about the decrease in reading ability? *No*, because you have no way of knowing which occurs first, watching television or poor reading. Your survey of viewing and reading habits has only measured one variable at a time. Maybe poor reading ability brings about more watching of television. You have established a relationship between variables but only at one point in time; to say that one variable causes another, the effect must follow the cause. If this is appropriate for your research question or hypothesis, then the cross-sectional design was adequate. Many times, however, a different design is needed.

Longitudinal Designs   A design that allows for observations over time is labeled *longitudinal.* Longitudinal designs permit you to make statements about which variables occur first, although they do not allow you to make statements about which variable causes another variable. Only experiments, discussed in following chapters, allow you to draw causal conclusions about the relationship between two variables.

Trend and panel are two basic types of longitudinal sample designs. *Trend* designs allow you to collect *different samples at different points in time* (see Table 8.3). For example, you want to find out what people think about nuclear power plants, and you have coincidentally collected data before a major nuclear disaster (Chernobyl in the Soviet Union or Three Mile Island in the United States). If you wanted to see if perceptions about nuclear power changed after the disaster you would collect a second sample of people from the *same* population.

In the same way, you might be interested in how people's attitudes about using computers change over time. Because some members of your first sample will probably move away, some will die, while others will change their names through marriage or divorce, you will have to sample again from the *same* general population. If you wanted to trace what happened to people who went to college during the late 1960s and early 1970s (the baby boom generation), you would locate some data that measured students attitudes and feelings at that time, and collect another sample from people who were now in their 40s and went to college. You would then compare the results.

This study uses a *cohort trend* design. It is a cohort design because you are examining people who come from the same subgroup of the population over time. In this instance the cohort would be age. Trend designs are often necessary because of changes in your sample over time and are relatively easy to carry out (you simply ensure that your sample reflects the population), however, they do not permit

Table 8.3 THE DIFFERENCE
BETWEEN TREND
AND PANEL
DESIGNS

January	June
People sampled—Trend design	
Linda	Debbie
Susan	Patricia
David	David
Mike	Ed
Joe	Jill
People sampled—Panel design	
Linda	Linda
Susan	Susan
David	David
Mike	Mike
Joe	Joe

actual examination of change over time. What you can measure, however, is how two *different* groups sampled from the same population perceive your topic of interest.

Panel designs are those that measure the *same individuals over time* (see Table 8.3). This powerful design permits you to make statements of change. Panel designs are typically used in two ways. First, you might identify some condition (an intervening variable, or a variable that may cause people to change in some way) that is about to occur, sample and measure how people feel about the condition prior to the event, then measure the same people after the event has occurred. Second, you might follow a sample through a given time period to see what change, if any, has occurred regardless of specific events. The former design examines the impact of a specific event (condition or intervening variable) on a population while the latter examines simple change over time. The result, however, is the same: You can examine *how* people changed because you have studied the same sample over time.

An example of an intervening variable panel design is found in an unpublished study of the impact of the made-for-television movie, *The Day After,* on attitudes toward nuclear war. Hocking and McDermott, interested in how this movie, which dramatized the effect of a nuclear attack on a city in Kansas, would affect U.S. perceptions about nuclear war, hypothesized that the movie might have a large impact on people in the United States and decided to test that hypothesis by a panel design of people contacted by telephone. The survey was run twice. The researchers contacted people two days before the broadcast, and then called the respondents back the day after the broadcast—a time-1, time-2 panel design. With this design the researchers would be able to note any change (or lack of change) due to seeing the movie.

Could it be said with assurance, however, that the broadcast *caused* the changes? Maybe the respondents simply changed from day one to day three. Maybe they were changed by the first set of questions. Maybe they were changed by interpersonal communication with others about the movie and not the movie itself. What if the design had included a separate sample of people who did *not* watch the broadcast? Could we then compare the two samples? No, because the respondents who watched may have been different from those who did not watch the broadcast; maybe those who watched the broadcast were more prone to change. Even though the time-1, time-2 design is valuable for investigating naturally occurring events, it does not permit us to infer causality.

Use of the second panel design might answer the question addressed earlier about reading and television habits. You might select a sample of children and follow them through preschool and elementary school and observe both their television habits and their reading ability. You could measure their television viewing and reading ability at regular intervals and note any changes over time. This type of sampling design is extremely powerful. If done properly you can make inferences of change and suggest causality; however, other factors— factors you cannot control—might influence your findings. (More about *control* will be discussed in the chapter on experimental method.)

Although panel designs are more powerful, they are also much more expensive to conduct. You must locate and follow people across time. You must begin with an initial sample large enough so that when you lose sample members, you will still have a sample that is representative at a later time. Political studies that examine the electorate over a long period of time (say before the primaries, through the primaries, and after the general elections) are extremely time-consuming to conduct but tell the researcher much more than those that select separate samples at each surveying point.

COLLECTING THE DATA

There are three basic ways of getting information from people in a survey: in person, by mail, or by telephone. Each of these methods has its advantages and disadvantages. In-person and telephone interviews, however, require another person, usually someone other than the researcher, to help gather the data. The degree to which your interviewers are trained will affect how the data are collected. Before examining each of the collection methods, we need to look at training the interviewer.

Training

You cannot simply give interviewers a questionnaire and start them on their way. The way in which the questionnaire is delivered, is presented to the respondent, will often introduce subtle biases and can alter the way the respondent chooses to answer each question. Also, as discussed in Chapter 6, variations in the way questions are asked can detract from measurement reliability. In general, all interviewers must go through a training phase, which includes an understanding of the questionnaire, how to deal with contingencies that may occur, and several practice rounds. First, the interviewer must understand what you are asking your respondents. He or she must be aware that the questionnaire must be followed *as it is written;* if not, the responses may be due to things other than the questions you have created. Second, the interviewer needs to know how to handle people. You are asking for their cooperation, so the interviewer must understand that the respondent may have other things to do at that time. In such cases you might instruct your interviewer to ask for a better time to call back. A respondent may, halfway through the interview, decide not to complete the interview; how should the interviewer tackle this? A respondent may wish to speak to "someone in authority"; prepare the interviewer for such contingencies.

Finally, the interviewer must practice the questionnaire and the situation until he or she is at ease with both. In this mode of the training the interviewer should practice with other interviewers, both as interviewer and interviewee. After each session there should be a discussion of what was done right and what was done wrong. At this stage you could create different problems and have the interviewers work their way through them. Only after the interviewers feel comfortable with the questionnaire, understand how to conduct the interview, and have practiced the interview, should you allow them to contact a respondent.

There are five things interviewers need to be reminded of while contacting respondents. These are presented in Box 8.1. It is probably most important that the interviewer remember that the questionnaire is his or her "bible." The questions must be asked in a matter-of-fact, businesslike fashion, even if they differ from the interviewer's own personal feelings or beliefs. In the same vein, the interviewer must refrain from commenting on the respondent's responses, unless the comment is built into the questionnaire as a way of getting open-ended responses, or with probing questions. The questions must be asked as they are written, even if the interviewer thinks he or she could phrase them better (sometimes practice sessions actually produce better questions than those originally written). And, finally, when confusion is apparent (or the respondent asks for clarification), the question should be repeated exactly as written—do not allow an interviewer to interject his or her interpretation of what the question is supposed to mean. Additionally, responses that require a reply, such as Strongly Agree, Agree, Disagree, Strongly Disagree, or Uncertain, should be stated each time the question is asked, just as if the respondent were responding to the *written* questionnaire.

Following these simple guidelines will produce an interview and data about which you can feel confident. As with most things, practice makes perfect. One final comment. If possible, as the researcher, you should be present when data collection is occurring. This provides you with an insight into any problems that may crop up *and* you will be available when questions arise. Your presence also ensures that the interviews are actually conducted. (Some researchers make random follow-up calls to ensure that the call was made and that the interviewer conducted him- or herself in the manner trained.)

Interviewing Methods

In-person interviews, done door-to-door, on a street corner, or in a mall, allow for the greatest flexibility in terms of the type of information requested, but they are often the most time-consuming, difficult, and expensive to conduct. This method of collection also is most prone to *interviewer effects*, those outcomes that are produced in the responses as a result of behaviors of the interviewer, which may bias the answers a respondent provides. Showing approval or disapproval of responses, even with a smile, nod, or verbal hesitancy may influence the type and even the length of the response. Even the type of clothing worn may have a significant influence on answers.[7]

In-Person Interviews   There are several advantages to the in-person interview. One advantage is that in-person interviews usually generate a good *response rate* (usually 80 percent or better), compared with mail or telephone interviews, which are usually around 60 percent or lower.[8] Another advantage is that the interviewer can write down items that may be too sensitive to ask—like a person's race or income—and make notes on what he or she observes, such as house type, possessions, and so forth. Finally, the in-person interview allows for immediate feedback so the interviewer is able to probe when a respondent is having trouble with a response.

There are important ethical procedures that should be followed when conducting an in-person interview. The respondents are not anonymous in the strictest sense of anonymity and thus, as a researcher, you should provide some guarantee that the identity of the respondent, his or her name and address, will be kept in strictest confidence or not even be noted. Second, you must consider where you will send an interviewer to gather data. Random sampling requires that all possible respondents be included in your sample—including those living in undesirable and even dangerous neighborhoods—and they must be interviewed if selected. You must also take into consideration possible unpleasant weather and vicious animals when conducting the in-person interview.

Mail Surveys   Mail surveys are virtually free of interviewer effects because the respondent answers a paper questionnaire he or she receives in the mail. However, some of the advantages of the in-person interview are not available with this method: There is no possibility for feedback or for probing, observations of the respondent and his or her environment are not possible, and the response rate is lower. Response rate can be increased if a self-addressed and stamped return envelope is included, the questionnaire is sent a second time to "jog" the respondents, or by added incentives such as a gift or money.

Mail surveys are usually cheaper to conduct and have the advantage of respondent anonymity, which takes care of some of the ethical concerns expressed earlier. This is especially helpful when the questions you ask are sensitive. When a person is asked to respond to a sensitive question, he or she may be reluctant to do so in person and may even distort the answer to make it socially desirable. For example, suppose you wanted to study the potential conflict married couples have over money matters. If you went up to someone's door and started asking questions

Box 8.1 # Asking the Questions

The questions are generally direct and straightforward. Emphasize the underlined words as you read them, and give the answers that are included in the wording of the question. circle the capitalized response that is closest to the answer given. If you cannot clearly classify a response with one of the available choices, write it out in the margin. YOU, OF COURSE, HAVE FEELINGS ABOUT THESE ISSUES. THEY *MUST NOT* INFLUENCE YOUR RECORDING OF RESPONSES OR YOUR BEHAVIOR DURING THE INTERVIEW.

USE THE QUESTIONNAIRE, BUT USE IT INFORMALLY

The interview should be conducted in a relaxed manner; the interviewer should avoid creating the impression that the interview is a quiz or cross-examination. PLEASE BE CAREFUL NOT TO IMPLY CRITICISM, SURPRISE, APPROVAL, OR DISAPPROVAL OF THE QUESTIONS ASKED OR THE RESPONDENT'S ANSWERS.

But don't be sloppy in asking the questions. Know the questions so you can read each one smoothly and move on to the next without hesitancy. This means you should study the questionnaire carefully and practice asking the questions *aloud,* perhaps by doing a practice interview with someone.

ASK THE QUESTIONS EXACTLY AS WORDED IN THE QUESTIONNAIRE

Since exactly the same questions must be asked of each respondent, the interviewer should MAKE NO CHANGES IN THE PHRASING OF THE QUESTIONS. Also, guard against trying to be conversational by inadvertently adding a few words at the end of a question or leaving a few words out. The respondents should be aware of all of the alternatives on a particular question (except for yes/no questions).

Ask the questions in the order presented in the questionnaire. Question sequence is carefully planned for continuity and promoting a conversational atmosphere. The sequence is also arranged so that early questions will not have a harmful effect on the respondent's answers to later questions. Furthermore, the question order needs to be standardized from respondent to respondent if the interviews are to be comparable.

ASK EVERY QUESTION SPECIFIED IN THE QUESTIONNAIRE

In answering one question, a respondent will sometimes also answer another question appearing later in the interview. Or, from time to time, the interviewer needs to ask a series of apparently similar questions. In either case, DON'T SKIP QUESTIONS WHICH ARE APPARENTLY ANSWERED BY AN EARLIER RESPONSE.

REPEAT QUESTIONS WHICH ARE MISUNDERSTOOD OR MISINTERPRETED

Questions may be repeated just as they are written in the questionnaire. If you suspect that the respondent merely needs time to think it over, simply wait and don't

> press for an immediate answer. If you think the respondent just needs reassuring, you may want to add to the question a neutral remark, such as: "We're just trying to get people's ideas on this," or "There are no right or wrong answers, just your ideas on it."

regarding this, what would happen? Outside of the respondent's actual refusal to participate in the research, you would be likely to get answers stating that they (the couple) have no conflict because it is not socially desirable to admit to money problems, especially to strangers.

Telephone Interviews   Telephone interviews strike a happy medium between in-person and mail surveys. They are very inexpensive (at least with local samples), easy to conduct, and not very time-consuming—no need to wait for questionnaires to be returned nor spend time driving around town to go door-to-door. They allow for feedback, yet minimize some in-person interviewer effects. They also have the advantage of guaranteeing some anonymity, if the respondents are assured of such and believe it. However, they typically do not generate the high response rate achieved by in-person interviews.

Telephone surveys have become the most used data-collection technique. Most researchers have access to telephones, they can train their interviewers and be at the interview location while the data are collected, and *most* respondents have telephones. You can also contact people in problem or dangerous areas via telephone. The problems of anonymity can be overcome via random digit dialing techniques so that the interviewer can tell the respondent that his or her telephone number was selected at random. You can also stratify your sample by requesting that the "man of the house," the "person of voting age," or "the person watching television at your household" respond to the questionnaire.

STRUCTURING THE SURVEY

The foregoing discussion about data collection has pointed out the need to provide some structure to the survey. You have to have either an interview schedule or a questionnaire to ensure that each respondent gets the same interview so that you can compare responses across people.

Survey Types

An *interview schedule* is a guideline for asking questions in-person or over the telephone. A *questionnaire* contains the exact questions and measures an interviewer uses to survey through the mail, in person, or by telephone. The interview schedule differs from a questionnaire only in that precise measures are not given to the respondent, but rather guidelines for eliciting information are requested. Both can be used in any data-collection method, but each has its own advantages.

Suppose you are interested in getting an idea about the communication patterns physicians have with terminally ill patients. You have examined the literature in the area and found that there is no adequate description of the types of experiences patients have. You have no knowledge of such matters yourself and few ideas for the kinds of experiences or precise messages that might be exchanged between a physician and patient. Since you are engaging in rather preliminary work, and you do not have concrete ideas of what constitutes key messages, you want to explore the patient's experiences to find out what they are. Therefore, you develop a series of topics you want to cover. You want to find out what the patient's relationship with the doctor has been. So, you might begin by asking how often they have seen the physician. Then you might ask them what happened during the visits.

As they begin to relate their experiences they may tell you that they had trouble with one of the visits. You are now cued by the respondent and may ask, what kind of trouble. You have asked a question that was dependent on the earlier response. You may not have identified this issue if it were not for the loose nature of the interview. Thus, this example points out the main advantage of using a schedule: You are able to gain insight and some depth into the area chosen. You also get the respondent's experiences in his or her own words. (Here you must consider how to actually record the data—writing notes, using a tape recorder, or even videotaping.)

The disadvantage with the interview schedule is found in interpretation. Although interpretation across respondents may be difficult, you have the advantage of finding new topics brought to your attention by the respondent or probe for further information. The interview schedule is most amenable to humanistic or exploratory research, in which you want to concentrate on individuals and are not overly concerned about generalizing to a larger population. Note, however, that the selection of respondents can be as scientific as ever.

The most commonly used method in communication research is the second type, the *questionnaire.* With a questionnaire, the interviewer has a list of precise questions to ask the respondent. These questions can be either closed or open-ended. *Closed* questions are similar to multiple-choice test questions in that responses are provided from which the interviewee may select the most appropriate. *Open-ended* questions are similar to essay or short answer questions, allowing the respondent to answer in any way he or she wishes. An example might be the type of questions mentioned earlier in reaction to the nuclear war film study. One way to tap viewer reaction would be to ask the closed question, How much did watching the film affect you emotionally? Responses might be provided as: A Lot, Somewhat, or Not at All. If you wanted more general responses, however, you would use an open-ended question, such as, How has viewing the film, *The Day After,* affected you emotionally? and let the respondent say whatever he or she wants. Answers to the open-ended question require some type of categorization and content analysis. But you get the responses as the respondent feels them: "Saddened, shocked." "Just feel that nuclear war is senseless." "Hadn't affected me." "No." "Trouble sleeping and thought provoking—very thought provoking—very frightening—worth watching." Obviously, you may have trouble quantifying these responses as they differ in type and magnitude of feeling.

Typically you will use both open-ended and closed-ended questions in a questionnaire. For instance, you may ask a person's age (open-ended) and their marital status (Married, Never Married, Divorced, Separated, Widow/Widower—closed-ended). In general, it takes longer and your responses are less easily analyzed with open-ended questions. You must train your interviewers more with open-ended questions, making certain that they write down *all* that was said. In some instances you may wish to begin with a closed-ended question, use it as a filter, and then depending on response, go to the open-ended question. (For example, the closed-ended question might be, Do you smoke? Yes, No. If the respondent replied no, you would go to another question. If the respondent replied yes, then you ask, What benefits do you get from smoking?)

Designing the Survey Questionnaire and Schedule

The following discussion closes out our coverage of the descriptive methodology. Based on what we discussed earlier, careful consideration must be given to both the content and structure of the survey and to the design of the individual items within each survey. Only through careful consideration and construction of questions can we be assured that the questions we ask reflect the general questions guiding our research. Further, the quality of the question will to a great extent dictate the quality of the response. Use the following as guidelines in constructing your own questionnaires.

Content and Structure   Any interview or survey must include an introduction before the main questioning begins. This introduction is designed to introduce the study to the respondent. Several things should be included in the introduction:

1. An introduction of the interviewer and the affiliation of the sponsor of the study is necessary. For instance, you might begin with, Hello, I'm _____ calling from the University of. . . . This introduction should be written and followed carefully by each interviewer. It provides both a name for the respondent to refer to and the sponsoring agency.
2. An explanation of the nature of the questions to be asked. This need not be lengthy or specific, but should provide some indication of the subject matter to be requested of the respondent. For example, if you were doing a study of the effects of a televised debate on political attitudes, you might say, We're doing a study of peoples' feelings about the current political campaign. It is important, however, not to give away any hypotheses or specific research questions that might cue the respondent as to how to answer.
3. An estimate of the amount of time it will take the respondent to finish the survey. Keep in mind that each interview or respondent will differ in the amount of time it takes him or her to complete the information, estimate a reasonable amount of time (5 to 10 minutes is normal, unless the questions are very detailed or open-ended).
4. A request for the respondent's participation. Do not assume that a person

will help you; ask for his or her help. If he or she refuses, offer thanks anyway.

5. A statement about how they were selected for the study. If they were selected at random, be sure to state that.

6. A guarantee of confidentiality and/or anonymity.

7. Uses to be made of the data. Will it be prepared for a class project? A convention paper? For publication? A business report?

8. An expression of gratitude for their participation.

In the introduction, as well as throughout the survey, the interviewer should act the same way with each respondent. Every effort should be made to make the experience as pleasant as possible, even if the respondent becomes rude and abusive.

After the respondent has agreed to participate, begin the questioning, but always remember that questionnaire development is both a science and an art. Unless you have a reason for beginning with background information, avoid asking demographic questions early in your questionnaire. Respondents may refuse to answer when you ask their race, educational level, age, income, and so forth. Begin with a simple and interesting question and work the respondent through the questionnaire. For the rest of the questionnaire or schedule, you should keep the following in mind when developing the questions: the pace of the questions (how long it takes to go through each question or block of questions), the ordering of questions (keep it logical, have one set lead to the next), keeping interest, and making sure that you get all the information you need.

To complete the questionnaire and to control the amount of relevant communication from the respondent, questions must be put together so that the interviews are paced to finish within the planned time limit. Interviewers must be instructed to move along from question to question, and not get sidetracked on irrelevant issues brought up by the respondent. When a respondent spends too much time talking, you or the interviewer may have to interject that you've got to go on to the next question. Overly long replies are often a problem with telephone surveys because the respondent cannot be guided through nonverbal behavior (facial expression and body language).

Ordering is important for pace, as well as ensuring that the respondents are not biased to give answers to questions toward the end of the interview as a result of questions asked near the beginning. For instance, suppose you want to measure a variety of campaign issues discussed in an election. But you also are interested in determining who is a viable candidate. You do not want to ask issue questions before you ask about the person's preference for candidates. The issues identified in your questionnaire, even if they were not normally associated with a candidate, may become salient in determining who a viable candidate is. Suppose you wanted to find out what people thought of Gary Hart for president of the United States, but you also wanted to know if there was any connection between certain race-related issues and people's attitudes toward presidential candidates. You know that Hart marched in a racial protest march in Georgia in 1987. If you started your questionnaire with a question asking what the respondent thought about Hart's participation in the protest march, you have made that issue an important one for evaluating him. After all, the respondent probably would not have been aware of that fact, and given that they are now made aware of it, this knowledge may influence their evaluation of him later in the questionnaire.

Keeping interest is sometimes difficult, especially with either relatively complicated or relatively uninteresting topics. Questions about television viewing are relatively interesting and usually keep people's interest; questions on political ideology may not. You should avoid redundancy in question content and form to keep the respondent interested enough to complete the questionnaire (something that is essential so you have the full range of data you need to answer your research question[s] or hypotheses). You may have to occasionally include some throw-away questions that will not be analyzed but are designed to keep interest. This is particularly true when working with children. In many instances the researcher needs to ask questions that appear quite similar but are different. To a child, however, they may appear the same. Thus, they may tire of answering and therefore would either answer them all in the same way, skip some, or quit altogether. Therefore, you might include questions about their favorite television shows (which would not be analyzed) and perhaps schedule a break during which they could stand and stretch for a few minutes.

Making certain you get all the information you need is sometimes one of the most difficult tasks. You want to make sure that each respondent finishes the questionnaire, but you also need to make sure there is an answer for *every single question* within the questionnaire. To do this, a little encouragement on the part of the interviewer is sometimes required. With a reluctant respondent, an interviewer might have to say, If you had to give some opinion, what would it be? You should strategically place such prompts within the questionnaire, especially when you are almost finished with the major questions and transitioning to demographic information. It sometimes helps to use transitions between major bodies of questions, such as "Now we are going to ask you a few questions about. . . ."

Designing the Questions   Designing questions requires careful consideration of a variety of factors that may lead to erroneous findings. Questions need to be direct, clear, and unambiguous. One or more questions should be used for each area you wish to study. Questions that contain two parts (referred to as *double-barreled* because the respondent may respond to either or both of the parts rather than the one idea you are attempting to analyze) may be ambiguous and should be avoided. Examples of *bad* questions include:

1. Do you think the United States should support Spain and the Common Market?
2. What is your attitude about George Bush and his staff?
3. Do you believe in America and vote?

Instead, each question could be split in two. For example, you might ask, What is your attitude toward George Bush? and follow up with a second question asking What is your attitude toward Bush's staff?

Leading questions also produce poor results. They are the questions that most often bias the respondent in a certain direction. Examples of leading questions include:

1. Don't you think that rich university professors should be denied a pay raise?
2. Isn't it true that most Southerners are bigots?
3. Do you think the Brotherhood March was successful?

Question 1 claims that university professors are rich. Question 2 implies by the phrase, "Isn't it true," that Southerners *are* bigots. And, question 3 has included "brotherhood," a term that some respondents may find emotionally loaded. Instead, the questions should be phrased:

1. Do you think university professors should be denied a pay raise?
2. Are Southerners bigoted?
3. Do you think the march of June 15th in San José was successful?

As discussed earlier, you also must guard against social desirability, even within a question. You must be careful to word questions so that the respondent does not give answers just to please you or others. For instance, if you ask people if they are influenced by commercials, they may say no (even though we know people are). Similarly, there is the "Gilligan's Island Effect." If you survey people about what television shows they watch at a particular time, and you know that there are four programs that are shown at that hour, including "Gilligan's Island" and "Masterpiece Theatre," you will find that virtually no one will claim to be watching "Gilligan's Island," while more people than actually watch "Masterpiece Theatre" will claim they do so.

"Journalistic" Surveys   A new technique, the "journalistic" telephone survey or opinion polls, which are sponsored by many local television stations, also has problems, especially in the area of social desirability. These television stations typically ask one question and require the viewer to call one of two telephone numbers to indicate if they agree or disagree. Many times the anchor will read the question to the audience; in so doing, he or she may bias the results through vocal or facial expression, or by the fact that it follows a news story on the issue in question.

In addition to social desirability, these surveys and polls have other equally serious problems. First, many of the questions asked are neither well written nor pretested. Second, the results are invalid because they do not keep track of how many times a particular person responds. Another problem should be apparent by now: The sample is self-selected, therefore the principles of randomization discussed earlier cannot apply and the sample is no longer reflective of an identifiable population. Unless carefully constructed, such surveys are largely worthless.

When others report the results of such surveys and polls, remember to look for the following things: (1) the question as it was asked, (2) the number of respondents, (3) how the respondents were selected, (4) how the respondents were contacted (by telephone, in person, by mail), (5) the error rate (3 percent, 5 percent, 10 percent), (6) who sponsored or cosponsored the survey or poll, and,

(7) what social desirability factors might have been present. You should include the same information when reporting your own surveys.

OTHER CONSIDERATIONS

This chapter has introduced descriptive social science research, primarily through the use of survey methodology. It should be remembered that the selection methods introduced can be used by both the humanistic researcher and the social science researcher. In closing out this chapter, a few comments need to be made. First, you are probably different than your sample. Your education and interests may differ from those you seek to describe. Imposing your own feelings and ideas on their responses will not provide the impartial analysis you need. Always remember that although you are like some of your respondents in some ways, you are not much like some of your respondents in others. If you are conducting a survey, remember that you have *a lot* of information about the subject of your survey while many of your respondents may not. In addition, your vocabulary may not be suitable for your respondents. This is, of course, obvious in research dealing with children, but even adults may have trouble with the vocabulary of college students. Take special care to avoid jargon. Replace terms that may be stated more directly and more clearly with simpler, less obtuse terms. A respondent who does not understand a term in a question will most likely try to fake it to save face; thus, you may have an invalid response.

Before actually surveying your sample, pretest the questionnaire on your classmates, or on a subset of the population under study. Ask for feedback during a session following the pretest administration of the questionnaire. Get reactions, ask how they interpreted each question, and find out if they have comments about the questions. You will find this extremely helpful in designing the final draft of your questionnaire.

SUMMARY

This chapter has introduced a form of research that is very popular. Almost every time a major political figure makes an important speech, surveys are conducted to gauge reaction to both the speaker and the message. By understanding what descriptive research does, and the questions it answers, you should be prepared to evaluate those findings. Further, you have the necessary information to begin to conduct your own research. This chapter has attempted to provide: (1) an understanding of what a sample is and how it reflects a population; (2) an understanding of how to sample that population in a way that accurately reflects the population's parameters within a prescribed confidence level and with an acceptable degree of error in the responses; and (3) information about how to collect data, whether it be by questionnaire or interview.

Descriptive methodology can be used by the historian and rhetorician as well as the social scientist. Understand also that descriptive research is rigorous; it provides a way of describing how people think and feel about a subject and begins to address the question of causation. In sum, descriptive research allows you to begin to understand how variables may relate to each other and—in particular—describe their isomorphism with real-life settings.

PROBES

1. Survey methodology seeks to canvas a number of people to gain insight into their perceptions regarding selected variables or concerns. If you were asked to critique this method as a way of gaining understanding about human behavior, what would you say? What does survey tell us that other methods do not? What limitations are placed on the survey researcher? Are these limitations important?

2. One of the more complex areas of survey research deals with the sampling design. Assume for a moment that you want to know who will be the next president of the student body, what type of design would best provide the data with which to answer that question? What if you wanted to establish how the students at your college or university had voted over time—which design(s) would you choose? What if you wanted to know how a particular group of people voted over time?

3. What does it take to conduct *good* survey research? Does the researcher have to concern him- or herself with more than just questionnaire development? What are the needs of interviewer training? What about the type of interviewing method proposed? If you were going to interview people about a marketing concern in the local area, what method would be *best*? What method would be *worst*? Why?

4. What is a double-barreled question? What problems do we have with such questions? Thinking back to Chapter 6 (Measurement), what are the *best* types of questions for a mail survey? A telephone survey? An in-person survey?

5. There are several minimal things that should be dealt with when reporting the results of a survey. What are they? Which is *most* important? Why? Which have you observed to be violated the most? Why might it be violated? How would you report the results of a survey, for instance, on the five o'clock news?

SUGGESTED READING

Babbie, E. R. (1973). *Survey research.* Belmont, CA: Wadsworth.

Backstrom, C. H., & Hursh, G. D. (1963). *Survey research.* Evanston, IL: Northwestern University Press.

Bradburn, N. M., & Sudman, S. (1979). *Improving interview method and questionnaire design.* San Francisco: Jossey-Bass.

Brady, J. (1976). *The craft of interviewing.* Cincinnati, OH: Writer's Digest Books.

Frey, J. H. (1983). *Survey research by telephone.* Beverly Hills, CA: Sage Publications.

Mishler, E. G. (1986). *Research interviewing: Context and narrative.* Cambridge, MA: Harvard University Press.

Payne, S. L. (1951). *The art of asking questions.* Princeton, NJ: Princeton University Press.

Roll, C. W., Jr., & Cantril, A. H. (1972). *Polls: Their use and misuse in politics.* New York: Basic Books.

Slonim, M. J. (1960). *Sampling.* New York: Simon and Schuster.

Weisberg, H. F., & Bowen, B. D. (1977). *An introduction to survey research and data analysis.* San Francisco: W. H. Freeman.

NOTES

1. Steven T. McDermott and Bradley S. Greenberg, "Black Children's Esteem: Parents, Peers, and Television," in Robert Bostrom, ed., *Communication Yearbook 8* (Beverly Hills, Calif.: Sage, 1984): 164–177.
2. See Earl R. Babbie, *Survey Research* (Belmont, Calif.: Wadsworth, 1973).
3. Philip Meyer, *Precision Journalism* (Bloomington, Ind.: University Press, 1973), 123.
4. Bradley S. Greenberg and Steven T. McDermott, "The Debut of a Black Television Station: Adoption of an Innovation," paper presented to the Association for Education in Journalism and Mass Communication, Madison, Wisconsin, 1977. (ERIC ED 153–227.)
5. Don W. Stacks and Ricky T. Gordon, "Does Public Speaking Exist Outside of Academia? A Look at One Southeastern Community," *Georgia Speech Communication Journal,* 2 (1974): 77–85.
6. Babbie.
7. See R. W. McPeek and J. D. Edwards, "Expectancy Disconformation and Attitude Change," *Journal of Social Psychology,* 96 (1975): 193–208; and Judee K. Burgoon and Thomas J. Saine, *The Unspoken Dialogue: An Introduction to Nonverbal Communication* (Boston: Houghton Mifflin, 1978): 273–301.
8. John Goyder, "Survey on Surveys: Limitations and Potentialities," *Public Opinion Quarterly,* 50 (1986): 27–41.

Chapter 9

The "True" Communication Experiment

*T*he experiment is surely one of the most ingenious creations in human history. The logic is elegant. To observe what effect a particular independent (manipulated) variable has on a dependent (measured) variable, the researcher creates two situations in which all factors are made constant except the independent variable, which is carefully manipulated to take on different values. Then the effect of this manipulation on the dependent variable is carefully observed. If the research has been successful in holding other relevant factors constant, observed differences on the dependent variable may be attributed to the manipulation of the independent variable(s). Few ideas are simpler or more straightforward than the logic that underlies the experiment. Many of the advances in sciences, ranging from physics and chemistry to educational and social psychology to communication, have come from the skillful application of experimental method.

The value of the experimental method lies in the *rigor* of the comparisons that are made possible. *Comparisons* are fundamental to establishing empirical relationships between variables, and, therefore, are fundamental to scientific inquiry. For example, if we want to know if the amount of self-disclosure in a relationship is related to the amount of relational satisfaction experienced by partners, we need to *compare* relationships with varying amounts of disclosure to see if they differ in amount of satisfaction. If we want to know if one type of organizational culture results in higher productivity than others, we need to *compare* various organizational cultures to see if they differ in productivity. If we want to know if exposure to political campaign advertising has an effect on voting, we need to *compare* the voting behavior of voters with high exposure to political ads with those of voters who have lower amounts of exposure. If we want to know if wearing seat belts saves lives, we need to *compare* states with high and low seat belt use to see if they have differing levels of traffic accident deaths. Whenever we want to know the relationship between variables we need to make comparisons; this is true whether the method used is field observation, survey, or experiment. What the experiment allows us to do is make more carefully *controlled*, more *systematic*, more *rigorous* comparisons. By comparing two sets of circumstances that are highly similar in every respect, except with regard to the independent variable, the effects of that variable can be *isolated.* Because experiments can allow careful, rigorous comparisons, they provide the researcher with a uniquely powerful tool for establishing the relationships between variables under study.

This chapter introduces the logic associated with the experiment. We begin by describing the advantages of the experiment and then examine the critical link found in all research methods—asking the appropriate research question. After this we examine how the experiment *controls* potential sources of error (variance) to make the analysis of proposed relationships as pure as possible. Then we describe, step-by-step, the procedures involved in conducting the *laboratory* experiment. Chapter 10 then extends the study of experiments to quasi-experiments, and attempts to show that the elegant logic and power of the experiment has widespread applicability outside the laboratory.

Experiments have two related strengths or advantages over all other research methods. Of all methods, experiments can provide the best evidence that two variables are, in fact, related. And, importantly, in those situations where we want to make *causal* statements about the relationship between variables, the experiment can provide the strongest possible evidence that a particular independent variable *causes* an effect on a dependent variable. Secondly, if two independent variables both appear to be related to a dependent variable, the experiment provides a means of sorting out whether one or both independent variables are related to the dependent variable; and, if both are related, an experiment can tell us which of the variables is the more powerfully related to the dependent variable.

ESTABLISHING RELATIONSHIPS

As we noted, establishing relationships between variables is at the core of scientific inquiry. However, because the point is so important and related specifically to experimental method, a brief review is in order. Theories are composed of systematic statements about the nature of relationships between variables and, as discussed in Chapter 2, the purpose of scientific inquiry is the creation of theory. The statements contained in a theory provide explanations for, and allow predictions about, the phenomenon the theory concerns. All communication theories contain statements of the relationships between variables.[1] Useful theories define variables and state their interrelationships in ways that are consistent with actual observation. Theories that do not do this are not useful. Thus, the purpose of empirical research can be viewed as establishing whether variables in theories are, in fact, related or not.

There are a variety of sources of evidence that can be marshaled to determine if variables are related in the way stated by a theory. *The most powerful form this evidence can take comes from the results of a well-conducted experiment.* Whenever we make observations that indicate two variables are related, there exists the possibility that the observed relationship is *spurious*—that the apparent relationship lacks validity, it is false. If an experiment indicates that a particular independent and dependent variable are related, we can be confident that, at least within the context of the procedures and the rigor with which the experiment was conducted, the relationship is not spurious. Rather, the variables are indeed related. Let us examine why.

Assume for a minute that we have a theory about the relationship between touching behavior and interpersonal attraction. Specifically, we believe that some individuals engage in more casual touching of other people than do other individuals. Furthermore, our theory states that those who engage in high amounts of casual touching will be better liked than will individuals who engage in low amounts of touching. One way to test this theory would be to conduct a field study. This approach would involve making observations in a naturally occurring environment, such as in a college dorm, sorority or fraternity house, or a public place where many people congregate. We would observe the communicative behaviors in the particular environment(s) chosen, taking particular care in noting the amount of touching engaged in by each person. After a period of time we might be able to categorize those in the environment(s) according to the quantity of their casual touching of others. Some individuals would be "high touchers," others would be "moderate touchers," and yet others would be "low touchers." Next, we would need to assess our dependent variable—how well liked each of the individuals was by others in the environment(s). The amount of interpersonal attraction could be operationalized in a variety of ways (see Chapter 6). We could count the number of people with whom our touchers communicated. We could measure the total amount of time they spent talking to others. We could conduct interviews with the participants and ask how well liked each of our touchers was. Better, we could do all three, and have the opportunity to obtain a more valid measure of the participants' amount of attraction for our touchers.

Assume that our observations confirm that the variables *touching* and *interpersonal attraction* are related. The high touchers are the most liked, the low touchers are the least liked, and the moderate touchers fall somewhere in the middle. Our theory, then, is supported by our observations. However, we still must be quite cautious in concluding that touching is actually the variable that accounts for the differences in the amount of interpersonal attraction felt for our high, medium, and low touchers. This is because there are many other variables that might be related *both* to amount of touching and to interpersonal attraction; each of these unknown and unmeasured variables could be accounting for what we have observed. For example, some people are more friendly and outgoing than others. These individuals probably communicate with more people, perhaps smile more, have more eye contact, more open body postures, better senses of humor, and so on, all in *addition* to touching others more.[2] Each of these other behaviors, or all of them, could be accounting for the observed relationship between touching and interpersonal attraction. It is possible that the amount of touching is just incidental, that it has no effect whatsoever on how well liked someone is. It is even possible that, other factors being equal, touching is negatively related to interpersonal attraction, that high touching makes someone less attractive, but that other behaviors associated with high touching overcome the negative impact of touching (i.e., smiling, eye contact, increased posture, etc.). Although seemingly unlikely, it is possible that the high touchers are liked better *in spite of* engaging in large amounts of touching.

Extraneous Variables

In the natural setting where these observations were made the researcher does not have much control over *extraneous variables*—variables that although present, are not the focus of the study. Extraneous variables muddy up the waters, so to speak, and make it difficult to observe clearly the relationships between the independent and dependent variables. Controlling for extraneous variables is the major advantage that experiments have over field studies and surveys. In the experiment, extraneous variables are held *constant* across the various conditions (manipulations of the independent variable[s]) of the experiment, and thus the effects of such variables are the same in *each* experimental condition. In our example, imagine if our field researcher could somehow magically hold all variables *except* touching and interpersonal attraction constant. Everyone would be *equally* friendly and outgoing, would communicate with the same people, would smile the same amount, have equal amounts of eye contact and open body postures, and have equally well-developed senses of humor, regardless of their amount of touching. If all possible extraneous variables could be made equal and the high touchers were still found to be better liked than their low or moderate touching counterparts, then the researcher would be in an excellent position to conclude that touching and interpersonal attraction are related.

The Classic Experimental Design

How might an experiment to address this question be conducted? Sixty people could, one by one, be brought into the researcher's environment—his *laboratory*—and be randomly assigned to either the experimental group (touch) or to a *control group* (no touch). Each participant could be introduced to a confederate, an individual who, although appearing to the participant to be another participant, is actually someone who is working with the researcher. Next, they could be given tasks in which they must sit together at a table for an hour or more and solve a series of problems cooperatively.

All confederates employed in the study would be carefully trained to behave identically in both touch and no-touch conditions, except that in the experimental group, during the course of the hour, the confederate would casually touch the participant in subtle, natural ways. In the control group the confederate would not touch the participant. Additionally, based on observation or the research literature, the number of touches would be carefully planned, practiced, and introduced during the experimental sessions.[3] This careful manipulation of touch increases the *rigor* of the study and ensures that the touch condition is effective.

After completing the tasks, each participant's degree of liking for their new friend, the confederate, could be assessed. For example, they could be given a questionnaire that asked such questions as: "If you were required to work on a similar problem-solving task in the future, how much would you like to work with your partner from this session?" "How much would you like to spend time with your partner in another setting?" Scaled response options ranging from Not at All to Very Much could be provided. Or, Likert-type scales, such as those devised by McCroskey and McCain that measure peer attraction on three levels, could be used to check the created scales' validity and to gain a different perspective[4]:

1. I think he(she) could be a friend of mine.

Strongly Agree _____:___:___:___:___:___ Strongly Disagree

2. I think he(she) is quite handsome/pretty.

Strongly Agree _____:___:___:___:___:___ Strongly Disagree

3. I couldn't get anything accomplished with him(her).

Strongly Agree _____:___:___:___:___:___ Strongly Disagree

Thus, the degree of liking for the partner could be assessed and the responses of those in the experimental (touch) group could be compared to those of the control (no touch) group.

If the participants were assigned to the two groups at random, if the other conditions (such as amount of confederate smiling) were indeed held constant in both conditions, and if the difference between the two groups' average amounts of liking for the confederate was great enough that statistical analysis indicated that the interpersonal attraction difference was not a result of random chance, the researcher could conclude that the variables touch and interpersonal attractiveness were related, *at least for these participants and under these conditions.*

The *design* of this simple two-group experiment is generally referred to as a *classic experiment.* It is shown symbolically as Design 9.1. The *R* represents the fact that the participants have been randomly assigned to the two conditions of the

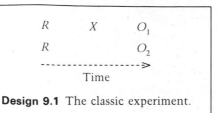

Design 9.1 The classic experiment.

experiment. The X is used to refer to exposure to a stimulus of some kind. While in this case it represents exposure to a confederate who engages in a high degree of touching, it could represent another kind of communication message, the communication channel through which information was received, the characteristics of a person delivering a message—in short, anything to which research participants are exposed. Note, however, that the X is not by itself an independent variable because it does not vary; it is a constant, representing only one level of a variable. (If there were other levels of the variable, as examined in the next chapter, there would be other lines composed of R's and X's.) An O refers to an observation, that is, a measurement. Symbols that appear on the left represents events that precede in time events represented by symbols on the right. The X's and O's on the same horizontal rows are applied to the same individuals or objects. This notation system was first presented in 1963 by two educational psychologists, Donald T. Campbell and Julian C. Stanley. This notation system is general, flexible, and useful, and we shall rely on it throughout the next chapter to illustrate and clarify various experimental and quasi-experimental designs.[5]

The classic experimental design provides a graphic illustration of what has been said verbally. Note the rigor of the comparisons allowed by the design and the resulting *potential* confidence that may be placed in the results. (We say potential because the experiment still must be run in a carefully planned manner. It is not the design per se that allows confidence; rather, it is the design, plus the care with which the researcher conducts all aspects of the experiment.) In Design 9.1 we see two groups of participants, illustrated by the two horizontal lines, the members of which have been randomly assigned, indicated by the R. One group then receives the experimental stimulus, exposure to the confederate who engages in high amounts of touching, represented by the X. The second group does not receive the experimental stimulus, represented by the absence of an X. Each group's degree of interpersonal attraction for the confederate is observed (measured) as represented by O_1 and O_2 and determine if the variables are indeed related and the strength of the obtained relationship.

ESTABLISHING CAUSATION

Frequently, researchers want to establish *causal relationships* between variables. They want to assert that variable X causes a change in the value taken by variable Y. Just as experiments have the potential to provide evidence that two variables are related, experiments also have the potential to establish that two variables are causally related.

Criteria for Establishing Causation

Three criteria need to be met to provide convincing evidence of causality. First, *the variables need to be shown to be empirically related to one another.* A change in the value of one variable must result in a change in the value of the other. If touch and liking are related, a change in the amount of touching should result in a change in the amount of liking. If smoking causes cancer, increases in smoking should lead to increases in the incidence of cancer. If violence on television causes violence in society, then increases in violence on television should lead to increases in violence in society. Unless the two variables covary they cannot be causally related.

Second, *the effect must follow the cause in time.* When we run our electric can opener, our cats come running into the kitchen. Since the can opener was started first, the running cats cannot be the cause of the can opener being used. While this second criterion is conceptually simple, sometimes establishing time order is very difficult. The problem is not unlike the thorny issue posed by the question, Which came first, the chicken or the egg? Concerning touching and liking, it could be that people who are already well-liked respond by emitting more touching behaviors than those who are less well-liked. Similarly, perhaps it is the violent tendencies of individuals that results in their choosing to view television programs with violent content, rather than the opposite. In both these examples, the variable that was thought to be the cause might be the effect. In other words, which of the variables was independent and which was dependent might be confused.

Establishing time order is especially difficult when both variables are attributes of individuals that may have taken a lifetime to develop. Self-esteem and communication apprehension are two variables that are *inversely* related. Individuals who have high self-esteem tend to have low communication apprehension, and vice-versa. But which came first? The time order between these variables is not apparent. This is a limitation of the experimental method. Attributes of individuals cannot normally be manipulated. And, when they are manipulated, care must be taken to establish theoretically the expected causal ordering prior to the experiment.

Finally, to establish causality, possible alternative explanations that could account for the observed relationship between two variables must be discounted. Specifically, *the relationship cannot be accounted for by a third variable.* In other words, is there something else, some other variable, that could be causing covariation of both the independent and dependent variables? This is the most difficult criterion to meet. In fact, some would argue that it can never be met absolutely, beyond any doubt.[6] For example, the number of bars located in towns and cities shows high correlation with the number of churches. Towns that have only a few bars also have only a few churches. Towns with many bars also have many churches. It might be tempting to conclude that churchgoers are heavy drinkers, or vice versa. Or that churches spring up to combat the evil caused by bars. Or that bars spring up to combat the good caused by churches. In reality, a third variable—town size—accounts for both the number of bars and the number of churches. The apparent church/bar relationship is spurious.

Meeting the Causation Criteria

A well-conducted experiment can meet all three criteria necessary to establish causation. The experiment does so by ensuring that covariation occurs, that the assignment of subjects is truly random, and that the researcher has controlled extraneous variables.

Covariation   First, if the dependent variable takes on different values in the experimental and control groups, covariation has been shown. The variables are related empirically.

Randomization   Second, prior to the manipulation of the independent variable, the value taken by the dependent variable is made equal in both the experimental and the control group. This is accomplished by randomly assigning participants to both groups. An important distinction needs to be made between a random *sample* and *random assignment.* See Chapter 8 for a discussion of various kinds of sampling and samples. The purpose of sampling is to draw a subgroup from a population that is *representative* of the population. Drawing a sample from a population at random provides a means of increasing the likelihood that the sample is indeed representative of the population from which it is drawn.

Participants in experiments are rarely drawn at random from any population. Rather, they are almost always availability or convenience samples (see Chapter 8). However, once the sample is in hand, so to speak, regardless of the method by which its members were obtained, random *assignment* refers to the method by which participants are assigned to the various conditions in the experiment. If *every* participant has an equal opportunity of ending up in *every* experimental condition, then random assignment has been achieved. (We will have more to say about how random assignment is accomplished in practice later, when we discuss the steps in conducting an experiment.)

To illustrate how random assignment equalizes the initial value of the dependent variable, suppose, for example, that we were interested in assessing the impact of a particular type of persuasive argument on attitudes toward smoking in public places. Initially, before any of our participants are assigned to a condition and before they hear any persuasive message about smoking, they will have a variety of views on this topic. How do we know that it is our message and not their initial views that result in the observed changes? By randomly assigning the participants we can be confident, within the limits of statistical probability, that the two groups are about equal in terms of their preparticipation attitudes. Some participants will be in favor of smoking in public places, others will be more neutral, and still others will be against it. By randomly assigning the participants to treatment and control groups we can be sure that each of these different attitudes will be represented *about equally in each group.* Therefore, any substantial differences that are observed after the receipt of the persuasive message can be attributed to the messages themselves. Time order has been established. The manipulation of the independent variable preceded the change in the dependent variable.

Control Finally, an experiment can allow the researcher to eliminate extraneous variables as the cause of observed differences on the dependent variable. A critical determinant of whether an experiment can rule out *all possible* alternative explanations for the relationship between the variables under study is the extent to which the effects of other variables are controlled by being made equal in both the experimental and control groups.

How are the effects of all possible extraneous variables made equal? This is accomplished in two ways. First, the conditions under which the experiment is run are made as similar as possible in all conditions. Let us take the example of a researcher studying the impact of the use of humor in a persuasive speech on the effectiveness of the speech. If she were conducting an experiment on the effects of the use of humor in a persuasive speech, the only thing that would be varied across conditions would be the humor in the speech. Thus, in both "humor" and "no humor" conditions, the speaker would be the same, the room and audience sizes would be the same, the introduction would be the same. She would attempt to make even seemingly irrelevant factors the same in both conditions. Time of day, for example, might not seem important, but it is possible that the participants might find the speech funnier and therefore more (or less) persuasive in the morning than right after lunch. *Any* differences between the experimental and control conditions, besides the purposefully manipulated independent variable, are potential rival explanations for any observed differences on the dependent variable and must be as controlled for as much as possible.

Second, conditions in the experimental and control groups are made equal by randomly assigning participants to conditions. This point was made earlier when illustrating how an experiment establishes that the manipulation of the independent variable occurs earlier in time than any changes in the dependent variable. However, an understanding of the importance of randomization is so essential to understanding how an experiment can provide the best possible evidence that two variables are related that it deserves special emphasis. In fact, randomization is so important that Campbell and Stanley only apply the word experiment to studies in which participants have been randomly assigned to experimental conditions. The term quasi-experiment is used to describe those studies that, although identical in other respects, have been unable to randomize subjects.[7]

Assume that in our study of the effects of humor on persuasion the theme of our persuasive speech is that basketball players are better athletes than participants in other sports. All sorts of extraneous variables that may affect how they feel about this topic and how susceptible they may be to being influenced by a humorous or nonhumorous speech on the topic are floating around in our participant pool. The most obvious extraneous variable is their initial feelings about the theme of the speech. Before hearing the speech the participants are likely to have all sorts of differing views on this theme. Some probably think that it is true, that basketball players are the best athletes; others may think that football or soccer or baseball players are better athletes than basketball players. Others may have no opinion whatsoever and, in fact, may not even care. Obviously, we want to be sure that we get as equal a number of participants holding all these views in both the humorous and nonhumorous speech conditions as possible. If the humor condition was full of participants who already agreed with the theme of the speech and the nonhumor condition was full of participants who thought football players were most athletic, these differing views would likely account for any differences on the dependent variable. Random assignment takes care of this problem. It assures that those in both the humor and nonhumor conditions will have about equal initial feelings on the speech topic.

It may not be so obvious how other extraneous variables could affect the outcome of the experiment. Some participants might be taller than others and therefore more receptive to a particular kind of speech about basketball, a sport in which height is an advantage. The list of ways in which our pool of participants differ is almost endless—some have high self-esteem, others low; some are affluent, others poor; some are high media users, others low; some are Republicans, others Democrats; and so forth. Any of these seemingly irrelevant variables *could* influence how someone feels about the theme of our speech and/or his or her susceptibility to a humorous or nonhumorous speech on this particular theme. How can we rule out this endless list of extraneous variables, each of which represents an alternative explanation of an apparent relationship between the independent variable (use of humor) and dependent variable (attitude towards the speech topic)? The answer, once again, is random assignment of participants to conditions. If the number of participants is large enough, usually between 50 and 60 in a classic two-group experiment, random assignment assures that the participants in both the experimental and control groups will be highly similar in terms of variables, which obviously may affect the outcome of the experiment. Furthermore, the groups will be highly similar in *all possible ways.* Thus, random assignment allows *all* possible alternative variables to be ruled out as alternative explanations for the observed relationship between the independent and dependent variables.

Summary

An experiment has the potential to provide the strongest possible evidence that two variables are related, and related causally, stronger than field studies or surveys. However, to conduct such an experiment the researcher must be able to accomplish five things: (1) Assign participants randomly to both experimental and control conditions; (2) structure the environments in the various conditions so that they are similar in every respect; (3) expose one group of participants to one level of the independent variable (usually called a *treatment*) and expose the other groups to the other levels of the independent variable, that is, to a different treatment; (4) employ a control group(s), which receive(s) no treatment; and (5) measure the dependent variable so that the effect of the independent variable on the dependent variable can be assessed. In short, to conduct a rigorous experiment—what we shall call, along with Campbell and Stanley, a true experiment—the researcher must have a great deal of control over the experimental participants and their environment. This means that, in general, the most rigorous experiments take place in the researcher's carefully structured environment, his laboratory.

QUESTIONS APPROPRIATE FOR EXPERIMENTS

As noted in Chapter 1, the first step in conducting any research project is selecting a research question. Reviewing this process is important because selecting a good research question can be one of the most difficult parts of the entire research process.

Questions about human communication are plentiful. One of the things we like about our discipline and that differentiates it from, say, chemistry, is that we can study the social world around us. Ideas for interesting, important, and research-able questions about human communication can come from many sources. They can come from examining previous research literature, from classroom discussions, from reading a popular magazine, from asking someone for a date, from a conflict with a roommate or coworker; in short, research questions may come from almost any life experience.

Selection Criteria Appropriate for Experimental Questions

Once a question has been selected (and the related literature reviewed), an appro-priate method to answer it needs to be devised. The method should always follow the question, not the reverse. While it is extremely difficult to state hard-and-fast rules that assert which questions are appropriate for experimental method and which ones are not, we will suggest a few guidelines.

Experiments are particularly appropriate for research whose aim is to provide explanations for phenomena by establishing causal relationships between variables, for sorting out real relationships from spurious ones. Thus experiments are appro-priate for testing hypotheses derived from theories. Relatively narrow, focused questions lend themselves to experimentally derived answers. If we were interested in the causes of relationship satisfaction, a broad question, we probably would be better off, at least in the beginning of our study, observing or interviewing some couples involved in relationships than we would in conducting an experiment. On the other hand, if we wanted to know how accurate married couples were in detecting lying by their partner, a more narrow question, we might be able to address this question with an experiment.

Many questions can be addressed using different methods, each with its own set of advantages and disadvantages. A theoretical proposition that is supported empirically over and over with different methods is one in which you can have a good deal of confidence. Examples include the propositions that smoking causes cancer and media violence causes viewer violence. These questions have been addressed using many methods, including experiments. As noted in Chapter 7, the examination of the same basic research question using several different methods is called *triangulation*.[8]

A good many questions simply are not amenable to experimentation. Exploratory investigations into new areas are probably best tackled with other methods: field studies, focus group interviews, surveys, and so on. Obviously, questions about past events, such as the impact or content of President Roosevelt's fireside chats, are not appropriate for experimentation. Similarly, questions involving large populations of people are not appropriate for experiments—How do Americans feel about a joint Russian-American space mission to Mars? is better answered via survey methodology.

Finally, if it is not possible to manipulate a variable, that variable cannot be the independent variable in an experiment. (And we might add, if it is not possible to measure a variable, that variable cannot be the dependent variable in an experiment. In fact, it cannot be in *any* kind of scientific study.) Many variables of interest to communication researchers are characteristics or attributes of people. These variables may have taken a lifetime of experience to create. *Attribute variables* must be measured.[9] Examples of attribute variables include: physical characteristics such as sex, height, body shape, physical attractiveness, and psychological characteristics such as attitude, self-esteem, machiavellianism, self-monitoring, and androgyny. All of these variables may be treated as independent variables, but strictly speaking, since they must be measured and not manipulated, doing so involves a survey, not an experiment.

We should note, however, that the impact of an attribute variable *on others*, as opposed to on those who possess the attribute, can sometimes be manipulated. For example, the impact of a person's physical attractiveness on others could be studied by exposing people to individuals of varying levels of attractiveness. Or the effect of interacting with someone having differing levels of self-concept on a partner in a dyad could be studied by training a confederate to *behave* as if he or she had a high or low self-concept—and then observing the effects of this manipulation on the participant.

THE *LABORATORY* EXPERIMENT

Theoretically, communication experiments, like other kinds of communication research, can be conducted in any environment in which human beings or their artifacts are present. In practice, however, most experiments take place in the experimenter's laboratory. A laboratory study is often contrasted with a *field study*. If a study is conducted with people in a location where they are routinely and normally present, it is generally called a field study (see Chapter 7 and Chapter 8). Thus, research conducted in shopping malls, in businesses or organizations, in public school classrooms, at professional association conventions, in short, any environment in which the research participants are present naturally, is taking place in the field. On the other hand, if the research participants are brought into the researcher's environment, it is called a *laboratory* study. Thus, if participants are moved from where they would otherwise be and brought to a place under the researcher's *control*, the research is taking place in the laboratory.

The distinction between laboratory and field studies is not an either/or dichotomy, but rather should be conceived as existing on a continuum ranging from pure field research to pure laboratory research. If a researcher causes people to report individually at a specified time to a special facility called the Communication Research Lab, attaches them to a galvanic skin response (GSR) machine, and then measures their degree of physiological arousal as they were exposed to various erotic and violent television programming, the research would be an example of relatively pure laboratory research. On the other hand, if the researcher phoned the participants in their homes and asked them questions about their reactions to a particular television show, it would be an example of relatively pure field research. Many studies fall somewhere in the middle of the continuum. For example, if members of an organization were brought into a room that was at their place of work, but which they did not normally visit, to fill out a questionnaire, the setting would have some of the elements of a field study and some of a laboratory study.

With rare exceptions, true experiments, that is those that meet the four criteria discussed earlier—random assignment, conditions held constant, manipulation of the independent variable(s), and systematic measurement of the dependent variable(s)—occur only in the laboratory. With this in mind, we present the basic steps in conducting an experiment.

To conduct a laboratory experiment the researcher must: (1) present to the participants a plausible cover story; (2) assign participants randomly to conditions; (3) manipulate the independent variable(s), while holding other conditions constant; (4) measure the dependent variable and the success of the manipulation of the independent variable; and (5) debrief the participants. We will examine, briefly, each of these in turn.

The Cover Story

The phrase *cover story* implies, quite accurately, that experiments involve deception. Frequently the deceptions are matters of omission—as when participants are not provided with complete information about the research; for example, participants are not routinely told that they are, in fact, participating in an experiment in which other participants are receiving a different experimental stimulus. Other times the deception involves outright misrepresentation of fact. In either case, research participants are typically quite curious to know all about the research. The requirements of obtaining informed consent (see Chapter 3) prior to allowing individuals to volunteer to participate necessitates telling the participants in *general* terms what participation involves. However, if the participants knew *exactly* what was being studied, this knowledge would be likely to affect their behavior and invalidate the results. The cover story is designed to make all features of the experiment plausible to the participant, yet maintain any deception that may be necessary to obtain responses similar to those that would be obtained if the participants actually were confronted with this same situation in their normal lives.

A relatively simple cover story was used in a recent *intra-audience* effects study. Intra-audience effects refer to the impact that audience response to a speech (or some other kind of stimulus) has on *other* audience members. Participants in this study were students enrolled in basic public speaking classes. They were brought into the laboratory during a regular class meeting. In this case the laboratory consisted of a large classroomlike room, which already had about 12 participants seated randomly about, waiting for the research to start. In reality, these individuals were confederates, individuals working with and trained by the researcher. Specifically, they had been instructed to provide either positive or negative feedback to the speech and speaker. The cover story stated that the purpose of the research was to examine people's reactions to various public speeches (slightly untrue) and explained that the individuals already in the room also were participants who happened to be enrolled in another public speaking course which met at the same time (patently untrue).

Depending on the needs of the experiment, cover stories may be simple or elaborate. The counterattitudinal advocacy experiments described in Chapter 3 had extremely elaborate cover stories and typically included several levels of deception embedded within one another. Other cover stories may be very straightforward and simply state in general, but truthful terms, what is being studied. Because it provides a potential difference in how the participants may react to the experimental stimulus, the cover story is always reported in the method section of an experimental study so that others can replicate it exactly as it was conducted.

Assign Participants Randomly to Conditions

The experimental and control groups need to be made as nearly equal as possible in every possible way. This is done through random assignment of participants to conditions. Each person must have an equal probability of being assigned to both the experimental and control groups. This can be accomplished by flipping a coin, pulling names from a thoroughly shaken hat, assigning those with even Social Security numbers to one condition and those with odd numbers to the other, or, probably best, through the use of a table of random numbers. With the random numbers table, the first person may be assigned the first number in the table, the second is assigned the second, and so on. If there are two groups in the experiment, those with even numbers would be assigned to one group and those with odd numbers to the other. If there were three groups, those with numbers ending in 1, 2, or 3 could be assigned to one group, those with numbers ending in 4, 5, or 6 could be assigned to the second group, and those with numbers ending in 7, 8, 9 could be assigned to the third group. Those with numbers ending in 0 would be reassigned another number. If one group received one-third of the participants before a second group, those subsequently assigned to the full group would be randomly assigned to one of the two remaining groups, and so on, until all groups had equal numbers of randomly assigned participants. With a little thought and creativity, a table of random numbers can be used to assign people randomly to conditions, regardless of the number of conditions. Additionally, most microcomputer statistical packages now have a random number generator that can be used in place of the random numbers tables found in most statistics books.[10]

Assigning *intact* classes, or those participants who arrive first to an experimental session, to one group and other intact classes, or those who arrived later, to a second group does *not* constitute random assignment. Similarly, participants should not be allowed to select to which of several groups he or she will be assigned.

On the surface it may seem perfectly random to allow participants to choose for themselves whether to participate on, for example, a Wednesday or Thursday night, and to then administer the experimental treatment on one of these nights and the control condition on the other. However, it could well be that something is systematically different about people who select one night over another. And, this possibility creates a potential extraneous variable, a rival explanation for any differences observed on the dependent variable between the experimental and control groups. Therefore, if a research project must be run over several days, each condition should run each day to ensure that randomness is achieved.

Manipulation of the Independent Variable

Once people are randomly assigned to conditions, the members of each group must be exposed to the various levels of the independent variable. Elliot Aronson and J. Merrill Carlsmith in a thorough, detailed paper on experimentation emphasize three concerns faced by the experimenter as he or she tries to operationalize the independent variable.[11] The first asks what specific event corresponds to his theoretical independent variable.[12] That is, the operationalization of the independent variable needs to capture some of the meaning of the conceptual definition of the variable. For example, if the independent variable is audience feedback, what specific behaviors in a given situation constitute positive and negative feedback. If the variable is a fear appeal message, what specific message content constitutes high and low fear appeals. If the variable is relationship disengagement strategies, what specific strategies are consistent with the variable's conceptual definition. Or, if the variable is physical distance between interactants, how are participants made to assume various distances?

Second, how can the levels of the variable be presented to the participants to produce the maximum effect? The impact of a variable that exists in the real world can seldom be recreated in the communication researcher's laboratory. He or she can show films that either do or do not depict violent content, but however violent the laboratory stimulus, it pales before the hundreds and hundreds of hours of exposure to violent media content available to people outside the laboratory. Similarly, the audience feedback that could plausibly be emitted by students listening to a speech in a classroom setting is probably negligible in intensity and effect compared to the audience response possible at a political rally, sporting event, or rock concert. Thus, the researcher's task is to expose the participants to the levels of the independent variable in as powerful a form as possible.

Finally, Aronson and Carlsmith note that on occasion the manipulation of the independent variable may tip off "cooperative" participants to provide the responses that they think the researcher wants. This is also a problem during the measurement phase of an experiment.

Unfortunately there are few, if any, widely accepted techniques for manipulating a particular independent variable. Although studying previous research in an area as part of the literature review may provide clues about how to proceed, the researcher must frequently create unique manipulations to fit his or her situation. Aronson and Carlsmith note that there are basically two ways to present the manipulation of an independent variable: Participants can be presented with a set of verbal *instructions* or they can be presented with an *event* of some kind. Assume that we are interested in assessing the effect the height of a person has on perceptions of his or her credibility in a job interview setting. An instructions manipulation might involve telling participants that the male job candidate whose credentials they were examining was either 5'3" tall or was 6'3" tall. An event manipulation would involve actually presenting the participants with a job candidate who was actually either 5'3" or 6'3" tall. Clearly, an event manipulation will, in general, be more realistic and have more impact than an instruction manipulation. Not surprisingly, Aronson and Carlsmith argue for event manipulations whenever possible.

An especially realistic and effective event manipulation was carried out by James Stiff and Gerald Miller in their study of lying and truthful communication behavior.[13] They needed to create a situation in which participants either lied or told the truth as they were being interrogated. Participants were told in the cover story that the purpose of the research was to study "dyadic problem solving." Thus, it seemed quite natural to the participants when they were placed with another participant (really a confederate) and given a problem to solve. Further, they were told that the dyad that scored the highest on the problem-solving task would receive a substantial financial reward. Soon after each dyad had begun work on the task, the researcher was called out of the room. For half the dyads the confederate proceeded, as instructed by the researcher, to attempt to convince the participant to cheat on the task by looking at the answer, which had been conveniently left in a folder on the researcher's desk. (Almost all participants in this condition did collaborate in the cheating episode.) For the other half of the participants, cheating was not induced; that is, the confederate and the participant simply completed the task together. The researcher then returned, scored the completed task, and feigned great surprise at how well they had done. The participants were subsequently interrogated about how they had done so well. Of course, half of the participants, those who had been induced to cheat, were forced to lie in response to the interrogator's questions. This technique resulted in a realistic and relatively powerful manipulation. Note also the role of the cover story in setting up a situation that allowed a smooth and plausible manipulation of the independent variable.

As important as presenting a valid and powerful manipulation of the independent variable to participants is, it is equally important to take great care to assure that this is the *only* difference between what happens to those in the groups that make up the conditions of the experiment. Participants must be treated identically, or as nearly identical as possible, in every other way. Thus, for example, in Stiff and Miller's experiment, the researcher was called out of the room in *both* the lying and truthful conditions; and the confederate was carefully trained to behave in the same ways in both conditions, except for the cheating incident. Further, the person who interrogated the participants was *blind* (unaware) as to whether a particular participant had cheated or not. Sometimes, care is taken to assure that even the experimenters—anyone part of the research team who comes into contact with the participants—are blind to the experimental condition of which specific participants are part of. This is called a *double-blind* experiment and is done to reduce *demand* biases that the experimenter may introduce by unconsciously treating participants in different conditions differently. Equal care in holding conditions constant is taken in every well-controlled experiment.

Measuring the Dependent Variable and the Success of Manipulation of the Independent Variable

The measures discussed in Chapter 6 have potential applicability for assessing the impact of the experimental manipulation on the dependent variable. Basically, there are two kinds of dependent measures: *paper and pencil* measures, in which participants respond to scales and/or open-ended questions; and *behavioral* measures, which are generally unobtrusive, that is, the participant is unaware that he is being measured. Unfortunately, the measurement process has the potential to tip off the true purpose of the experiment to the participants, which, in turn, could influence their responses. Thus, if the experiment involves deception, the measurement procedure frequently needs either to appear to the participant to be consistent with the cover story, to be unobtrusive, or to appear to be unrelated to the research project entirely.

Thus, for example, in studies of the effectiveness of various persuasive messages, the relevant dependent measure could be embedded in a large attitude survey distributed in class a week or so after the exposure to the experimental stimulus. In the Stiff and Miller deception experiment, participants were surreptitiously videotaped as they lied or told the truth, and their behaviors were later coded by observers. In a study on the impact of personal space violations and persuasion, Don Stacks and Judee Burgoon administered the attitude-change questionnaire (the actual attitude scales were buried amid ten other attitude statements) as part of a larger study being conducted on campus at the same time. [14] They informed their participants that because so many students were participating in their study (the cover story concerned an examination of human-human and human-machine interaction) the researchers conducting the attitude survey wanted to canvas them also. They even went so far as to ask if any of their participants had completed the survey before. Debriefings indicated that the cover story worked for both the procedures and the posttest attitude measure.

Whenever possible, it is important to assess the success of the manipulation of the independent variable by directly measuring participants' perceptions of this variable. Such measures are called *manipulation checks*. For example, if source credibility has been manipulated, the measuring instrument would include a direct measure of participant perceptions of source credibility. If the amount of conflict in a small group discussion was manipulated, member perceptions of the amount of conflict present would be assessed. Manipulation checks are especially important whenever the results of an experiment indicate that an independent and a dependent variable are *not* related. Whenever such an outcome is observed there are two possible explanations: Either the variables really *are* related, but something about the procedures of this particular experiment failed to allow this relationship to be revealed empirically, *or,* the theory is wrong and the variables are not related. The purpose of the manipulation check is to provide evidence bearing on these explanations. If the independent variable and dependent variable are *not* found to be related and the manipulation check indicates that the manipulation was perceived as intended, this evidence suggests that the theory *may* be wrong.[15] On the other hand, if the manipulation check demonstrates that the manipulation was *not* perceived as intended, then this is evidence that the experiment has not provided a good test of the theory, that the procedures were inadequate.

Debriefing

In Chapter 3 we emphasized the importance of the debriefing for ethical reasons—specifically to undo any deception, restore or maintain a positive relationship between the experimenter and the participant, and to make research participation a positive educational experience for the participant. Here, we will briefly mention a fourth purpose: to provide the researcher with information about the efficacy of the experimental procedures. Was the participant suspicious about the research? What did he or she think was the reason for the research? Why did he or she display that particular behavior? Answers to questions such as these can help the researcher make adjustments to these procedures (particularly if they are asked in sessions following participation in a pilot test of the experimental procedures), make corrections in the procedures used in future research, and even provide clues relevant to the accuracy and thoroughness of the theory being tested. As noted earlier, Stacks and Burgoon used the debriefing to check if participants were suspicious of the procedures, especially the additional "survey" completed at the end of the study. Debriefing, then, is more than an ethical consideration; it has practical applications also.

ROLE-PLAYING AS AN ALTERNATIVE TO DECEPTION IN EXPERIMENTS

Role-playing involves telling participants about a situation and asking them to pretend that they are really in that situation. Role-playing can be used as an experimental method because different groups of people can be asked to imagine that they find themselves in different circumstances. There are two reasons why a researcher might use role-playing as an alternative to deception in an experiment: Ethical reasons and practical reasons. We will discuss the ethical reasons first.

Ethical Concerns

Although we discussed the ethical treatment of human participants in research projects in some detail in Chapter 3, the impression should not be created that once considered, ethics can be put on the back burner. Rather, ethical concerns are an integral part of all phases of research projects. This point can be made in no better place than here, in the context of discussing experiments, because experiments involve deception. Whenever we lie to a research participant it is a serious matter. The deception must be justified on the grounds that (1) there is no reasonable alternative that will allow the researcher to answer the research question(s) without using deception, (2) neither the deception nor its revelation during the debriefing will bring harm to participant, and (3) the research question is an important one and the knowledge gained by answering it is substantial.

Social psychologist Herbert Kelman has been an outspoken critic of the use of deception. He argues that [16]:

> Serious ethical issues are raised by deception *per se* and the kind of use of human beings it implies . . . Yet we seem to forget that the experimenter-subject relationship, whatever else it is—is a *real* interhuman relationship, in which we have a responsibility toward the subject as another human being whose dignity we must preserve.

Kelman goes on to advocate role-playing as an alternative to deception. But the problem with role-playing, as a research methodology, is that it provides information about what people *think* they would do, not necessarily what they would do if actually confronted with a particular situation. As Jonathon Freedman notes, "experimental results are not always easy to predict; people do not always behave the way that they or we expect them to." [17]

Nonetheless, some research questions may involve deceptions that are so severe that role-playing is the only alternative to abandoning the research question entirely. If, for example, we were interested in assessing the impact of a serious news event, we could not falsely tell participants that certain serious events, such as, for example, a major earthquake in California, had occurred. In such a situation role-playing would be our only alternative. We should add that the more realistic the role-playing situation we are able to create, the more valid will be the data our pretending participants provide.

Practical Concerns

Some important independent variables simply cannot be operationalized adequately in the laboratory. For example, suppose we were interested in which of several relationship dissolution strategies resulted in the least damage to the self-concept of the disengagee. We simply could not realistically bring in 100 intimate couples, assign half to one condition and the other half to another condition and then enlist one partner as a confederate and have him or her use one or the other strategy to end the relationship, then measure the other partner's self-concept. Even if this procedure were not patently unethical, it would be impossible to conduct this, and many other communication studies, for purely practical reasons. In such situations, role-playing may be an alternative. If we ask people to imagine a situation, such as a date with their intimate partner, make the situation as realistic as possible, and ask them to imagine that their partner then ended the relationship with one of the strategies, we may obtain results approximating those of actual relationship disengagement.

LIMITATIONS OF THE LABORATORY EXPERIMENT

Type of Questions

A good many questions simply are not amenable to experimentation. As noted earlier, exploratory investigations into new areas are probably best answered with other methods, such as field studies and focus groups. Questions involving large populations of people—such as, How do Americans feel about the creation of a Palestinian state in the Middle East?—similarly are not appropriate for experiments.

Generalizability of Findings

Laboratory experiments frequently are conducted in a highly contrived environment, one that may bear little resemblance to the circumstances typically faced by individuals as they communicate in their normal lives. This *artificiality*, especially when extreme, requires that great caution be used in generalizing the findings to more realistic circumstances. However, as sociologist George C. Homans notes, "The laws of human behavior are not repealed when a man leaves the field and enters the laboratory."[18] With this weakness in mind, we should strive to make the laboratory environment as realistic as possible.

A related concern involves the population from which participants in laboratory experiments are typically drawn. In Chapter 8 the importance of sampling was emphasized. It was noted that the ability to generalize from samples to populations was limited by the sampling procedures and estimates of sampling error. You learned that probability samples are most likely to be representative of, and thus generalizable to, the population from which they are drawn. From what population is the sample of respondents who participate in most communication research randomly drawn? None. They are almost always an *availability sample* —and most commonly an availability sample of undergraduate college students. Is this problem so serious that it eliminates our ability to generalize the findings to other populations? Not nearly to the extent that some critics of experimentation would suggest. The key question is: Are college students, and even more specifically, volunteers enrolled in introductory communication courses, different, *with regard to the variables being studied*, than human beings in general?

Assume for a moment that we are interested in determining the effect of taking a pin and pricking a person's finger on the production of blood on the fingertip. Does it matter whether we use a college student or not? Of course not. Blood is going to appear, no matter who we study. Now take an example of something we might actually study. Are individuals involved in intimate relationships that are characterized by high amounts of self-disclosure more satisfied in these relationships than those who are in relationships that have lower amounts of self-disclosure? Although this is an empirical question, we are going to venture an answer based on the use of reason. Our best guess is that in many ways, and specifically in this case with regard to self-disclosure and relational satisfaction, college students are a lot like other human beings. Most relationships observed between communication variables in samples drawn from college students probably exist in other human beings, even in populations from which our sample was not randomly drawn. Unless there is a good reason to think that college students are different with regard to the variables under study than the population to which we want to generalize the findings, it is reasonable, in our opinion, to proceed to generalize.

This is not to say that caution in generalizing our findings should not be exercised. Caution is fundamental to science. Limitations on findings should be emphasized; weaknesses and artificiality should be pointed out explicitly; caveats should abound; results should be interpreted conservatively and generalized cautiously. Whenever possible, findings should be replicated using different (and more realistic) methods (triangulation of the results based on the use of different methods) and populations. Until the results of such replications are available, claims of relationships between variables should be met with skepticism. *However*, experimental results should not be dismissed casually, as occasionally has happened, simply because the research context was the laboratory and the sample studied consisted of college students.

Weakness of the Independent Variable

Kerlinger asserts that "the greatest weakness of the laboratory experiment is probably the lack of strength of the independent variables."[19] In spite of Stiff and Miller's success at creating a realistic situation in which participants lied or told the truth, the consequences for the participant of being caught in the lie were minor compared to that which would exist in many normal life situations. If caught, they would have lost the financial reward they thought they were about to receive and would perhaps have suffered considerable embarrassment. Compare this to being caught lying to one's spouse about being involved in an extramarital affair, or to the IRS about an income tax return.

Communication can have powerful effects in our daily lives. Communication can create elation and depression; it can cause or prevent love or hate; it can change significant attitudes and behaviors. Yet these powerful outcomes are rarely, if ever, obtainable with the relatively weak manipulations of independent variables that are achievable in the laboratory. Thus, if a variable *can* be shown to have an effect in a laboratory, this might well be taken as suggesting that this variable will have more powerful effects in our daily lives.

SUMMARY

This chapter introduced what some consider to be the ultimate form of research: the laboratory experiment. In particular, we have introduced the classic experiment, the true laboratory experiment. The experiment, a controlled manipulation of an independent variable whose effects are measured on a dependent variable, allows us to go one step further in the research process: We not only gain under-standing, but we now can predict the relationships between the effects of the independent and dependent variable. The experiment is a systematic, controlled, and rigorous test of the relationships between variables.

The chapter also introduced the procedures and concerns of experimental researchers. A general overview of the laboratory experiment was provided, with emphasis on establishing the cover story, random assignment, manipulation of the independent variable(s), dependent variable measurement, and deception and de-briefing. Finally, an alternative method to deception was discussed and the limita-tions and disadvantages of the method presented. This chapter has focused on the simple, classic, experiment, and has presented the material necessary to carry out an experiment.

PROBES

1. What advantages does the experimental method present the communication researcher, compared to field studies? Compared to surveys? What are the disadvantages?

2. The experiment typically addresses empirical questions. Based on your area of interest, what are some *significant* research questions amenable to experimental method? Why are they more appropriate to this method than others?

3. The concepts of control and causation are important to experiments. Why? Can you establish causation without control? Why or why not? What do you give up to achieve control?

4. What are the ethical implications of the well-designed experiment? Are there certain research questions that might be unethical to test using experimental method? From your area of interest, what questions might *not* be ethically appropriate for experimental testing? Why?

5. Suppose that you are interested in the possibility that violence on television contributes to spousal abuse. Design an experiment to test this relationship; what is your independent variable? What are the levels or conditions you will use? Set up your experimental procedures by first using a pencil and paper dependent measure and then by a behavioral dependent measure. What cover story will you use? What type of debriefing will you employ? Critique your study.

SUGGESTED READING

Campbell, D. T., & Stanley, J. C. (1963). *Experimental and quasi-experimental designs for research.* Chicago: Rand McNally.

Jones, Russell A. (1985). *Research methods in the social and behavioral sciences.* Sunder-land, MA: Sinauer Associates. Chapters 7, 8, & 9.

Kerlinger, F. N. (1986). *Foundations of behavioral research* (3rd ed.). New York: Holt, Rinehart and Winston.

Miller, G. R. (1970). Research settings: Laboratory experiments. In P. Emmert and W. D. Brooks (Eds.), *Methods of Research in Communication.* Boston: Houghton Mifflin.

Rosenthal, R. *Experimenter effects in behavioral research* (2nd ed.). New York: Halsted Press, 1976.

NOTES

1. We are defining theory here as we did in Chapter 2. See Fred N. Kerlinger, *Foundations of Behavioral Research*, 3rd ed. (New York: Holt, Rinehart, & Winston, 1986), 9.
2. For a discussion of such variables and their impact see Mark Hickson, III, and Don W. Stacks, *NVC: Nonverbal Communication Studies and Applications*, 2nd ed. (Dubuque: William C. Brown, 1988), Chaps. 2 and 4.
3. For a good study that used touches as the independent variable, see Beth E. Pressner, "The Therapeutic Implications of Touching During Articulation Therapy," M.A. Thesis, University of Florida, 1978.
4. James C. McCroskey and Thomas A. McCain, "The Measurement of Interpersonal Attraction," *Speech Monographs*, 41 (1974), 261–266.
5. Donald T. Campbell and Julian C. Stanley, "Quasi-Experimental Design for Research on Teaching," in N. L. Gage, ed., *Handbook of Research on Teaching* (Chicago: Rand McNally, 1963). This paper has become one of the most influential and widely cited contributions to research methodology in the social sciences. The treatment of research design presented in this book, like those in many of the methodology books published in the last 20 years, is based on Campbell and Stanley's treatment. For those students particularly interested in experimental design, this reading is essential.
6. Kerlinger, 361.
7. See: Campbell and Stanley.
8. Earl C. Babbie, *The Practice of Social Research*, 4th ed. (Belmont, Calif.: Wadsworth, 1986), 90.
9. Kerlinger, 34–35.
10. See, for example, James Boulding's program, Statistics with Finesse (P.O. Box 339, Fayetteville, Ark.).
11. Elliot Aronson and J. Merrill Carlsmith, "Experimentation in Social Psychology," in Gardiner Lindzey and Elliot Aronson, eds., *Handbook of Social Psychology*, Vol. 2 (Reading, Mass.: Addison-Wesley, 1954), 1–79.
12. Aronson and Carlsmith, 42.
13. James B. Stiff and Gerald R. Miller, "'Come to Think of It . . .': Interrogative Probes, Deceptive Communication, and Deception Detection," *Human Communication Research*, 12 (1986), 339–357. This procedure was originally used by R. V. Exline, J. Thibaut, C. B. Hickey, and P. Gumpert, "Visual Interaction in Relation to Machiavellianism and an Unethical Act," in R. Christie and F. Geis, eds., *Studies in Machiavellianism* (New York: Academic, 1970), 53–75.
14. Don W. Stacks and Judee K. Burgoon, "The Role of Nonverbal Behaviors as Distractors in Resistance to Persuasion in Interpersonal Contexts," *Central States Speech Journal*, 32 (1981), 61–73.
15. It is not *definitive* evidence; no one study, by itself, can determine conclusively whether a theory is correct or incorrect. Rather, each study adds evidence to patterns which ultimately increase the confidence with which conclusions are drawn. See Chapter 2 for a review of the process of science.
16. Herbert C. Kelman, "Use of Human Subjects: The Problem of Deception in Social Psychological Experiments," *Psychological Bulletin*, 67 (1967), 5.

17. Jonathon L. Freedman, "Role Playing: Psychology by Consensus," *Journal of Personality and Social Psychology,* 13 (1969), 110.
18. George C. Homans, *Social Behavior: Its Elementary Forms* (New York: Harcourt, Brace, & World, 1961), 15; cited in Gerald R. Miller, "Research Settings: Laboratory Studies," in Philip Emmert and William D. Brooks, eds., *Methods of Research in Communication* (Boston: Houghton Mifflin, 1970), 81.
19. Kerlinger, 367.

Chapter
10

Experimental Strategies and Designs

*R*esearch often requires trade-offs between what the researcher really wants to do and what he or she can realistically impose on the variables and participants in the study. This chapter examines the impact of such trade-offs on the rigor and control of the experiment. We begin with an overview, a synthesis of previous discussion, then we move to an examination of what Donald T. Campbell and Julian C. Stanley have termed quasi-experimental design.[1] We will then examine more complex "true" experimental designs and discuss the advantages and limitations of these more complex experiments.

As we noted in Chapter 9, comparisons are central to establishing the relationships between variables, and therefore central to scientific inquiry. The most rigorous comparisons are possible in well-controlled experiments in which participants are randomly assigned to experimental and control groups; conditions are held constant, except for the manipulated independent variable, and the effect of the manipulation on the dependent variable is observed. This ideal experiment is usually only possible in the laboratory. However, for a variety of reasons, there are many times when we want to study the relationships between variables but cannot meet this ideal. We cannot design and conduct a true experiment that adequately addresses our research question. Sometimes we are unable to assign participants to conditions at random. Sometimes we are unable to hold conditions constant in two groups. Sometimes we are unable to manipulate a particular independent variable in the confines of the laboratory. Under these circumstances we may have no alternative (other than to choose a different research question) but to conduct a study that has some of the elements of a rigorous laboratory experiment, that resembles the design of such an experiment and allows us to make comparisons that help us answer our research question, but falls short of meeting all the criteria of the true experiment. Such studies are called *quasi-experiments.*

QUASI-EXPERIMENTAL DESIGN

Quasi-experiment is a broad term, which refers to *any research project in which, although one or more features of a true experiment are not present, the effect of an independent variable is studied by making comparisons between groups exposed to different levels of the independent variable.* Subsumed under quasi-experiments are field experiments, in which a researcher is able to manipulate a variable in a natural setting, and natural experiments, in which the researcher is able to observe the effects of some naturally occurring event. True experiments and quasi-experiments have the same basic goal: to study the relationships between variables. The quasi-experiment, however, attempts to *approximate* the rigorous comparisons allowed by a true experiment as closely as possible. As the number of features present in a true experiment that are absent in a quasi-experiment increase, that is, as the resemblance between the two is diminished, the confidence that can be placed in the results must be reduced accordingly. We begin our discussion of quasi-experiments with an attempt to apply the logic of experimentation to a naturally occurring event.

On October 19, 1987, the Dow Jones Industrial Average of the New York Stock Exchange, the most widely followed index of stock price movements, dropped over 500 points, by far the biggest drop in its history, even including the disastrous "crash" of 1929. Stock prices in general, and "the Dow" in particular, are widely assumed to be indicative of the economic health of the country. The 1987 drop was taken as almost irrefutable evidence that the long run of the bull market and of a healthy, growing economy was over. Journalists, politicians, and many ordinary people spent considerable time discussing possible causes of this event. Democrats in Congress said the cause was President Reagan's economic policies, tax cuts for the rich, and so on. President Reagan blamed the crash on the Democrats' unwillingness to enact his economic policies fully, such as agreeing to even deeper cuts in domestic spending. Almost everyone agreed, however, that the crash had something to do with the large federal deficits, at that time approaching nearly

$2 hundred billion a year. Other causes to which the crash was attributed included a large international trade deficit, policies of the Federal Reserve Board, an over-valued dollar, an undervalued dollar, and the Iran-Contra affair.

What caused the stock market crash? It could be any of the factors mentioned, some combination of them, or none of them. We do not know, and worse, we do not have a good way to find out. The problem is that we do not have anything with which to *compare* the stock market crash, and the circumstances that preceded it. We do not know what would have happened to the stock market if President Reagan had different economic policies, or if the Democrats had agreed to more domestic cuts, or if the trade deficit had been smaller. There is no convenient set of *different* circumstances against which to compare what we know actually did happen. And, as noted in Chapter 9, comparisons are essential to establishing with confidence that variables are related. In turn, the kinds of comparisons that a particular *experimental design* allow us to make are what differentiates *true* experiments from *quasi-*experiments, inferior from superior designs. A research design is a structure or model of the relationships among variables being studied in a research project. As noted in Chapter 9, it is the design's structure that allows us to make comparisons that warrant confidence in the conclusions about the relationships being studied.

In Chapter 9 we demonstrated the design of the classical experiment. In the following sections we will continue to illustrate various designs using Campbell and Stanley's notation system. Recall that an R represents random assignment, and the lack of an R means there has not been random assignment. An X is used to refer to a stimulus of some kind. It could represent an economic policy, marijuana use, rock music, a speech—in short, anything to which research participants are exposed. An O refers to an observation, that is, a measurement. The X's and O's on the same horizontal rows are applied to the same individuals or objects. The main criterion by which designs are examined is the rigor of the comparisons that can be made. We now examine how a variety of designs, which when used in research, stack up in terms of this criterion.

One-Shot Case Study

The most basic design presented by Campbell and Stanley is the one-shot case study (see Design 10.1). This design can be used in two forms: The X can happen first and then the O is observed, or the O is observed and then the researcher goes

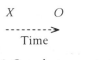

Design 10.1 One-shot case study.

looking for an X. In the first form, something is made to happen or is observed happening naturally and something else is observed. For example, to study the impact of a persuasive speech, the researcher might expose a group of participants to it and then measure their attitudes toward the topic. The researcher wants to attribute the postspeech attitudes to the impact of the speech. Unfortunately, this design does not allow such an attribution to be made. It really does not even qualify as a quasi-experimental design. The reason: *No* comparisons are possible and therefore this design provides no evidence about the impact of the speech. The participants' postspeech attitudes might be a result of anything.

The other form of this design is that something happens and then, after the fact, the researcher goes looking for causes, a post hoc explanation of the relationship between stimulus and observation. Examples of use of this design are not hard to find. In each case the researcher observes an outcome and then looks for events that preceded the event to which to attribute causality. In the earlier stock market example, the researcher observes a 500-point drop in the Dow Jones Average and looks for the X's that explain the drop. Frequently, there is a strong temptation to conclude that because something preceded something else in time, it must be the cause of what it preceded—that if X preceded Y, X *must* have caused Y. This is especially true when the causal relationship is one that is consistent with our preconceived prejudices or is in our political self-interest. Thus, when something bad happens, as with the stock market crash, we find politicians conveniently and confidently attributing the cause to the X's created by the other party.

Other examples might include a study in which a psychotic killer is interviewed in prison and indicates that he viewed pornography as an adolescent. The interviewer then concludes that exposure to pornography causes violent behavior. But, even assuming the killer is being truthful, we do not know what the individual's behavior would have been if his life had been identical in every way, except with regard to exposure to pornography; even though we can *infer* that there are some similarities, we have not controlled the study on that variable. Or, a researcher finds that 984 out of 1000 pregnant, unwed teenaged girls conceived their babies (O) while listening to rock music (X) and concludes that rock music causes premarital sexual activity. Even assuming that the statistic is factual, there is no way to know if *these* mothers would have ended up pregnant if the rock music had been removed from their lives.

The problem with this design is fundamental: There is *nothing* against which to compare our observations, that is, the O. Thus, we are unable to conclude that the X and the O are related. We may speculate that they are, we may use other "methods of knowing" such as tenacity, intuition, or authority to conclude that they are, but scientifically we have *no* evidence that the X and the O are indeed related. [2]

One Group Pretest-Posttest Design

To improve the design and raise it to the level of minimal scientific respectability *we must be able to make at least one comparison.* The "one group pretest-posttest" design allows for such a comparison (see Design 10.2).

$$O_1 \qquad X \qquad O_2$$
-------------------->

Design 10.2 One group pretest-posttest design.

With this design, observations are made both before and after exposure to a stimulus. For example, to study the effects of taking a course in public speaking on communication apprehension, we could measure student communication apprehension, then expose the students to the stimulus (the X—that is, they would take the course), and then measure apprehension a second time. This is an obvious improvement over the one-shot case study because we now can compare the audience's postcourse apprehension with their precourse apprehension. Any changes *might* be a result of taking the course and, therefore, might be attributed to the course. To the extent that we can confidently attribute any changes between O_1 and O_2 to X, our study has *internal validity*. Internal validity refers to whether a stimulus—the public speaking course in this case—had a known effect in *this particular study*. To the extent that observed results are attributable to the course, the study is internally valid. However, we emphasized the word "might" because there are other possible explanations that could account for the differences between O_1 and O_2. Each of these other explanations represents a threat to the study's internal validity.

Threats to Internal Validity   There may be other things, many other things, hundreds of other things, that happen to participants between a pretest (O_1) and a posttest (O_2) in an experiment besides exposure to the independent variable (the public speaking course). In the public speaking study, the students could have observed a skilled speaker, or had a successful speaking experience in a nonclassroom setting, or undergone psychological counseling, or terminated a relationship, or begun a relationship, and so on—the list is endless. The point is not that any of these events necessarily had an impact on the subsequent amount of communication apprehension experienced by the participants, but rather, we *do not know* if they did or not. Thus, all of these events are part of the participants' *history* between O_1 and O_2 and are threats to the study's internal validity.[3] That is, they threaten the degree to which changes between O_1 and O_2 are known to be a result of X—the stimulus.

Second, the participants may simply change with the passage of time. They certainly will grow older, but also may become bored, sleepy, energetic, smarter, hungrier, and so on, completely independent of the fact that they are involved in a research study. Our public speaking students are likely to mature somewhat during the course of a 10- or 15-week term and this maturation process would occur whether they were enrolled in a public speaking course or not. Since this *maturation* process could result in reduced—or increased—communication apprehension, it is a threat to the study's internal validity.

Third, the measurement of the participants at O_1 may affect the scores they receive on the second measure at O_2. Assume that we measured communication apprehension at O_1 by having each student make a speech, which was videotaped and shown to trained observers who coded a variety of verbal and nonverbal indicators of anxiety. At O_2, after completing the public speaking course, they deliver the speech again. Any difference between O_1 and O_2 could be a result of the speech made as part of O_1. Participants might display less (or more) anxiety at O_2, regardless of whether they took a public speaking course or not. Again, the point is not that the O_1 measurement necessarily affected the O_2 measurement, but rather that we *do not know* if it did, and thus it also is a threat to the study's internal validity. Alternatively, we might have measured communication apprehension with a paper and pencil measure. Responding to the Likert-type items on this measure might affect how someone would respond to these same items 10–15 weeks later. Perhaps they would cause some participants to dwell on their communication apprehension and this introspective process might affect the subsequent responses, even if they were not enrolled in the public speaking class. The effects of a measure on subsequent applications of the same measure is commonly called a *testing* effect, a term derived from educational research, where the effects of taking a test may have an effect on the scores of subsequent testings. Testing is a threat to the internal validity of Design 10.2.

Fourth, depending on the measurement technique selected, the rules for assigning numbers to observations may not be applied in exactly the same way at O_1 and O_2. For example, if the participants' speeches were being observed and coded for the amount of apprehension displayed, the observer might become bored or fatigued. This, and any other such changes, might affect the way the coders evaluate the O_2 speeches. Campbell and Stanley term this threat to internal validity *instrumentation*, "in which changes in the calibration of a measuring instrument or changes in the observers or scorers used may produce changes in the obtained measurements."[4]

Fifth, if the participants have been selected to participate in the research because of their extreme scores on O_1, there is a tendency for them to receive less extreme scores at O_2. This is because extreme scores are extreme, in part because of measurement unreliability; that is, random chance. If someone scores extremely well on an exam, frequently they do not do quite as well on the next one. Similarly, someone scoring extremely low on an exam will frequently do better the next time. In other words, extreme scores tend to *regress* toward the mean of all scores on a second testing. If all 4000 freshmen entering a particular university were given a particular test for some variable, and those 50 students who scored the highest were selected for the study, it is almost certain that they would score lower on the second application of the measure, whether they took public speaking or not. Campbell and Stanley call this phenomenon *statistical regression.*

Sixth, some participants may drop out of the research project. If they did so randomly, that is, if those who were lost were representative of all the participants, this would not be a problem. The problem is that those who drop out may be systematically different in ways relevant to what is being studied from those who complete the project. In the public speaking study, it seems probable that those students who have severe communication apprehension are much more likely to drop the class than those who do not. These same students may be the ones who would have been the most affected by the experience of taking the class. However, since they are not around to provide scores at O_2, we would never know. Their absence is a threat to the internal validity of the design. Campbell and Stanley label this threat *mortality*. We prefer the label *attrition*, since death is rarely the cause of a subject failing to complete a research project in the social sciences.[5]

Thus, while the pretest-posttest design is a marked improvement over the one-shot case study, it still possesses major threats to its internal validity. History, maturation, testing, instrumentation, statistical regression, and attrition all provide potentially rival explanations for differences between O_1 and O_2, other than X.

Nonequivalent Group Comparison

The nonequivalent group—or static-group comparison design (see Design 10.3)—provides some good and some bad news for the internal validity of the experiment. The good news is that it allows us to rule out some of the alternative explanations; the bad news is that it opens the door to others.

In this design, a group of participants that have been exposed to a stimulus is compared to a group that has not. Consider the earlier example, in which we examined the impact of a public speaking course on communication apprehension. To answer the research question posed in that study (Does a course in public speaking change student's communication apprehension?) with a static-group comparison design, a group of students that had a course in public speaking is compared to a control group that did not. To the extent that the groups are equivalent, except with regard to exposure to the stimulus, O_1 - O_2 differences can be attributed to the X. If the public speaking veterans have less communication apprehension, the researcher can conclude with some confidence that the class *reduced* communication apprehension.

How can we come to this conclusion? Assuming group equivalency, *history* is not a problem because extraneous events happen to both groups equally. *Maturation* is not a problem because both groups are measured at the same point in time, thus any maturation *should* be the same for both groups. Any *instrumentation* effect should affect both groups equally. *Testing* is not a problem because there is no pretest given. *Statistical regression* is eliminated as a possible rival explanation because, since both groups are measured only once, neither could be selected for participation based on their extreme scores.

However, some problems still occur. If, for instance, the stimulus caused some

$$X \qquad O_1$$
$$\text{-------->}$$
$$O_2$$

Design 10.3 Nonequivalent group comparison.

participants to drop out, as would likely be the case in the communication appre-hension study, *attrition* would still be a problem; that is, the students high in communication apprehension might be inclined to drop the class, therefore drop-ping out of the research. Their counterparts in the control group would not be enrolled in the class so they would not drop out. Thus, the initially equivalent groups might become nonequivalent through attrition. But on the whole, *assuming initial equivalency,* this design looks pretty good. Unfortunately, the bad news is that we cannot assume equivalency. *Intact groups are almost always unique.* They are different from other groups. And, it could be the fact that the groups are different that accounts for differences between O_1 and O_2, and not the fact that one group received the treatment—the X.

For example, students enrolled in a public speaking class are different from students not enrolled in such a course. In fact, we know that students who have extremely high communication apprehension will go to great lengths to avoid enrolling in such a class. It would not be surprising to find that students enrolled in an interpersonal communication class would report more communication appre-hension as measured on the Personal Report of Communication Anxiety (PRCA) than students in the public speaking class.[6] But this difference would not be because of the experience of taking the class—the X—it would be because of the method of *selection* of the participants. In this case they themselves have selected whether they are in the control group or the experimental group.

It may be that the two groups are quite similar; and, the more similar they are, the better this design. However, while we might marshal evidence that they are similar, without *random assignment* we will never know definitely that they are and, thus, the rigor of our comparisons is reduced.[7] Our O_1 - O_2 comparison may really be comparing apples to oranges, cheese to Tuesday, seashells to Germans. The point is that the *nonequivalency of the groups,* the selection problem, pro-vides a *major* threat to the internal validity of the design.

Any group that we find existing intact is likely to be different from any other group. Let us look at two examples. First, a researcher is interested in assessing the effects of the physical attractiveness of a speaker on attitude change toward the speech topic. Two videotapes are made of an individual making the same persuasive speech. In one condition the source's physical attractiveness has been lowered through the use of makeup. In the second condition the source has been made to be as physically attractive as possible. One version of the tape is shown to one intact public speaking class, while the other is shown to another intact public speaking class. After viewing the speech the students in both classes fill out a questionnaire on which they indicate their attitudes toward the speech topic. On first glance it may appear that two public speaking classes are likely to be highly similar. How-ever, most certainly, they are not. Every event that happens in one class but not in the other, contributes to the groups being nonequivalent. For example, one class may have an instructor who emphasizes the importance of a conversational deliv-ery style while the other does not. This could alter the effectiveness of the speech in that class. Or, perhaps the speech topic was discussed in one class but not the other. The discussion could have systematically affected the participants attitudes towards the topic. What if the experiment took place the first day of class, before the groups had a chance to experience unique histories? The groups might be equivalent, but without random assignment the researcher could not know if they were or not. One section might have filled during preregistration, while the other section filled during a drop-add period. Any such factors could affect attitudes towards the speech topic. We simply do not know.

A second example: In 1987, the United States government allowed each state to increase the speed limit on rural interstate highways from 55 to 65 miles per hour. (The limit had been reduced to 55 miles per hour in 1974 as an energy conservation measure.) Opponents of the increase argued that the higher speed limit decreased highway safety and that states should keep the limit at 55 miles per hour. Nevertheless, many, but not all, states quickly increased the limit to 65 miles per hour. One way to examine the effect of increasing the speed limit (X) is to compare states that increased the speed limit (O_1) to those that did not (O_2). Doing so involves a quasi-experiment and, more specifically, since the independent variable is manipulated *naturally* and not by the researcher, a natural experiment. To the extent that the states are equivalent in other ways that might contribute to interstate traffic deaths (weather, population, speeding enforcement, driver propensity for drunken driving, etc.), a large difference in traffic deaths between the states observed might plausibly be attributed to the speed limit. However, while such an observed outcome can be taken as one piece of evidence for this conclusion, it is not definitive evidence because the states are not equivalent. To improve the design, we need to be able to provide evidence about how similar the two groups are. The nonequivalent group pretest-posttest design shown in Design 10.4 provides this evidence.

Nonequivalent Group Pretest-Posttest Design

We round out our examination of quasi-experimental design with the nonequivalent group pretest-posttest design (Design 10.4). This design has been commonly used in all of the social sciences, including communication. Two groups exist intact: One group is assigned to an experimental treatment and the other is assigned as a control. The more similar the two groups, the better this design. To provide evidence bearing on the degree of similarity between the two groups, the dependent variable is measured in both groups before *and* after the experimental group is exposed to the experimental stimulus. If the pretest measures O_1 and O_3 are highly similar, the comparison between the posttest measures (O_2 versus O_4) determine

$$O_1 \quad\quad X \quad\quad O_2$$
$$\text{-----------------} \rightarrow$$
$$O_3 \quad\quad\quad\quad O_4$$

Design 10.4 Nonequivalent group pretest-posttest design.

the results. To the extent that $O_1 - O_3$ differences are not the same as $O_2 - O_4$ differences, this outcome may be attributed with considerable confidence to the treatment, X.

In the example involving traffic deaths, if the states had similar levels of deaths prior to one state raising the speed limit to 65 miles per hour and then this state had increased deaths, this would be better evidence that the speed limit and traffic deaths were related. As with the other examples, the addition of the pretest provides us with some control over history, maturation, testing, instrumentation, selection, and attrition. *History* is controlled, at least somewhat, because the treatment group can be compared to a nontreatment group that will be similar in many respects, except for exposure to the stimulus. The states may have different weather, different enforcement, and so on. *Maturity* is also controlled in that we know that what happens over both groups will be similar. *Testing* and *instrumentation* are controlled for by comparing the control and treatment groups to see if any observable differences occurred because of either the materials used or the way in which they were administered. *Attrition* is known because we know how many participants we had when we began and how many we had when we ended. *Selection* is poorly controlled to a degree. The groups may be different with regard to their susceptibility to being influenced by the experimental stimulus. There is no problem due to *statistical regression,* unless the participants in one group have more extreme scores than those in the other groups.

There are many other quasi-experimental designs we can study. An examination of the works of Campbell and Stanley is highly recommended to those interested in pursuing other, more complex designs. Nonetheless, while pretesting can *help* establish initial equivalence, it can do this *only* with regard to the variable measured in the pretest. Random assignment, in contrast, can assure equivalence not only in terms of the variables measured, but in terms of all extraneous variables which were not measured as well.

EXTERNAL VALIDITY

Before we turn to the more complex true experimental design we need to discuss the other aspect of experimental validity: *external validity.* External validity concerns the questions of *generalizability.* As noted in Chapter 9, the results of most experiments must be generalized cautiously. In many cases we seek to begin a program of organized research in the laboratory, where we can try to isolate our variables in as pure an environment as possible. At this stage of our research generalizability is extremely limited. And, when we get to the stage where we are confident enough to test our variables in the natural world, we enter the domain of quasi-experimental design. As a general way of seeing things, external validity concerns are a trade-off for internal validity concern. Designs that control for external validity may loosen their control of internal validity; designs that control for internal validity may reduce their control of external validity. In sum, it is a trade-off. As Campbell and Stanley note, "While *internal validity* is the *sine qua non,* and while the question of *external validity,* like the question of inductive inference, is never completely answerable, the selection of designs strong in both types of validity is obviously our ideal.''[8]

MORE COMPLEX DESIGNS

So far, we have been talking about the simplest form of a true experiment—the classic two-group experiment in which one group receives an experimental stimulus and another group does not. The experimental and control groups are made equal through randomization and both groups are treated identically, except for their exposure to the independent variable, after which the dependent variable is measured. This same logic applies to more elaborate experiments. What one gains from the use of more complex true experimental design is both the potential to control all sources of invalidity and the possibility of testing more than one treatment within the study. For this reason, and because many times we use designs that are more complicated than the classic experiment, we now turn to more complex designs.

True Experimental Designs

Suppose that instead of an experimental and a control group, in which case the experimental stimulus would be present or absent, we have three levels of an independent variable: high, medium, and low. In our example of the experiment examining the effects of touching presented in Chapter 9 (the impact of touch and interpersonal attraction), we might have a high-touch condition, a moderate-touch condition, and a no-touch condition. This design is depicted in Design 10.5. If the researcher kept the circumstances as nearly identical as possible in all three conditions and randomly assigned participants to the three conditions, the effect of all three levels of the independent variable (high touch, moderate touch, control [no touch]) could be assessed. Although there are practical limitations on the number of levels that feasibly might be manipulated in one experiment, the underlying *logic* generalizes to any number of levels of an independent variable.

Consider the following example. A communication education researcher is interested in assessing the effectiveness of six different approaches to teaching public speaking at one-day seminars. That is, she has an independent variable—type of teaching approach—that has six levels. She has a large pool of partici-

$$R \qquad X_1 \qquad O_1$$
$$R \qquad X_2 \qquad O_2$$
$$R \qquad \qquad O_3$$

Design 10.5 The three-group true experiment.

$$
\begin{array}{ccc}
R & X_1 & O_1 \\
R & X_2 & O_2 \\
R & X_3 & O_3 \\
R & X_4 & O_4 \\
R & X_5 & O_5 \\
R & X_6 & O_6 \\
\end{array}
$$

Design 10.6 A six-group experiment.

pants and randomly assigns them to six groups. One group (X_1) receives lectures—that is, they hear lectures about how to give public speeches. A second group (X_2) receives lectures and delivers one public speech. A third group (X_3) receives lectures, delivers one speech, and receives feedback about the speech from the instructor and the class. A fourth group (X_4) receives a lecture, delivers a speech, and watches a videotape of their speech, and receives no other feedback. A fifth group (X_5) receives a lecture, delivers a speech, watches a videotape of their speech, and receives feedback about the speech. A sixth group (X_6) receives no lecture, delivers a speech, and receives no feedback. A week later, all participants give a speech under identical circumstances. The dependent variable is assessed by having experts evaluate the quality of the speeches. This design is shown in Design 10.6.

Again, the basic logic is identical to that of simpler designs. In a large enough group of participants, between 25 and 30 per condition, for a total of 150 to 180 participants, who are assigned at random, all six groups can be expected to be highly similar initially in all ways. Note that there is no control group in this design. This is perfectly acceptable if the research question or hypothesis concerns how the various treatments (types of public speaking training sessions in our example) differ from each other in terms of the dependent variable, and not how they differ from a situation in which participants receive no training whatsoever. If this latter question were important, the research should include a true control condition in which a group of randomly selected participants received none of the six one-day seminars that constituted the experimental conditions.

Factorial Experiments

So far our discussion of experimentation has assumed there is only one independent variable. However, the logic of the experiment is easily extended to more complex research problems in which the researcher wants to examine the independent and conjoint effects of two or more independent variables on a dependent variable(s). (*Note:* Any experiment—regardless of the design—can have multiple dependent variables.) An experiment that has at least two independent variables is called a *factorial experiment.* If two (or more) independent variables both appear to be related to a dependent variable, the experiment provides a means of sorting out whether only one or whether both of these independent variables are related to the dependent variable; and if both are related, an experiment can tell us which of the two independent variables is the more powerfully related. Let us examine how this is possible.

In the mid-1960s, James C. McCroskey conducted a series of experiments with the purpose of empirically examining the relationships between variables that were suggested commonly as advice in public speaking texts.[9] One of his studies was designed to determine if the quality of evidence in a speech increased persuasive effectiveness. To test this research question, he constructed two speeches: one that used extremely good evidence to back up claims that were made—relevant statistics, and so on; the second speech was identical to the first, except that the evidence used was poor—irrelevant statistics, and so on. Groups of participants were randomly assigned to the two speech conditions, exposed to the speeches, and asked to indicate their attitudes toward the speech topic. Surprisingly, contrary to 2000 years of prescriptive advice about public speaking, the quality of evidence did not affect attitudes toward the speech topic.

McCroskey tried again. It is hard to let the results of one experiment tell you that something this seemingly obvious is not true; that a theory consistent with common sense is deficient. He noted that, in his experiment, the speech had been attributed to a speaker who was perceived as highly credible by the participants. He speculated that perhaps source credibility (generally called *ethos* at that time) was so powerful that it made the quality of evidence irrelevant. To test this possibility he needed to examine *simultaneously* the effect of high- and low-quality evidence across different levels of source credibility (high and low). To do so he conducted a *2 × 2 factorial experiment;* that is, within the same study he manipulated both evidence quality (high and low) *and* source credibility (high and low). The design of his study is shown in Design 10.7, and also in Figure 10.1 using a graphic representation that shows the factorial nature of the design more clearly. The first number following the X represents the first independent variable (evidence quality [see Figure 10.1]). The second number represents the second independent variable (source credibility). Thus X_{11} represents a treatment group in which randomly assigned participants are exposed to a speech with high-quality evidence delivered by a highly credible speaker. The X_{12} represents a high-quality speech and a low credible source; X_{21} represents a speech with low-quality evidence

R	X_{11}	O_1
R	X_{12}	O_2
R	X_{21}	O_3
R	X_{22}	O_4

Design 10.7 2×2 factorial design.

Source credibility

Figure 10.1 A 2×2 factorial design.

delivered by a highly credible source; and, finally, X_{22} represents low-quality evidence and a low credible speaker.

Looking at Design 10.7 and Figure 10.1, the first factor represents the first independent variable—evidence quality—and the fact that it is observed at two levels, as opposed to a three or some other number, means that there are two levels of evidence: high and low. (If the number were a three, this would mean that there were three levels of this variable, perhaps high, medium, and low.) The second factor represents the second independent variable (source credibility) and again, because it is composed of two levels, we know that there are two levels of this variable. Thus, by saying that the design is a 2×2 factorial experiment, we are saying that there are two independent variables, each of which has two levels. In this particular design, there are four experimental conditions, or cells. Each of the four groups of randomly assigned participants receives one of the four treatment combinations for that cell.

If McCroskey's speculation was correct, he would find that under conditions of high credibility, evidence quality would not make a difference. Equal amounts of attitude change toward the message topic would result. However, under conditions of low credibility, evidence quality *would* affect the amount of attitude change. Thus the $O_{11} - O_{21}$ comparison was expected to be negligible, while O_{12} was expected to show relatively more attitude change than O_{22}. And, in fact, these were the results. As a result of this experiment, and various replications conducted by McCroskey and his colleagues, we now know that evidence is an important factor in speech effectiveness, especially under conditions of low or moderate source credibility. Note that only by simultaneously manipulating both independent variables within the same experiment, was he able to answer his research question adequately; he had to conduct a factorial experiment to answer his question adequately.

McCroskey's research used the simplest factorial experiment possible—a two-by-two factorial design. Figures 10.2(a), 10.2(b), and 10.2(c) show, respectively, 2×3, 3×3, and $2 \times 2 \times 2$ factorial designs. The 2×3 design has two independent variables, one with two levels and the other with three levels, and a total of six separate conditions, or cells. The 3×3 factorial design has two independent variables, each with three levels, and a total of nine cells. The $2 \times$

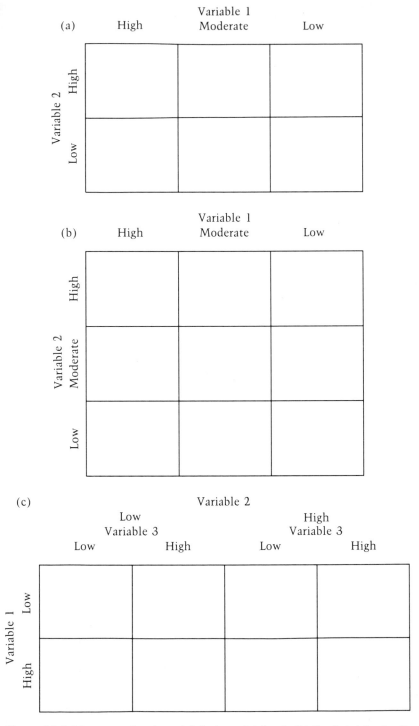

Figure 10.2 More complex factorial designs: (a) 2×3, (b) 3×3, (c) $2\times2\times2$.

2×2 has three independent variables, each with two levels, and a total of eight conditions. Manipulation of three independent variables is probably the maximum number of variables that should be manipulated in one experiment. It is extremely difficult to interpret the results of more complex experiments.

Figure 10.3 shows a 2×2 factorial design with an *offset control group*. The control group is referred to as offset because it is not given a stimulus treatment. Design considerations allow for all the treatment conditions to be *collapsed,* that is, averaged, and compared against the control group or, when appropriate, each separate condition can be tested against the control, thus ensuring that the treatments—manipulations—not only differentiated between themselves, but also against a group that received no treatment. Special statistical tests are required when employing an offset control group design.[10]

Determining the results of an experiment with one independent variable is simply a matter of comparing the scores in each of the groups. Typically, these scores are compared against what could have occurred by random chance. If the differences between the scores are so large that it is improbable that chance could account for them, the difference is attributed to the manipulation of the particular independent variable under study. Determining the results of a factorial design experiment is similar, but more complicated.

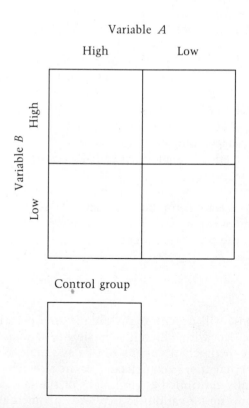

Figure 10.3 Factorial design with offset control group.

Main and Interaction Effects   Let us take the 2×2 design used by McCroskey as an example. First, there is a result for evidence usage, ignoring credibility. Secondly, there is a result for credibility, ignoring evidence quality. These results are determined by examining the means (the average of the responses for each level of the variable), respectively, at the bottom of the columns—O_{1c} versus O_{2c}—and at the end of the rows—O_{1r} versus O_{2r}. These comparisons, called *main effects*, allow the effects of the two independent variables to be examined without regard to the levels of the other independent variables (high *versus* low credibility main effect; high *versus* low evidence main effect). Figure 10.4a shows hypothetical means that would be interpreted as main effects for both variables. Figure 10.4b illustrates the results graphically.

To determine if the effect of one independent variable is different, depending on the level of the other independent variable with which it is combined, requires an examination of the individual cell scores. Such an examination is called an *interaction effect comparison*. There are two kinds of interaction effects. One occurs if the *magnitude* or the size of the effect of one independent variable varies, depending on the level of the other independent variable with which it is combined. Figure 10.5(a) and 10.5(b) shows hypothetical data for such an interaction effect. Note, also, a main effect is also shown for both independent variables. Interpretation of this would be that with a low credible source, evidence quality made no difference on participants' attitudes toward the speech; for a highly credible source, however, high evidence quality produced more attitude change than low evidence quality.

The second type of interaction effect occurs if the *direction* of the effect of one independent variable is different, depending on the level of the other independent variable with which it is combined. A hypothetical example of such an outcome is shown in Figures 10.6(a) and 10.6(b). Note that in this example there is *no* main effect for either of the independent variables; that is, each cell produces significantly different attitude scores depending on the interactive effect of *both* independent variables. This interaction effect is sometimes called a *classic crossover* interaction effect.

Thus factorial experiments provide the researcher with a powerful tool for examining simultaneously the relationship between several independent and dependent variables. Tests of more complex theories are made possible without the loss of the rigor provided by the true experiment.

SUMMARY

The type of design you choose will depend upon the research question you are attempting to answer and the rigor with which it is possible to examine the effects of the manipulations. True experimental designs can be as simple as a one-level treatment/control group experiment or as complicated as the research can make it. As we move from the carefully controlled environment of the laboratory to the field, we lose our ability to control for various sources of experimental invalidity. Still, through careful consideration of the experimental design, some control is possible; research questions, however, sometimes require less rigorous designs.

(a)

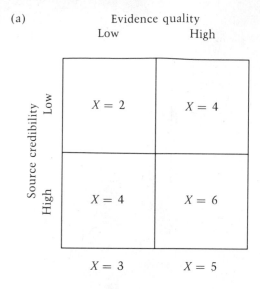

(b)

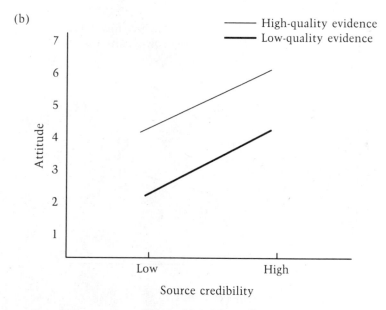

Figure 10.4 Main effects.

Knowledge of the limitations of these designs helps in interpretation of the findings.

Due to the nature of the questions asked, some research must examine the impact of manipulating two or more independent variables *simultaneously*. These factorial designs are more complicated but follow directly from the true experimental designs discussed earlier.

This chapter has introduced several designs, quasi-experimental and more

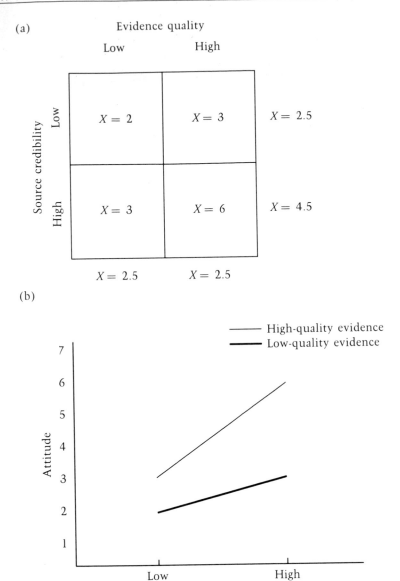

(a)

Evidence quality

	Low	High	
Low	$X = 2$	$X = 3$	$X = 2.5$
High	$X = 3$	$X = 6$	$X = 4.5$
	$X = 2.5$	$X = 2.5$	

Source credibility

(b)

Attitude

Source credibility

——— High-quality evidence
—— Low-quality evidence

Figure 10.5 Magnitude interaction effect.

complex true experimental. There are many more. We pick the design most appropriate to the research question or hypothesis. Experimental research, as noted previously, allows us not only to establish relationships, but also to establish causation among those same relationships. This advantage, however, is often limited by the stringent procedures we must employ to ensure that the relationships obtained are truly caused by the stimuli introduced.

(a)

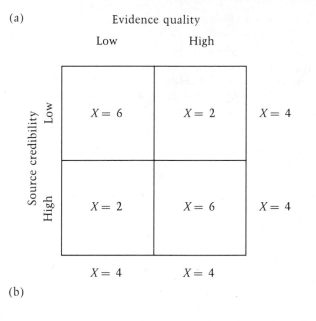

(b)

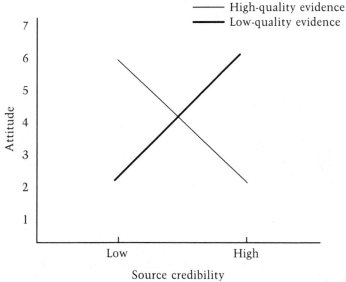

Figure 10.6 Direction-interaction effect.

PROBES

1. Although the one-shot case study is not a true experimental design, why might communication researchers still use it? What does it tell us? Can you think of any potential studies from your particular area of interest for which this design would be most appropriate? Why?

2. Is internal validity more or less important than external validity? What is the tension between the two types of validity?

3. What research questions are best answered from a quasi-experimental design? What can you do with this type of design that you cannot do with the true experiment? From your area of interest and reading, who has conducted quasi-experimental research? What have they found that they could not find with the true experiment?

4. When would you consider a factorial design experiment? Why would you even consider this type of design? Would an offset control group add anything to your study? Why or why not? Given this design, how many independent variables are you studying? How many dependent variables are you assessing? How many levels of the independent variable do you have? Will there be any main effects? Any interactions? Why?

5. Why is an experimental design with over three independent variables not recommended? Would the same recommendation be valid for dependent variables? Why or why not? Examine some of the research in your area of interest; how many factors do *most* of the studies have? How does this affect interpretation?

SUGGESTED READING

Campbell, D. T., & Stanley, J. C. (1963). Quasi-experimental design for research on teaching. In N. L. Gage (Ed.), *Handbook of research on teaching.* Chicago: Rand McNally.

Kerlinger, F. N. (1986). *Foundations of behavioral research* (2nd. ed.). New York: Holt, Rinehart and Winston.

Kidder, L. H. (1981). Qualitative research and quasi-experimental frameworks. In M. B. Brewer and B. E. Collins (Eds.), *Scientific inquiry and the social sciences.* San Francisco: Jossey Bass.

Kirk, R. E. (1968). *Experimental design: Procedures for the behavioral sciences.* Belmont, CA: Brooks/Cole.

Ricken, H. W., & Boruch, R. F. (Eds.). (1974). *Social experimentation: A method for planning and evaluating social intervention.* New York: Academic Press.

NOTES

1. Donald T. Campbell and Julian C. Stanley, "Quasi-Experimental Design for Research on Teaching," in N. L. Gage, ed., *Handbook of Research on Teaching* (Chicago: Rand McNally, 1963).
2. See sections on tenacity, authority, and intuition in Chapter 1.
3. Campbell and Stanley (p. 5) list eight threats to internal validity. This treatment is based on theirs.
4. Campbell and Stanley, 5.
5. Suggested by Russell A. Jones, *Research Methods in the Social and Behavioral Sciences* (Sunderland, Mass.: Sinauer Associates, 1985), 225.
6. See Don W. Stacks and John D. Stone, "An Examination of the Effect of Basic Speech Courses, Self-Concept, and Self-Disclosure on Communication Apprehension," *Communication Education,* 33 (1984): 317–331.
7. Of course, even with random assignment we will never know *absolutely* definitively

that the groups are highly similar. Random assignment is always subject to the limits of probability. It is possible that all the individuals who are, for example, tall, will end up in one condition. However, it is *extremely* unlikely that, given adequate sample size, this will happen. With random assignment we will know as definitely as it is possible to know anything in science that the groups will be equal.

8. Campbell and Stanley, 5.

9. James C. McCroskey, "Individual Scholar Presentation," presented at the Southern Speech Communication Association Convention, Houston, Texas, 1986. See also James C. McCroskey, "A Summary of Experimental Research on the Effects of Evidence in Persuasive Communication," *Quarterly Journal of Speech,* 55 (1969): 169–176.

10. Control to experimental groups are compared by using Dunnett's multiple comparison statistic. See Roger E. Kirk, *Experimental Design: Procedures for the Behavioral Sciences* (Belmont, Calif.: Brooks/Cole, 1968): 94–95.

Chapter
11

Content Analysis

One of the most important distinguishing characteristics of research in communication is its focus on human symbolic exchanges; that is, on communication *messages, both verbal and nonverbal.* As communication researchers we are interested in the antecedents of messages, the effects of messages, and, frequently, in the messages themselves and the inferences we can make about their creators or the circumstances under which they were created. One special method of communication research, which focuses specifically on such messages in a systematic and rule-governed way, is *content analysis,* a research method or measurement technique that involves the systematic study of the content of communication messages. As we will see, a content analysis involves the creation of categories that are designed to allow a particular research question to be answered by counting the instances of content within a message which fall within each category.

Before we examine content analysis in detail a short overview of the method will provide a perspective on why content analysis is conducted and how it fits with the scientific study of communication. We begin with its uses and an example.

USES OF CONTENT ANALYSIS

Any message of which there is an obtainable record can be content analyzed. Speeches, dialogue (as in a play, film, or television show), conversations, letters, mail appeals to sell a product or support a cause, and newspaper or magazine articles or editorials are potential sources for content analysis. Other messages might include fiction or nonfiction books, music lyrics, poetry, courtroom testimony, advertisements (in newspapers, magazines, or on television, radio, or billboards), editorial or humorous cartoons, graffiti in restrooms or on mass transit cars, and so forth; all can be content analyzed. Of course, it is important to keep in mind that while any kind of communication message can be content analyzed, there must be a good reason to do so; that is, the analysis must help us answer an important research question. Content analysis can be used in research projects that seek to explain or describe communication. We will examine each of these in turn.

Description

Many research projects have as their goal the description of some communication phenomenon. In Chapter 7, we examined field research techniques. The researcher's goal was to observe behaviors and then write down what he or she observed. Similarly, a researcher might be interested in observing communication content and describing what was observed. Content analysis can be used to add accuracy and precision to such observations.

In Chapter 2 and Chapter 5 we pointed out that researchers who take a qualitative (historical/critical) approach are frequently interested in describing a particular event. Content analysis provides a method for quantifying the messages that were produced during the event. For example, Franklin Roosevelt's fireside chats were an historically important use of the mass media. What did he say in them? Skillful use of content analysis could answer such questions as: What topics did he speak about? What was the frequency of selected topics? What types of persuasive appeals did he use? And, by drawing inferences, we could also consider such questions as Whom did he address? and What were his motives?

An important use of content analysis as a descriptive method is as a starting point for establishing the effects of particular messages. A researcher who wanted to study the effects of Roosevelt's speeches might first want to know their precise content. Similarly, if a researcher was interested in examining whether rock music contributed to drug use among teenagers, he or she would first want to know the content of the lyrics under scrutiny. Or, a researcher who was studying whether violence on Saturday morning television shows aimed at children contributed to viewer violence would probably first want to know exactly the quantity of violence on the selected shows under study. Thus, description is an important use of content analysis.

Explanation

Content analysis can be used in research that has as its purpose the explanation of observed communication phenomena. In this way, it can be used as a measurement technique to provide measures of independent and dependent variables in research designed to test hypotheses derived from theory. Good explanatory research questions compare something to something else; that is, as we have discussed, they involve examining the relationship between variables. Careful study, for instance, might reveal that 23 percent of the "Doonesbury" comic strips sampled over the past year contained attacks on the Bush administration. As a descriptive method this finding may be interesting, but it begs the question. Why do we want to know this? On the other hand, if we suspected that "Doonesbury" was harsher on the Bush administration than it was on the Carter administration, we could then compare the 23 percent finding with a figure derived from analyzing "Doonesbury" comic strips when Carter was president. If 23 percent attacked Bush and only 10 percent involved attacks on Carter, this might be interpreted as evidence that the strip was biased. In other words, bias would help *explain* something—the percentage of "Doonesbury" cartoons that attacked the administration in power.

In this example, and in the majority of studies using this method, content analysis is used to measure the *dependent* variable. To compare violence on television now versus ten years ago, a researcher might content analyze a random sample of current programming and compare the incidence of violence on these shows with shows that were on ten years ago. The amount of violence would be the dependent variable, while time, "now" or "ten years ago," would be the independent variable. Or, to assess the effect of the manipulation of an independent variable in an experiment, a researcher might have participants in experimental and control groups write essays, which then could be content analyzed and compared.

Although done less frequently, content analysis also can be used to measure the independent variable. Several prominent researchers have operationalized the variable *cognitive complexity* by content analyzing essays written by their participants. Cognitive complexity is then used as a predictor of a wide number of dependent variables, including communicator effectiveness. [1]

Steps in Content Analysis

The methods of content analysis follow directly from and are largely guided by the research question. The steps in conducting a content analysis are outlined briefly here and explained in detail in the rest of the chapter. The first step in any content analysis is a review of the literature, a review that helps focus and clarify the research questions or hypotheses that guide the study.

The second step is to define exactly *what* messages are to be studied. Here your *population* or *universe* of messages is defined. In the "Doonesbury" example this would probably be all the strips created during the Carter and Bush administrations. Basically, this step simply involves limiting the study by creating workable boundaries and parameters.

Although it would be possible to answer some research questions by analyzing all available relevant messages, more commonly the messages are so numerous as to be difficult to study in their entirety. Thus, a third step, in which a sample is selected, is required. The sample consists of messages that are representative of the entire body of messages available for analysis. The sample must be large enough to be representative, yet small enough to be studied feasibly with available resources.

After you have defined and selected the messages, the fourth step involves defining the *units of analysis,* the thing that is actually counted and assigned to categories. Units of analysis might include a word, a sentence, a paragraph, a theme, a yell (at a football game, for instance), a television news story, and so forth. In the "Doonesbury" example, the *theme* of the comic strip would be the unit of analysis, but since there usually is but one theme per strip, the strip also could be thought as the unit of analysis.

Fifth, categories into which each unit of analysis is assigned are created. The creation of categories that are valid, that allow you to measure what you want to measure, is critical to a successful content analysis. Creation of categories is reflected by the research questions posed or hypotheses advanced. Frequently, however, the researcher begins with some preliminary categories and then refines or modifies them during a pilot-test phase of the project. In the "Doonesbury" example, the categories could be as simple as Attacks the Administration in Power/Does Not Attack the Administration in Power, or as complex as a semantic differential scale reflecting the degree of pro- or antiadministration sentiment. This leads to the sixth step, the creation of reliable coding procedures. As noted earlier, clear operational definitions must be provided and training procedures created that will ensure that coding reliability is high.

Finally, the actual coding is done. Coding is conducted carefully, systematically, and objectively. After the messages have been coded the results are tabulated, analyzed, and interpreted. With this in mind, we now turn to a more detailed examination of content analysis.

DEFINING THE METHOD

Content analysis is a systematic, objective, and quantitative method for measuring variables. It is systematic, in part, because it relies on rules that follow closely those of survey sampling. It is objective because the content analyst follows specific and predetermined rules and guidelines of *what* is to be studied. Finally, it is quantitative because content analysis yields numbers that are placed in categories designed to reflect the content of the communication.

Just what *is* content analysis? Ole R. Holsti notes that definitions of content analysis changed as new techniques have been developed.[2] Contemporary uses of content analysis, for instance, have moved from the earlier held notion that the method should be tied to the descriptive level of analysis. As Bernard Berelson defined it, content analysis is "a research technique for the objective, systematic, and quantitative description of the *manifest* content of communication [emphasis added]."[3]

What is the *manifest* content of communication? Why is it important? Consider the following question: How many times is the reader referred to as "you" in this text? To answer this question you must count the number of times the word *you* was used. *You,* in this regard is *manifest* in that it is the content exactly as it appears. The researcher can assign numbers and determine the frequency of the use of *you* by the communicators (the authors). Further suppose that you know that one or two chapters were written by others. Could the frequency of use of the word *you* provide an indication of which chapters were written by whom? Perhaps.

Other researchers argue that content analysis can be approached on a *qualitative* level. Based on such analyses you might seek to move one step further: to understand the *latent* content, or the deeper meanings that are intended or perceived. Holsti contends that content analysis *at the coding level* must be limited to manifest content; that is, by being objective and systematic we are limited to coding that which we observe.[4] The latent question comes in when content analysis is used with research questions that go beyond the *pragmatic aspects of the messages themselves.* This approach, which opposes that offered by Berelson, has been advanced by Charles E. Osgood as a way of approaching questions dealing with the intended uses of the message or their intended effects.[5] Holsti argues, however, that such definitional problems are overcome when you remember that content analysis is *objective,* it must deal with the manifest nature of the material observed. He also suggests that the latent meaning of a message may be inferred, but must be corroborated by independent evidence.[6]

This chapter concentrates on the manifest end of content analysis. When necessary the researcher may make inferences based upon the objective and systematic study of the messages in question. You have, however, just seen one of the outcomes of content analysis; many times it functions as a preliminary mode of investigation to research from a different method.

An Illustration   Suppose, for instance, that you were interested in finding which research methods were being used in articles published in communication journals. There are a number of methods available to address this question. You might survey communication professionals for their opinions. But what you would get would be attitudes or beliefs regarding the methods they *thought* were being published, not the actual content of the journals. What you want to know is which research methods are actually being used in articles published in communication journals. The best way to answer this type of research question would be through a content analysis whereby you could carefully select communication journals and systematically check each for the research methods published in each article.

The key element here lies in the *content* of the journals. In answering this question you may be assuming that certain research methods may be more prevalent than others. You might also keep track of who is using what methods or when the method was employed (assuming that the date of publication represents a valid estimation of when the research was conducted). By identifying the major research methods thought to be prevalent in the journals, you might construct categories such as rhetorical/critical, historical, experimental, survey, content analysis, and so on. You might also have other subcategories, which could include, for example, the discipline of the author(s) (English, psychology, history, etc.). The content analysis will provide a listing within each category that will help you to answer your research question, and tell you which methods are used in empirical articles published in communication journals. It may also tell you who (from the identification of researchers employing each method) is using which method and which researchers employ more than one method. You may also want to report trends over time.

Content analysis, then, is a method of observing the communication of others and categorizing it according to some rigorous set of rules. Such rules determine what the content is we are analyzing, determine what categories we create to sort the content, and are created to sample adequately the content under study.

CONDUCTING THE CONTENT ANALYSIS

In preparing to analyze any communication event or variable you must first decide *what* you will be studying, you must select your *unit of analysis*. Based on the unit of analysis you must then decide how to sort the data, you must create your category system. Both decisions, however, are guided by the research question and are dependent on the amount of data with which you can work. After selection of the units of analysis and creation of the category system, a sampling procedure must be established. Finally, you must actually acquire the data.

Research Questions

We conduct a content analysis if the method best answers the particular research question. As with other approaches to the study of communication, the research question helps the researcher define just what he or she will study. Conducting a content analysis just because the material exists does not help us to understand communication better; content analysis should be employed in research because it is best suited to answer the questions posed by the researcher.

The creation of the research question begins with a thorough literature review, which leads to either specific research questions or hypotheses that point out the category system ultimately employed. The research question *delimits* the content to be analyzed in such a way as to make the research doable and valuable to the researcher. Questions that can be answered primarily with content analysis include:

> Does sexism exist in public school textbook portrayals of "appropriate" male and female roles?

> Has the amount of sex and violence in rock music videos changed in the past ten years?

> Do individuals who are lying engage in more self-references than their counterparts who are telling the truth?

Delimiting the Population

After deciding that a content analysis is the most appropriate method to answer a specific research question, the first step is to establish certain boundary conditions that will limit your search. Assuming that you still want to know which research methods are used in articles published in communication journals, you must first determine two things: what constitutes the "outlets" for publication and how far back in time you will go to establish a starting point. In determining the population under study, then, you must decide which journals are appropriate for publication of communication research. Look back over the journals listed in Chapter 4. Could you possibly cover *all* those journals? Or, are there certain journals that are more likely to publish communication research (as opposed to predominantly psychology or sociology research) or are more important to your specialty or field? Further, are you interested in communication as a general discipline or is your concern with one of the subdisciplines? In so doing you have established a boundary for your population: Perhaps you will look at only the ten most representative journals for speech communication. Obviously, this selection will limit the generalizability of your findings.

The second boundary you might consider is how many years will be covered in your study. This decision may be based on practicality and dictated by the resources available, such as coding assistance, time, and the journals themselves. The decision may be based on previous research. It may be that previous study covers only the period up to 1980; therefore, you might choose the time period 1980 to 1990 as a second boundary on your population. (You should have a specific ending point—in this case one sufficiently close to the present but still allowing for at least, say, four issues *each* of your journals to be published and in circulation.)

In this example, then, let us say your population is composed of the ten journals you feel best represent where speech communication research has been published and will cover ten years. You are now ready to move to the second step, selecting the things you will count, your units of analysis.

Units of Analysis

The *unit of analysis* is what you actually *count* and assign to categories. How your unit of analysis is defined depends on how you *operationally define* the variable(s) under study. As noted in Chapter 6, the concept of an operational definition is crucial when creating the variables for study. In content analysis the variables under study (the ones being counted) should be distinct and identifiable by coders after training. Potential units of analysis might include: words, sentences, paragraphs, and themes in written material; phrases, sentences, and turns in oral material; scenes, acts, and plays in dramatic material; or names, institutions, and dates in other material.

A major consideration at this stage of content analysis is how the definition of the unit of analysis will relate to how it is ultimately coded. How can you select your unit of analysis? As a start, we might consider the five *major* units suggested by Berelson (see Table 11.1).[7] Keep in mind, however, that these units are suggestions and, at a minimum, will need further specificity. Berelson's smallest unit of analysis is the *word* or *symbol.* This can include units consisting of names, utterances, parts of speech, and so forth. The second unit of analysis is the *theme.* A theme consists of an idea, concept, or thesis. While the word is fairly simple to operationalize, the theme presents more of a problem. Kerlinger, however, suggests that careful use of the theme provides "an important and useful unit because it is ordinarily realistic and close to the original content."[8] For instance, if the unit of analysis is defined as an individual's self-concept, the theme would revolve around statements of self-esteem, self-worth, and so on. Within the major theme, then, we would have subthemes. Obviously, thematic variables are more difficult to use and should be carefully operationalized. Berelson notes that thematic units of analysis are more difficult to code reliably, a problem that can be minimized through clear definition, careful training, and the use of more than one coder.

Themes provide the researcher with an idea of the *latent* meaning of the

Table 11.1   UNITS OF ANALYSIS

Unit	Example
Word	Nouns
	Proper names
	Utterances (for example, "uh-huh")
Theme	Self-esteem
	Positive news promotion
	Democracy
Character	Sex (male/female)
	Occupation
	Race (black/white/Asian)
Time/Space	Column inches
	Type size
	Air time provided a program
Item	Speech
	Interview
	Television program

content at a quantifiable level of analysis. For example, if we assume that sexually related innuendo underlies more situation comedy today than in the 1960s, we could compare scripts of both periods. Our analysis would look for the absence or presence of innuendo, coded as "sexual" or "nonsexual." A count of use would provide support as to which was prevalent. For example, sexual innuendo might include such nonverbal *quasi-courtship* behaviors as long, lingering glances, eyebrow raises, or pelvis rotation (both sexes), breast thrusts or touching (females), pelvis thrusts or unbuttoned shirts (males).

The third unit of analysis discussed by Berelson is the *character.* The character is defined as an individual. In most research the character unit is composed of specific people, such as whites/blacks, males/females, or married/unmarried. However, you could define the character as being composed of specific communicative behaviors identified with a specific type of person. Suppose that you are analyzing the transcripts of a group discussion. You may choose as your unit of analysis the particular *roles* as the characters employed by members during the discussion. Hence, you might find that certain roles emerge at different points in the discussion. In literary and some historical research characters as units of analysis take special importance.

The fourth unit of analysis is an increment of *time* or *space.* Just as it suggests, this reflects some physical or temporal measure. Spatial/temporal measures of content are often employed in media research. Wurtzel, for instance, used the amount of air time given a particular event.[9] Other time/space variables might be defined as the size of different pictures used in media, number of column inches a given story is allocated, or even the page a particular story is placed on in the paper.

The final unit of analysis in Berelson's system is the *item.* An item consists of an entire communication message. In Wurtzel's study of air time given an event, the story (Republican-oriented or Democrat-oriented) was an item unit of analysis, while the time aired per story was a time unit of analysis. One advantage of item units is that they can be presented to trained judges (coders) with rating scales and compared on a dimension or range of dimensions.

Sometimes the researcher must use two or more different units of analysis. Again, it is important to keep in mind that the choice of the most appropriate units should reflect the research questions or hypotheses being tested. Use of multiple units can provide extra information and may help validate the measures.

Creating Categories for Analysis

Once you have decided on your units of analysis, the next step is to establish the categories in which to place them. The concern here is establishing how to separate the units of analysis into *meaningful* categories. As with selecting unit(s) of analysis, the decision of *which* and how many categories to use must reflect the objectives of the research project. Quite simply, choosing the proper category system is critical in conducting a content analysis.

Guidelines   When creating a category system, five general guidelines should be followed.[10] Content analysis categories should (1) reflect the purpose of the research, (2) be exhaustive, (3) be mutually exclusive, (4) allow for independence (assigning an item to one category should not influence the assignment of other items to other categories), and (5) all categories within the system should reflect one, *single* classification principle. These guidelines underlie the systematic and objective nature of content analysis, which makes it a scientific method.

At the core of categorization, then, is the definitional process. Suppose again that your research project deals with identifying different *types* of research methods published in communication journals. The unit of analysis is the article published. The categories might reflect those established in this book: historical/critical, survey/descriptive, participant-observation, descriptive, experimental/quasi-experimental, and, of course, content analysis. Given this category system, will all units identified fit into only one of the categories? If they do you have created a category system that is *mutually exclusive,* a particular entry will fall into one of these five areas and only one of these five areas.

What will you do with an item that fits none of your categories? In this case you might have a sixth category: Other. Another problem might evolve around different types of surveys. If it is important to understand the types of research being reported, it may be important to know that there are several different types of surveys. In this case you might want to divide your category of survey/descriptive further into several different subcategories. You might do the same with historical/critical and experimental/quasi-experimental.

In creating the subcategories you have created a category system that is not only *exhaustive* but also exclusive. Each unit now has a home, even if that home is other. Roger D. Wimmer and Joseph R. Dominick suggest that researchers keep careful track of the miscellaneous or other category; when the total entries in such a category exceed 10 percent of the total units placed, something may have been overlooked in the categorization process.[11] Creating categories, then, involves making choices as to whether or not you will have the right number of categories. Sometimes it is necessary to pretest or pilot test a study to get a feel for the content and the *appropriate* number of categories necessary to answer the research question adequately.

Counting In our earlier example, a pilot study was conducted that further limited the sample to only those people who had published at least five *total* articles. Once you have created your categories you will need to consider how you will "count" the items to be placed in each category. To illustrate, consider the following research project, which is examining which individuals have published in major communication journals. The major research questions concerned finding out who the "top" publishers in communication journals are. The universe for this study, then, consists of people publishing in speech communication journals; specifically, by those publishing in journals recognized by the Matlon *Index.*[12] This index includes only "major" communication journals. Our unit of analysis is the equivalent to the "word" in Berelson's system, the author's name. Each author's listing, regardless of whether or not he or she was the sole author, was entered as well as the number of articles in each of the selected journals. By using the *Index* we have been able to reduce the time it takes to draw our sample based on the earlier work put into the *Index.*

The most obvious and simple quantification system is simply to count the units being analyzed in each category. Typically, the researcher will create a tally sheet. In this example, the tally sheet would include those authors included in the journals. Hence, our category system is more complex and takes in a bigger picture than simply identifying the top authors.

Counting also may take the form of examining how many different times a particular word or phrase is used in a message. In counting, no discrimination is made regarding subdivision within a category. If you were interested in how a writer perceived himself in his writing and thought that as the writer gained self-respect and reduced apprehension more personal pronouns would appear in his writing, a simple count of the number of personal pronouns would constitute the results. Note that no further discrimination between what *types* of personal pronouns is made. In the "top authors" study, a simple count of citations was used for each journal regardless of *what* the article might have been about or what method was used.

SAMPLING

As with survey research, content analysis may require that the elements chosen be representative of the larger universe or population. Although there are times when it is possible to include *all* messages in your content analysis, many times there is just too much material with which to work efficiently. Thus, the principles of sampling presented in Chapter 8 apply.

Sampling Concerns

If the population you will be studying either is not large or is composed of a limited number of messages, sampling may not be of concern. In such cases you would in effect simply take a *census* of the material available—including all messages—as part of the content analysis. This may be possible with some content analyses, but usually there are more messages than can be efficiently and reliably studied. Of concern here is whether the messages are such that *any* message or item is representative of all possible messages. The following sections review different ways to draw sample messages from some population.

Random and Systematic Sampling   A simple random sampling of works written or spoken by a communicator could be conducted. The research question here would concentrate on understanding the messages of this particular person. If you are concerned with messages from a variety of sources, and you have no reason to believe that your sources are unsimilar with regard to whatever attributes are of importance, then simple random sampling may be appropriate. If your research question concerns the content produced by one individual—a long complex speech, a book, or text of some message—then sampling may not be a major concern.

Simple random sampling, however, is both time-consuming and prone to error. As discussed in Chapter 8, you might want to consider a systematic sampling of the content. Since you already have copies of the messages (in written, audiotape, or videotape form), systematic sampling may be a better approach. Systematic sampling involves compiling a list of messages and the selection of a random starting point and a constant skip interval. Based on the starting point, the next message for inclusion in the sample will be determined by the skip interval. Perhaps there are several hundred presidential speeches over the term of a single president. If you are not concerned with *change* in messages over time, a systematic random sample would be an efficient and accurate way to select the messages for content analysis. Thus, we might select every tenth speech (the skip interval chosen randomly) from the first speech of the second year (again, both—as starting points— chosen randomly).

As discussed earlier, there is a problem with systematic sampling. *Periodicity*, or the way in which the items are chosen based on their location in the population, may bias the sample. If a research project is to examine media content, for example, systematic sampling may be a major problem. Decisions must take into account both time and space factors. For example, content during electronic media *sweeps* weeks is different from that during *nonsweeps* weeks. (Sweeps weeks are those periods during which advertisers examine statistics showing how many viewers are watching the different networks. These statistics help to determine advertising rates. Because of this the networks often broadcast blockbuster programming or new programs.) Regarding sports events, reporting may vary with the season (or preseason) period. In the same way, television news on the weekends differs greatly from Monday through Friday newscasts; in the print media, weekend newspapers also may differ from those published Monday to Friday.[13]

Stratification Sampling   Sometimes a stratified sample may yield a more representative sample of the content under study. Stratified sampling is concerned with selecting messages that have an *identifiable* characteristic or segment of interest. We may be interested in only those presidential messages during the period 1965 to 1974 which deal with the Vietnam War as an economic argument, a matter of national defense, or as a way to stop communism. Those messages dealing with that period and those topics would be included as possible items for selection. If our research question also concerned the content of the messages during the first third, second third, and final third of the presidency, we could then sample equally from each time period. As pointed out in earlier chapters, the major problems associated with stratified sampling concern a good knowledge of ways in which the strata are more homogeneous than the entire population under study.

Cluster Sampling   Sometimes the population of possible message sources differs significantly enough to warrant breaking the sample into representative subsamples or clusters. It may be possible, and even desirable, to sample, say 15 major newspapers, in an analysis of news content on the national level. But the same may not be true of a multilevel analysis of front page news. The *Cheboygan Tribune*'s perception of what is news may differ significantly from that of the *New York Times.* Although headlines may be similar, the actual content may differ. Hence, you might consider clustering according to newspaper size or circulation, a single-stage cluster sampling. Thus, a delimiting factor in the study would be the daily circulation of the paper. You might want to go one step further and establish other clusters, which further identify the population. You might cluster first by region, then by type of newspaper (daily and weekly, for instance), and then by circulation.

In the same way, an analysis of company newsletters may differ by industry, whether or not they are one of the Fortune 500, or whether they have public relations departments. A simple random selection, then, may be inadequate and a cluster sampling may be more appropriate. When working with the texts of speeches this is especially true. If the speech is short, a census of the entire speech can be taken; however, if you are looking at a large volume of speeches by one person or party, sampling will be required. A simple random selection may not produce results representative of the entire *population* of speeches. Here you would cluster your sample according to introduction, body, and conclusion, sampling from each speech randomly within the three areas. [14]

Availability of Data   Another consideration in sample selection is the availability of data. Suppose, for instance, that you are examining the mudslinging campaign of one candidate for a statewide political office. In this state there are five major cities, each with a population over 100,000. In four of the five cities the major media consists of one newspaper, in the other there are two newspapers. Assume also that four of the five newspapers are clumped in a geographic area about 150 miles from the largest city and the fifth is some 250 from the closest city. Can you ignore the fifth city? Not if your questions deal with statewide impact, even though getting the paper may pose a problem. If, on the other hand, you are interested only in the coverage of newspapers from the large, perhaps more political parts of the state, then you might consider excluding the fifth paper.

Decisions regarding availability of sources should be considered at the research question/hypothesis stage. The availability of sources also should be considered before the sample is selected. In some instances you have available an existing data base from which to draw your sample. Suppose that you are interested in what type of article is written in the popular press (magazines) following an important news event. One source to consider might be *Reader's Guide to Periodical Literature,* which is indexed by topic and title, for the content of the particular areas you need. In the "top authors" study mentioned earlier, the Matlon *Index* might be considered as the data base, assuming that it is a reliable compilation of the data; however, care should be taken to double-check the accuracy of all the entries. [15] As noted in Chapter 4, there are many abstract sources that provide potential sources of data; care must be taken, however, to ensure that they are representative of the population required for your research questions.

Quantification

How do we "enter" the data collected in a content analysis? That depends on the category system employed. The decision of how to quantify should be approached early in the planning process. Remember, one of the major goals of the method is that all data should be potentially quantifiable.[16] Given today's use of microcomputers, simple and straightforward coding has become even more important (we will cover this in more detail and depth in a later section of this chapter). This section will discuss ways to approach this stage of the content analysis.

Nominal Quantification Coding requires that some distinction be made in the content. This distinction could be defined as simply as male/female or more complexly as in the case of personal pronouns, which might be first person, second person, or third person. As discussed in Chapter 6, a nominal variable does not assume that one category is more or less, better or worse, higher or lower than any other category. Assume for a moment that you are evaluating a number of messages written by respondents after exposure to a persuasive message with which they did not agree. You might code each respondent's message's arguments according to the strategy he or she employed in reacting to the persuasive message. In coding each message you would assign an appropriate letter, number, or phrase to the particular message. The same could be done if your unit of analysis was paragraphs. For example, messages may be of three types: one-sided, two-sided, or emotional appeal. Coding of these messages could employ any of several strategies: 1 (one-sided), 2 (two-sided), 3 (emotional appeal); Type I, Type II, Type III; and so on. Another example of nominal quantification is found in Table 11.2.

Ordinal Quantification A second method of coding requires some decision regarding ranking the data. Ranking requires that the content be placed in categories that are mutually independent and ordered in some way. If you were working with a number of student news releases you might rank them as Excellent, Good, Bad, or Terrible. Each release could be coded as E, G, B, T or 4, 3, 2, 1. Or you could assign a grade (A to F) for each. Other sample codings are found at Table 11.3.

Interval Quantification A third method of coding is that of rating each item in the analysis according to some scale. These scales could be of any of the types

Table 11.2 NOMINAL CODING

Content: Newspaper Editorials	
Units	Nominal Coding
Domestic affairs	1
International affairs	2
Environment	3
Local issues	4

Table 11.3   ORDINAL CODING

Amount of violence depicted
in a television show

Category	Coding
A lot	1
A little	2
None	3

Sexual appeal in a magazine
cigarette advertisement

Category	Coding
Blatant	1
Moderate	2
Slight	3
Subtle	4
None	5

discussed in Chapter 6. Often you will want to code your content according to some degree of something, perhaps positive to negative. In that case we are no longer simply creating a dichotomy but actually placing the item on some continuum:

Positive ___:___:___:___:___:___:___ Negative

Or, we could use multiple rating scales:

Positive ___:___:___:___:___:___:___ Negative

Hot ___:___:___:___:___:___:___ Cold

Active ___:___:___:___:___:___:___ Passive

Obviously, you obtain finer distinctions or categories from such scales. However, the price you pay is in the increased difficulty of establishing reliability. Content analysis, unlike earlier uses of these scales, requires that coders agree with one another regarding, for example, how positive or negative the message was.

Coding Reliability

When your content analysis calls for simply counting manifest content, for example, the number of times a particular word appears, reliability is fairly easy to establish. [17] However, when more difficult judgments are required, increased atten-

attention is necessary to assure that coders place items in the correct categories with a degree of consistency.

When quantification requires that judgments be made, the researcher must be prepared to establish that the coders are consistently placing data into the correct categories. (Even with counting, it is advisable that someone other than the researcher double-check the counting.) Coding reliability is enhanced when the units of analysis are clearly defined and they are assigned to mutually exclusive and exhaustive categories. Even when these two conditions are met, there may be times when coders will be unable to agree upon the category in which the item should be placed. In such cases it is helpful to have all agree in which category the items should go, achieving a common frame of reference toward the content.[18] That is, when coders have problems deciding where the particular item(s) go, they should talk over their differences and agree on a category for the item(s); if the category system has been adequately pretested, however, this should be a fairly uncommon occurence.

Intercoder reliability can be enhanced in several ways. Perhaps the most important of these is to make certain that all coders understand and can use the coding categories. It is important that they understand the definitions of the categories and how and why the units of analysis were chosen. Coders must understand the project well enough to make decisions about content but not so well as to know what the researcher is seeking. Thus, it is important that a balance between an understanding of the coding system and the actual research questions or hypotheses be maintained for coders. For example, if the material being analyzed was derived from people who had participated in an experiment, the coders should be blind to (unaware of) the experiment's particular conditions (treatments). It is also important that they understand that certain items may not easily fit into the categories, that they might need to "talk it over" and agree where the item should be placed when such an item appears. For this purpose a pilot test phase of research should be undertaken during which the categories and operational definitions are tested and coders trained.

After the coders have a good understanding of the project's definitions and categories, practice sessions should be run. In these sessions material randomly selected from the population under consideration should be presented and coded. Any disagreements over coding should then be discussed and agreements reached concerning the appropriate categories (if the researcher has reviewed the area well enough, category ambiguity should be minimal, but it should be expected that some content may still cause problems). The practice session should be used to work out procedures for solving disagreements and to ascertain whether or not the categories meet Holsti's criteria of reflecting the research question, being properly subdivided into useful groups, being exclusive and independent, and reflecting a single classification principle.[19]

Coding reliability is usually enhanced when coders use a standardized coding form. Such a form provides the necessary categories and allows for standardization.

Reliability Coefficients   Once the data have been gathered some estimate of coding reliability must be determined. Hand-calculated reliability coefficients are not difficult to compute. Holsti's reliability formula is fairly straightforward, requiring only information about the number of coding decisions the coders must make and the total number of decisions made by each coder[20]:

$$\text{reliability} = \frac{2M}{N_i + N_j}$$

where M = total items agreed upon
  N_i = total items coder i selected
  N_j = total items coder j selected

This assumes that independent coders have been employed. In some cases you may use only one coder. *Intra*coder reliability may be computed the same as *inter*coder reliability; the coder codes the *same* material *twice*, without being aware of how it was coded the first time, and coefficients of reliability are then computed on both sets of data. Of course, this assumes a fairly large number of messages have been coded so that the coder would not remember how he or she coded it the first time.

Some coding requires more than simple categorization. This is especially true when the data is being coded for specialized computer analysis. For instance, H. Wayland Cummings' Syntactic Language Computer Analysis (SLCA) program takes messages and analyzes them for syntactical content.[21] Box 11.1 presents an actual message and its SLCA-coded counterpart. Obviously, coding such messages can be quite complex and requires both extensive training sessions and checking of the coding by the researcher.

Coding Validity

As noted in Chapter 6, reliability is a necessary but not sufficient condition for establishing measurement validity. Validity is most commonly defined as whether a coding system measures what you want it to measure. As with other methods, validity can be a real concern with content analysis. This concern can be traced to three possible sources of invalidity: definition, category, and sample.

Definitional Sources of Invalidity   By now it should be apparent that the definitional process involved in determining what the units of analysis will be is critical to validity in content analysis. When units of analysis are defined, a set of boundary conditions are created which serve to limit what you will accept in the analysis. In setting these boundaries you may or may not reflect the same definitions others would have chosen. Many times definitional problems come up in training sessions; once pilot testing commences it is discovered that the definition decided on will not work with the material or the coders. If this occurs, your definition needs revision.

If your research project was interested in how communication apprehension was manifested verbally and nonverbally in an initial public speech, it would be

---

Box 11.1 **Computer-assisted Coding for Content Analysis: Syntactic Language Computer Analysis**

MESSAGE AS WRITTEN

Local officials met Tuesday with a chemical company about the development of a new chemical plant in the Tuscaloosa Area.

Dayton Chemical Inc. was named a "serious polluter" in 1984 by the Environmental Protection Agency. It produces many products, among them are compounds used in manufacturing medicines. Dayton is a pioneer in research on synthetic interferon, a compound some predict will be a significant breakthrough in the treatment of cancer.

In 1985, Dayton settled a damage suit over toxic waste dumping near the headquarters in Ohio. The total settlement was for $1.4 million.

Dayton could create as many as 200 new jobs for Tuscaloosa residents.

MESSAGE AS CODED FOR COMPUTER ANALYSIS

LOCAL + OFFICIALS − MET ++ TUESDAY WITH A CHEMICAL + COMPANY ABOUT THE ++ DEVELOPMENT OF A NEW CHEMICAL + PLANT IN THE ++ TUSCALOOSA + AREA. ++ DAYTON ++ CHEMICAL ++ INCORPORATED WAS − NAMED A SERIOUS + POLLUTER IN + 1984 BY THE ++ ENVIRONMENTAL ++ PROTECTION ++ AGENCY. + IT − PRODUCES MANY + PRODUCTS, AMONG + THEM − ARE + COMPOUNDS − USED IN + MANUFACTURING + MEDICINES. ++ DAYTON − IS A + PIONEER IN + RESEARCH ON SYNTHETIC + INTERFERON, A + COMPOUND + SOME − PREDICT WILL − BE A SIGNIFICANT + BREAKTHROUGH IN THE + TREATMENT OF + CANCER. IN + 1985, ++ DAYTON − SETTLED A DAMAGE + SUIT OVER TOXIC WASTE + DUMPING NEAR THE + HEADQUARTERS IN ++ OHIO. THE TOTAL + SETTLEMENT − WAS FOR 1 MILLION + DOLLARS. ++ DAYTON COULD − CREATE AS MANY AS 200 NEW + JOBS FOR ++ TUSCALOOSA + RESIDENTS./

---

important to define apprehension in such a way that it could be codeable in a manner consistent with your definition. Such coding might yield different results if we defined apprehension as a *fear of communication* rather than as an *unwillingness to communicate* or *shyness*. Conceptually, there are major differences between being fearful of communication and being unwilling to communicate; being shy may be an altogether different reason for being apprehensive about communicating. Clearly, the way we define our units of analysis will alter how they are perceived by the coders, thus becoming a potential source of invalidity. Additionally, we need to examine *what* content is being analyzed. If we were to take the actual text of the speeches, to include hesitations, stutter-starts, and so forth, as the content, our definition would need to incorporate such instances of apprehension. Assume that our content is the self-statements made during the speaking situation. Although the definitions may appear similar, they really point to three different perspectives of apprehension. The same is potentially true of many concepts, such as violence, conservatism, liberalism, or even self-concept.

Your theoretical perspective will serve as the guiding force in definition. If your approach to apprehension is from a perspective suggesting unwillingness, then that definition will be valid for you. The validity of the analysis, then, lies primarily within the areas of face or content validity.

Category Sources of Invalidity   As should be evident by now, definition is closely tied to category selection. Creating a category system that is valid presents a second problem. Category systems should be exhaustive and mutually exclusive. To the degree that you are able to place units in categories without overlap, validity is increased. Here, validity is closely related to reliability. If your reliability is high, your validity should be increased. As noted earlier, *the categories must reflect the purpose of the research.*

For example, if you were interested in the portrayal of sex on MTV, and you have a category that is defined as instances in which a female is treated violently—the category does not accurately reflect the variable per se. It is not valid. Or, if the number of times certain words—devil, Satan—were used as a measure of the extent of devil worship content it might not be valid. Christian rock might use the words "beat the devil" or "defeat Satan" and the category would validly reflect the variable. Thus, simple word counts would be inadequate to assess the content. Themes would probably be more appropriate.

Sampling Sources of Invalidity   The third problem facing the researcher deals with the sample. If your sample represents the universe or population from which it was drawn and the analysis of the sample is valid, inferences about the population should be valid. However, care must be taken to make sure that your sampling procedure reflects the aims of the research. This is especially true in content analyses that look at parts of a speech, newspapers, or sampling one week of TV shows to find out about violence in prime time—whose validity was destroyed because one network ran a miniseries that week on one channel. Choosing the first 100 words of a number of randomly selected messages for analysis could invalidate the sampling procedure if your research question does not deal with just the introduction. If the research question deals with the *total* message, random sampling from sections of the message is probably more valid than fixing on a certain number of words at the beginning of the message. In general, if you are examining a number of messages, your sample should consist of the *population* of messages; if you are examining certain messages, the sample should be the *message itself*; and, if you are examining a specific message, you should examine the *entire* message.

USE OF COMPUTERS IN CONTENT ANALYSIS

The computer has allowed content analysis to accomplish things never thought possible 25 years ago. Computer programs such as The General Inquirer provided the first computerized analysis of messages and subsequently a number of other content analysis programs have become available. [22] Two of interest are the SLCA program discussed earlier and Roderick P. Hart's Diction program, which produces descriptive analyses of speech content. [23] Although the computer has made content analysis easier to conduct, the problems of reliability and validity are still present; careful definition and creation of categories for the units selected is still necessary. If anything, the advent of computerized content analysis makes sample selection even more important.

Computerized content analysis often demands complex coding procedures. SLCA coding, for instance, while not difficult, still provides a challenge to anyone who attempts it. Coding of the messages also requires that the messages be altered in some instances. Spelling errors can cause problems, some programs require punctuation correction, and others require that the messages be rewritten to fit its coding procedures (see Box 11.1). Use of these programs does not eliminate the need to read each message before coding. The human computer, the brain, may be the best content analysis tool yet devised.

Computerized content analysis provides precision in analysis. It does *not* replace anything that the researcher could do, but does make it easier to accomplish the often tedious chores associated with coding the data. Any of the research questions suggested earlier *could* be addressed through computerized content analysis. Obviously, the computer is an excellent tool for counting; but it has problems with establishing the *meaning* of the content. With advances in artificial intelligence programs, however, even this may soon be conquered. Until then, questions addressing the latent content of messages may best be approached by a noncomputerized method.

ADVANTAGES AND LIMITATIONS OF CONTENT ANALYSIS

Like any method, there are certain advantages and limitations to content analysis. By now you should be aware that content analysis can be both time-consuming and complex. The key point to remember is that content analysis *describes* the content of a message, but the message can be part of (or derived from) a larger study that has explanation as its goal. Content analysis provides the researcher with the *manifest* message content, which *may* lead to future research on the *latent* meaning of that content. In many ways content analysis should be considered a heuristic tool—serving to establish future research.

Finally, it should be emphasized that content analysis does not, and cannot, assess the *effects* of communication messages. Occasionally we hear, for example, that certain song lyrics advocate Satan worship or worse. This may or may not be true. But, if it is true, nothing has been learned about the effects of these lyrics on those who listen to them. In this regard, content analysis could be the impetus for other research questions that require different methodologies to arrive at the appropriate answer.

SUMMARY

Content analysis is an important measurement tool, which can be used in conjunction with other methods discussed. It can be used historically and critically to examine messages people have produced. It can be used in both qualitative and quantitative descriptive research and to measure either the independent variable or dependent variable in exploratory research. As a measurement tool it can assess concepts included in research using other methods, such as experiments. As a method itself, content analysis can tell us a lot about the type of messages we see.

Content analysis can be a complex and time-consuming method of research. Its advantages lie in an ability to describe the messages under study, to make inferences about the creator of the message, and in providing a heuristic function to research. As with any method, however, its use should be carefully considered and used when the research questions or theoretical perspective call for it.

PROBES

1. As noted in opening sections of this chapter, content analysis focuses on messages. Are there *any* messages that may be inappropriate or impossible for content analysis? If there are, which ones and why?

2. What is the difference between *manifest* and *latent* content? Is the distinction really important, or is it something that should be considered a secondary consideration? Why or why not?

3. From your area of communication interest, state a research question that is amenable to content analysis. Based on this question, what *type* of content will you be analyzing (How would you operationalize the categories)? What unit(s) of analysis would you use? How would you sample the content, or would a census be best?

4. Assume that you are interested in conducting a content analysis of network news promotions. Specifically, you are interested in the types of promotions and the frequency with which they are used during prime time to hype the evening news. What would be an interesting question that content analysis would best answer? Based on this question, what category system(s) might you employ? What would your units of analysis be? Would you want to consider some time frame? Would you have to *sample* the content? If so, how? How would you analyze the data?

5. What reliability and validity concerns does content analysis present? Are these concerns unique to content analysis, or are they present in other research methods as well? Do you think that computer-assisted content analysis has any impact on reliability? Validity? Why or why not?

SUGGESTED READING

Berelson, B. (1952). *Content analysis in communication research.* Glencoe, IL: Free Press.

Bowers, J. W. (1970). Content analysis. In P. Emmert and W. D. Brooks (Eds.). *Methods of communication research.* Boston: Houghton Mifflin.

Budd, R. R., Thorp, R., & Donohew, L. (1967). *Content analysis of communications.* New York: Macmillan.

de Sola Pool, I., (Ed.). (1959). *Trends in content analysis.* Urbana, IL: University of Illinois Press.

Gerbner, G. et al. (1969). *The analysis of communication content.* New York: John Wiley.

Holsti, O. R. (1969). *Content analysis for the social sciences and humanities.* Reading, MA: Addison-Wesley.

Krippendorff, K. (1980). *Content analysis: An introduction to its methodology.* Beverly Hills, CA: Sage.

Stone, P. et al. (1966). *The general inquirer: A computer approach to content analysis.* Cambridge, MA: MIT Press.

NOTES

1. For several excellent examples, see *Communication Monographs* 46 (1979), 231–281. Four articles using content analysis are presented.
2. Ole R. Holsti, *Content Analysis for the Social Sciences and Humanities* (Reading, Mass.: Addison-Wesley, 1969), 2.
3. Bernard Berelson, *Content Analysis in Communication Research* (New York: Free Press, 1952), 18.
4. Holsti, 12–14.
5. Charles E. Osgood, "The Representational Model and Relevant Research Methods," in I. De S. Pool, ed., *Trends in Content Analysis* (Urbana,: University of Illinois Press, 1959), 33–88.
6. Holsti, 14.
7. Berelson, 508–509.
8. Fred N. Kerlinger, *Foundations of Behavioral Research,* 3rd ed. (New York: Holt, Rinehart & Winston, 1986), 480.
9. Alan Wurtzel, "Review of the Procedures Used in Content Analysis," in Joseph R. Dominick and James E. Fletcher, eds., *Broadcasting Research Methods* (Boston: Allyn and Bacon, 1985), 11–12.
10. Holsti, 94–126.
11. Roger D. Wimmer and Joseph R. Dominick, *Mass Media Research: An Introduction,* 2nd ed. (Belmont, Calif.: Wadsworth, 1987), 177.
12. Ronald J. Matlon, *Index to Journals in Communication Studies Through 1984* (Annandale, Va.: Speech Communication Association, 1985). A problem with indices such as Matlon's, however, is that they often contain errors, errors that will affect both the validity and the reliability of the study.
13. Wimmer and Dominick, 174.

14. John Waite Bowers, "Content Analysis," in Philip Emmert and William D. Brooks, eds., *Methods of Communication Research* (Boston: Houghton Mifflin, 1970), 294.

15. Mark Hickson, III, Don W. Stacks, and Jonathon H. Amsbary ("An Analysis of Prolific Scholarship in Speech Communication: 1915–1985: Toward a Yardstick for Measuring Research Productivity," *Communication Education*, 38 [1989]: 230–236) recently asked the research question, "who are the most prolific communication researchers of all time?" Their content analysis used the Matlon *Index* as its basic data base.

16. Kerlinger, 481.

17. Berelson, 512–514.

18. Guido H. Stempel, III, "Content Analysis," in Guido H. Stempel, III, and Bruce H. Westley, eds., *Research Methods in Mass Communication* (Englewood Cliffs, NJ: Prentice-Hall, 1980), 127.

19. See Holsti, 94–126.

20. Holsti, 140.

21. H. Wayland Cummings and Steven L. Renshaw, "SLCA III: A Meta-theoretic Approach to the Study of Language," *Human Communication Research*, 5 (1979): 291–300.

22. P. Stone, Dexter C. Dunphy, Marshall S. Smith, and Daniel M. Ogilivie, et al., *The General Inquirer: A Computer Approach to Content Analysis* (Cambridge, Mass.: MIT Press, 1966).

23. Cummings and Renshaw "SLCA III"; Roderick P. Hart, *Diction* Mimeograph, "Seminar on Computerized Language Analysis," presented at the Speech Communication Association, 1984.

THREE

Modes of Analysis

*O*nce we have acquired data from surveys, experiments, or content analyses, what next? This section explores how we analyze the data gathered from quantitative methods. In so doing we address a topic about which many students seem most apprehensive: The manipulation of numbers. As we move through this section keep in mind that our aim is *understanding.* Understanding modes of analysis does not require the memorization of complex formulas, or difficult computations. Understanding requires that you make *intelligent* decisions about how to analyze the data you have collected and what conclusions, if any, you can draw from those analyses.

In preparing these chapters we have limited our discussions to those analytical tools you will most likely need in both reading others' research, and in proposing and conducting your own. This section provides you the *basic* information from which to work and provides hints of where to go for future help. Perhaps some students will find this introductory treatment interesting enough to enroll in a statistics class. Our approach, however, is to attempt to meet three important objectives: (1) We want you to understand what types of analysis you have available to you, (2) We want you to understand which types of analysis are most appropriate for your particular research question/hypothesis/ theory, and (3) We want you to be able to interpret the results.

To meet these objectives we introduce you to data analysis. Where it is appropriate we provide you with formulas. However, we believe that being able to choose the most appropriate mode of analysis is more important than applying the specific formula or equation. Our approach is conceptual.

Understanding also requires the ability to *read* the results of the analysis. Much like driving in a new area, you need a road map to guide you. Inability to read that map, however, precludes its usefulness. Thus, we will provide you with maps to interpreting printouts. Most researchers use computers— mainframe or personal—to do their analyses; we present examples of printouts based on popular personal computer programs. The ability to read one or two should make it easier to read others, including those of large mainframes.

Chapter 12 introduces the concept of data and simple *description* of the data set. We discuss the way data points are arranged and how they spread. Modes of analysis discussed in this chapter include, for ordinal and nominal data, frequency and percentage, and for interval and ratio data, range, mean, mode, median, variance, standard deviation, standard error, and curvilinearity. Types of simple descriptive analysis covered include tabulation, crosstabulation and rank-order analysis.

Chapter 13 moves from simple description to inferential analysis and introduces inferential statistics. Specific statistical tools discussed include parametric tests such as *t*-tests, analysis of variance, correlation, and regression, and nonparametric tests such as the chi-square test and nonparametric correlation are also covered.

Chapter 14 introduces the personal computer—explores the use of computers, how they operate, and how you can use them. Based on the discussions in earlier chapters, you should have an idea of the computer's usefulness as a research aid. This chapter explores the uses of the computer and examines the advantages and limitations of the personal computer in research.

Finally, Chapter 15 brings together the research process by focusing on the final product: The research report. This chapter brings us full circle. We began by asking questions and we end by examining the processes involved in reporting your answers and the formats appropriate for your report. Finally, we review the research process.

Part Three, then, bring us to the climax of learning about research that generates quantified data. We began the journey by learning how research relies on theory, how theory leads to research questions, how questions lead to method, and, now, in turn, this section demonstrates how method leads to analysis. But remember, the research process does not end there. All research, especially social scientific research, is cumulative and ongoing. It serves to build toward more and better theory, further questions and research, still better theory, and on and on.

Descriptive Statistics

After data from a survey or an experiment have been collected, the results must be summarized, organized, and analyzed. *Statistics* is the branch of applied mathematics that provides the tools to accomplish these goals. Our experience has been that many communication students are intimidated by statistics and, perhaps because they believe that quantitative research methods and statistics are one and the same, even fearful of quantitative research methods in general. If you feel this way, several points may help allay your fears. First, statistics are merely a *tool*, a set of techniques that have only one overall purpose: to help answer research questions. They are not an end in themselves, they are a means to an end: Understanding the results of a research study. Second, understanding most statistical analyses does not require high levels of mathematical sophistication. Rather, the ability to think conceptually—to understand the underlying logic of the tool—is more important than knowing specialized mathematical techniques. Third, data analysis—statistics—is a relatively small part, albeit an important part, of the overall research process. Identifying an important question, designing the study, and creating adequate operationalizations of the variables are all *more* important than data analysis. Why? If these stages of research are poorly carried out, if an unimportant research question is addressed, if the research design is seriously flawed or the variables are inadequately operationalized, all the sophisticated analysis in the world will not create a good study.

There are three major distinctions that are helpful in understanding statistical analyses used by social researchers. First, statistics are used to *describe* and to *infer*. The goal of descriptive statistics is the reduction and simplification of the numbers representing research to ease interpreting the results. For example, when we read that "participants in the experimental group had a mean score of 4.2 on the dependent measure and participants in the control group had a mean score of 2.5," or that two variables "had a correlation of .45," we are being presented with *descriptions* of the results. Inferential statistics, on the other hand, have as their goal the presentation of information that allows us to make judgments. These judgments concern whether the research results observed in a sample *generalize* to the population from which the sample was drawn. Thus, when we hear that the difference between two groups' means was "significant at the .05 level" we are able to make *inferences* to the population from which the sample was drawn. Specifically, we know that there is less than a 5 percent chance that the result observed in the sample would *not* generalize to the population.

A second important statistical distinction concerns the *type of data* we are making inferences about or describing. We noted in Chapter 6 that measurement occurs at four levels: Nominal, ordinal, interval, and ratio. Numbers resulting from nominal and ratio measures are described, and inferences from samples to the population made, with one class of statistics: *Nonparametric*. Numbers resulting from interval and ratio measures are treated with *parametric* statistics.

Third, we may describe, or make inferences about, nonparametric or parametric variables by themselves (univariate), as two variables relate to one another (bivariate), or as three or more variables interrelate (multivariate). Table 12.1 summarizes and gives examples of the kinds of statistics available to the researcher within each of the categories mentioned. In this chapter we present both nonparametric and parametric descriptive statistics.

We begin now by reviewing the types of data used in research. After this we examine the nonparametric and parametric analyses available to make sense out of the numbers generated in the research.

TYPES OF DATA

As noted, measurement creates data consisting of one of four types—nominal, ordinal, interval, and ratio. For analytical purposes, data can be broken into two broad categories. Data that come from nominal categories (nominal measurement) or ordered categories (ordinal measurement) are classified as categorical, or *nonparametric*. These analytical tools rely on establishing proportions or percentages

Table 12.1   EXAMPLES OF TYPES OF STATISTICS

	Descriptive (Chapter 12)		Inferential (Chapter 13)	
	Nonparametric	Parametric	Nonparametric	Parametric
Univariate (one variable)	Percentages e.g., 17% Yes 30% No 3% ?	Mean Median Mode Range Standard Deviation	Confidence intervals (percent) e.g., 95% sure, 56%–40% +/− 3%	Confidence intervals (range) e.g., 95% sure, mean between 4.5 & 4.0
Bivariate (two variables)	Comparison of percentages Crosstabulations Spearman rho correlation	Comparison of two means e.g., 4.5 > 3.1 Pearson correlation	Chi-square	*t*-test test of significance
Multivariate (three or more variables)	Comparison of percentages Crosstabs (three or more variables)	Comparison of means, (two or more independent variables) Partial correlation Multiple regression	Chi-square	Analysis of variance Multivariate analysis of variance

based on simple categorization principles. Data from interval or ratio measures are classified as continuous, or *parametric.* They are assigned some arbitrary (interval) or absolute (ratio) zero point. Parametric analysis examines the dispersion of the data or the data's *central tendencies.* These categories (nonparametric, parametric) provide a workable distinction between descriptive data types.

If, for instance, our purpose in conducting a research project is to ascertain if a woman might be elected president, we might consider a survey of registered voters. Our survey would include some basic information about the sample. Here, nominal and ordinal measures come into play. They help us to classify people into groups, understand when they fall into different categories, and generally provide frequency and percentage data about the sample.

Box 12.1 presents some of the variables we might consider in surveying people about voting. Note that some of the variables are measured at the nominal level (sex, race, marital status), others at the ordinal (education) or interval ("voting is important") level, and still others at the ratio level (age). The nominal and ordinal data are analyzed with nonparametric statistics; the interval and ratio data with parametric statistics.

Several variables could be treated as nonparametric *or* parametric. For example, although age is a ratio variable, ranging from 18 years (remember, our question concerns voting behaviors and people must be at least 18 years of age to vote) to

---

Box 12.1 **Categorizing Data**

Sex: ____Male (1)   ____Female (2)

Age: _____Years

Race: ____White (1)   ____Black (2)   ____Other (3)

Income After Tax: $ _____

Years of Education: _____Years

Highest Degree Earned: ____High School   ____Community College
                        ____University   ____Graduate Degree
                                            ____No Degree

Occupation: _____

Occupational area: ____White Collar   ____Blue Collar
                    ____Student   ____Not Applicable

Years on the job: _____ Years

Married? ____Yes   ____No
(or
Marital Status: ____Married   ____Single   ____Divorced)

Instructions: Please circle the response which best reflects how you feel about the following statements. Circling SA means that you strongly agree with the statement, A means that you agree with the statement, N means that you neither agree nor disagree with the statement, D means that you disagree with the statement, and SD means that you strongly disagree with the statement.

SA A N D SD   Voting is important.

SA A N D SD   The next president of the United States should be a woman.

---

the age of the oldest voter, we could also place age in one of several ordinal categories:

____under 20   ____20–30   ____31–40
____41–50   ____51–60   ____over 60

This category system suggests that people under 20 should be grouped together, as should be people over 60, and that there are naturally occurring breaks

Table 12.2 CATEGORICAL AND CONTINUOUS DATA LEVELS OF MEASUREMENT

Data type	Measurement level	Example
	Nominal	Sex (Male=1/Female=2) Race (White=1/Black=2)
Categorical (Nonparametric statistics)	Ordinal	Larger > Smaller Agree > Disagree
Continuous (Parametric statistics)	Interval	Agree (5) to Disagree (1) Believe (5) to Disbelieve (1)
	Ratio	Age Hours of television viewing

that are meaningful in answering the particular research question. It also suggests that there is some reason for placing those between 20 and 60 in categories of 10-year increments. How "age" is defined will determine the category system. Although age is normally a ratio measure, we defined it here as ordinal; we ordered the age groups from youngest to oldest.

Consider the ways we can approach the survey's attitudinal statements. Responses to the statement, "Voting Is Important," for instance, consist of Strongly Agree, Agree, Neither Agree nor Disagree, Disagree, and Strongly Disagree. We could treat each as a category and count the number of respondents who Strongly Agree, Agree, Disagree, Strongly Disagree, or Neither Agree nor Disagree with the statement. Our analysis would take the percentage or proportion of respondents falling in each category. Or, we could treat the responses as continuous data, assigning numbers to the intervals as Strongly Disagree=1, Disagree=2, Neither Agree nor Disagree=3, Agree=4, and Strongly Agree=5. This scale, as noted in Chapter 6, is a Likert-type measure, one that is treated as interval data.

Table 12.2 presents examples of data types found within categorical and continuous data. Note that as we move from nominal to ratio measures, precision increases. But, it is often more difficult to get participants to respond to more complex measurement scales. Sometimes we must trade off precision (interval and ratio measures) for accuracy (nominal and ordinal measures.)

DISTRIBUTIONS

Regardless of what type of data you collect, it will be distributed in some way. When describing research findings we frequently find both types of data, although as Kerlinger notes, quantitative social science research seems more predisposed to continuous data than frequency data.[1] A quick perusal of communication research might find, however, that categorical data analysis is undertaken, especially in the mass communication area. Political communication research, for instance, reports many categorical descriptions of how people perceive different candidates. Communication education research also employs categorical data analysis. Examples include research reporting what educators are doing in introductory courses (types of activities, books in use, types of basic courses) and how educators use different educational strategies in the classroom.

We now turn to the question of how to use data to answer research questions. We discuss how to prepare for the analysis, identify the various descriptive statistics available, and interpret what they mean. We begin with nonparametric data descriptors.

Table 12.3 presents a fictitious subset of data for the questionnaire found at Box 12.1. In this data set we have two variables, sex and score1 (the first column contains the *participant number* which could be considered a third variable). For the rest of this chapter we present calculations based on two programs available for the personal computer which emulate the larger mainframe computers. One, *SPSS/ PC+*, is available for use on IBM, IBM-compatible, and Macintosh personal computers.[2] The second—*Statistics with Finesse (SWF)*—is available for IBM, IBM-compatible, and Apple II series computers.[3] Each presents a different type of data

Table 12.3   SAMPLE DATA SET

Data lines
1   1   5
2   2   5
3   1   4
4   2   4
5   1   4
6   2   3
7   1   3
8   2   3
9   1   3
10   2   3
11   1   2
12   2   2
13   1   2
14   2   1
15   1   1
16   2   9
17   1   9
18   2   9

Note: Response number (1–18), sex (1=Male, 2 = Female), and data (interval scale: 1 = Strongly Disagree, 2 = Disagree, 3 = Neither Agree nor Disagree, 4 = Agree, 5 = Strongly Agree).

entry and analysis procedure, procedures representative of many statistical packages available for personal computers.

CODING DATA FOR ANALYSIS

Before the data can be analyzed it must be coded. Coding requires that the researcher systematically take the responses from the questionnaires, scales, or observers' check sheets and assign numbers to them. For example, our scale might consist of responses to a yes/no question. We might enter this on the coding form as Y and N or we might enter it as 1 (Yes) and 2 (No). Usually, *the simpler the coding, the fewer the errors.* Errors are the major problem with coding data and the data must be carefully proofread after transfer to the coding sheet and again after being entered into a computer file.

Sometimes a respondent or participant fails to answer a question or complete a scale. Most computer programs today allow us to enter a special notation for missing data. Typically, we use a 0 or a 9 to represent missing data. These programs then compute the analysis without including an entry for the missing case. As a general rule, it is best to code the data using numbers (1 for male, 2 for female; 1 for white, 2 for black, 3 for Asian; etc.) and then add values or labels later. Although most computer packages allow for both alphabetical and numeric data, many analyses require the data to be entered as numbers only.

The key to coding data is to establish a coding system (much like that discussed in Chapter 11) that includes all possible ranges when the data are categorical. When the data are continuous, the actual numbers can be entered. Care must be taken when creating your coding forms that there are enough spaces or columns on the form for the particular variable. If you are coding sex as M or F, 1 or 2, only one space or column is needed. However, if you are coding an 11-point scale, you must reserve two columns. It is a good idea to get used to coding these data as 01, 02, 03, . . ., 11.

Once the data have been coded and entered into the computer, we are ready for analysis.

DESCRIBING NONPARAMETRIC DATA

Nonparametric data, as was noted earlier, are data that have been placed in mutually exclusive categories. We can take the same data presented earlier and categorize responses to the questions; we can then break them into smaller units for comparison. These analyses range from *univariate* analysis, in which only one variable is examined, to *multivariate* analysis or *contingency* analysis, where two or more variables are analyzed simultaneously.[4] Our focus will be limited to univariate and bivariate (two variable) analysis. We will present each of these in turn.

For the purposes of our discussion, suppose that we are interested in studying how voters feel about a woman being elected president in the next election. Our research question might be: Do males and females differ in their feelings about a woman president? The best method to answer this question is to survey randomly selected voters.

Univariate Descriptive Analysis

When conducting an univariate descriptive analysis we analyze the ways our respondents scored on one variable. Table 12.4 presents a simple univariate analysis. It analyzes the sample according to the category, *sex*. As you can see, there were nine males and nine females. These statistics are simply the frequency distribution; that is, the number of responses that fall in each category. We could analyze the same data as *percentages*, assuming that the total number is finite, and then describe the data in terms of *proportions*. We find that one half (50 percent) of our sample is male and the other half is female. Both descriptions tell us something about the sample.

Table 12.5 presents the categorical analysis of the Likert-type scale described

Table 12.4   PRINTOUT: UNIVARIATE STATISTICS
             Sex

```
                          SPSS/PC+
------------------------------------------------------------
SEX
------------------------------------------------------------

                                          Valid     Cum
   Value Label    Value  Frequency  Percent  Percent  Percent
MALE               1         9       50.0     50.0     50.0
FEMALE             2         9       50.0     50.0    100.0

                          -------   -------  -------
              TOTAL        18       100.0    100.0
------------------------------------------------------------


                           SWF

            ------------------------------


            File name:  DATA1S


            ------------------------------


      Variable:  SEX
      ------------------------------
      Code         Frequency    Percent
      ------------------------------
          M            9         50.00
          F            9         50.00
                    ------      -------
      Total          18         100.00
```

Table 12.5   PRINTOUT: UNIVARIATE STATISTICS
Score1

SPSS/PC+

SCORE1   RESPONSE TO ATTITUDE STATEMENT

Value Label	Value	Frequency	Percent	Valid Percent	Cum Percent
STRONGLY DISAGREE	1	2	11.1	11.1	11.1
DISAGREE	2	3	16.7	16.7	27.8
UNDECIDED	3	5	27.8	27.8	55.6
AGREE	4	3	16.7	16.7	72.2
STRONGLY AGREE	5	2	11.1	11.1	83.3
	9	3	16.7	16.7	100.0
TOTAL		18	100.0	100.0	

Note: The printout for SWF is identical to this (see Table 12.4).

earlier. Listed in one column are all possible responses, including those who failed to respond. Notice that while the frequencies are the same, the percentages differ. In the case of Table 12.5, our analysis would conclude that 27.8 percent of the respondents were undecided about electing a woman president. Notice that the figures in columns Percent and Valid Percent are identical; that is, the results are calculated as if *any* response, in any category, should be tabulated. All *18* respondents were included in the analysis. Actually, only those who responded (15 of the 18 respondents) should be included in the analysis. The Valid Percent column in Table 12.6 differs from the Percent column in that the former takes into account respondents classified as Missing, Incomplete or Other.

We can visualize the univariate analysis by examining the frequencies in ways other than reported percentages. Figures 12.1(a), 12.1(b), and 12.1(c) present one such analysis of the data, a *bar chart*. (Figure 12.1(a) represents the actual printout, Figures 12.1(b) and 12.1(c) present the data as they might be graphed for actual presentation.) We see that more people responded as "undecided." Furthermore, an equal number of respondents agreed and disagreed with the statement, as was the case of those "strongly disagreeing" and "strongly agreeing." A second analysis, the *histogram*, provides not only the frequency of responses, but also the percentages and proportions (percent × 100) associated with each category. These descriptive tools show the responses visually. Interpretation, assigning meaning to the responses, is still up to the researcher.

Bivariate Analysis

Usually, the data have to be divided into subgroups to describe the results of the research adequately. While it may be informative to report the number or percentage of males and females in a sample, we do not know if the males and females

Table 12.6   PRINTOUT: UNIVARIATE STATISTICS
            Score1

SPSS/PC+

SCORE1   RESPONSE TO ATTITUDE STATEMENT

Value Label	Value	Frequency	Percent	Valid Percent	Cum Percent
STRONGLY DISAGREE	1	2	11.1	13.3	13.3
DISAGREE	2	3	16.7	20.0	33.3
UNDECIDED	3	5	27.8	33.3	66.7
AGREE	4	3	16.7	20.0	86.7
STRONGLY AGREE	5	2	11.1	13.3	100.0
	9	3	16.7	MISSING	
	TOTAL	18	100.0	100.0	

SWF

File Name: DATA1S

Variable: SCORE1

Code	Frequency	Percent
1	2	11.11
2	3	16.67
3	5	27.78
4	3	16.67
5	2	11.11
Missing	3	16.67
Total	18	100.00

Note: SWF does not take missing values into account with a "valid percent" column. You are forewarned of Missing values, but they are calculated in with the other frequencies as if they were part of the analysis.

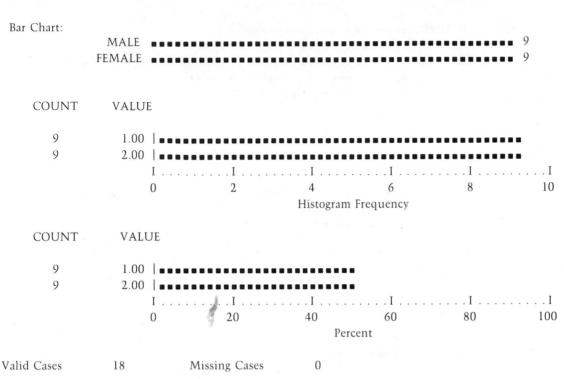

SPSS/PC+

SEX

Bar Chart:

MALE   ■■ 9
FEMALE ■■ 9

COUNT   VALUE

9   1.00 |■■■
9   2.00 |■■■
             I . . . . I . . . . I . . . . I . . . . I I
             0   2   4   6   8   10
                          Histogram Frequency

COUNT   VALUE

9   1.00 |■■■■■■■■■■■■■■■■■■■■■■■■■■■■
9   2.00 |■■■■■■■■■■■■■■■■■■■■■■■■■■■■
             I . . . . I . . . . I . . . . I . . . . I I
             0   20   40   60   80   100
                             Percent

Valid Cases   18   Missing Cases   0

Figure 12.1a Printout: Bar charts and histograms.

responded differently to the Likert-type statement concerning electing a woman president. By breaking sex into two categories and reanalyzing the data it is possible to address this question. Table 12.7 presents a 2 (M-F) × 5 (Strongly Agree to Strongly Disagree) *contingency table.* This table shows how males and females responded to the attitude statement.

There are several ways to interpret this table. First, we can examine the frequency of males and females who responded to the statement and the resulting percentages or proportions. Our tables are constructed in such a way that the columns represent the variable sex and the rows the responses to the statement. As a general rule, it is best to establish your independent variable as the columns (usually there are fewer categories with this variable and this makes for easier reading) and the dependent variable's categories as the rows. Initial analysis of the data indicates that eight males (53.3 percent of the sample) and seven females (46.7 percent of the sample) responded to the statement (see Tables 12.8 and 12.9). Analysis also indicates that two people (13.3 percent) strongly agreed, three people (20.0 percent) agreed, three people (20.0 percent) disagreed, two people (13.3 percent) strongly disagreed, and five people (33.3 percent) were undecided about a women being elected president. This analysis is the same as conducting two univariate analyses, one for sex and one for attitude.

SCORE1   RESPONSE TO STATEMENT

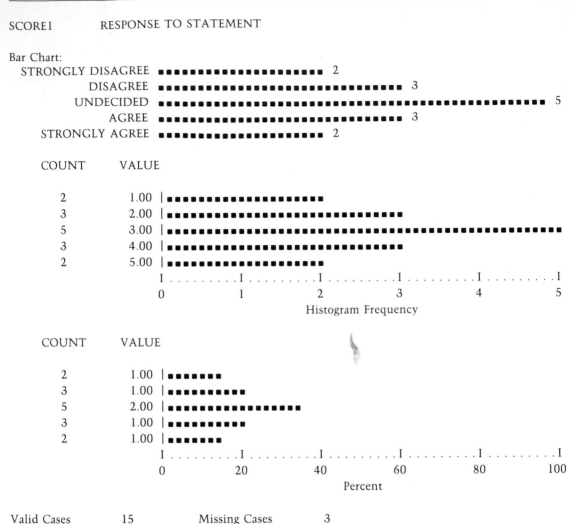

Bar Chart:
    STRONGLY DISAGREE ■■■■■■■■■■■■■■■■■■■■ 2
              DISAGREE ■■■■■■■■■■■■■■■■■■■■■■■■■■■■■ 3
             UNDECIDED ■■■ 5
                 AGREE ■■■■■■■■■■■■■■■■■■■■■■■■■■■■■ 3
        STRONGLY AGREE ■■■■■■■■■■■■■■■■■■■■ 2

    COUNT   VALUE

      2   1.00 |■■■■■■■■■■■■■■■■■■■■
      3   2.00 |■■■■■■■■■■■■■■■■■■■■■■■■■■■■■
      5   3.00 |■■■
      3   4.00 |■■■■■■■■■■■■■■■■■■■■■■■■■■■■■
      2   5.00 |■■■■■■■■■■■■■■■■■■■■
                       I . . . . I . . . . I . . . . I . . . . I I
                       0   1   2   3   4   5
                                        Histogram Frequency

    COUNT   VALUE

      2   1.00 |■■■■■■■
      3   1.00 |■■■■■■■■■■■
      5   2.00 |■■■■■■■■■■■■■■■■■■
      3   1.00 |■■■■■■■■■■■
      2   1.00 |■■■■■■■
                       I . . . . I . . . . I . . . . I . . . . I I
                       0   20   40   60   80   100
                                             Percent

Valid Cases   15   Missing Cases   3

Figure 12.1a (*Continued*)

Analysis of the *crossbreaks,* or a comparison of the frequency of responses in individual cells, provides three different types of analysis. [5] In each case the individual cell frequencies (number of males choosing each response category and number of females doing the same) will remain the same, what changes are the percentages or proportions. If you are concerned with describing how *each* cell related to the *total,* you would interpret Table 12.8a, which shows that 6.7 percent of the males (1 out of 15) strongly disagreed with the statement, as did the same percentage of females. Twenty percent of the females, however, were undecided; as were 13.3 percent of the males.

The second way to interpret this table is by analyzing each cell as a percent

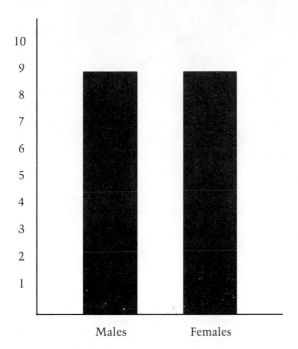

Figure 12.1b Bar chart.

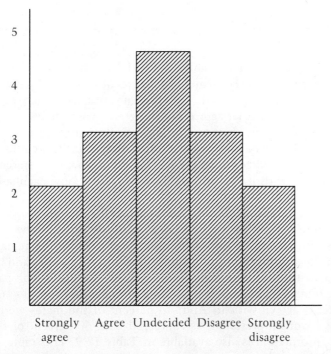

Figure 12.1c Likert-like scale ($n = 15$).

287

Table 12.7 CONTINGENCY TABLE

	Sex	
Score	Male	Female
Strongly agree		
Agree		
Undecided		
Disagree		
Strongly disagree		

of each *column,* as presented in Table 12.8b. Here descriptions of the data focus on how each sex responded. For males, 12.5 percent strongly disagreed, 25.0 percent disagreed, 25.0 percent agreed, 12.5 percent strongly agreed with the statement, and 25.0 percent neither agreed nor disagreed. For females, the percentages differ: 14.3 percent strongly disagreed, disagreed, strongly agreed, or agreed with the statement; 42.9 percent neither agreed nor disagreed. You could also further collapse the rows and analyze which sex was uncertain about the statement, agreed with it, or disagreed with it. Your focus, however, is on how each sex responded to the statement.

The third analysis shows (Table 12.8c) each cell as a percentage of each *row.* Here we are interested in how each response category differs between males and females. Thus, 50 percent of the males and 50 percent of the females strongly disagreed with the statement, the same percentages as with males and females who strongly agreed with it. Of the males, 66.7 percent disagreed, compared to 33.3 percent of the females. The same percentages of males and females (66.7 percent and 33.3 percent) agreed with it. And, 40 percent of the males were undecided about electing a woman president, as compared with 60 percent of the females.

The same information is also available in Table 12.9. This table, however, is more complex and harder to interpret—*it combines all three analyses into one*

Table 12.8 (a)   PRINTOUT: CONTINGENCY TABLE
Cells Related to Total

```
                          SWF

    ------------------------------------------

              File name:  DATA1S

    ------------------------------------------

Missing some value:    3

Rows  = SCORE1, Columns  = SEX
    ------------------------------------------
Codes          M          F        Total
    ------------------------------------------
     1          1          1          2
     %         6.7        6.7       13.3

     2          2          1          3
     %        13.3        6.7       20.0

     3          2          3          5
     %        13.3       20.0       33.3

     4          2          1          3
     %        13.3        6.7       20.0

     5          1          1          2
     %         6.7        6.7       13.3
              ------     ------     -------
Total          8          7          15
     %        53.3       46.7       100.0
```

table. When constructing tables, remember that your research question guides both the way each is created and how each is interpreted. In our example we are interested in how males and females responded to electing a woman president. For instance, we can report the *number* of responses per cell for each sex, the *percentage* of responses per cell based on which *marginals* (the row or column totals, interpreted as row marginal and column marginal, respectively, or the total) for each sex, or the proportions (as calculated by the percentages) responding for males and for females. In one case you might say that two males and one female agreed with the statement. In another you might report that 66.7 percent of the males agreed with the statement, while only 33.3 percent of the females agreed with it. Or, finally, you might note that males agreed with the statement either twice as

Table 12.8(b)   PRINTOUT: CONTINGENCY TABLE
                Cells Related to Column Marginals

```
                          SWF

        ------------------------------------------

                  File Name:   DATA1S

        ------------------------------------------

    Missing some value:      3

    Rows  = SCORE1, Columns  = SEX
    ------------------------------------------
    Codes          M            F          Total
    ------------------------------------------
       1           1            1            2
       %          12.5         14.3         13.3

       2           2            1            3
       %          25.0         14.3         20.0

       3           2            3            5
       %          25.0         42.9         33.3

       4           2            1            3
       %          25.0         14.3         20.0

       5           1            1            2
       %          12.5         14.3         13.3
                 -------      -------      -------
    Total          8            7           15
       %         100.0        100.0        100.0
```

much as did females, or that the proportion of males agreeing was twice that of females. All three would be correct.

Before completing this section we need to note two things. First, it is important that you report how many responses were not included in the tables, or were classified as missing. If there were 100 respondents to a survey and only 97 responded to a particular question, then that should be indicated in the table. Second, contingency tables can be confusing to construct and interpret. We have presented two *simple* cases consisting of only two variables with limited categories. We could just as easily have added a third variable, perhaps whether or not the respondents were married (just two levels or categories, Married and Not Married) and created a *multivariate* analysis. We would now have *six* potential tables to analyze: three for those married and three for those not married. Or, as shown in

Table 12.8(c) PRINTOUT: CONTINGENCY TABLE
Cells Related to Row Marginals

```
                          SWF

        ----------------------------------------

                  File Name:  DATA1S


        ----------------------------------------

        Missing some value:     3

        Rows = SCORE1  Columns = SEX
        --------------------------------------------
        Codes        M          F        Total
        --------------------------------------------
          1          1          1          2
          %         50.0       50.0      100.0

          2          2          1          3
          %         66.7       33.3      100.0

          3          2          3          5
          %         40.0       60.0      100.0

          4          2          1          3
          %         66.7       33.3      100.0

          5          1          1          2
          %         50.0       50.0      100.0
                   ------     ------    -------
        Total        8          7         15
          %         53.3       46.7      100.0
```

Table 12.10, the interrelationships between the three variables could be displayed in a considerably more complex table. Some computer programs, such as *SPSS/ PC+*, allow you to interpret only two tables, each like Table 12.9. Others, such as *SWF*, will create all six tables for comparison, such as Tables 12.8(a)–12.8(c). Some mainframe computer programs will create the full table, as shown in Table 12.10.

Summary

Nonparametric data analysis allows us to describe how scores are distributed in general classes or categories. At times it is more important to know that 62.2

Table 12.9   PRINTOUT: CONTINGENCY TABLE

SPSS/PC+

```
------------------------------------------------------------
Crosstabulation:      SCORE1   RESPONSE TO ATTITUDE STATEMENT
                    By SEX
------------------------------------------------------------
           Row Pct |MALE    |FEMALE  |
    SEX-> Col Pct  |        |        | Row
          Tot Pct  |     1  |     2  |Total
SCORE1    ---------|--------|--------|--------
                1  | 50.0   | 50.0   |    2
Strongly disagree  | 12.5   | 14.3   | 13.3
                   |  6.7   |  6.7   |
                   |--------|--------|
                2  | 66.7   | 33.3   |    3
Disagree           | 25.0   | 14.3   | 20.0
                   | 13.3   |  6.7   |
                   |--------|--------|
                3  | 40.0   | 60.0   |    5
Undecided          | 25.0   | 42.9   | 33.3
                   | 13.3   | 20.0   |
                   |--------|--------|
                4  | 66.7   | 33.3   |    3
Agree              | 25.0   | 14.3   | 20.0
                   | 13.3   |  6.7   |
                   |--------|--------|
                5  | 50.0   | 50.0   |    2
Strongly agree     | 12.5   | 14.3   | 13.3
                   |  6.7   |  6.7   |
          ---------|--------|--------|--------
          Column   |    8   |    7   |   15
          Total    | 53.3   | 46.7   |100.0
```

Number of Missing Observations = 3

percent are undecided about an issue than to know that the sample surveyed average a score of 3.45 on a Likert-type scale.

DESCRIBING PARAMETRIC DATA

What do we know about the data presented in Table 12.3, other than how many people—the number, percent, or proportion—responded to the categories Strongly Agree, Agree, Disagree, Strongly Disagree, or Uncertain regarding our statement? If we want to examine the characteristics of the data for the entire sample we can begin by asking what the central tendencies of the respondents' answers are and how much dispersion there is in the scores.

Table 12.10   MORE COMPLEX CONTINGENCY TABLE

Score	Married		Not Married	
	Male	Female	Male	Female
Strongly agree				
Agree				
Undecided				
Disagree				
Strongly disagree				

Figure 12.2 presents the same data as Table 12.3, but graphically. Note that it approximates the *normal curve* discussed in Chapter 8. In this case there are five scores at the midpoint of the Likert-type scale (3), three scores on either side (2 or 4), and two scores at the extremes (1 or 5). This is a *frequency distribution* of the data. It tells us at a glance that there is a score that is the *average* response. Obviously, not all data will be normally distributed. Note that three people failed to respond to the statement. The ramifications of missing data will be more apparent later, for now we omit them from the analysis.

How would you describe the data in Figure 12.3? One way is to describe the data distributed over the entire scale. Our first descriptive analysis is visual: We can label it in at least two ways—by degree of *flatness* (bell-shaped, peaked, or flat) or by the degree of *skewness* of the data (the peakedness of the data to one side of the midpoint of the scale or the other).[6] Figure 12.4 indicates five possible descriptions of the data. Note that our data distribution is *normal;* that is, it is bell-shaped and equally distributed on both sides of the peak.

If two of the scores were shifted from 4 to 2 we would skew the curve toward the higher end of the scale. This curve is described as having a positive skew. Why? We label the curve by the direction of the *tail* away from the peak. If the data cluster at the negative end of the scale, the skewness is positive; if the data cluster at the positive end, the skewness is negative.

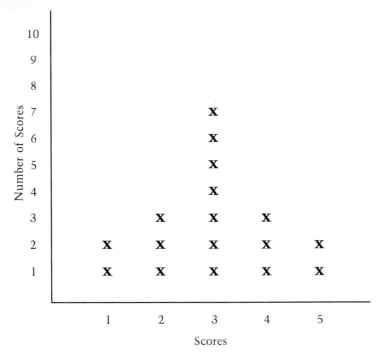

Figure 12.2a Graphic representation of data for SCORE1.

Univariate Indicators: Mean, Median, Mode

Now that we have graphically described the data, we want to describe the average score for our sample (see Table 12.11). There are three indices of *central tendency* that provide information about the average response.

The *arithmetic mean* is one type of average response. It is calculated by summing all scores and then by dividing by the number of scores:

$$M = \frac{\Sigma X}{N}$$

where M is the mean (sometimes represented as $\overline{X}$, or "x-bar"), Σ is the notation for summation, X are the individual scores, and N is the number of scores being summed.

By adding all data for SCORE1 from our survey data and dividing by 15 (the number of people *answering* the question), we get a mean response of 3.00. Note what happens if we add in the scores coded as 9s, a frequently used missing numbers indicator: The mean changes from 3.00 to 4.00. Thus, our first warning when dealing with measures of central tendency: *Extremes in the data influence the mean response.*

Sometimes it is best to examine the data for another kind of average: the *mode.* The mode is the most frequently occurring score. In this example it happens to be

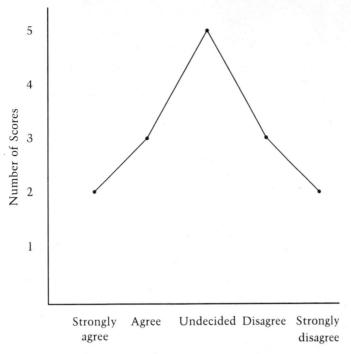

Figure 12.2b Frequency polygram.

the same as the mean, 3.00. Some data sets will have more than one mode, in this case we might describe the data as being bimodal or even trimodal (see Figure 12.5).Figure 12.4 If the sample yielded six people responding to the statement as undecided and another six as strongly disagreeing, then the data would be described as bimodal (two modes of six responses each). The mean is always influenced by the mode and by all other scores; in contrast, the mode is uninfluenced by small numbers of extreme scores.

The third measure of central tendency is the *median.* The median is the score representing the midpoint of all scores. It is the score above which lie one-half of

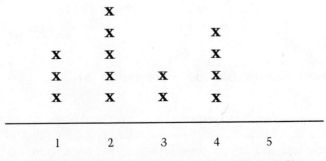

Figure 12.3 Graphic representation of hypothetical data.

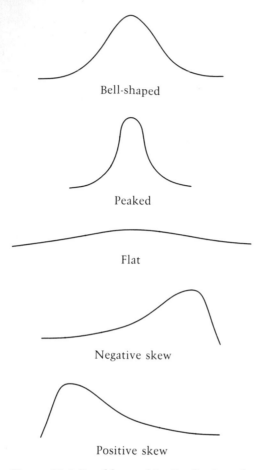

Figure 12.4 Possible graphic distribution of continuous data.

the scores and below which lie the other half of the scores. Our median also is 3.00 (remember, the scores are "normally" distributed). In this case the median is a whole number; that is, there are an odd number of participants and the midpoint fell on one score. Where there are an even number of scores, you take the average (or mean) of the two scores that fall around the midpoint (a median of 3.5, for instance).

Understanding Dispersion: Range, Standard Deviation, and Standard Score

A second way to describe data is to examine how the data points or scores spread out around the mean. Put another way, we can describe how the data are dispersed between the highest and lowest points. Again, we have three commonly used

Table 12.11   PRINTOUTS: STATISTICAL INDICATORS
             Score 1

SPSS/PC+

With ''missing data'' included

SCORE1   Score on Likert-like statement

Mean	4.000	Median	3.000
Mode	3.000	Std Dev	2.567
Skewness	1.151	Variance	6.588
Range	8.000	Minimum	1.000
Maximum	9.000		

Valid cases   18   Missing cases   0

Without ''missing data''

Mean	3.000	Median	3.000
Mode	3.000	Std Dev	1.212
Skewness	0.000	Variance	1.471
Range	4.000	Minimum	1.000
Maximum	5.000		

Valid cases   15   Missing cases   3

SWF

File name: DATA1

Variable	N	Mean	Std Dev	Low	High
SCORE1	15	3.00	1.21	1	5

Missing data were coded as blanks (^).

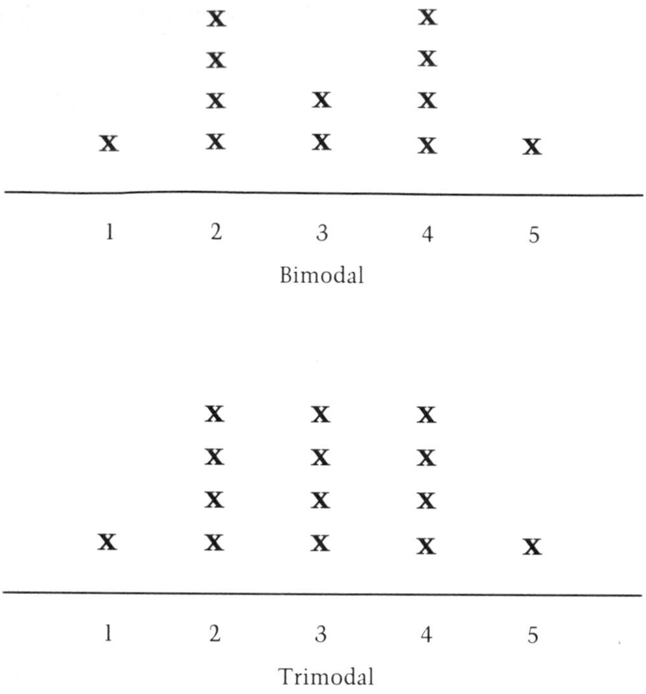

```
    X                 X
    X                 X
    X        X        X
X   X        X        X        X

_____

1        2        3        4        5

              Bimodal



    X        X        X
    X        X        X
    X        X        X
X   X        X        X        X

_____

1        2        3        4        5

              Trimodal
```

Figure 12.5 Bimodal and trimodal distributions.

indices of the distribution. The *range* is simply the difference between high and low scores. Since we have scores between 1 and 5, our range is 4 (5−1=4).

While the range tells us the distance between data points, it does not tell us much about the dispersion of scores within the data. A more precise analytical tool is the *standard deviation* (usually signified as *s* or σ). It provides us with a more workable description of the data. It also has another advantage—the standard deviation can be used to estimate the number of responses that lie within the various points of the data:

$$s \text{ or } \sigma = \sqrt{\frac{\Sigma(X - M)^2}{N}}$$

The standard deviation tells us how dispersed the data points are from the mean. The more closely the scores cluster around the mean, the more reliability you have in your analysis and the smaller the standard deviation will be. Calculation of the standard deviation is not difficult, you simply subtract the average score from each score, square the result, and sum the *deviations*. You then divide this score by the number of scores. The standard deviation tells us how normally dispersed the data are. A more general measure of dispersion is the *variance*, from which the standard deviation is calculated. The variance (s^2 or σ^2), then, is the square of the standard deviation (see Table 12.12).

The normal curve was introduced in Chapter 8 as predictable areas under the

Table 12.12   VARIANCE CALCULATIONS

Participant	Score	Mean	$X-M$	$(X-M)^2$
1	5	3	2	4
2	5	3	2	4
3	4	3	1	1
4	4	3	1	1
5	4	3	1	1
6	3	3	0	0
7	3	3	0	0
8	3	3	0	0
9	3	3	0	0
10	3	3	0	0
11	2	3	-1	1
12	2	3	-1	1
13	2	3	-1	1
14	1	3	-2	4
15	1	3	-2	4
Σ (sum)	45		0	22

Note: $\sigma^2 = \dfrac{22}{15} = 1.47.$

curve where scores might be expected to fall. In our example the curve we obtained from our sample was normal, in that it was bell-shaped and tapered out symmetrically at both ends. This curve yielded a standard deviation of 1.21 ($\sigma^2 = 1.47$), where the number of scores that fall between ± 1.21 points from the mean response (3.00) accounted for 68 percent of the total number of scores, or between 1.79 and 4.21. As Figure 12.6 demonstrates, over two-thirds of the scores should fall within

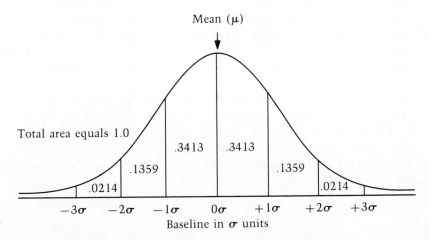

Figure 12.6 The normal curve.

one standard deviation either side of the mean. Ninety-five percent of the scores should fall within two standard deviations of that mean.

The standard deviation provides an index of how the majority of the scores spread out around (deviate from) the mean. Additionally, it provides one more tool for data description. Suppose for a moment that we have not *one* but *two* measures of respondent attitudes toward something. The first is the Likert-type, 5-point measure we have been describing. The second is a semantic differential scale consisting of seven equal-appearing intervals. How can scores derived from two different scales be compared? We might want to know how the two scores describe the same attitude object. Obviously, the 5-point and 7-point measures will yield different distributions. Are we comparing apples to oranges? A *standardized score* provides us with a way of describing the attitudes by translating each individual score into a score that reflects standard deviation units.

To *standardize* the scores so that they may be described together, a simple calculation is necessary. The *Z-score,* or standardized score, takes each participant's score, subtracts the mean from it and then divides that number by the variable's standard deviation:

$$Z = \frac{X - M}{\sigma}$$

In our example, the mean response for the 15 people answering was 3.00 and the standard deviation, 1.21. We can calculate Z-scores for each participant and then take the mean of those scores, providing a standardized mean score for comparative or descriptive purposes. Suppose, for instance, that a score on the Likert-type measure was a 2.00, subtracting the mean from this (2.00 − 3.00) produces a numerator of − 1.00, dividing this score by 1.21 yields a Z-score of − .826. Assume that a score on the semantic differential measure was a 3.00 and the standard deviation for the measure was a 2.42. The standardized score for the semantic differential would be ([3 − 4] ÷ 2.42) or − .413. Both standardized scores describe the score as falling within one standard deviation *below* the mean response. You can do the same for all the scores on each measure.

For example, what if we have scores for ten people on two different measures reflecting beliefs and attitudes toward a persuasive message? The data may have been gathered from an experiment in which the participants were exposed to a persuasive message employing high fear appeals. Table 12.13 presents both the attitude measure scores (a belief scale ranging from 1 to 11 and a 7-point semantic differential scale tapping attitude toward the speech). By standardizing the scores we can better describe how the sample perceived the high fear appeal. Note the similarities between the Z-scores among the participants. Note also the discrepancy when the participants evaluated the speech differently on the two scales (participants 3 and 10).

Summary

Describing single parametric variables provides us with a starting point in our research. A research report will frequently report means, standard deviations, and

Table 12.13   *Z*-SCORES FOR TWO ATTITUDE MEASURES

Participant	Belief score[a]	Z score	Attitude score[b]	Z score
1	2	−1.022	2	−0.909
2	4	−0.292	3	−0.303
3	3	−0.657	1	−1.515
4	6	0.438	4	0.303
5	2	−1.022	3	−0.303
6	11	2.262	7	2.121
7	5	0.073	3	−0.303
8	7	0.803	5	0.909
9	3	−0.657	3	−0.303
10	5	0.073	4	0.303
	Mean	4.80	Mean	3.50
	Std Dev	2.74	Std Dev	1.65

[a]Scale = 1 (low belief) to 11 (high belief).

[b]Scale = 1 (low attitude) to 7 (high attitude).

ranges. This allows the reader to examine other research that describes similar circumstances and make comparisons. Although social scientists make regular use of descriptive analyses, purely descriptive studies are still rather rare because reporting single variable average responses, responses that cluster around some central tendency of the sample or population, do not adequately answer the research question. Sometimes it is more important to know the distribution of responses than the average response in some distributions. When researchers are more interested in the frequency with which the participants are able to name candidates, categorical analyses may be more appropriate. Consider, for instance, what it means to report that the average family consists of 2.33 people; unless the researcher is trying to describe the variance in family size, a categorical response is more appropriate here. On the other hand, reporting that 22.3 percent of the respondents reported earning between $15,000 and $19,999 a year may be less revealing than knowing that the average respondent earned $24,242.54, with the sample's median income reported as $26,500. And almost always, descriptions of the results for single variables do not adequately answer complex research questions. Usually it is necessary to analyze the relationship between two or more variables, a topic to which we now turn.

Bivariate: Correlational Analysis

As we have noted repeatedly, the purpose of science is to build theories that state the way in which variables are *related*. Probably no statistic in all of empirical communication research has been more widely employed than the Pearson *r*, (the Pearson correlation coefficient). This statistic provides an index of the extent to which ordered pairs of observations (measurements) covary or share variance; that is, the correlation tells us if and to what degree individual scores on two variables are related.

Correlations range from $+1.00$ through 0 to -1.00, from a perfect positive correlation, to no correlation, to a perfect negative correlation. Seldom, however, do we find perfect positive or negative correlations in the social sciences, but to the extent that respondents who score high on one variable also score high on the second, correlations will be positive. Thus height and weight are usually positively correlated because tall people tend to weigh more than shorter people. Self-disclosure and the degree of trust in the person to whom the disclosure is addressed are usually positively correlated; that is, people self-disclose more to people they trust highly than they do to those whom they trust less. Thus self-disclosure and trust are positively correlated. On the other hand, if people who score high on one variable score low on the second variable, or vice versa, the variables are negatively correlated. High blood pressure and longevity are negatively correlated; people with high blood pressure do not live as long as those with lower blood pressure. Communication apprehension and success in many professions such as law, teaching, and sales are negatively correlated. People with high communication apprehension do not do as well in these professions as those with lower levels of apprehension.

Of course, sometimes tall people are quite skinny and light, while a short person may be plump and heavy. Occasionally individuals will self-disclose to those they do not trust and will withhold disclosures from those they do. A few people with high blood pressure will live to ripe old ages while some with lower blood pressure will die at younger ages. And, some individuals with high communication apprehension will do well in law or teaching or sales, while others with low apprehension will do poorly in these professions. These aberrations reduce the strength of the correlation. As the number of aberrations increase, the resulting correlations will move toward zero. And, in fact, if the two variables were unrelated, the correlation would be close to zero.[7]

What constitutes a strong versus a moderate versus a weak correlation? Interpretation guidelines are somewhat arbitrary and vary with both the type of study undertaken and the purpose of the analysis. For example, if we used a correlation to estimate the reliability of two related measures, we would look for a good correlation of .70, while a .85 correlation or higher would be considered excellent. On the other hand, if the relationship between theoretical variables was being examined in an exploratory study, we might be pleased to find *any* correlation. A correlation of .20 might be considered a worthwhile finding. With this in mind, when examining relationships between two variables, correlations below $\pm.30$ are *generally* considered weak or slight, $\pm.30$ to $\pm.50$ are moderate and above $\pm.50$ are strong correlations.

Scatter Diagrams   A useful graphic depiction of the relationship between two variables is the scatter diagram, or *scattergram.* One of the two variables is represented by the X axis, while the other is represented by the Y axis. Each respondent's score on both variables is plotted and the resulting pattern of points on the graph provides the opportunity to inspect their relationship visually. Figure 12.7 shows a series of hypothetical scattergrams. Scattergram (a) shows a positive corre-

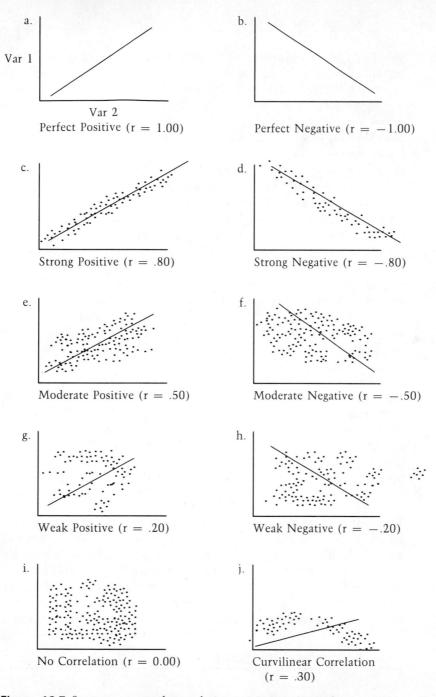

Figure 12.7 Scattergrams and correlations. (a) Var 2, perfect positive ($r=1.00$); (b) perfect negative ($r=-1.00$); (c) strong positive ($r=.80$); (d) strong negative ($r=-.80$); (e) moderate positive ($r=.50$); (f) moderate negative ($r=-.50$); (g) weak positive ($r=.20$); (h) weak negative ($r=-.20$); (i) no correlation ($r=0.00$); (j) curvilinear correlation ($r=.30$).

lation of 1.00; the plotted points fall perfectly along a straight line. Note that the individual with the highest score on variable 1 also had the highest score on variable 2; the individual with the next higher score on variable 1 also had the next highest on variable 2, and so on, for all the individuals measured. Scattergram (b) shows a negative correlation of -1.00. Again, the points fall along a straight line; however this time the individual with the highest score on variable 1 had the *lowest* score on variable 2, and so on, for all the individuals. Both of these scattergrams show a *perfect* relationship between variables 1 and 2.

Scattergrams (c) and (d) show, respectively, strong correlations of $+.80$. Note that some of the plotted points deviate from the straight line. Scattergrams (e) and (f) show moderate correlations of $+.50$. Deviations from the straight line, aberrations, have increased. The plots in scattergrams (g) and (h), which show weak correlations of $+.20$, indicate many wide deviations from the straight line.

Scattergram (i) shows the case when two variables are *not* related. There is no systematic pattern whatsoever, only randomness. An individual's score on one variable is unrelated to his or her score on the other. The correlation is *zero.*

Finally, scattergram (j) shows a curvilinear correlation; that is, two variables are related in a positive fashion for low to moderate scores, but as scores represented by plots on the *X* axis continue to increase from moderate to high, scores on the *Y* axis begin to go down again. A curve results. Note that although the pattern is very regular and very closely follows a curving line, the correlation is quite low: .30. This is because the correlation coefficient assumes that variables will be *linearly* related; it assumes that as one variable increases the other either increases *or* decreases, not increases *and* decreases. *The Pearson correlation provides no information about curvilinear relationships.* Thus, the scattergram becomes an important analytic technique, providing information that the correlation cannot: Specifically, information about the *shape* of the relationship.[8]

The Correlation Matrix   A correlation matrix is a table that presents the correlations among three or more variables. Each variable's correlation with every other variable is shown. If there were five variables being measured in a survey, variable 1 could be correlated with variables 2, 3, 4, and 5. Variable 2 could be correlated with variables 1, 3, 4, and 5, and so on. With 5 variables there are 10 different correlations. With 10 variables there are 45 separate correlations.[9] Table 12.14 shows a simple correlation matrix. In addition to the correlation itself, correlation

Table 12.14   SAMPLE CORRELATION MATRIX

	(1)	(2)	(3)	(4)	(5)
(1) Monetary donations	1.00	.10	−.08	.09	.25
(2) Age		1.00	.08	.09	.19
(3) Sex			1.00	.26	.10
(4) Times voted				1.00	.94
(5) Policical activity					1.00

matrices frequently contain the sample size (e.g., $n = 85$; 85 would be the number of *pairs* of scores used to calculate a particular correlation).

Nonparametric Correlations   The Pearson correlation is a parametric statistic and thus requires interval or ratio data. Correlation techniques are also available for both nominal and ordinal data. Probably the most commonly used correlation for ordinal data is the *Spearman rho rank* correlation. This technique is employed when the scores to be correlated are rank ordered. [10] There are specific correlations available for special cases, such as when the data for one variable are continuous and the data from the second are dichotomous, or even for a situation in which both variables are dichotomous. [11]

   A final note on correlations: Correlation is *not* causation. It is important to remember that there are three criteria for the establishment of causality (see Chapter 10): covariation, time order, and ruling out alternative explanations. Correlation provides evidence bearing only on the first of these criteria, *covariation.* It could be that the relationship is spurious, that a third variable is causing the observed relationship. Or, it could be that the variable thought to be the cause and the variable thought to be the effect are reversed. Correlation, by itself, does not help determine time order.

SUMMARY

This chapter introduced the concepts of data analysis and data interpretation. It also has introduced the most elementary form of data analysis: descriptive analysis. Descriptive analysis has as its goal the simplification of research results so that patterns can be detected and conclusions made regarding those patterns. We noted that descriptive analysis is an important first step in most research; we also noted that some type of descriptive analysis is found in most research.

   We observed that data can take on two basic forms or types: it can be categorical or continuous. Categorical data are representative of nominal or ordinal category systems. Continuous data are representative of interval or ratio scale data. They describe the sample or population differently. When describing a sample containing continuous data, we rely on measures of central tendency; usually the mean, median, and mode. We can also describe the data as to their dispersion through variance and standard deviations. We can display our data graphically and describe their skewness and peakedness.

   Sometimes our research questions are more appropriately answered with a categorical analysis. Categorical analysis establishes categories from which we can describe our sample. Simple frequency counts and calculation of percentages and proportions can be used to describe how the population falls into each category. We noted that there were several types of analysis available: Univariate analysis allows you to examine how scores fall across the categories of one particular variable, while bivariate or multivariate analysis breaks the analyses into finer distinctions. Finally, we noted that the correlation allows us to establish a simple relationship between two variables.

PROBES

1. In what ways can statistics be used in communication research? Are there methods where statistics, in general, are *never* employed? If you think so, which? Why?

2. What is meant by the concept of descriptive statistics? What do these data tell us about our research? Do they *really* mean anything, or are they merely points of reference suggested by some theory? Why or why not?

3. What is meant by nonparametric analysis? When might you employ a nonparametric analysis? What might this analysis tell you about the data you collected? What inferences can you make?

4. When we measure via continuous data we rely on parametric statistics. What do these statistics tell us that nonparametric statistics do not? When and where might we want to use such statistics?

5. Differentiate between the use of univariate and bivariate statistics. How do the parametric and nonparametric tools discussed differ with each type of analysis? When would you use one and not the other?

SUGGESTED READING

Huck, S. W., Cormier, W. H., & Bounds, W. G., Jr. (1974). *Reading statistics and research.* New York: Harper & Row.

Kerlinger, F. N. (1986). *Foundations of behavioral research* (3rd ed.). New York: Holt, Rinehart, and Winston.

Pedhazur, E. J. (1982). *Multiple regression in behavioral research: Explanation and prediction* (2nd ed.) New York: Holt, Rinehart and Winston.

Phillips, J. L., Jr. (1973). *Statistical thinking: A structural approach.* San Francisco: W. H. Freeman.

Rosenthal, R., & Rosnow, R. L. (1984). *Essentials of behavioral research: Methods and data analysis.* New York: McGraw-Hill.

Williams, F. (1986). *Reasoning with statistics: How to read quantitative research* (3rd ed.). New York: Holt, Rinehart and Winston.

NOTES

1. Fred N. Kerlinger, *Foundations of Behavioral Research,* 3rd ed. (New York: Holt, Rinehart & Winston, 1986), 131.
2. Marija J. Norusis, *SPSS/PC+ for the IBM PC/XT/AT* (Chicago: SPSS Inc., 1986).
3. James R. Boulding, *Statistics with Finesse* (P.O. Box 339, Fayetteville, Ark.).
4. Compare Earl Babbie, *The Practice of Social Research,* 4th ed. (Belmont, Calif.: Wadsworth, 1986), 342–354; Kerlinger, 161.
5. Kerlinger, 149.
6. Frederick Williams, *Reasoning with Statistics: How to Read Quantitative Research,* 3rd ed. (New York: Holt, Rinehart & Winston, 1986), 28–30.
7. For a detailed presentation of the formula for the Pearson correlation see Elazar J.

Pedhazur, *Multiple Regression in Behavioral Research: Explanation and Prediction,* 2nd ed. (New York: Holt, Rinehart & Winston, 1982), 12–44. The formula is:

$$r_{xy} = \frac{N\Sigma XY - (\Sigma X)(\Sigma Y)}{\sqrt{N\Sigma X^2 - (\Sigma X)^2}\,\sqrt{N\Sigma Y^2 - (\Sigma Y)^2}}$$

where N is the number of pairs of observations, X and Y are the individual scores on the two variables, and Σ means "sum to what follows."

8. There are statistical techniques for examining nonlinear relationships, and are beyond the scope of this book. See Pedhazur, 404–435.
9. The formula for determining the number of correlations is $N(n\text{-}1)/2$, where n is the number of variables and N the number of respondents.
10. See Robert Rosenthal and Ralph L. Rosnow, *Essentials of Behavioral Research: Methods and Data Analysis* (New York: McGraw-Hill, 1984), 214–222.
11. See Rosenthal and Rosnow pp. 214–222, for a discussion.

Chapter
13

Inferential Statistics

*I*n Chapter 12 we examined statistics as percentages and proportions, measures of central tendency, variability, and correlations. These statistics provide descriptions of the samples studied. Frequently, however, the researcher is interested in knowing if the results observed for a sample are indicative of the population. (See Chapter 8 for a review of sampling.) *Inferential statistics* allow the researcher to make this determination.

Before examining specific statistical models, we need to look at the reason for employing inferential statistics. What is the purpose of inferential statistics? When we observe that two variables are related in a sample, the question arises: Are the variables related in the larger population from which the sample was drawn? They either are or they are not. It is one or the other. How do we decide? It is on inferential statistics that we base this decision. Let us return for a moment to the classic experimental design discussed in Chapter 9. Suppose that we conduct an experiment in which one group of 30 participants receives an experimental treatment—say exposure to a persuasive message advocating the legalization of marijuana—while a second group of 30 serves as a control and receives an unrelated message. Then both groups are given a questionnaire that contains semantic differential scales measuring attitudes toward the legalization of marijuana. The results indicate that the mean scores of the people in the experimental group are 5.5 (on a 7-point scale), while those in the control group are 4.5, a difference of 1.0. Thus, it looks as if the independent and dependent variables are systematically related. Exposure to the message apparently changed attitudes. However, there is another possibility. It could be that, just by random chance, we put people who felt more favorably toward the legalization of marijuana in the experimental group, while the control group, again, just by chance, consisted of people who felt less favorably toward this issue. Inferential statistics allows us to state the *probability* that our observed difference of 1.0 was the result of exposure to the persuasive message, or alternatively, that it was the result of sampling error—of random chance.

An observed result in a study is said to be *statistically significant* if sampling error accounts for the result in fewer than a specified number of cases (usually 5 percent) if the study were run over and over again. This chapter deals with several basic tests of statistical significance. There are inferential statistics to test the statistical significance for both nonparametric and parametric analyses. Thus, we can estimate the probability that research results such as percentages, frequencies, correlations, and differences between means are the results of the fact that the variables under study are *actually* related in the population from which the sample studied was drawn. Again, the alternative is that although the variables appear to be related in the sample, in fact this appearance is the result of sampling error.

USING STATISTICS TO TEST HYPOTHESES

Inferential statistics tell us whether results that we have observed in our study are indicative of what would have been obtained if we had studied a larger group, that is, the population from which the sample (the group we have studied) was drawn had been studied in its entirety. Employing a statistical test, however, is not the crux of research. It is important to remember that research is driven by the questions we ask. When conducting a research study we attempt to predict the relationships between variables. Thus, our statistical *analyses* are tests of the hypothesized relationships between variables of interest. Hypothesis testing involves four steps: (1) specifying the specific hypothesis to be tested, (2) picking a significance level for the tests, (3) calculating the appropriate statistics and probability levels, and (4) concluding whether the null hypothesis is rejected or not. We will examine each.

Specifying the Hypothesis

As we have noted in earlier chapters, a hypothesis is a statement of a relationship between two or more variables. It is a prediction of how the variables are related.

As the values for an independent variable change, the hypothesis predicts what will happen to the values for the dependent variable. Examples include:

Individuals who have had a course in public speaking will experience less communication apprehension than individuals who have not.

Increases in amount of touching will result in increases in liking for the toucher.

As cognitive complexity increases, self-monitoring increases.

Participants exposed to a message that contains a single vivid example of a homeless person's situation will be more favorably disposed toward helping the homeless in general than will participants exposed to a message that contains abstract statistics about the homeless.

Although it may seem somewhat odd, classical statistical inference hypotheses such as these are tested by predicting that the variables are *not* related, and then examining the probability that this prediction is false. These predictions of no relationship are called *null hypotheses.* The researcher hopes that the null hypothesis will be rejected and the alternative, or theoretical hypothesis, will be supported. The null hypothesis is tested because an assumption of science is that, logically, a hypothesis can never be proved; it can only be disproved. Thus, the null hypothesis is tested in an effort to reject it, providing evidence for its alternative. For the previous examples the null hypotheses would be:

Individuals who have had a course in public speaking will experience the same amount of communication apprehension as individuals who have not.

Increases in amount of touching will result in no change in liking for the toucher.

As cognitive complexity increases, self-monitoring is unaffected.

Participants exposed to a message that contains a single vivid example of a homeless person's situation will feel equally favorable toward helping the homeless in general as participants exposed to a message that contains abstract statistics about the homeless.

Once the hypothesis has been stated, a decision must be made regarding the level of error we will tolerate in testing the null hypothesis; that is, we must specify a level of confidence for our statistical tools or specify an accepted level of significance.

Specifying a Significance Level

The level of significance specified in a research study represents the confidence we have in our predictions. Most researchers have adopted a fairly stringent level of significance. If the results are said to occur by chance no more than 5 times out of 100 then those results are statistically significant. Put another way, we would say that selection of the *.05* level of significance expresses confidence that our findings occur due to expected differences *95 percent* of the time and that chance accounts for only *5 percent.* Some researchers report their level of significance as an *alpha (α)level;* thus, we might report a particular test being significant at the $\alpha=.05$ or $\alpha=.01$ level.

We have now expressed the degree to which we believe our results provide a basis for rejecting the null hypothesis. What is so magical about the .05 level of significance? Actually, nothing; the figure is commonly accepted as being appropriate. You might want to be more stringent about the amount of error you will accept in your results. In this case you might specify the .01 level of significance; now chance could account for the observed results only 1 time in 100. Perhaps your research is still at the exploratory stage and the accepted .05 level of significance is too stringent. You might choose to increase your probability of error to .10, or allowing chance to account for the results as often as 10 times out of 100 occurrences.

There is no magic significance level. Accepted levels include .05, .01, and .10 in some instances. The .05 and .01 levels of significance approximate two and three standard deviations from a mean; thus, they represent the "tail" ends of the probability curve. (See Figure 13.1; for a review of the probability curve, see Chapter 8 and Chapter 12.)[1]

Research Questions versus Hypotheses

How you interpret your level of significance is confounded by whether your research hypothesis predicts simple differences or establishes direction. For instance, suppose that we predict that males and females will differ in their reactions to physically attractive females. This statement suggests that males and females will differ, but not which sex will perceive the attractive female as "more" attractive (as indicated on some measure). Like the research question, this is a *two-tailed test of significance* (see Figure 13.2). In actual practice you have said that some differences will be found, but you have not specified how the differences will occur.

If you had hypothesized that males would score higher on your measure than females, the test for significance would be *one-tailed* (see Figure 13.3). In other

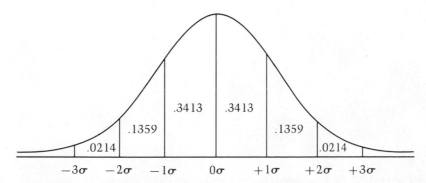

.3413   .3413

.1359   .1359

.0214   .0214

−3σ −2σ −1σ 0σ +1σ +2σ +3σ

Figure 13.1 Probability curve.

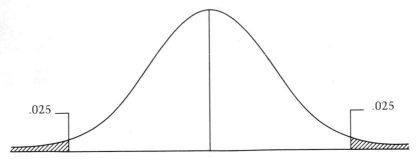

Figure 13.2 Rejection curve: two-tailed ($\alpha = .05$).

words, specification of direction or magnitude in a hypothesis gives you a better chance for significance (the area under the curve indicating significance is larger) than when you simply make a claim of difference. In some ways you are rewarded for making the specific prediction, but in actual practice the two-tailed test simply must account for differences at *both* ends of the probability curve, while the one-tailed test is looking for results at one and only one end of the probability curve.

Research questions, like nondirectional hypotheses, are usually examined as if they are two-tailed. Practically, this means that the level of significance is .025 ($.05 \div 2$) for *either* end of the probability curve. Unless your theory is developed enough to specify direction or magnitude, one-sided tests of significance should be avoided. Frederick Williams goes so far as to state[2]:

> a one-tailed test is never used (or should never be used) unless there is very good reason to make a directional prediction. This reason is not especially a function of wanting to make directional predictions, but is mainly based on the confidence that an outcome in the opposite direction will not be obtained. If a one-tailed test is made in the absence of such confidence, the researcher is assuming the hazard of never really testing statistically an outcome that would be opposite to the predicted direction.

This leads us to the two types of error possible when we test hypotheses.

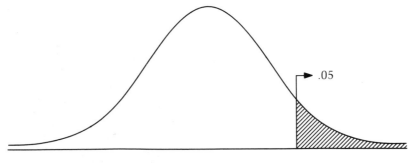

Figure 13.3 Rejection curve: one-tailed ($\alpha = .05$).

Type I and Type II Errors

There are two basic mistakes researchers can make when interpreting statistical tests of their hypotheses or research questions (see Figure 13.4). A *Type I error* occurs when a researcher claims that relationships exist when in fact they do not. This is an inappropriate rejection of the null hypothesis. A *Type II error* is just the opposite. The researcher fails to reject the null hypothesis and claims that relationships do not exist when in fact they do. Both types of error are important and are to be avoided. In general, error is associated with sample size. As illustrated in Figure 13.5, the larger the sample, the smaller the probability of Type I error. Thus, we might note that the *power* of the test, the ability to detect differences that are truly different, is a function of sample size.

Calculating Statistics and Probability Values

Most computer programs provide both the obtained statistical test values and the level of significance. Some, however, still require that you look up a calculated value and compare it to a tabled value. Regardless of how you proceed, you must understand how to interpret the statistics you calculate or obtain on a printout.

Reading of statistical tables requires an understanding of three things: *calculated values, critical (tables) values,* and *degrees of freedom.* An understanding of these things is necessary whether you do your statistical tests manually or use a computer. Both parametric and nonparametric statistical tests use similar concepts, although the labels may differ.

Degrees of Freedom   Fundamental to inferential analysis is the understanding of *degrees of freedom,* correction factors that allow for a type of probability to be computed and analyzed. Degrees of freedom provide information about the "latitude of variation a statistical problem has."[3] The assumption is that, by holding one condition, group, or category constant, we can predict what the other conditions will be. In other words, by fixing the degrees of freedom we can then calculate

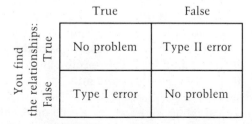

The relationships are really:

	True	False
You find the relationships: True	No problem	Type II error
You find the relationships: False	Type I error	No problem

Figure 13.4 Relationship of Type I and Type II error to research. (*Source:* After Fred N. Kerlinger, *Foundations of Behavioral Research,* 3rd ed. [New York: Holt, Rinehart & Winston, 1986], p. 117. Reprinted by permission.)

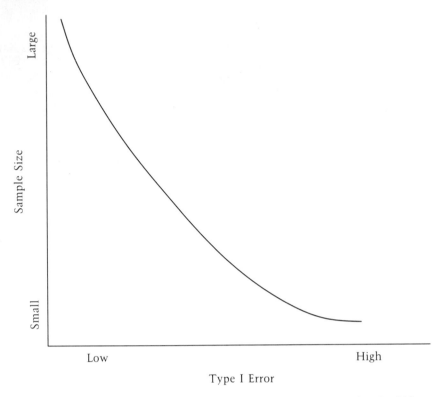

Figure 13.5 Relationship of Type I error to sample size. (*Source:* After Fred N. Kerlinger, *Foundations of Behavioral Research,* 3rd ed. [New York: Holt, Rinehart & Winston, 1986], p. 117. Reprinted by permission.)

scores from the nonfree condition. You will need to know how many degrees of freedom are associated with your test in order to interpret the results. Understanding degrees of freedom leads us to the calculated and tabled values associated with the study's sources of variation.

Rejecting and Accepting the Null Hypothesis Statistical tests yield calculated values. These may be in the form of F-values, t-values, r-values, chi-square values, or whatever. Calculated values are tested against a tabled value at the particular degree(s) of freedom associated with the specific analysis. The tabled value is the *critical value* that the calculated statistic must equal or surpass to be significant at the designated level of significance.

Table 13.1 presents two critical tables, one for a N-1 type distribution (one in which the only concern is for a homogeneous sample [Table 13.1(a)]) and one in which the sample is composed of two or more groups (Table 13.1[b]). Interpretation of Table 13.1(a) is straightforward. Assume that your calculated value is 12.22 and your degrees of freedom are 99 (100 respondents minus 1). If the critical value in the table is less than your calculated value, you can say that the results were significantly different at that level of significance.

Which level of significance? Significance levels are found at the top of the table, broken into one-tailed (α) and two-tailed (2α) tests. In the middle of the table is the column $\alpha=.05$. For a *one-tailed test* you would look down the column to the appropriate row for your degrees of freedom. Notice that 99 degrees of freedom is not present in this table. For this analysis you would either have to find a more complete table or extrapolate between the tabled values for 60 and 120 degrees of freedom (your calculated value would have to be greater than 2.00 but could be less than 1.98). If your computer program calculates the significance level, you need not worry about it. Be forewarned, however, that unless otherwise indicated, most computer programs assume a one-tailed test; thus, you may have to reinterpret the results based on the next column to the right.

Table 13.1(b) is more complex. It assumes that there are more than two groups in your study. Reading this table requires that you know the degrees of freedom associated with the groups and the sample. Assume that your study examined the impact of the sex of speaker (male, female) and message intensity (high, moderate, low) on persuasiveness. The degrees of freedom for this test would be sex of speaker$=1$ (2 groups $-$ 1), message intensity$=2$ (3 groups $-$ 1), and the interaction of message intensity and sex of speaker$=2$ ($2_{[3 \text{ groups} - 1]} \times 1_{[2 \text{ groups} - 1]}$). To test for each *effect* first find the appropriate column for groups or categories (m) (2, for message intensity) and then the degrees of freedom for the sample (N - 1). Supposing that we have 31 people, our denominator (n) degrees of freedom would be 30. To be significant at the $\alpha=.05$ level, a calculated value greater than 3.32 would be necessary.

Assumptions

Before we look at specific statistical tests, we need to look at several assumptions statistical tests make about data. Although different statistical analyses interpret them differently, we should note that inferential statistics assume that for both the sample and the population the variables of interest are independent, each variable is normally distributed, and that the variances for all groups are equal. *Independence* simply means that any participant selected in the sample does not preclude another participant's selection (see Chapter 8). *Normality* refers to the peakedness of the data distribution (are the data found under a normal dispersion or a curve?), as would be the data in the population. We assume that our sample's data for each variable are normally distributed, as are the population's data. Finally, if the sample is representative of the population, each group's *variance* will be equal. To the degree that our data do *not* meet these assumptions, we introduce error to our analyses.

Summary

Statistical analysis that goes beyond description and tests for differences between groups is frequently a necessary step in answering research questions. In testing for differences among participants, researchers must make decisions regarding how they approach their problem. We noted that the researcher will derive hypotheses or state research questions and then test these relationship statements by the null

Table 13.1(a) CRITICAL VALUE TABLE: *N*-1

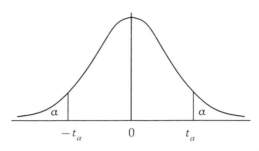

df	$\alpha =$ .25 $2\alpha =$ .50	$\alpha =$ .20 $2\alpha =$ .40	$\alpha =$ .15 $2\alpha =$ .30	$\alpha =$ .10 $2\alpha =$ .20	$\alpha =$ .05 $2\alpha =$ .10	$\alpha =$ .025 $2\alpha =$ .05	$\alpha =$ .01 $2\alpha =$ .02	$\alpha =$ .005 $2\alpha =$ .01	$\alpha =$ .0005 $2\alpha =$ .001
1	1.000	1.376	1.963	3.078	6.314	12.706	31.821	63.657	636.619
2	.816	1.061	1.386	1.886	2.920	4.303	6.965	9.925	31.598
3	.765	.978	1.250	1.638	2.353	3.182	4.541	5.841	12.924
4	.741	.941	1.190	1.533	2.132	2.776	3.747	4.604	8.610
5	.727	.920	1.156	1.476	2.015	2.571	3.365	4.032	6.869
6	.718	.906	1.134	1.440	1.943	2.447	3.143	3.707	5.959
7	.711	.896	1.119	1.415	1.895	2.365	2.998	3.499	5.408
8	.706	.889	1.108	1.397	1.860	2.306	2.896	3.355	5.041
9	.703	.883	1.100	1.383	1.833	2.262	2.821	3.250	4.781
10	.700	.879	1.093	1.372	1.812	2.228	2.764	3.169	4.587
11	.697	.876	1.088	1.363	1.796	2.201	2.718	3.106	4.437
12	.695	.873	1.083	1.356	1.782	2.179	2.681	3.055	4.318
13	.694	.870	1.079	1.350	1.771	2.160	2.650	3.012	4.221
14	.692	.868	1.076	1.345	1.761	2.145	2.624	2.977	4.140
15	.691	.866	1.074	1.341	1.753	2.131	2.602	2.947	4.073
16	.690	.865	1.071	1.337	1.746	2.120	2.583	2.921	4.015
17	.689	.863	1.069	1.333	1.740	2.110	2.567	2.898	3.965
18	.688	.862	1.067	1.330	1.734	2.101	2.552	2.878	3.922
19	.688	.861	1.066	1.328	1.729	2.093	2.539	2.861	3.883
20	.687	.860	1.064	1.325	1.725	2.086	2.528	2.845	3.850
21	.686	.859	1.063	1.323	1.721	2.080	2.518	2.831	3.819
22	.686	.858	1.061	1.321	1.717	2.074	2.508	2.819	3.792
23	.685	.858	1.060	1.319	1.714	2.069	2.500	2.807	3.767
24	.685	.857	1.059	1.318	1.711	2.064	2.492	2.797	3.745
25	.684	.856	1.058	1.316	1.708	2.060	2.485	2.787	3.725
26	.684	.856	1.058	1.315	1.706	2.056	2.479	2.779	3.707
27	.684	.855	1.057	1.314	1.703	2.052	2.473	2.771	3.690
28	.683	.855	1.056	1.313	1.701	2.048	2.467	2.763	3.674
29	.683	.854	1.055	1.311	1.699	2.045	2.462	2.756	3.659
30	.683	.854	1.055	1.310	1.697	2.042	2.457	2.750	3.646

CRITICAL VALUE TABLE: *N*-1 (*Continued*)

df	$\alpha = .25$ $2\alpha = .50$	$\alpha = .20$ $2\alpha = .40$	$\alpha = .15$ $2\alpha = .30$	$\alpha = .10$ $2\alpha = .20$	$\alpha = .05$ $2\alpha = .10$	$\alpha = .025$ $2\alpha = .05$	$\alpha = .01$ $2\alpha = .02$	$\alpha = .005$ $2\alpha = .01$	$\alpha = .0005$ $2\alpha = .001$
40	.681	.851	1.050	1.303	1.684	2.021	2.423	2.704	3.551
60	.679	.848	1.046	1.296	1.671	2.000	2.390	2.660	3.460
120	.677	.845	1.041	1.289	1.658	1.980	2.358	2.617	3.373
α	.674	.842	1.036	1.282	1.645	1.960	2.326	2.576	3.291

Source: Table 13.1(a) is taken from Table 3 of Fisher and Yates: *Statistical Tables for Biological, Agricultural and Medical Research,* published by Longman Group UK Ltd., London (previously published by Oliver and Boyd Ltd., Edinburgh) and by permission of the authors and publishers.

hypothesis, or hypothesis of no difference. Depending on the level of theory or confidence in relationship development, the researcher will establish a probability level with which he or she feels comfortable. Finally, the researcher will test the data by the appropriate test and compare the test statistic to a tabled value.

We can now turn to inferential analyses. The first set of tests examined will be nonparametric. These are analyses appropriate for *both* dependent and independent variables that are composed of *only* categorical data. After this we will examine parametric analyses, which consist of continuous data dependent variables and categorical independent variables.

NONPARAMETRIC ANALYSES

As you will recall from Chapter 6, the way we operationalize our variables requires us to make certain decisions. One of those decisions is whether the data collected will be categorical or continuous. Categorical data are derived from nominal or ordinal measurement. This choice also affects later analysis decisions. As we saw in Chapter 12, categorical data analysis provides gross distribution analysis; continuous data analysis allows measures of central tendency and dispersion. Assuming that all the variables of interest are categorical, the *appropriate* data analysis tests are nonparametric. To understand better what nonparametric tests are and what they can do we will discuss their advantages and limitations and examine specific nonparametric tests.

Advantages and Limitations

Roger Kirk suggests the advantages to nonparametric analyses are threefold.[4] First, nonparametric tests are fairly simple to conduct. However, with the advent of computerized statistical packages the value of this advantage diminished; but the amount of *time* the computer must take to "crunch" the data and the rather simple choices (e.g., placement of scores or observations into predefined categories) it

Table 13.1(b)   CRITICAL VALUE TABLE: MULTIPLE GROUPS

	F distribution 95th percentile						
n/m	1	2	3	4	5	10	20
1	161.40	199.50	215.70	224.60	230.20	241.90	248.00
2	18.51	19.00	19.16	19.25	19.30	19.40	19.45
3	10.13	9.55	9.28	9.12	9.01	8.79	8.66
4	7.71	6.94	6.59	6.39	6.26	5.96	5.80
5	6.61	5.79	5.41	5.19	5.05	4.74	4.56
6	5.99	5.14	4.76	4.53	4.39	4.00	3.87
7	5.59	4.74	4.35	4.12	3.97	3.84	3.44
8	5.32	4.46	4.07	3.84	3.69	3.35	3.15
9	5.12	4.26	3.86	3.63	3.46	3.14	2.94
10	4.96	4.10	3.71	3.48	3.33	2.98	2.77
11	4.64	3.98	3.59	3.36	3.20	2.85	2.65
12	4.75	3.69	3.49	3.26	3.11	2.75	2.54
13	4.67	3.81	3.41	3.18	3.03	2.67	2.46
14	4.60	3.74	3.34	3.11	2.96	2.60	2.39
15	4.54	3.68	3.29	3.06	2.90	2.54	2.33
16	4.49	3.63	3.24	3.01	2.85	2.49	2.28
17	4.45	3.59	3.20	2.96	2.81	2.45	2.23
18	4.41	3.55	3.16	2.93	2.77	2.41	2.19
19	4.38	3.52	3.13	2.90	2.74	2.38	2.16
20	4.35	3.49	3.10	2.87	2.71	2.35	2.12
21	4.32	3.47	3.07	2.84	2.68	2.32	2.10
22	4.30	3.44	3.05	2.82	2.66	2.30	2.07
23	4.28	3.42	3.03	2.80	2.64	2.27	2.05
24	4.26	3.40	3.01	2.78	2.62	2.25	2.03
25	4.24	3.39	2.99	2.76	2.60	2.24	2.01
26	4.23	3.37	2.98	2.74	2.59	2.22	1.99
27	4.21	3.35	2.96	2.73	2.57	2.20	1.97
28	4.20	3.34	2.95	2.71	2.56	2.19	1.96
29	4.18	3.33	2.93	2.70	2.55	2.18	1.94
30	4.17	3.32	2.92	2.69	2.53	2.16	1.93
40	4.08	3.23	2.84	2.61	2.45	2.08	1.84
60	4.00	3.15	2.76	2.63	2.37	1.99	1.75
120	3.92	3.07	2.68	2.45	2.29	1.91	1.66
—	3.84	3.00	2.60	2.37	2.21	1.83	1.57

Source: Reprinted with permission from S. M. Selby, *CRC Standard Mathematical Tables,* 23rd ed. (West Palm Beach, FL: CRC Press, Inc., 1974). Copyright CRC Press, Inc.

must take still makes simplicity an advantage. Second, nonparametric tests are less restricted by their assumptions about the data. Nonparametric tests can be conducted on "nonnormal" populations, populations with large variances for instance.[5] Third, in experimental designs, nonparametric analyses are appropriate where parametric (continuous) analyses are not. This last advantage comes from the ability of the nonparametric analysis to use a "crossbreak type analysis" in the experiment. A crossbreak analysis allows us to see the percentage of responses of various kinds in each experimental condition or cell.

There are severe limitations to nonparametric analysis. One limitation stems from the advantages: Nonparametric tests cannot tell us as much about differences between groups or categories as can parametric tests. Because the level of measurement is nominal or ordinal, the analysis will be less refined. We only know that scores or observations are found in particular categories—in terms of the count or frequency of occurrence—but we have no real way of assessing the *relationships* between the scores and observations and the categories. This causes difficulty in attributing differences when they are found. Finally, power (the probability of Type II error) is low. The probability of accepting your null hypothesis when in fact it is false is increased with nonparametric tests.

Although there are many nonparametric tests, we will only cover only a few. These include *chi-square* tests and measures of association.

Testing for Differences: The Chi-Square Test

Probably the most used of all nonparametric tests, the chi-square (we use the notation χ^2 in equations) tests for differences between the frequency of occurrence between different categories. In general there are two types of chi-square tests: simple or *one-sample* (univariate) tests and *two-sample* (bivariate) tests. We will begin with the one-sample test.

One-Sample Chi-Square Test   The one-sample chi-square examines the differences in the category selection when the sample has been selected for purposes of homogeneity; that is, people are expected to fall into categories based on some common characteristic. Assume, for instance, that we are interested in the occurrence of communication apprehension in public speaking students. We could survey students enrolled in public speaking courses on a measure designed to tap perceptions of communication apprehension.[6] Although there are several parametric indices that might interest us, we are mainly concerned with placing students into one of three categories: highly communication apprehensive, moderately communication apprehensive, and lowly communication apprehensive. Furthermore, we are interested in whether highly apprehensive students enroll in public speaking courses.

(The nonparametric test will examine the proportions of students falling into each category. These students, as in our case, are the *observed* frequency per category of apprehension. The students will fall into either high, moderate, or low apprehension categories. But, there is an *expected* frequency that, all things being equal, would suggest that an equal number of students would fall into each category of apprehension.)

After considerable research we derive the following hypothesis:

> There will be fewer high communication apprehensive students enrolled in public speaking courses than moderate communication apprehensive students and more low communication apprehensive students than moderate apprehensives.

Note that our hypothesis is directional, it specifies that there will be more people in two groups than in one group. For this one-tailed test we will set our level of significance at $\alpha = .05$.

The distributions of 66 students who participated in the study by enrolling in public-speaking courses are found in Table 13.2. Reading the table is straightforward: 4.5 percent of the sample report high communication apprehension, 36.4 percent report moderate communication apprehension, and 59.1 percent report low communication apprehension.

A simple inspection of the data indicates that there are different frequencies in the three categories. But are they significantly different statistically? That is, could our results be the result of sampling error? To test for differences between the categories we must calculate the chi-square statistic. Calculation of the chi-square is fairly simple. Table 13.3 reports the computer-generated chi-square statistic. Of importance are the "cases observed" and the "expected" columns. The cases observed column reflects the number of participants placed in each category. The expected column reflects the theoreticallyexpected frequency. What we test for in the chi-square is the *difference* between expected and observed frequencies.

Although most computer packages calculate the expected frequencies, it is important you understand how they are computed. (Remember, the expected frequency is what is expected if the independent variable has had no effect—the null hypothesis.) The expected frequency is the number of observations divided by number of categories. In our case we have 66 cases observed and three categories: expected $= (66 \div 3) = 22$. If we had 60 cases our expected frequency per category would be $(60 \div 3) = 20$.

Calculation of the chi-square (χ^2) takes each category and subtracts the expected from the observed, squares that difference, and divides it by the expected frequency:

$$\chi^2 = \frac{(O - E)^2}{E}$$

Or, in our case, $\chi^2 = [(3 - 22)^2 \div 22] + [(24 - 22)^2 \div 22] + [(39 - 22)^2 \div 22] = 29.72$.

Our chi-square calculated value is 29.72, but is that a value higher than the tabled value? To interpret the chi-square *statistic* we must compare it to the tabled value found in the chi-square Critical Value Table. First, however, we must calculate the degrees of freedom associated with the statistic. The formula for one-sample chi-square is the number of categories minus 1, or $(3 - 1) = 2$ in our case.

Table 13.2   PRINTOUT: FREQUENCY COUNT
            Communication Apprehension in Public Speaking Courses

```
                              SPSS/PC+
-----------------------------------------------------------------

APP     Communication Apprehension
-----------------------------------------------------------------

                                          Valid      Cum
    Value label    Value  Frequency  Percent  Percent  Percent
-----------------------------------------------------------------

high             1.00        3        4.5      4.5      4.5
moderate         2.00       24       35.8     36.4     40.9
low              3.00       39       58.2     59.1    100.0
                  .          1        1.5    Missing

                         -------  -------  -------
                 Total       67     100.0    100.0
-----------------------------------------------------------------

Valid Cases    66    Missing Cases    1
-----------------------------------------------------------------


                    Statistics With Finesse


            ---------------------------------


                 File name:  APPSWF


            ---------------------------------


                 Variable:   APPSCORE
            ---------------------------------
                 Code     Frequency    Percent
            ---------------------------------
                 HIGH         11         6.67
                 LOW          74        44.85
                 MOD          75        45.45
            Missing           5         3.03
                          ------     -------
                 Total      165       100.00
```

Reading a chi-square critical value table for the $\alpha = .05$ column and then down to the row for degrees of freedom (df)$=2$, we arrive at a tabled value of 3.84. Since 29.72 is greater than 3.84 we can interpret the categories as being statistically significantly different. This information was provided by the computer-generated values listed in Table 13.2.

But which groups are different? Here the chi-square analysis reveals a limitation. Inspection of the frequencies clearly indicates that there were fewer high apprehensive students than those who indicated moderate or low degrees of appre-

Table 13.3 PRINTOUT: CHI-SQUARE TABLE: PUBLIC SPEAKING
COURSES

SPSS/PC+[1]

APP Communication Apprehension

	Category	Cases Observed	Expected	Residual
high	1.00	3	22.00	−19.00
moderate	2.00	24	22.00	2.00
low	3.00	39	22.00	17.00
	Total	66		

Chi-square	D.F.	Significance
29.727	2	.000[2]

[1]There is no equivalent test with Statistics with Finesse.

[2]Printout indicates $p < .0001$, but is printed only to three digits.

hensiveness. Examining the *residual* column in Table 13.3 provides further information. The residual is simply the difference between the observed and expected frequencies. Notice that the residuals are calculated as -19, 2, and 17 for the high, moderate, and low apprehensive categories. We might interpret these as follows: Both high and low apprehensive groups differed from expected frequencies, with far fewer high apprehensives than expected and far more low apprehensives than expected. The frequency of moderates was not greatly different than expected.

Two-Sample Chi-Square Tests   The two-sample chi-square test adds a second set of categories from a second sample. Suppose that we have access to a course in which no speaking is done; instead, the students enrolled in this course simply learn about speakers in the past. If we were to give them the same communication apprehension measure, would they differ from the speaking course students?

The results of this analysis are found in Table 13.4, which presents a 2 (course) ×3 (apprehension) crosstabulation design similar to those presented in Chapter 12. The table provides the observed frequencies in each of the six possible categories; the category, column, and row percentages; the marginals; and the expected frequencies. Also given are the computer-calculated chi-square value, the degrees of freedom, and the level of significance for the test.

Calculation of the chi-square is similar to that of the one-sample test. In this case the expected frequencies are a little more complicated to calculate. Expected frequencies are the result of multiplying the row and column *marginals* (or totals for each row and column) for that particular category and then dividing the result by the total frequencies for the table. Thus, the expected frequencies for the category, high/nonspeaking is (11 [row frequency]×94 [column frequency]

÷160 [total frequency]) or 6.5. Each particular category's expected frequency must be calculated and then the chi-square calculated. In this case

$$\chi^2 = ([8-6.5]^2 \div 6.5) + ([3-4.5]^2 \div 4.5) + ([51-44.1]^2 \div 44.1)$$
$$+ ([24-30.9]^2 \div 30.9) + ([35-43.5]^2 \div 43.5) + ([39-30.5]^2 \div 30.5)$$
$$= 7.54$$

The degrees of freedom associated with this particular chi-square take into account variation due to both rows *and* columns. The formula for degrees of freedom is (columns $-1) \times$ (rows -1). In our case the degrees of freedom associated with the 2×3 table are $(2-1) \times (3-1)$ or 2. Comparing this against the tabled critical value indicates that 7.54 is greater than that value. The conclusion is that some cells are significantly different than would be theoretically expected. Interpretation of the chi-square could end here. However, we can go one step further and examine the relationships between categories.

We have already examined the frequency of occurrence for the speaking course (see Table 13.3). We can now do the same for the nonspeaking course. Table 13.4(a) presents the observed frequency, expected frequency, and residuals for the three categories of apprehension found in the nonspeaking course. The chi-square calculated is significant (30.149 with 2 degrees of freedom). Here we may infer that the moderate and high apprehensive students differed from the expected frequencies but the lows did not. We could, of course, run chi-squares between courses to see if the frequency of high apprehensives differs from course to course, and then do the same with moderate apprehensives and the same with low apprehensives. Your decision to do so, however, is dependent on your research question and hypotheses (see Table 13.5.) (Notice that the observed frequencies differed significantly from theoretical expectations only for the *moderate* apprehensive student.)

Problems Associated with Chi-Square   The chi-square test is very sensitive to sample size (effect size, E.F.). When the number of expected frequencies is less than 5 in a category, the chi-square value and level of significance may be incorrect. Some computer programs will warn you if this problem exists. Table 13.4 warns us that one cell was found with an expected frequency less than 5. The table tells us that this accounted for 16.7 percent of the categories or cells, and gives us the *minimum* effect size for all cells.

Kerlinger suggests that for 2×2 chi-squares a correction of .5 from the absolute difference between expected and observed frequencies *before squaring* corrects for this (this is the Yates Correction as calculated by some computer programs). For designs greater than two columns or two rows, this correction is not necessary; nor, for that matter are all statisticians convinced that the correction is necessary at all. The correction, however, almost always yields a smaller chi-square value. Use of the correction is considered a conservative approach to the analysis (see Table 13.6).

Coefficient of Contingency   What we have found so far is that differences have occurred, but we do not know about the *magnitude* of the differences. Here the coefficient of contingency can be of help.[7] This statistic provides a *relative* measure of magnitude of the relationship between variables on a .00 to $+1.00$

Table 13.4 PRINTOUT: TWO-SAMPLE CHI-SQUARE

SPSS/PC+

Crosstabulation: APP   Communication apprehension
                   By COURSE

Course->	Count Exp Val Tot Pct	NON- SPEAKING 100	SPEAKING 123	 Row Total
APP				
High	1.00	8 6.5 5.0%	3 4.5 1.9%	11 6.9%
Moderate	2.00	51 44.1 31.9%	24 30.9 15.0%	75 46.9%
Low	3.00	4335 21.9%	3039 24.4%	4674%
	Column Total	94 58.8%	66 41.3%	160 100.0%

Chi-square	D.F.	Significance	Min E.F.	Cells with E.F. < 5
7.53985	2	.0231	4.537	1 OF 6 (16.7%)

Statistic	Value	Significance
Cramer's V	.21708	
Contingency Coefficient	.21214	

Number of Missing Observations   =   5

scale. Its calculation is simply the square root of the chi-square value divided by that value plus the total observed frequencies:

$$C = \sqrt{\frac{\chi^2}{\chi^2 + N}}$$

For the one-sample test of the speaking course, C is the square root of (29.-727÷95.727)=.55. A C of .49 was obtained for the nonspeaking course. For the two-sample test C was only .21. Note, however, that the *direction* of relationship is not assessed. That is, we do not know if the relationship is positive or negative; we only know the relative degree of relationship. This is a severe limitation.

Table 13.4 (*Continued*)

```
                    Statistics with Finesse

        ------------------------------------------
        Missing some value:       5

        Rows  = APPSCORE,    columns  = COURSE
        ------------------------------------------
        Codes    NONSPK         SPK        Total
        ------------------------------------------
         HIGH       8            3           11
           %       5.0          1.9          6.9

          MOD      51           24           75
           %      31.9         15.0         46.9

          LOW      35           39           74
           %      21.9         24.4         46.3
                 ------       ------       -------
        Total      94           66          160
           %      58.8         41.3        100.0
        ------------------------------------------

        Chi-square                        7.5399

        Coef. of Contingency               .2121

        Significance Level                 .0231

        Degrees of Freedom                 2
```

Interpreting Chi-Square Tests   Interpretation of the chi-square test, like that of most nonparametric tests, is not easy. Care must be taken in making conclusions, especially if the test for magnitude indicates less than moderate ($< .30$) association. The best way to interpret the data is first to calculate the chi-square statistics, then the percentages, and then the measure of association. Use all the information you have to make such decisions as to which category or categories are making the difference.[8]

Summary

Nonparametric analyses are appropriate when the data collected are categorical. The chi-square test was examined, both in one-sample and two-sample formats, where the test statistic examines whether the frequency of scores or observations into categories is statistically greater than the expected frequency, assuming no

Table 13.5   PRINTOUT: ONE-SAMPLE CHI-SQUARE

HIGH APPREHENSIVES

Course	Category	Cases Observed	Expected	Residual
non-speaking	1.00	8	5.50	2.50
speaking	2.00	3	5.50	− 2.50

	Total	11		

Chi-square	D.F.	Significance
2.273	1	.132

MODERATE APPREHENSIVES

Course	Category	Cases Observed	Expected	Residual
non-speaking	1.00	51	37.50	13.50
speaking	2.00	24	37.50	− 13.50

	Total	75		

Chi-square	D.F.	Significance
9.720	1	.002

LOW APPREHENSIVES

Course	Category	Cases Observed	Expected	Residual
non-speaking	1.00	35	37.00	− 2.00
speaking	2.00	39	37.00	2.00

	Total	74		

Chi-square	D.F.	Significance
.216	1	.642

----

effect for the variable(s) under study. Finally, the coefficient of contingency statistic, a rough measure of association related to nonparametric statistics was examined. The advantages and limitations of the nonparametric analysis were also discussed for each nonparametric statistic examined.

The next section examines a more powerful set of analytical tools: Parametric analyses. Based on measures of central tendency and following the assumptions of normality and equal (homogeneous) variances, parametric statistics provide powerful tools for data analysis.

PARAMETRIC ANALYSIS

An extremely important inferential statistic is *Analysis of Variance,* or *ANOVA.* Historically, ANOVA is the method in which the results of experiments were almost always analyzed. It is a technique for studying the various sources of variance associated with a *dependent* variable consisting of interval or ratio data. Our goal here is to present a conceptual treatment of ANOVA, keeping formulas to a minimum. After the basic ideas of ANOVA have been explained, we will turn to the very practical matter of reading and interpreting ANOVA results, focusing on the dependent variable's mean responses, which may differ according to the levels or conditions associated with the independent variable. We begin by reexamining variance, move to a simple ANOVA, then, finally, to the more complex multiple factor ANOVA.

Variance

Whenever we measure a variable, different numbers will result. Whether we measure height or cognitive complexity or amount of positive self-disclosure, or any variable, different people receive different scores—they vary. This variability is called *variance* (s^2 or σ^2). We have already introduced the statistical concept of variance, but its importance to parametric analysis of data requires a short review. The variance of any measure is defined as follows:

$$\text{Variance} = \frac{\Sigma(X - M)^2}{N - 1}$$

where X is each individual's score, M is the mean of all scores, and N is the number of scores. In other words, this formula says that the mean of all scores is subtracted from each score, then these deviation scores are squared, added together, and finally divided by the number of scores minus one. (You will recall from Chapter 12 that if we took the square root of this result we would have the standard deviation, another measure of dispersion.)

In an experiment, if we took *all* the scores on the dependent measure and calculated the variance we would come up with the total variance. Of course, we do not actually cluster these scores together as one group of data; rather, they are grouped together within the various experimental conditions. ANOVA sorts out the sources of variation into its component parts. Some of the variability is due to *error.* Participants who are in the same experimental condition, yet who receive different scores, are the sources of this error. From the experimenter's point of view, participants in each experimental condition were all treated identically; thus, he or she does not know why they vary on the dependent variable measurement, yet

Table 13.6   PRINTOUT: SAMPLE YATES CORRECTION FOR CHI-SQUARE

SPSS/PC+

Crosstabulation: APP   Communication Apprehension
                     By CRS

Count	GRT SPKR	PUB ADDR	
CRS-> Exp Val	S	ESS	Row
	1.00	2.00	Total

APP			
1.00 high	8 5.6	3 5.4	11 12.9%
3.00 low	35 37.4	39 36.6	74 87.1%
Column Total	43 50.6%	42 49.4%	85 100.0%

Chi-square	D.F.	Significance	Min E.F.	Cells with E.F. <5
1.56462	1	.2110	5.435	None
2.47752	1	.1155	(Before Yates Correction)	

Statistic	Value	Significance
Phi	.17073	
Contingency coefficient	.16829	

Number of missing observations   =   0

they do. Thus, some of the total variance, specifically this *within-group* variance, is due to error. However, some of the total variability may be due to the fact that the independent variable had an effect on the dependent variable. If participants in one group had a mean of 4.5 (on a 7-point scale) and those in the other had a mean of 5.5, this is *between-group* variance—this difference of 1.0 is systematic variance. Thus, the total variance consists of two parts, systematic (between group) and random or error (within group) variance:

$$V_{\text{total}} = V_{b(\text{etween})} + V_{e(\text{rror})}$$

If the systematic source of variance (between groups) is larger than the error variability (within groups), the ANOVA will indicate that the independent variable accounted for the difference between the means. Because ANOVA is an inferential statistic, the differences reflect not *only* this particular *sample*, but *also* the

Table 13.6 (*Continued*)

```
                Statistics with Finesse


        ---------------------------------------
            Chi-Square Test of Independence
        ---------------------------------------

        Observed frequencies:
        ---------------------------------------
            10              5

             5             10
        ---------------------------------------

        Expected frequencies:
        ---------------------------------------
           7.50           7.50

           7.50           7.50
        ---------------------------------------

        Number of observations              30

        Chi-Square                      3.3333

        Yates Correction                2.1333

        Degrees of Freedom                   1

        Significance Level              0.0679

        Contingency Coef                0.3162

        Cramer's Phi prime              0.3333
```

population from which the sample was drawn. On the other hand, if the error variance is larger than the systematic variance, then the group mean differences are probably due to sampling error.

How do we calculate which source of variance is larger? The within-group variance (error) is divided into the between-group variance (systematic):

$$F = \frac{V_b}{V_e}$$

The result is an *F*-ratio, a value that can be looked up in a table of critical values to determine the statistical significance of the differences between means. (Most computer programs now automatically supply both the *F*-value and its related significance level.) If the results of the experiment were a result of sampling error, or put another way, if the null hypothesis that there was no difference between the means of the groups in the population is accurate, we would expect the error variance and the systematic variance to be about equal and the *F*-ratio would be about 1.0. However, as the systematic variance increases in relation to the error variance, our *F*-value increases, as does the probability of achieving significance. The following examples illustrate this point:

V_b is small
V_e is large   : no significance   (13.1)

V_b is large
V_e is equally large   : no significance   (13.2)

V_b is small
V_e is equally small   : no significance   (13.3)

V_b is large
V_e is smaller   : *significance*   (13.4)

As indicated, no significance will be obtained if the variance between groups and within groups is equal, regardless of whether the variance is large or small. Any differences in the means observed in the sample do not reflect population differences. It also follows, as shown in (13.1), that if the variance within groups is larger than the variance between groups, no significance will be found. Significance is *only* obtained when the variance is larger between groups than within groups.

Oneway ANOVA

A *oneway* ANOVA is used when there is one independent variable. The test can be used to determine the significance of the results regardless of the number of levels the independent variable takes. This statistic takes the average within-group variability in each experimental condition and compares it with the average between-group variability. In experiments involving three or more groups, if the overall *F*-test yields significance, subsequent tests that examine the pairs of mean differences need to be performed to determine which mean differences account for the significant *F*-value. Most computer programs offer several different group comparison tests as a follow-up to the analysis; how these are conducted will be discussed later. Table 13.7 shows the output of a oneway ANOVA with three groups and hypothetical data that failed to reveal significant results, while Table 13.8 shows the same experiment with data that achieved significance.

The oneway ANOVA table is read as follows. The first column shows the Source of Variation—there are always two sources of variation for a oneway ANOVA: between groups and within groups. The between-groups variation is that

Table 13.7   PRINTOUT: ONEWAY ANOVA AND CELL MEANS

Source of Variation	Sum of Squares	df	Mean Square (Variance)	F	p
Between	8.00	2	4.00	1.0	ns
Within	348.00	87	4.0		
Total	356.00	89			

Cell means

Group 1	Group 2	Group 3
3.2	3.9	3.6
($n=30$)	($n=30$)	($n=30$)

Note: SPSS/PC+ and SWF report oneway ANOVAs similarly.

Table 13.8   PRINTOUT: SIGNIFICANT ONEWAY ANOVA AND CELL MEANS

Source of Variation	Sum of Squares	df	Mean Square (Variance)	F	p
Between	30.00	2	15.00	5.0	$< .01$
Within	261.00	87	3.0		
Total	291.00	89			

Cell Means

Group 1	Group 2	Group 3
2.1	4.5	6.7
($n=30$)	($n=30$)	($n=30$)

attributable to the experimental treatments; the within-groups variation is error. The second column shows the *sums of squares* (SS) associated with each source of variation. The sums of squares are the results of the numerator in the formula for the variance ($\Sigma[X-M]^2$). The third column indicates the *degrees of freedom* associated with the analysis (abbreviated "df"). The total number of degrees of freedom is always the number of participants minus one. In this hypothetical example there were 30 participants per experimental condition, for a total of 90. Thus, there are 89 total degrees of freedom. These are then partitioned into two subsets, with two being assigned to the between-groups source of variation (3 groups minus 1=2) and the remaining 87 being left to the within-groups variation (error). The *mean square* (MS), which is also the variance, is the sum of squares divided by the degrees of freedom. (Since the sums of squares can be calculated by multiplying the mean square by the degrees of freedom, some computer programs omit the sums of squares column.) The next column is the obtained F-value. As shown earlier, this is calculated by dividing the mean square associated with the between-groups source of variation by the mean square associated with the within-groups source of variation. Finally, the level of probability is printed. This is the significance level with which to associate the F-value. Most computer programs will provide this value, but some still require that the researcher look up the F-value in the critical value table where the m is the $df_{between}$ and the n the df_{within} (see Table 13.1[b]).

Table 13.8 illustrates an example of an hypothetical significant oneway ANOVA result. Note that the mean square between groups is 15.0 and the mean square within groups is much smaller, 3.0. Thus, the calculated F-value of 5.0, with 2 and 87 degrees of freedom is significant at the .01 level. This is interpreted as meaning that differences between the means shown in the cells of the experiment are so large that they could have been obtained by random chance in fewer than 1 case in 100. An examination of these means intuitively supports this interpretation. Assuming the hypothetical data represent responses to a 7-point scale, mean differences of between 2 and 4 scale points seem quite large. Thus, it is highly *probable* that the results of the experiment are *not* a result of sampling error. They do generalize to the population.

The differences shown in Table 13.7 are not statistically significant. Note that the mean squares between and within are identical; that is, the variances within and between conditions are equal. Thus the F-value is 1.0. Again, this is consistent with an examination of the cell means that are shown below the ANOVA table. They differ only by fractions of a scale point. Note that the ANOVA table, by itself, does not reveal which cells have higher scores, or which cells are significantly different from each other. ANOVA source tables and tables that show cell means are necessary to interpret the results of the experiment.

Multiple Factor ANOVA

In Chapter 10 we introduced the notion of the factorial experiment—an experiment with two or more independent variables—and gave examples of the various factorial designs, such as the 2×2, 3×2, and $2\times2\times2$. We showed how the results of such experiments are interpreted, in part, by examining the patterns of the means obtained, and further, how graphs help display these patterns visually. We say "in part" because the patterns of means provide descriptive statistics only. As with the oneway ANOVA, we still do not know if these patterns are a result of our manipulations of the independent variables or, alternatively, of sampling error. Factorial ANOVA is the statistical tool that helps us decide whether we can make inferences from the patterns of means observed in the sample *to* the population from which the sample was drawn. Like the oneway ANOVA, the factorial ANOVA is based on the idea that the total variance of a data set can be divided into component parts. However, the factorial ANOVA has more parts. An ANOVA with two independent variables has the following components contributing to the total variance:

$$V_{\text{total}} = V_A + V_B + V_{A \times B} + V_{\text{error}}$$

As can be seen from this conceptual formula, the error variance still comes last, but the between-groups variance has now been divided into (1) the variance associated with variable A, (2) the variance associated with variable B, and (3) the variance associated with the interaction of variables A and B. A factorial ANOVA table reflects these increased sources of systematic variance, but otherwise is conceptually similar to a oneway ANOVA table. The only difference is that there are two or more (depending on the number of independent variables) additional sources of systematic variation.

Table 13.9 shows a source table for a 2×2 factorial design experiment, which contains the results of a 2×2 ANOVA. The within-groups source of variation remains unchanged from the oneway ANOVA error—the numbers in this row still reflect the variance of scores within each individual cell. However, the between-groups variance that characterized the oneway ANOVA has now been divided into three parts. Independent variable A can be a source of dependent variable variation. Independent variable B can also be a source. (As noted in Chapter 10, these are called *main effects.*) Finally, the interaction of variables A and B can be a source of variation. Thus, there are three different tests of statistical significance in this table. In this example the only significant F-value (4.96, df = $1_{[\text{between}]}$ and $116_{[\text{within}]}$) is associated with variable A. Note that these results are consistent with the cell means shown in the table below the ANOVA source table. Variable A has main effect means of 4.0 and 6.0, a 2-point difference (see Figure 13.6a). Variable B's main effect means are 4.9 and 5.1, only a .20 difference (see Figure 13.6b). Examination of the individual cell means reveals that neither the magnitude nor the direction of the effect of one variable varies with the level of the other variable with which it is combined (see Figure 13.6c). Thus, it makes intuitive sense that no interaction effects were revealed in the ANOVA. Note that to interpret the results of an ANOVA fully requires both an examination of the ANOVA source table *and* an examination of a table of means.

A Priori and *Post Hoc* Tests of Pairs of Cell Means

In a complex experiment in which there are three or more experimental conditions it is frequently necessary to conduct tests of statistical significance between pairs of cell means. Suppose, for example that we conduct a oneway ANOVA and the

Table 13.9   PRINTOUT: 2 × 2 ANOVA

Source of Variation	Sum of Squares	df	Mean square (Variance)	F	p
Main Effect					
A	12.40	1	6.20	4.96	< .01
B	.95	1	1.10	< 1.0	ns
Interaction					
A × B	.90	1	1.20	< 1.0	ns
Within	145.00	116	1.25		
Total	159.25	119			
Cell Means					

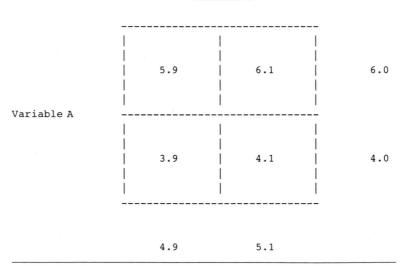

	Variable B		
Variable A	5.9	6.1	6.0
	3.9	4.1	4.0
	4.9	5.1	

Note: Reported for SPSS/PC+; SWF reports main effects as columns and rows, in this case *A* would be the row variable and *B* the column variable. SWF labels "within" as error.

results indicate overall significance. How do we know which of the group means, if any, are significantly different from the other. If, before the data were collected, we had specifically predicted that one cell will differ from another, we can conduct an *a priori* test, a planned comparison to see if the two means differ in the population. Planned comparisons are liberal tests in the sense that they minimize the

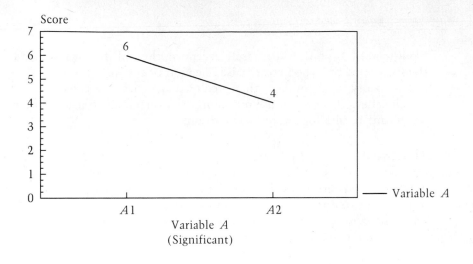

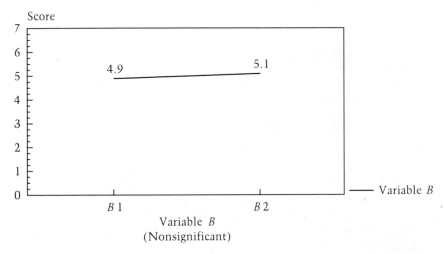

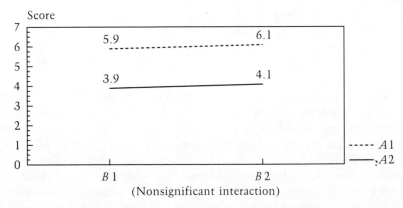

Figure 13.6 Breakdown of 2×2 ANOVA: (a) variable A main effect, (b) variable B main effect, (c) $A \times B$ interaction.

likelihood of Type II error (falsely accepting the null hypothesis) and maximize the likelihood of Type I error (false rejection of the null hypothesis). Because we had a theory, a hypothesis, that predicted which cell means would differ from which other cells, we can use procedures that maximize our chances of obtaining significant results for a given comparison.

The *t*-test   The most liberal a priori test is the *t*-test for difference between population means. Although the computational procedures are different, the logic on which the *t*-test is based is similar to the ANOVA. Within-cell variation is used to calculate an estimate of the sampling error. This estimate, called the *standard error of the mean*, is used in the denominator in an equation while the difference between the two means is in the numerator:

$$t = \frac{M1 - M2}{\text{standard error}}$$

The result is a *t*-value that expresses in standard error units how far apart the two means are. If they are about 1.68 or more standard error units apart, the difference is significant at the .05 level (one-tailed, df > 40).

An important point to note is that in simple two-group experiments such as, for example, the classical experimental design, the *t*-test can be and usually is used in lieu of ANOVA to analyze the results. Of course, like the ANOVA, the *t*-test requires interval or ratio dependent measures.

Multiple Comparison Tests   *Post hoc*, or multiple comparison, tests are appropriate when specific differences between cell means are not predicted ahead of time; rather, the researcher wants to examine several, or even all, possible cell mean comparisons. The number of comparisons possible is calculated by the now familiar formula: $n\ (n-1) \div 2$, where n is the number of experimental conditions or cells. Thus, in the three group experiment there are three possible comparisons: group 1 versus group 2; group 1 versus group 3; group 2 versus group 3, or $[3\ (3-1)] \div 2 = 3$ comparisons. For a 3×2 factorial experiment, there would be six cells and 12 possible cell mean comparisons—$[6(5-1)] \div 2 = 12$; for a $3 \times 2 \times 2$ factorial experiment there are 12 cells and 55 possible comparisons—$[12(12-1)] \div 2 = 55$.

Since achieving the .05 level of significance means that an observed outcome could be a result of sampling error in 1 case in 20, if we conducted 55 *t*-tests of significance, we would expect about three significant results by chance alone. Clearly, we are in grave danger of committing Type I error in such a case—of thinking we have found a significant relationship when actually we have found sampling error. This problem is addressed by using more *conservative* tests whenever we are conducting post hoc or multiple comparisons. These tests, if properly applied, can provide us with what is called *experiment-wise error protection*. Experiment-wide protection means that we can be sure that no matter how many multiple, post hoc comparisons we conduct, the chance that any *one* of them will be statistically significant is still .05. We are protected against Type I error. However, the price of conducting many post hoc tests, and thus having to use these conservative tests, is the increased probability of Type II error—of failing to iden- tify mean differences that actually *are* indicative of mean differences in the popula- tion. Theory should be used to make a priori predictions whenever possible.

Although discussions of the various post hoc tests are beyond the scope of this book, many computer packages offer the researcher several alternative ways to test for differences between cells; therefore, a short discussion of what is offered may help to understand and interpret the output of the oneway ANOVA programs.

After the oneway ANOVA table has been produced, most computer packages will list the cell means and indicate which are significantly different from the others. Table 13.10 demonstrates the output from one such test. Note that the cell means are listed in column form, from lowest to highest. The cells are identified in a matrix format and those cells that differ significantly from each other are indicated by an asterisk (*). We find Group 1 is significantly different from Group 2 and Group 3, and that Group 2 and Group 3 also differ significantly (see Figure 13.7). Table 13.11 demonstrates an instance where groups fail to differ significantly (see Figure 13.8). Sometimes significant ANOVAs fail to yield actual differences between groups; the reason for this is the way the tests are computed.

Table 13.10   PRINTOUT: SIGNIFICANT ONEWAY ANOVA AND CELL
             MEANS

Source of Variation	Sum of Squares	df	Mean Square (variance)	F	p
Between	30.00	2	15.00	5.0	< .01
Within	261.00	87	3.0		
Total	291.00	89			

(*) Denotes pairs of groups significantly different at the .05 level

Mean		Group 1	Group 2	Group 3
2.1	Group1			
4.4	Group2	*		
6.7	Group3	*	*	

More complex factorial designs can also be tested. When main effects that consist of only two levels are tested, the *t*-test is appropriate. However, when the independent variable consists of three or more groups, multiple comparisons are necessary and are computed as discussed earlier. To test for differences between means from the interaction, if significant, the cells are compared as if consisting of a combination of the independent variables. Thus, if there were two independent variables with two levels each (a 2×2 experimental design), cell A_{11} would become Group 1, cell A_{21} would become Group 2, cell B_{12} would become Group 3 and cell B_{22} would become Group 4. These groups would then be tested for differences.

In general, post hoc analyses range from extremely liberal (any differences between groups, even if there is substantial error, will be detected) to extremely conservative (it takes a large difference between means and minimal error, to detect significant statistical difference). Understanding how conservative individual tests are helps in interpreting the results. Basically, there are six post hoc tests (Scheffe, *L*east *S*ignificance *D*ifferences, Honestly Significant Difference, Tukey's Multiple Range Test, Duncan's Multiple Range Test, and the Student-Neuman-Keuls). The conservative tests require that the overall *F*-value be significant before the cell means can be tested. Of these the Scheffe test is most conservative and the LSD test is the most liberal.[9]

SUMMARY

This chapter introduced the concepts of inferential statistical analysis. We noted that inferential statistics go one step further in analyzing the data collected in research, allowing the researcher to test whether the sample's results are indicative of the larger population from which it was drawn.

We began with a general discussion of what inferential statistics do. We then

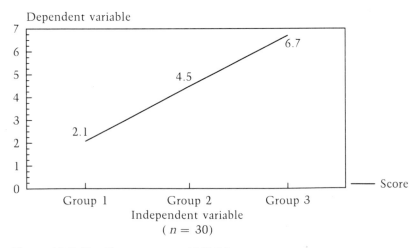

Figure 13.7 Significant oneway ANOVA.

Table 13.11   PRINTOUT: ONEWAY ANOVA AND CELL MEANS

Source of Variation	Sum of Squares	df	Mean Square (variance)	F	p
Between	8.00	2	4.00	1.0	ns
Within	348.00	87	4.0		
Total	356.00	89			

(*) Denotes pairs of groups significantly different at the .05 level

---

	G r o u p 1	G r o u p 2	G r 0 u p 3
Mean			
2.1	Group1		
4.4	Group2		
6.7	Group3		

examined the related concepts of hypotheses, probability, and error. Hypotheses, null and otherwise, and research questions were examined in light of inferential analysis, probability was reexamined, and Type I and Type II error were discussed. With these interrelated concepts in mind, the logic behind the statistical table was discussed with the concepts of critical values, tabled values, and degrees of freedom explored.

Nonparametric and parametric inferential statistics were then covered. We began with an examination of the chi-square statistic as a way of examining univariate (one-sample) and bivariate (two-sample) nonparametric research. We then examined Analysis of Variance and a priori and post hoc multiple comparisons as analytical procedures for parametric tests of differences, both in terms of the oneway ANOVA (univariate) and the multiple factor ANOVA (bivariate and multivariate). This chapter introduced more advanced analysis techniques. Remember that this is an introductory treatment of a complex area. An in-depth understanding of the assumptions discussed earlier, the various nonparametric and parametric statistical analyses and more advanced statistics (such as multiple regression and multivariate analysis of variance) require other courses.

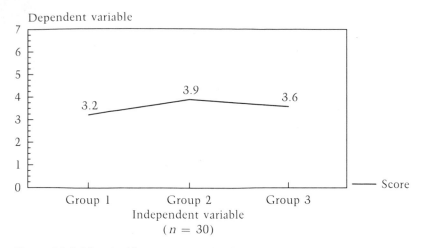

Figure 13.8 Nonsignificant oneway ANOVA.

PROBES

1. What is the purpose of the null hypothesis? Why do we test the null hypothesis?

2. How do hypotheses and research questions differ in the way probability operates in the use and interpretation of inferential statistics? Is it important to let the readers of research know whether the test statistic was tested one-tailed or two-tailed? Why?

3. What is the relationship between Type I and Type II error? Why are researchers concerned with both types of error? How does each affect the way in which we can interpret research findings? How can we control for Type I error in our design considerations?

4. What types of research are *best* analyzed via nonparametric analyses in your area of interest? Why? Can you think of any univariate and bivariate examples from the research you have read? Are they used appropriately? Why or why not? What limitations exist in analyzing nonparametric data? Why are they limitations?

5. What types of research are *best* analyzed via parametric analyses in your area of study? Why? When might you want to use a *t*-test? Why a *t*-test instead of an Analysis of Variance? When should we use a multiple comparison test? Why might a researcher use a liberal multiple comparison test? Why? What is the major difference between a post hoc and an a priori test? Why might a conservative researcher, even when an *a priori* test might be appropriate, choose to test for significance between means with a *post hoc* test like Scheffe?

SUGGESTED READING

Kerlinger, F. N. (1986). *Foundations of behavioral research* (3rd ed.). New York: Holt, Rinehart and Winston.

Kirk, R. E. (1968). *Experimental design procedures for the behavioral sciences.* Belmont, CA: Brooks/Cole.

Williams, F. (1986). *Reasoning with statistics: How to read quantitative research* (3rd ed.). New York: Holt, Rinehart and Winston.

NOTES

1. Fred N. Kerlinger, *Foundations of Behavioral Research*, 3rd ed. (New York: Holt, Rinehart & Winston, 1986), 156.
2. Frederick Williams, *Reasoning with Statistics: How to Read Quantitative Research*, 3rd ed. (New York: Holt, Rinehart & Winston, 1986), 64.
3. Kerlinger, 155.
4. Roger E. Kirk, *Experimental Design Procedures for the Behavioral Sciences* (Belmont, Calif.: Brooks/Cole, 1968), 503.
5. Kerlinger, notes, however, that this "advantage" really is not a reason for using nonparametric analysis. He suggests that any time variances from groups drawn randomly from a population are greatly different, nonparametric analysis is just as prone to error as is parametric analysis.
6. The data reported here were collected and analyzed as part of a project in progress. Actual design required students enrolled in three public speaking courses ($n = 66$) and one mass lecture course that emphasized written speeches from "great speakers" ($n = 94$) to complete the PRCA-24, a communication apprehension scale developed by McCroskey. For more information see James C. McCroskey, *An Introduction to Rhetorical Communication*, 5th ed. (Englewood Cliffs, N.J.: Prentice-Hall, 1986).
7. For a more in-depth discussion, see Kerlinger, 158–159, or Williams, 138–139.
8. For an excellent example of the use of the chi-square statistic, see Michael J. Beatty, "Communication Apprehension as a Determinant of Avoidance, Withdrawal, and Performance Anxiety," *Communication Quarterly*, 35 (1987): 202–217.
9. For an excellent review of these tests, see William Hays, *Statistics* (New York: Holt, Rinehart & Winston, 1963), 456–489; B. J. Winer, *Statistical Principles in Experimental Design*, 2nd ed. (Chicago: McGraw-Hill, 1971), 196–201; Kirk, 87–97; and Kerlinger, 218–221.

Use of Computers in Research and Analysis

*T*hroughout this book references have been made to computers and their use in research. This chapter formally introduces the computer, and familiarizes you not only with the basics needed to operate the machine but also to make *intelligent* use of it. We begin by providing an overview of computer uses and a description of what a computer *is.* After this, we will look at what the computer *does* and why these functions are important. We then examine the role of the computer in the various methods of research discussed earlier and in the preparation of the research for dissemination. We also examine some of the problems inherent in the use of computers, problems arising from both the conceptual perspectives of what the computer is and how the computer operates, and its day-to-day use.

A conscious decision was made to place this chapter late in the book. We did so for two very important reasons. (1) We are more concerned that you understand which research methods are most appropriate regardless of the ease of their use. If we had introduced the computer earlier, the computer might influence how you approached your research, rather than the research question you were addressing. (2) We view the computer as a *tool* the researcher may use to make his or her work more efficient. The computer is *not* essential to conducting research; social research was conducted before the advent of the computer. The computer makes counting easier, performs the mundane analytical steps associated with certain aspects of research quickly and with fewer errors, and may increase the efficiency of the research process. But it is not essential to the research process. Prior to the advent of the computer most statistical analysis was done by hand; it was long, arduous, and unpleasant work, requiring an understanding of what was required (analyses, for instance) and why and how it worked. Because the computer offers great speed and because the computer often makes decisions for us, some researchers worry that the computer may begin asking the research questions—or at least determining which questions should be asked and how they should be answered.[1]

Although we do not particularly agree with this assessment, we do recognize the danger in using the computer to plan and execute research. Before the computer is considered, the entire research process must be thought out, conceptualized. The availability of an analytical computer package is *not* the determinant to research; although lack of computer assistance today may hinder the researcher, it should not dictate what or how the research is carried out or analyzed. In the end, human reasoning, insight, and interpretations can never be totally replaced by the computer.

AN OVERVIEW OF COMPUTER USES

Why use a computer in the first place? As strange as this may sound, there are people who still are computer-phobic. Over the past 45 years a revolution in how research can be conducted has taken place. At the center of this revolution has been the advent of the *mainframe computer,* a large machine capable of doing millions of calculations or making millions of decisions per second, and simultaneously serving many users. Mainframe computers are often described according to the millions of instructions they can process per second (*MIPS*), with an average mainframe running between 20 and 136 MIPS.

Mainframe and Personal Computers

Until the late 1970s computer use was limited to the mainframe, requiring the researcher to become involved in what today would be viewed as a cumbersome and time-consuming process. In 1977, for instance, input to mainframe computers by most social scientists was by key-punched computer cards, fed manually into the computer via a card reader, a machine whose reliability at reading the punched holes seemed at times questionable. When used, the mainframe would take a job (your requested program which would read the data for analysis), assign it a number, queue it up according to some predetermined priority, and then analyze the data. Results were typically printed out at the computer center. Depending on the computer center and the user's priority, this process could take anywhere from 15 minutes to several days. Typically, this meant that a researcher either had to work at the computer center or return there several times to check if the results were ready.

This same process today, using similar mainframe computers, is almost instantaneous and much more reliable. Instead of card input, data are entered directly into a file via terminals. Many users have access to the same computer and programs. When you request an analysis, depending upon the number of other users on the system, turnaround from input to output may be instantaneous—or close to it. And, in many instances, the output can be routed to a variety of locations. It is important to note that until the late 1970s the computer was basically a *computational* device. Report *generation*—word processing—was still primarily a function of pencils and typewriters.

Today, most of the functions found in the 1970s mainframe computer are available through the *personal computer.* The personal computer can do almost all the tasks that were once computed only on mainframes (limited primarily by memory size and speed of computation—limitations being eliminated rapidly). One advantage of the personal computer over the mainframe is the *word processing* capability of today's personal computers. (You can use the mainframe for word processing, however this is not the most efficient use of mainframe computing.) Another advantage of the personal computer is that it *is* personal—you determine access to it and can work on it as you need. Even in computer labs with a number of personal computers, you can reserve the *same* terminal for sessions; thus, you will become familiar with its particular quirks and operating style. And, for the most part, you can schedule sessions at your convenience.

Examples of Daily Use

Virtually all social scientists use personal computers in their daily activities. Their computers are used in *writing* notes and letters, research results for publication, and, obviously, books. Social scientists *communicate* with each other and other professionals through computer networks over telephone lines; they have computerized *statistical packages* that analyze data and have programs that help in conducting content analyses. Grades are kept on spreadsheet programs which sum, average, find standard deviations, and even assign a letter grade based on a computed average, although there are computer programs written specifically for this task. Even such mundane things as files for telephone numbers and addresses and automated calendars are available at the touch of a few keys on a personal computer.

The advantages of the computer should be evident by now. Consider, for example, the data provided in Table 14.1. The 100 fictional data entries could be units from some category based on a content analysis, scores on an instrument from an experiment, responses to a survey, or even counts of behavior from an observational study. Assume for a moment that you need to compute a frequency count for all columns and a total frequency count for those entries that are greater than

Table 14.1   SAMPLE DATA

A		B	
1	2	1	2
5	2	6	1
2	9	1	3
7	3	3	7
0	1	6	3
5	1	9	9
8	0	1	1
5	2	8	4
6	0	4	7
1	8	4	1
9	3	2	6
1	6	6	1
6	8	3	2
4	0	6	1
2	7	1	9
4	1	7	8
9	3	5	2
3	4	2	5
7	5	7	3
5	1	0	5
6	8	1	0
1	4	6	8
2	5	8	2
7	2	6	0
9	3	1	9
5	8	3	8

5. How long will it take? How *reliable* are your computations (even with a hand-held calculator)? Once the data have been added, divided, and computed, can you then easily calculate a population mean, standard deviation, variance? Column means, standard deviations, variance? Test for differences? The computer conducts these analyses quickly and reliably. The computer efficiently reduces the time it takes to perform repetitive tasks, whether they involve numbers, such as in the example, or words.

The primary disadvantages of the computer come from this very efficiency. Sometimes we let the computer decide what is best or appropriate. In the case of statistical analyses, failure to conduct a required test may be due to the fact that this procedure is missing in the computer package used. Or, failure to find significance with one analysis may result in a temptation to try another, and another, and another; after all, it may only take seconds to run the extra tests. A major trap is the belief that the computer can do it all. Analysis is not necessarily correct or right simply because it was done on a computer.

With this in mind, we move to a survey of the characteristics common to all computer systems, thus learning what a computer *is*. Then, we examine how computers work and the steps necessary for efficient and proper use. It is not the purpose of this chapter, however, to introduce everything there is to know about computers or about programming; should you become interested in these topics, there are many courses and publications that can serve to further your knowledge. [2] This chapter will not focus on any particular model or make of computer; there are simply too many to cover all adequately, but the information presented is relative to *all* personal computers—IBM, IBM-compatible, or Apple compatible or Macintosh. There are certain basic functions of computers that are universal.

COMPUTER BASICS

It is probably true that you need not understand a great deal about how the computer operates in order to use one, in much the same way you do not have to know how the engine works to drive a car. [3] Nonetheless, we have found that a basic understanding of the computer leads to more intelligent use. Hence, we begin with how the computer operates, what it *is* and what it takes to make it *run*.

Characteristics Common to Computer Systems

A computer, on the most elemental level, is an input-process-output *system*; that is, the computer takes data—numbers, symbols, designs—analyzes it and then presents it in some readable and usable form. As a system, all computers have at least five common characteristics that make them useful to research: speed, memory, universality, flexibility, and ductility. [4] These characteristics have been only touched upon thus far, but to understand the computer's *potential* for use in research we need to examine each in more detail.

Speed As should be evident by now, one of the major characteristics associated with computers is the speed with which they operate. Operations and judgments that would take hours or even days are done in seconds (in computer circles, however, even seconds are *slow*!). Speed is important in research when we analyze data via complex statistical procedures or, as in the case of content analyses, sort through categories to arrive at summaries of content.

Speed is extremely important when using the mainframe computer. Only a few years ago gaining access to the mainframe computer was frequently time-consuming. You could "connect" to the computer only indirectly, through the use of punch cards. Now access is almost unlimited, researchers can link up directly to the mainframe through *ports*, or dedicated lines. These ports can also be used by others through a system called *time-sharing*. In time-sharing systems high speed allows each user to access the computer, enter data, manipulate or analyze it, and receive output (in the form of printouts, plots, etc.). Time-sharing, however, is only as efficient as the speed of the computer. The faster the computer, the better the time-sharing.

Speed, then, serves two purposes. It allows the user to perform computations quickly and it allows many users to access the computer in a short period of time. When compared to personal computers, the mainframe computer is significantly faster; but because it must serve many users simultaneously, often over a hundred, it can seem to be quite slow. The personal computer's speed is tremendous and getting faster all the time. New applications of the personal computer have resulted in networking between personal computers via *LANs,* or *local area networks,* which allow several computers to be connected to each other, providing shared access to files, programs, and other devices.

Memory   A computer is only as efficient as its *memory.* All the speed in the universe is negated when a computer's memory is small. Memory sets the limit on the computer's ability to store information, act upon it, and produce results. Mainframe computers obviously have more memory than personal computers, but what can be accomplished with personal computers today rivals the mainframe computers of just 15 years ago. Again, more memory is being packaged with personal computers each day. The program limitations due to memory of just 5 years ago are now nonexistent, but new and more advanced or refined applications are requiring more and more memory as, for instance, personal computers become their own internal networks. Programs with *multitasking* abilities are becoming common. Such programs allow the user to work with two (or more) application programs at one time.

The latest Apple Macintosh and the IBM personal computers running the latest software allow the user to perform simultaneously multiple tasks on one machine. For instance, you may have your computer screen divided into three areas: One area may have a statistical program for data analysis, the second a word processor for writing up reports, and the third a calendar to remind you of important dates and meetings. A similar but more limited capability is offered by Microsoft Windows, which allows you to cut and paste from one window on the screen to another. And some advanced word processing programs allow you to work in many documents—in different windows—at one time.

Universality and Flexibility   While speed and memory are physical characteristics of the computer, universality and flexibility are characteristics of computer use. All computers, regardless of the brand, can be *programmed* or instructed to do all kinds of operations, as long as the operations can be defined in some form of recognized language (such as BASIC, PASCAL, FORTRAN, etc.). Programs are written for particular computers. The information each program produces is not compatible with computers using other operating systems. An Apple IIe's Wordstar program cannot read data produced on an IBM's Wordstar program. Often, different computers produced by the same corporation cannot read or work with data produced on different models—the Macintosh and Apple IIe or IIc, for example. However, the situation is rapidly changing. For example, both WordPerfect and Microsoft Word, popular word processing programs, originally produced for IBM and compatible machines are now written for the Apple Macintosh computer.

Flexibility means that computers can process these instructions in many different ways, each coming up with *similar* results. As we will note later, however, flexibility does not mean that all computer programs—or computers running the same programs for that matter—produce exactly the same results.

Ductility   Kerlinger uses the term *ductility* to refer to the computer's close ties with the people who use them.[5] No matter how good a computer is at solving a problem, it will only be as good as the human being who instructs it—programs it to do what must be done. What this means is that computers are only as smart as the people who use them. Relying on the computer to be correct in all cases is a problem all computer users face at some time or another. Take, for instance, a program that will read a text file, such as a term paper, correct misspellings it finds, and note major grammatical problems. Running the paper through this program may not find *all* misspellings and may not change the grammatical "errors" it finds. As of 1990, programs such as *Grammatik* could not make judgment calls about the "goodness" or "correctness" of the writing. As noted earlier, many users, both neophytes and old hands, have fallen into such traps. As Kerlinger so aptly notes, "The researcher can therefore depend on the machine's 'logic' and accuracy— within the finite limitations of the machine."[6]

The Physical Computer

The computer, as we know it *physically,* is usually composed of three components: input devices such as keyboards, mice, and scanners; the central processing unit (*CPU*)—the "body"—which either holds or accepts input from storage devices (*drives,* such as *floppy* and *hard disks*) and the silicon chips that serve as the "heart" or "brain" of the computer; and output devices such as printers, plotters, and monitors. In Figure 14.1 several different types of personal computers are depicted. Note that some are composed of three distinctly different components,

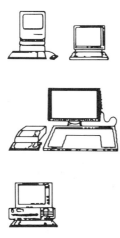

Figure 14.1 Personal computers.

others more, others less. The minimal physical computer "system" is composed of an input device, central processing unit, and output device.

Input Devices   The main input device associated with the personal computer is the *keyboard*, which functions much like a typewriter keyboard, except that unlike the typewriter, certain keys have specialized functions. When entering data, for instance, the alphabetical "l" key *cannot* take the place of the numeric "1" key and the capital letter, "O" is distinctly different from the number "0," which usually is slashed (Ø) to make a distinction between the two keys. The keyboard, however, is only one of several input devices.

Most personal computers can also accept input from a device called a *mouse.* The mouse, first popularly available on the Macintosh, allows a user to point to a physical location on the monitor or screen and click a button once or twice to initiate input functions. Usually, these mouse functions perform tasks that would require multiple keystrokes when entered from a keyboard. The mouse is particularly useful when working with graphics, drawing, and accessing and moving information from one part of the data set to another. Use of the mouse also reduces the already minimal time it takes to enter information to the computer and generally increases the ease of use. There are, however, some functions a mouse cannot perform, for example, entering word processing text.

Other popular input devices include the *scanner, light pen*, and *modem.* The scanner—or "optical character reader"—reads directly from a typed page, entering the information into the computer without the tedious task of retyping. The obvious advantage is the reduction in errors made in data entry; however, present scanners are not 100 percent accurate and they must be used with care. The light pen serves as a way to select information from the screen and to actually "write" on the screen. The computer screen, like a television, consists of hundreds of light "points." As a light point is activated and joined with others an image forms. The light pen activates the points, creating the information to be used by the computer.

The third input device is very different from keyboards, mice, and optical scanners and pens. The *modem* (*mo*dulate-*dem*odulate device) allows computers to "talk" to one another. As an input device, the modem allows people to send and receive data, usually across telephone lines. "Bits" of information are transferred between computers, coded and translated by a computer program at both ends of the connection, at incredibly high speeds. (*BITS*, or "binary digits of information" take the form of ones [1s] and zeros [Øs], which the computer reads as OFF [Ø] or ON [1]. Numbers, letters, graphic symbols, etc. are distinctly different combinations of ones and zeros.) A few years ago two computers might have communicated at about 30 characters (a space, letter, number, etc., created by the computer as it reads the data into *bits*) per second. This transmission speed is called a *baud rate.* Thirty characters per second closely approximates a 300 baud rate. Today, however, baud rates range anywhere from a low of 110 to a high of over *20,000* bits per second.

Use of a modem typically requires that one computer make contact with another. For a connection to be made, both computers must speak the same "language." Computer programs such as *Crosstalk, Red Rider,* and *Bitcom* provide the information necessary for computers to "talk" with each other. Once a connection has been made (and any special passwords or safety devices passed) the two computers may copy from each other. In this way many personal computers are able to tie into high-speed mainframe computers, share information with a number of other personal computers, and access programs and output devices.

The Central Processing Unit   The heart, brains, or guts of the computer is found in the central processing unit, or CPU, which is located in the "body" of the computer. Actually, the CPU is an electronic decision making system composed of storage systems, input-process-output systems, and memory systems. Information from the input devices is accepted by the CPU in the form of machine language or *bytes*. A byte, in turn, is composed of information called *bits*. Bytes, composed of a number of bits, are used to move information around the processing unit. Most older non-IBM-compatible computers use 7- or 8-bit combination systems to create numbers, letters, and so forth; IBM-compatible computers typically use 16-bits to create or *map* the character; newer computers are using 32-bit systems. Generally, the more bits used in the transfers, the faster the computer. Hence, we might expect that a 32-bit system would be three to four times faster than a 7- or 8-bit system.

A computer can only process so much information, regardless of how fast it is. The processing of information is closely tied to the computer's internal *memory*. Memory is simply the computer's storage capacity. There are several types of memory, some volatile and replaced as applications change, some permanent or *resident*. Either way, we measure memory in bytes, usually in combinations of thousands. If a computer's memory is 64K, it can hold 64,000 bytes of data (remember, a byte is composed of 8 bits of information). Internal memory can range from 64K to what is called 8 or more *megabytes* (M, Mb, or MEG). (A megabyte consists of 1,000,000 bytes of information.)

Internal memory can be divided into two types. RAM, or *random access memory*, is the volatile memory available for computation and data manipulation. Usually RAM serves as a temporary storage area for information as it is analyzed, computed, or changed. Information entered into RAM will disappear when the computer is turned off or will sometimes disappear if you have "overloaded RAM," as many computer users have learned. Many computer programs require a minimum RAM. At one time 64K of RAM was all that was available. To overcome the problem of limited RAM in older systems, you can add *expansion boards*, which increase your RAM in 16K to 64K increments. By 1990, most computer programs required at least 256K RAM, and most computer systems are being produced with a minimum 1 MEG of RAM or more. As RAM increases, so too does the potential to create more advanced, and easy-to-use, programs. RAM also allows for more advanced programming; increases in memory yield newer applications, which in turn, require more memory. For instance, the SPSS/PC+ statistical package discussed in the data analysis chapters requires a minimum of 512K RAM. Most popular word processors now require at least that much memory. Advanced applications require more.

The second type of internal memory is *permanent* memory. Permanent memory consists of two types, one of which is ROM, or *read only memory*, which cannot be changed or altered. It is preprogrammed and basically runs the system. It consists of the programming necessary to create, read, and manipulate file and programs (different computers often work on different systems, therefore making compatibility a potential problem). PROM, or *programmable read only memory*, is memory that can be changed by the user, but is normally treated as ROM.

External memory represents *storage* devices. Data stored in external devices includes data cards (now obsolete), computer tape (also including cassette tape), punched paper tape (quickly becoming obsolete), and magnetic or laser disks of varying sizes and types. The two storage forms most used today are floppy and hard disks. As of 1990, floppy disks range in size from 8 inches (obsolete) to 3½ inches, with the 5¼-inch and 3½-inch disk used most often. A typical floppy disk will hold between 360K and 1.44M bytes of information (see Table 14.2). The floppy disk can be carried from site to site, placed in storage boxes, and reused. The floppy disk is placed in a disk drive, located either in the computer itself or close by and "read" by the computer. Information is loaded, replaced, reloaded, and so on, into the computer's memory as needed. Floppy disks can be edited, purged of data, and generally used over again many times.

A hard disk, on the other hand, is a more physically fixed device. Typically, hard disks contain between 20 and 300 megabytes of information in a fixed location, located either in the body of the computer or in a separate unit. The major difference between the hard and floppy disk is the amount of information each holds, but differences in speed of information access generally give the hard disk user a significant speed advantage over the floppy disk user.

There are many other storage devices available today and even more in the planning stages. For instance, CD ROM disks offer the user almost unlimited storage space, but most still limit use to reading only. Steven Jobs' NEXT computer has a standard 280 MEG read/write CD ROM with replaceable CDs, just like floppy disks. Uses of CD ROM might include collections of ERIC entries for a decade, a specific set of abstracts, a listing of all books published during a given time period, and eventually, entire libraries of publications. Thus far, use of the CD ROM disk appears to be mainly for information retrieval, not information manipulation; but think of the speed with which that information could be accessed and used. Another type of disk is the *laser disk*, which writes data on the disk via light rather than magnetic manipulation. Like the laser telephone cable, much more information can be stored in this way. Even "removable" hard disk cartridges have appeared on the market.

When information is stored in memory and the computer begins its pro-

Table 14.2   INFORMATION STORAGE

Size	Page equivalent
1 3½ floppy = 800K	300 pages
1 megabyte disk	375 (= 1 book)
1 gigabyte (= 1000 MEG)	1000 books
1 terabyte (= 1000 GIG)	1,000,000 books

grammed analyses many things happen that serve to inhibit or increase the computer's speed and hence its efficiency. First, information is placed into waiting areas, or *buffers*. Buffers are temporary storage locations within RAM that serve to make transfer between input and output devices and between processing applications function smoothly. Typically, the more buffers a computer has, the faster and more efficiently the information can be processed.

At times, however, processing is bogged down in complex computations. Processing can be speeded up by installing either *coprocessors* or *combination boards*. A coprocessor is a computer chip that works with the main chips in the computer's CPU. A combination board is an integrated series of chips preprogrammed to do certain functions. For instance, running SPSS/PC+ without a mathematical coprocessor chip results in much slower computation. A coprocessor increases computational speed significantly, as much as four to five times normal processing speed.

Output Devices   To see what the computer has done requires an output device. Minimally, the personal computer requires a *monitor* (cathode ray tube, or CRT) or screen on which the information is relayed in some readable form. A monitor, as noted earlier, takes collections of light points and creates images. Monitors can be categorized according to several criteria. First, whether the display is in *monochrome* or *color*. Second, how "fine" the images on the screen are. For instance, ordinary television screens when used as monitors produce large block-like images, while true monitors produce pencil thin and refined images. And, third, whether the monitor can produce graphics. Most monitors today grade high. Many can be switched between monochrome and color modes, produce extremely fine characters, and can produce a host of graphics.

While a monitor is truly a necessity, a second output device is usually needed, especially if you want to have a *hard copy*—a printed copy—of your work. Hard copy devices usually are divided into two classes: printers and plotters. A printer acts like a typewriter, only controlled by the computer and, in many instances, with its own internal logic and memory. Printers are further divided into several classes. At the low end (both in cost and in quality of output) are the physical impact *dot matrix* printers. These printers print by creating a character with anywhere from 9 to 24 *pins*, which produce an image on paper according to a preset pattern of pin strikes (9-pin printers represent the lower end, while the 24-pin printers represent the high end). Dot matrix printers are generally quite fast and most can be run in two or more modes: draft, where the image is relatively unsophisticated, and letter or near-letter quality, where the image is sophisticated, darker, and more like typewriter copy. Most dot matrix printers also print graphics. For *real* letter quality, a *daisy-wheel* printer may be used. This printer actually has dedicated characters, much like a typewriter, that strike the paper and produce typewritten-like output. A disadvantage of the daisy-wheel printer is its inability to print graphics. At the high end we have the *laser printer*. Most laser printers create letter-quality output by using a 300×300 *point* matrix to form its characters. The laser printer is extremely fast and can integrate graphics with characters.

The plotter is used when you need to produce quality designs or graphics.

Plotters are specialized and produce extremely accurate representations of the data they are fed. Typically plotters are used to create graphs, charts, and diagrams.

Preparing and Using Computer Hardware

Before a computer can be used several actions must be taken. Although this may seem basic, the steps involved in using the computer are important enough to mention. After the computer has been assembled (all the cables must be attached to the various input and output devices) it is ready to run. Simply turning on the computer will not activate all computers. Computers that use floppy disks as their sole method of storage require that you first place a *DOS* (*disk operating system*) *disk* in the primary drive (drive 1 or drive A). Hard disk systems, on the other hand, have the system already resident on the hard disk and automatically access it. The system disk tells the computer how to store information and typically provides the user with data management programs. This step is sometimes called *booting* the computer; essentially, you are preparing the computer for use.

Typing at this stage will probably produce something on the screen, but that is about all. To use the computer you must use some form of programming, or *software*—programming done by an expert with specific applications in mind. Some programming, such as a basic computer language with which to write programs, may be included in the computer's ROM or PROM. Usually, however, you have to purchase such programs. *Programs are written for specific computers.* Although computers have as basic characteristics universality and flexibility, programs do not. Programs are written for particular computers and the storage devices on which they are "written" differ from computer to computer. This is a function of the *system* that is working. An IBM or IBM-compatible computer uses different operating system software than does an Apple or Macintosh. One cannot read the others' information without expensive additional equipment. Hence, you must have some knowledge of the system that operates the computer before purchasing the programs you desire to run. Even computers from the same company may run on different systems, such as the IBM PC/XT/AT and the OS versions. Apple and Apple Macintosh run on different systems. And, even programs written for one computer may not run on so-called compatible computers. Thus, a major disadvantage today is program compatibility, or, more accurately, program *in*compatibility.

Storage of *your* programs, text, or data is the function of an external or internal drive. Both floppy and hard disks must be *formatted* to accept the information you wish to store. Formatting is a function of the system, usually taking anywhere between a minute (floppy disk) to an hour (hard disk). Formatting prepares the disk for information reception; formatting also eliminates—erases—any information you might already have stored on it. Obviously, there is a danger inherent in formatting or reformatting a disk: You may erase needed information. With this in mind, all computer users routinely *back up* their disks, thus saving important data twice, once for use and once for protection in the case of unintentional erasure. It usually only takes one accidental erasure of important information to get the beginning user to back up his or her data on a regular basis.

Not only should you back up files after you have finished with them, but you should get into the habit of saving your files every 10 to 15 minutes. Many a time valuable data has been lost in the *entry stage* because of an inadvertent key stroke, power failure, or even disk overload. Saving an application every 10 to 15 minutes is an important habit to learn. Like accidental erasure, it only takes one or two experiences to learn the importance of temporarily saving your data during entry.

The computer—personal or mainframe—is a system of interrelated parts, an understanding of which can make life easier. In the end, however, the computer is a *machine*, a very efficient and usually accurate machine. As noted earlier, however, it is only as smart as the user. Computers rarely make mistakes, humans do—and do so for several reasons: (1) they fail to understand the limitations of the computer, (2) they use the wrong programs for the questions they are attempting to answer, or (3) they sometimes let the computer do their thinking for them.

SOFTWARE/PROGRAMMING

In some ways operating the computer is like driving a car. Once you learn its particular habits and quirks things go along fairly smoothly. The actual act of driving, however, is found in the use of programming—or in most of our cases, preprogrammed software. *Software* refers to ready-to-use computer programs. Software makes data analysis much easier because someone else has done the hard work for us. They have programmed the computer to do its calculations, make decisions, or present its output in a particular form or format.

The point is simple. As we grow to depend on software, we get lazy. It is much easier to use what we learn early and work within its limitations. This suggests, however, that the limitations are known. Computer centers normally update their mainframe software, eliminating bugs and problems. As personal computer users become more familiar with the products and more products become available, it is becoming easier to keep such equipment software updated. Since most of us are not programmers—in fact we really do not have to be as long as we can understand what the programmer did and basically how they did it—we must rely on the advice of others.

Using prepackaged software has several potential disadvantages. First, we can become too dependent on others' ways of doing things, of doing things the way the software makes us do them. Secondly, while we believe that the programs purchased are error free, they sometimes have bugs that limit their use.

With this in mind, a short overview of the available types of software and programming in general might help us make more intelligent decisions about software selection and use.

Programming

All computer programs are written in a form called a *language.* Computer languages include BASIC, PL/1, PASCAL, COBOL, and FORTRAN. Each program language is a system in and of itself. Each has its own way of arriving at a solution to the problem. Each differs in terms of the speed and structure. Some programs, such as FORTRAN, have been around for a long time, while others are much newer. Some programs appear in a series of *statements* and can be read and analyzed by the user. Others, however, are compacted into what is called *machine language.* The machine language program is faster than the statement-oriented form, but is harder to debug when problems occur. Machine language programs typically take up less disk storage space then other program forms, hence we typically prefer them over "basic" programming.

Although it is not necessary, some knowledge of computer programming would probably benefit any researcher. This is especially true if you, as the researcher, find a problem with a requested analysis and know that it *has* to be a function of computer malfunction or, more likely, of the programming. A basic understanding of the terminology and "structure" of the program used also helps when attempting to get some help from local computer consultants. This is clearly beyond the scope of *this* book. However, there are advantages to learning how to communicate with the programmer, including obtaining help when needed, knowing *what* to ask when getting help, and even requesting specialized programming. As with most things, even just a knowledge of vocabulary helps when problems are encountered.

Software

There are literally thousands of software programs written for the personal computer. Programs available to the researcher range between the extremely well-written package to the one that appears to work at first, only to cause problems later. Before covering the major packages now available, we should note that software should be selected based on several criteria. One excellent criterion is that it does what you need it to do. A second reason to choose a particular package is that the software comes well recommended by someone who has used it. One criterion you will hear often is that the software is *user-friendly.* This means that the programmer has taken the time to create a program that tells you what you are going to be doing and often provides specific help programs when you have a question or are not sure what to do next. User-friendly programs are preferable, but not a necessity. A fourth, and probably most important, criterion is that the software comes with *excellent documentation* and technical support. A toll-free telephone number and offers of assistance usually indicate quality programming and a manufacturer willing to help the user.

The software used by most researchers tends to fall into two categories: word processing and data manipulation. The following sections provide overviews of these important computer *tools.*

Word Processing   Word processing programs have evolved from relatively simple typewriter-like programs to programs that automatically footnote, format according to some style manual, and integrate graphics support. Most word processing packages today will italicize, underline, double-underline, super- and subscript, do red-line editing, and even do simple calculation of numerical data. These programs increase the ease of rewriting, moving sentences or entire sections, and even inserting other documents within the document.

A problem with word processing programs, like many other programs, is that they usually use their own system for creating your data. For instance, this book has been written on four *different* computers using four *different* word processing packages. None of the programs on their own can read the files of the other computers. Programs such as WordLink will translate between major word processors, but will not always pass on fancy style manipulations, such as automatic footnoting. Some word processing packages will unformat documents to a standard commonly accepted format (called *ACSII—American Standard Code for Information Interchange*). But many will not. In the case of this book, about half was written on an Apple Macintosh with Mindwrite, the other half on an IBM-compatible with Microsoft Word, and one chapter with an IBM version of DisplayWrite, and yet another with an Apple IIe version of WordStar.

Along with word processing packages, there are several accessory packages. For instance, there are spell-checkers, which check for misspellings. Most *integrated* word processors now possess that capability and allow authors to check their typing while still in the file. Nonintegrated spell-checkers, however, require that the file be saved and analyzed, errors marked, and then reedited. There are also grammar-checkers available. These accessories will check for errors in capitalization and punctuation, and a variety of other things, including warning of passive voice use and sexist language as well as provide summary statistics (readability indices, percent of certain word categories, number of words, etc.), and even compare the writing sample to other well-known samples.

Word processing also has progressed to the point where authors can actually incorporate "publishing" into their work. Packages available for IBM and IBM-compatibles, such as WordPerfect and Microsoft Word, and all Macintosh word processors allow graphics and text to be integrated and then printed on a laser printer for booklike quality. Future word processors will be even more powerful and time-saving.

Data Management   Data management programs fall into three general categories. Traditionally, there have been two main categories—*spreadsheets* and *data base* programs. The advent of larger memory and faster personal computers has added a third category: *statistical analysis* programs.

The spreadsheet is an electronic ledger, and performs calculations and makes decisions needed daily in business. Research uses of spreadsheets are less common. The best known spreadsheets are probably Visicalc, SuperCalc, Excel, and Lotus 1-2-3. Some spreadsheets also have become integrated, giving them varying forms of word processing capabilities.

Data base programs allow for the management of large amounts of information. Information entered can be easily accessed and the data bases' cross-referencing system allows for selection of unique sets of data. Data base programs include dBase IV, PC File, and Relational Database. Some data bases have become integrated, and now possess word processing capabilities.

The trend in data management programs has been toward integration of spreadsheet, data base, and word processor. Programs such as Symphony, Framework, Appleworks, and Microsoft Works are part of this trend. The major problem with such integration is, however, the price you pay in attempting to do too much, resulting in reduced specialization and specific program power when compared to nonintegrated software. It should be noted that most data management programs now do elementary statistical analyses. For the researcher, however, statistical analysis is best left to the specialized statistical packages available for the mainframe and personal computer.

There are many statistical packages available today, compared to just 15 years ago. Programs for the personal computer have mushroomed in the past 5 years alone. The three most powerful programs, SPSS/PC+, SAS, and SYSTAT, require hard disks of at least 10 Mb and large (512K–1M) memories. They also run best when the computer has a mathematical coprocessor. These programs will do almost all that the mainframe will do, not as fast of course, but probably more conveniently; additionally, each has its own idiosyncratic requirements. Smaller packages have been developed over the years, the best of which are probably Statistics with Finesse for both IBM and Apple computers and SL-Micro for the Apple (based on an SPSS format).[7] Good Macintosh statistics packages include Statview, CricketStat, Systat, and SPSS.

Additional software is available in the *public domain.* Public domain software is usually fairly inexpensive and many times includes either incomplete versions of the programs or trial programs whose bugs are still being worked out. Care should be taken when purchasing public domain software; the software—often thought of as noncopyrighted and many times called *freeware* or *shareware*—is still the property of the programmer. The major disadvantages of public domain software are found in the lack of comprehensive documentation and the unavailability of assistance when problems occur. Additionally, public domain software is often written for specific computers and may not operate well—if at all—on other systems or brands.

Using Software in Communication Research

By now you probably know more about computers, programming, and software than you ever thought necessary. But how can this software be used in research? Aside from the general descriptions of software given earlier, how can the computer help in *all* phases of the research program?

Remember that all research begins with a theoretical statement derived from some literature review. Today, the computer can not only make literature reviews easier but also help in preparing for the written product. We can begin by attaching our computer to the research library's computerized card files or specialized data bases, such as The Source. By asking for certain key words or authors we can establish a listing of available sources, which then can be copied and printed for later use. Using a data base program we might enter the citation and some cross-reference descriptors for later use in searching our literature.

As noted earlier, often we will use the personal computer as a *dumb* terminal, one linked to a mainframe computer serving only to communicate instructions to the mainframe. As a dumb terminal, the PC cannot process information, it only sends and receives commands from the user and the mainframe. In cases where the personal computer is used as a dumb terminal special software must be employed to emulate one of several industry-wide terminals (such as a VT-100 or an IBM 3101 terminal) so that the mainframe can communicate with the personal computer. Once you have coupled with the mainframe (through a modem or dedicated fiber optic line), you have the capabilities associated with mainframe use. You also have the potential to receive your analyses printed on your own printer. The speed at which your dumb terminal operates, however, will depend on the speed of the communications device (modem or cable) used.

Once we have access to the mainframe we can link to one of the growing *networks* dedicated to communication and other type of research and dissemination. In 1987, for instance, Thomas Benson of Pennsylvania State University began editing CRTNET (*C*ommunication *R*esearch and *T*heory *NET*work). Others include specific content networks such as PSYCHNET, CELEX, COMSERVE, and ISAAC and more general networks such as BITNET. Through interactive and downloaded (where messages are sent to the "host computer," like Benson's CRTNET) communications you might ask if anyone on the network knows of sources or information concerning your research area or specific research questions.

As with any research project, once the literature review is completed and the research questions or hypotheses posed, a method must be selected. Obviously, the computer can help the historical/critical researcher in much the same way it helped prepare the literature review. Notes can be placed in data bases and then searched. Quotations can be saved in files ready for inclusion in the written report. Cross-referencing can provide the historical/critical researcher with a new perspective on the event, person, or movement under study. The participant-observer can use the computer in much the same way. Entering field notes into files and then copying them into other files or searching the files for key words for later analysis is but one computer application available. Using graphics programs associated with data bases or word processors also may help prepare for the final report.

Obviously, statistical analysis packages are used with survey and experimental methods. These packages not only store the data, but many have special application programs available to table the results automatically for inclusion into word processing packages. Some statistical packages provide automatic random number generation, help assign participants to conditions, and will even help plan research designs. Concern over misuse of the computer, of conducting analyses previously not attempted because of limited time and ability is something that must be watched, both in experiment and survey methodology.

Content analysis, as a method, has probably gained a great deal from the availability of the computer. The computer's ability to take units placed in categories and do the mundane chores of counting has made the content analyst's life much easier. Special programs also allow the inclusion of much more complex content, as well as more messages, than possible previously. The computer, however, has caused concern for some in this area. The major fear here is that content analysis has become a function of finding some content and hammering everything *countable* out of it. Obviously, there is room for such concern, but if the researcher's emphasis is on the research question and not the tool, such concern should be minimized.

The computer has quickly become essential to the conduct of research. But we need to remember that the research question is the guiding force in the conduct of research, not the things the computer allows us to do. We also need to remember that we make conscious decisions of which analyses and tools we use in our research; mindless use of the computer is not in the research tradition discussed in this book.[8] In the end the individual researcher is responsible for what he or she produces and no computer in the world can reduce that responsibility.

Finally, researchers can benefit from the advanced word processing capabilities offered by the computer. One major advantage the computer provides is the ability to edit and revise the written word, allowing for a more polished and fine-tuned product. Editing others' research by swapping files stored on disks also makes the editing task easier. Even the ability to prepare tables and figures for publication is now possible. In the end, then, intelligent use of the computer can and will save time and yield a product that furthers our understanding of human behavior.

SUMMARY

This chapter has introduced you to the use of the computer. We began with an overview of the computer and its use. We then examined what the computer is and how it operates. The physical computer was described and the characteristics common to all computers were examined. Use of the computer was examined through software and programming available for most research projects. Throughout this chapter, however, it has been continually stressed that the computer is only as good as the user; the decisions it makes are a reflection of what it has been asked to do and the knowledge and ability of the programmer. We hope this chapter has sensitized you to not only the unlimited potential the personal computer provides the researcher, but to possible traps and problems as well.

PROBES

1. What has the computer done for research? Has it changed the *process* of research? If so, how?

2. Given the advances in microcomputer technology since 1980, where do you think computer technology will be in 1995? In 2001? How will this effect your chosen career area?

3. How would you use a bulletin board or a computer service specializing in research? Take an area of interest and generate the key words necessary to do a computer search in that particular area.

4. How computerized is your school's library? If it is computerized, how is it used? Take the concept and key words you generated for Probe 3 and use the library's computers to do a literature search. What additional elements would enhance that search? (Can you get a printout of the listings? Can you order a book or journal through the computer?) Where should libraries be after five years of computerization? Why?

5. Assuming that you had approximately $3000 to spend on a computer system for your personal use in research, how would you spend it? What are the minimal elements you would consider necessary for conducting research in your particular interest area?

SUGGESTED READING

Dertouzos, M. & Moses, J. (Eds.). (1979). *The computer age: A twenty-year view.* Cambridge, MA: MIT Press.

Etizoni, A. (1975). Effects of small computers on science. *Science, 189,* 1975.

Kerlinger, F. N. (1986). *Foundations of behavioral research* (3rd ed.). New York: Holt, Rinehart and Winston.

Moore, R. W. (1978). *Introduction to the use of computer packages for statistical analysis.* Englewood Cliffs, NJ: Prentice-Hall.

Weizenbaum, J. (1976). *Computer power and human reason.* San Francisco: Freeman.

NOTES

1. A. Etizoni, "Effects of Small Computers on Scientists," *Science,* 189 (1975), cited in Fred N. Kerlinger, *Foundations of Behavioral Research,* 2nd ed. (New York: Holt, Rinehart, & Winston, 1986), 634.
2. See, for example *PC Magazine, PC World, Personal Computing,* and *Byte* for more information about IBM and IBM-compatible computers; *Nibble, MacWorld,* and *A+* for Apple and Macintosh computers; other computer systems, such as Commodore and Atari have their own publications.
3. Roger D. Wimmer and Joseph R. Dominick, *Mass Media Research: An Introduction,* 2nd ed. (Belmont, Calif.: Wadsworth, 1987), 411.
4. Kerlinger, 626–629.
5. Kerlinger, 628–629.
6. Kerlinger, 629.
7. For a comparison, see Don W. Stacks, "Statistical Packages for the Personal Computer," *Communication Education,* 35 (1986): 419–429; Don W. Stacks, "Statistical Package for the Social Sciences/PC+ V3.0," *Communication Education,* 38 (1989): 387–393.
8. See Etizoni.

Chapter 15

Bringing It Together: Writing and the Process of Research

We have come full circle. The analysis of data gathered by whatever methodology, including qualitative methods, should yield new *questions*, questions arising from the answers to earlier questions. In sum, the quest is a continuous one; one we might even call the *never-ending process for knowledge, understanding, and prediction.* But, in reality, the research process is only nine-tenths complete. We began with a question derived from theory, selected the methodology most appropriate to collect the data to answer the question, and then analyzed the data. We now face the final step in making the results—including the theoretical rationale, method, analysis, and interpretation—available to others for further scrutiny. In completing this last step, we hope to move the research to the next plateau and add to the body of knowledge we know as science.

This chapter examines that final step. It also serves as a review of the process of research, and as such, is the culmination of a long journey from conceptualizing a problem, reviewing the relevant literature, posing the research question, selecting the most appropriate methodology, and analyzing and interpreting the data collected. But data collection and analysis is not the last step in a research project, preparing the research report for dissemination is.

PREPARING THE FINAL PRODUCT

For many researchers the final step of writing and presenting the results is the hardest. The research must be carefully reviewed and scrutinized before it can be published or presented. Even in informal, in-house presentations of research there are certain guidelines that help make the presentation as accurate as possible, and, at the same time, allow for comparison with other research. Let us begin by examining the importance of written research to the research process.

Importance of Writing to the Research Process

There are many reasons for writing and disseminating the results of research. The first is obvious: Data and interpretation of that data sitting in a computer file or on a desk do not help others addressing the same problems. One of the reasons for conducting research in any methodology is to let others know what has been found. The desire to share knowledge should be basic to the research process and this sharing comes from disseminating the findings of research to others, either in the form of published articles, monographs, and books, through presentations at professional societies and organizations, or through informal presentations to interested parties. In any case, the research must be written in a clear and accurate manner to ensure that the results and interpretations are clearly understood by interested others.

Second, research is written to advance the state of the knowledge about communication. In writing to advance theory, we seek to understand the relationships between variables. Which variables are related? In what ways? To what degree? Each research project disseminated to the field—and to other fields interested in the type of research or research questions we may be addressing—adds one more piece of evidence to our data base of knowledge concerning human communication. Research that does not get disseminated does not contribute to this knowledge base.

Third, and we believe this to be of major importance to academic researchers, dissemination of research allows for more informed and better teaching. As new research becomes available we change—modify or intensify—our views of how the world should be structured. This process is essential in relating human communication to students. Teachers are constantly revising their views of the essential *process* of communication through the knowledge of the research base(s) of their field and for research contributed by other fields.

Fourth, writing serves two *personal* purposes. (1) It is gratifying to see the end product of much labor and love (and sometimes grief) disseminated to interested others. Publication and presentation become an important part of life. (2) Disseminating the final reports enhances professional reputation. Although this may seem far from the original reasons for conducting research discussed in the first section of this book, professional reputations and livelihoods are an end product of the research process. This is especially true in academia; however, more and more, as we become an increasingly information-based society, the ability to produce and disseminate research will create careers. Examples of research-based careers include political polling, economic forecasting, marketing research, and advertising/media effect research, to name but a few.

Finally, as Raymond K. Tucker, Richard L. Weaver, II, and Cynthia Berryman-Fink point out, researchers "write for writing's sake."[1] That is, the process of writing helps us clarify the presentation of our research by ensuring that the focus is clear and the ideas are fully supported. Furthermore, the process of writing itself may serve a heuristic function; it may bring to mind new ideas or explanations that may have been lost among all the facts and ideas behind the research. Many times new or better tests of the theory come from the writing stage; many times entirely new theories originate at this stage. Writing, then, may serve as a way to balance the research from beginning to end, to bring the process of research full circle and motivate further theory and study.

Why write? There are many reasons, but from our perspective the most important reason is the dissemination of research in a timely and professional manner, one that allows for close scrutiny and replication. Writing the findings of a research project is the next step in a continuing *program* of research. Research, then, begets research.

Writing the Research Report

The process of writing research reports differs slightly from other forms of writing. The process of research reporting is much more formal than other forms of writing. There are certain elements that must be included in a research report, elements that may differ from method to method, such as identification of participants and definitions of variables. There are also approved *styles* for the way in which research is reported. Each particular discipline typically approves of one or more *style sheets* or manuals that researchers follow in reporting their research. The communication discipline, for instance, allows much more flexibility in the style sheets followed, typically differing between journal and association, than does the American Psychological Association (APA) or the Modern Language Association (MLA), each of which has its own particular style.

Style Sheets   There are a variety of style sheets and manuals available to the researcher. The communication discipline typically follows those of the Modern Language Association (*MLA Style Sheet*), the American Psychological Association (*Publication Manual of the American Psychological Association*), or a derivation of one or the other. In many journals the major format of one of these two style sheets is followed, but with minor modifications; these modifications are typically specified in the journal's editorial statement. By reading the different journals you should get a feel for the different style sheets appropriate for your area of study or methodology.

A major difference between these particular styles is the way they approach citation. As discussed in Chapter 3, all contributions by others must be carefully and fully credited. The *MLA Handbook for Writers of Research Papers* (3rd edition) calls for references to be *footnoted*, with reference citations placed in the text of the report as superscript numbers. (Usually footnotes are treated as *endnotes* in the draft report and are listed on a separate page at the end of the manuscript.) MLA style allows for substantiative additions and comments, as well as the actual source of the material. Box 15.1 provides a sample of MLA style. APA style cites by name and date within the particular line of text, a convention that MLA has adopted with some modification. Box 15.2 presents a sample of APA style. In MLA style the references are called Notes, while the APA style refers to both Notes (which elaborate or clarify a thought) and References, which are bibliographic in content.

Style sheets serve an important purpose in research reports. They allow a form of standardization and control over what could be a very individualized process. Imagine, for instance, an experiment being reported in free verse or iambic pentameter. The style sheet sets forth the required minimums of presentation and, as noted earlier, may be modified to meet the particular needs of specific groups.

Organization of the Report

Regardless of the style sheet followed, all research reports are organized in specific ways. The researcher, whether qualitative or quantitative, follows the general outline of introduction, body, and concluding statement. The specifics may differ by method, but in general the following outline provides a good starting point:

    I. Rationale
        A. Introduction
            1. Goal or purpose
            2. Significance of research
        B. Review of literature
            1. Review of related literature
            2. Statement of research question/hypothesis
    II. Method
        A. Research participants
        B. Procedures followed
        C. Measures used
    III. Results
    IV. Discussion
        A. Significance
        B. Flaws—limitations and qualifications
        C. Conclusion and extension of theory
        D. Future research

Box 15.1 **Sample MLA Style**

Both rhetorical and communication scholars have recently considered the relationships between the way in which the human brain functions and how human beings communicate. In *Symbolic Inducement and Knowing: A Study of the Foundations of Rhetoric,* Gregg suggests that a far more comprehensive view of the epistemic function of rhetoric is possible when "the principle of symbolic discrimination from the neurological level is recognized."[1] Similarly, Chesebro has argued that a neurophysiological view is especially useful when explaining the "epistemological functions of media in cultural systems."[2] Likewise, Shedletsky has isolated more specific relationships among language usage, information processing, and cerebral activity within the human brain.[3] Such explorations suggest that far more detailed examinations of the influence of brain hemispheres might now be appropriately considered in terms of specific variables such as source perception, message perception, and message intensity.

NOTES

[1]Richard Gregg, *Symbolic Inducement and Knowing: A Study of the Foundations of Rhetoric* (Columbia, SC: University of South Carolina Press, 1984) 44.

[2]James W. Chesebro, "The Media Reality: Epistemological Functions of Media in Cultural Systems," *Critical Studies in Mass Communication,* 2 (1984): 111–130.

[3]Leonard. J. Shedletsky, "Cerebral Asymmetry for Aspects of Sentence Processing," *Communication Quarterly,* 29 (1981): 3–11; and Leonard J. Shedletsky, "Cerebral Asymmetry for Aspects of Sentence Processing: A Replication and Extension," *Communication Quarterly,* 31 (1983): 78–84.

Sometimes the reference number is placed in-line; however, most communication journals superscript notes.

Source: From COMMUNICATION RESEARCH: STRATEGIES AND SOURCES by Rubin, R.B., Rubin, A.M. and Piele, L.J. © 1986 by Wadsworth, Inc. Reprinted by permission of the Publisher.

Additionally, the report should have a title page, a short abstract that presents the essential information such as basic theory, method employed, and results; references; and explanatory tables and figures.

In organizing and writing the report, use of subheads—subtitles of sorts—help to maintain a flow and direction of the writing. This book has employed the use of three levels of subheads within each chapter. Headers serve two functions: the *outline* function keeps the material in order and the *orienting* function tells the reader whether the material is a major idea, secondary idea, or even a tertiary

---

Box 15.2 **Sample APA Style**

Both rhetorical and communication scholars have recently considered the relationships between the way in which the human brain functions and how human beings communicate. In *Symbolic Inducement and Knowing: A Study of the Foundations of Rhetoric,* Gregg (1984) suggests that a far more comprehensive view of the epistemic function of rhetoric is possible when "the principle of symbolic discrimination from the neurological level is recognized" (p. 44). Similarly, Chesebro (1984) has argued that a neurophysiological view is especially useful when explaining the "epistemological functions of media in cultural systems." Likewise, Shedletsky (1981, 1983) has isolated more specific relationships among language usage, information processing, and cerebral activity within the human brain. Such explorations suggest that far more detailed examinations of the influence of brain hemispheres might now be appropriately considered in terms of specific variables such as source perception, message perception, and message intensity.

REFERENCES

Chesebro, J. W. (1984). The media reality: Epistemological functions of media in cultural systems. *Critical Studies in Mass Communication, 2,* 111–130.

Gregg, R. (1984). *Symbolic inducement and knowing: A study of the foundations of rhetoric.* Columbia, SC: University of South Carolina Press.

Shedletsky, L. J. (1981). Cerebral asymmetry for aspects of sentence processing. *Communication Quarterly, 29,* 3–11.

Shedletsky, L. J. (1983). Cerebral asymmetry for aspects of sentence processing: A replication and extension. *Communication Quarterly, 31,* 78–84.

---

idea. Experienced writers use subheads to maintain flow and coherence in their writing.

All research reports are *formal* presentations. Most style sheets suggest that the use of the first person be avoided; hence, the "I" becomes "the researcher" or "we." The report should be grammatically and syntactically correct, conforming to the rules and prescriptions of the language in which it is written (not all research is written in English—or American English). The report should flow with internal summaries and transitional sentences bridging the various sections of the report. Supporting evidence (tables and figures) should be discussed within the body of the report and, in unpublished reports, should include a statement as to where the table or figure should be inserted:

The means, as presented in Table 1, indicate that, although significant differences were not obtained for all analyses, the *pattern* of the means was as predicted: traditional males were most persuaded, traditional females followed next, nontraditional males next and, and nontraditional females being least persuaded by the message.

Insert Table 1 About Here

Introduction   The specific format followed in writing the results of a research project will differ according to the method you follow. For our purposes, we will look in more detail at the required elements of an experimental study. The introduction, obviously, introduces the reader to the general area of study and the importance of the study. Many times the problem that the research addresses is stated formally in the introduction. Most of the time, however, the introduction serves to acquaint the reader with the variables under study and prepares the reader for the rest of the report.

Literature Review   In Chapter 4 we discussed the literature review as a method in and of itself. All research reports, including the experimental report, contain a review of the literature that was used to formulate the general research question. The literature review formally presents the logic behind the theory or previous research or descriptions of the phenomenon under study. Supporting materials, often reduced to explanatory figures and tables, are frequently acceptable additions to the literature review, which also serves as a potential research base for future research. Again, in some instances, the literature review may *be* the final written project. The literature review should culminate in a *formal* statement of the research question(s) explored and/or hypotheses to be tested. Although it may differ according to style sheet, the research questions and hypotheses should be clearly set off in the report and stated as formal relationships between the variables under study.

For example, the literature review may seek to identify reasons for a possible relationship between two variables, say receiver sex and persuasibility. The literature review would describe the previous research for each variable and show why the relationship was expected. The literature review should serve as a transition between the actual literature review and the statement of the question, for example:

Based on this discussion the following research question was addressed.

Or, for the hypothesis:

Based on _____ theory, the following hypotheses were derived.

Frequently, the research questions and hypotheses are then stated as formal questions of relationships or predictions of relationships:

RQ$_1$: What is the relationship between sex of interviewer and expected distancing in interview situations?

RQ₂: What is the relationship between interviewer rate of speech and perceptions of interviewer credibility?

H₁: Male interviewees will be more disturbed by male interviewers adopting socially inappropriate seating distance than will female interviewees.

H₂: Speakers with faster-than-normal rates of delivery will receive higher evaluations of benevolence and trustworthiness than will speakers with slower-than-normal delivery rates.

The statement of research questions and hypotheses serves as a transition between theory and method in the report. The way in which the research question or hypothesis is stated may also help determine the methodology chosen to answer the questions or test the relationships between variables. *Remember,* however, both literature review and statement of research questions and/or hypotheses are actually stated prior to conducting the research. Often, as is the case of a research proposal or prospectus that seeks to conduct research, these have already been formally stated. (We cover the proposal/prospectus later in this chapter.)

Method   Critical to an understanding of the research and the results is a clear and concise description of the methodological design employed, the operationalization of the variables under study, the participants, and the procedures followed. In writing the method section keep in mind that someone should be able to *replicate* the research based on the way it is described in this section. The method section should begin with a statement of the particular methodology employed, whether it be experimental, survey, content analytic, or whatever. For example, suppose that our study explores the relationship of two independent variables (biological sex and message—language—intensity) and one dependent variable (persuasibility). We might begin the method section by stating that the "experimental design employed in this study was a 2 (sex of receiver—male or female)×2 (level of message intensity—high or low) factorial design with off-set control." This tells the reader that there were two independent variables in the experimental manipulation, the levels they took, and that a control group, which received no manipulation, was included in the design.

After the design has been explained, the participants should be described. It may be necessary to report demographic variables, although this practice is not as prevalent today as it once was. Typically, the number of male and female participants and where they were drawn from is important: "100 students, 50 male and 50 female, enrolled in beginning public speaking courses volunteered to serve as participants in this study." Or, "50 male volunteers from a large midwestern university participated in the study." Of importance is that the reader know *who* participated in the study, how many there were, and any important distinguishing characteristics (for example, university versus high school students, males versus females).

A careful description of the variables employed in the study must be included in the method section. Here you would describe how you operationalized the independent variables (sex could be *biological sex,* psychological sex orientation—

androgyny—if used might be operationalized as scores on the *Bem Sex Role Inventory;* distance as "the thigh-to-thigh seated distance adopted by the participant from the confederate"). Dependent variables should be described in terms of the type of data employed (e.g., number of violent themes in prime-time television, responses to a semantic differential or Likert-type scale). When describing the dependent variables you might want to include the bipolar terms employed in a semantic differential scale: "Persuasion was measured via responses to 7-step semantic differential scales which tapped the evaluation dimension of attitude. Scales were bounded by Good-Bad, Valuable-Worthless, Foolish-Wise, and Pleasant-Unpleasant." Likewise, we would need to know the number of intervals in the Likert-type scale and how they were operationalized (Strongly Agree, Agree, Undecided, Disagree, Strongly Disagree). Here, a reader could take your description and replicate the materials and manipulations employed.[2] Any messages employed should also be described in this section.

Finally, the procedures employed in the study should be briefly described. Again, the procedures should be stated in such a way that others can evaluate, and, if desired, replicate the research. As was discussed in Chapter 9, if the research required participants to report to a room, engage in a conversation, and then complete the dependent measure(s), this procedure should be outlined:

> Participants reported to the communications lab ostensibly to participate in an interview study concerning the basic speech course in which he or she was enrolled. Each was provided with a copy of the Subjects Signed Consent Form, which detailed the supposed reasons for the study and a basic overview of the procedures. After indicating that he or she understood the project and agreed to participate, each participant was taken to a second room where the "interviewer" was waiting. In reality, the interviewer was a confederate who "interviewed" all participants. The confederate was a female carefully trained in interview method, who asked the same questions of all participants and maintained the same vocal, facial, and gesticular communication throughout the study.
>
> The interview room was set up to approximate a standard interview room. The confederate sat behind a table with several résumés on it. The interviewee was shown one of two chairs, both situated across from the confederate, and told to sit down, and that the interview would begin shortly.
>
> After a few seconds the confederate arose and closed the door "accidentally" left open by the researcher. This manipulation allowed the confederate to adopt one of the two distance manipulations: norm—back behind the desk—or close—the other chair adjacent to the participant. The interview was then conducted with the confederate asking a series of pretested questions regarding participation in the basic speech course in which the student was enrolled.
>
> Immediately after the interview each participant was told that the real purpose of the research was to study *interviewer* behavior and asked if he or she would mind taking a few minutes to evaluate his or her interviewer via a series of scales. Upon completion of the dependent measures each participant was debriefed as to the real purpose of the research, afforded the opportunity to ask questions, and signed a statement indicating that he or she had read the debriefing statement, had a chance to discuss the study, and would remain silent as to its true purpose until later in the semester.

Based on this discussion a reader could replicate or improve upon the study. Where deemed necessary, figures that displayed the procedures or layout of the "lab" can be included.

Results   The results section presents the data analyses in both tabular and discussion format. Tables such as graphs, lists of means or data points, and charts should be included to make the reporting easier to follow. Tables and graphs, however, are less important than the written description of the analyses. Tables, for instance, make little sense without a written explanation as to what the data—numbers, points, and so on—mean.

Each hypothesis or research question should be addressed, beginning with the statistical method employed, the established alpha-level, and all relevant statistical information included. Suppose that we had completed the study created for the method section. We may have hypothesized that interviewees would rate the confederate as more professional when she stayed behind the desk. We would report the findings of the t-test between distance (norm-close) on professionalism (7-step semantic differential scaled bounded by Professional-Unprofessional) as follows:

> Hypothesis 1, that interviewees would perceive the interviewer as more professional when she remained at the norm, was tested with a t-test on the professionalism scale as the dependent variable and distance (norm or close) as the independent variable. Interviewers were rated as significantly more professional ($t = -4.51$, df$=87$, p $<.05$, one-tailed) when they maintained the expected norm than when they deviated to the close distance (the means are found in Table 1).

Notice that the results are simply presented, no discussion is offered. The results section should address the findings and provide the relevant information so that the reader can understand which analyses were employed and what the findings were.

Discussion   The final section typically begins with a short summary of the research: what was done and its importance to further understanding communication. Theoretical issues of import may be reviewed here, bringing them back into focus and reestablishing the purpose of the research. The discussion section serves to integrate the results with the theoretical rationale presented earlier. The discussion interprets the findings, extends them to other situations (if appropriate), and offers possible alternative explanations if the hypotheses were not supported. The discussion section should also include a frank discussion of any flaws or limitations to the research, especially in light of the findings. Finally, the discussion should suggest future research and the implications of such research for the field. In cases where the research is very complicated, a short summary of the research might end the discussion.

Tidying Up   There are three final elements to the research report remaining. First, the report should have a title. The title should reflect the purpose of the research and may reflect also the methodology employed. In instances where the study is part of a program of research, it might be indicated in the title, such as, "Power in the Classroom, II" or "Further Tests of the Mass Communication Writing Apprehension Measure (MCWAM)." Although it differs by style sheet, the title (and the names of the researchers and any other pertinent information) should appear on a title page, and on the first page of text. Second, the research should include an abstract of the study, usually 100–250 words, which serves as a preview of the study and includes the important findings (see Chapter 4). The abstract also may include key words, which index the research (such as Sex Differences, Proxemics, Violations of Expectations, Communication Apprehension). Placement of the abstract differs by style sheet, some require it on a separate sheet placed between the title page and text, others on the title page, and still others as the first page of text.

Finally, all research reports must be fully referenced. It is the writer's responsibility to give clear and fair credit to others' works (see Chapter 3). The reference section usually is found at the end of the report and may include substantiative statements that further explain points or arguments made in the report's body. Again, style sheets and journals differ on how references are presented.

THE RESEARCH PROSPECTUS/PROPOSAL

The way in which the research report is written is reflected in the purpose of the report. To this point we have assumed that the report reflects a completed research project. However, there is another type of research writing that is important, the research *proposal* or *prospectus*. The research proposal/prospectus follows the same general outline as provided earlier; however, it differs in that the method, results, and discussion are presented for discussion *prior to* the actual conduct of the research. In addition, in many areas it tends to be more detailed than the final report (see Box 15.3). The introduction and literature review, which culminate in the statement of research questions and/or hypotheses, are similar to the research report, typically taking about the same amount of space, but the method, procedures, and results are stated in the future tense ("Differences will be measured by. . . ." "Data will be analyzed via regression analysis." "Appropriate tables and figures will present the data obtained in the study."). The discussion section presents how the results will be discussed if hypotheses are supported or not supported. The proposal/prospectus is used to help identify any weaknesses in the proposed research prior to the actual acquisition of data. It also serves to prepare the researcher for the final report. In academic situations, a proposal or prospectus is normally required prior to the actual conducting of research needed for advanced degrees or when applying for funding to conduct the research. Specific funding organizations have specific guidelines that must be followed—as do universities and colleges for masters' theses and doctoral dissertations.

Box 15.3 **Proposal/Prospectus Outline**

In writing up a proposal to conduct research, answer the following questions as they pertain to your project.

I. Introduction (Statement of the Problem)
   A. What is the goal of the research project?
   B. What is the problem, issue, or critical focus to be researched?
   C. What are the important terms, what do they mean?
   D. What is the significance of the problem or issue?[1]
      1. Do you want to test a theory?
      2. Do you want to extend a theory?
      3. Do you want to test competing theories?
      4. Do you want to test a method or methodology?
      5. Do you want to replicate a method or methodology?
      6. Do you want to replicate a previous study?[2]
      7. Do you want to correct previous research that was conducted in an inadequate manner?
      8. Do you want to resolve inconsistent results from earlier studies?
      9. Do you want to solve a practical problem?

II. Review of Literature
   A. What does previous research reveal about the problem or issue?
   B. What is the theoretical framework for the investigation?
   C. Are there any complementary frameworks?[3]
   D. Are there any competing theoretical frameworks?
   E. What is (are) the research question(s) or hypothesis(es)?
      1. Clearly separate the research questions/hypotheses.
      2. Clearly state the research questions/hypotheses.

III. Participants/Materials
   A. Who (what) will provide (constitute) the data for the research?
   B. For quantitative research:
      1. What is the population being studied?
      2. Who will comprise the participants or respondents of the research?
      3. What is the sample size?
      4. What are the characteristics of the sample?
      5. Which sampling techniques will be used?
      6. If experimental research:
         a. How will participants be assigned to cells?
         b. What safeguards have you provided?
         c. Present a sample consent form and debriefing form in an appendix.
   C. For qualitative research:
      1. What materials and/or information are necessary to conduct the research?
      2. How will they be obtained?

3. What special problems can be anticipated in acquiring needed materials and information?
4. What are the limitations in the availability and reporting of materials and information?

IV. Methodology
   A. What methods or techniques will be used to collect the data?
   B. What procedures will be used to apply the methods or techniques?
      1. Be specific.
      2. Be practical.
      3. Be conservative.
   C. What are the limitations of this methodology?
   D. For quantitative research:
      1. What are the variables?
         a. The dependent variables?
         b. The independent variables?
      2. How will the variables be manipulated, controlled, measured, and/or observed?
      3. What instrument(s) (scales) will be used?
         a. If developed by others:
            (1) How reliable and valid are they?[4]
            (2) Why use this instrument or scale rather than others?
         b. If developing an instrument for this research project:
            (1) How will the scales be developed?
            (2) What format will be used?
            (3) How will reliability and validity be assessed?
            (4) Why develop a new scale or instrument?
   E. If an experiment:
      1. What factors will affect the study's internal validity?
      2. What factors will affect the study's external validity?
      3. How will plausible rival hypotheses be minimized?
   F. If historical/critical:
      1. What sources of bias will exist?
      2. How will bias be controlled?
   G. Will any ethical principles be jeopardized?
      1. If so, with what ramifications?
      2. If so, how will participants be informed of the true nature of the study?
      3. Will participants be debriefed? Given a copy of the results?
      4. Provided the name of someone to talk with if problems ensue?

V. Data Analysis — *quant*
   A. How will the data be analyzed?
   B. If quantitative research, what statistics will be employed?
   C. What criteria will be used to determine if the hypotheses are supported? (alpha-level?)
   D. If a pilot study was conducted, what was learned:
      1. About the question?
      2. About the data to be gathered?

3. About the methodology:
   a. Did the pilot study consist of another method?
   b. Which?
   c. What did it find?

VI. Conclusions
  A. How will the final research report be organized?
  B. In what form?
    1. Text?
    2. Tables?
    3. Figures?
    4. Bibliographies?
  C. What are the time deadlines imposed?
    1. For completing the literature review?
    2. For collection of the data?
    3. For analysis of the data?
    4. For writing the report?

VII. Summary (1 paragraph)

NOTES

1. Obviously, you may only answer one or two of these questions, but look at all to see what is appropriate.

2. In this case, why? What was wrong or flawed with the previous study? Or is it a case of time being the variable—things have changed over the ____-year period?

3. Here, be certain to point out any theoretical models developed if conducting a participant observation study or, in the case of content analysis, you may use already extant category systems.

4. Present other research reporting reliability and validity information. Be sure to indicate weaknesses in the scales and what you will do to improve them.

Source: Adapted from Rebecca B. Rubin, Alan M. Rubin, and Linda J. Piele, *Communication Research: Strategies and Sources* (Belmont, Calif.: Wadsworth, 1986), 46–48. © Copyright 1986 by Wadsworth, Inc. Reprinted by permission of the publisher.

SUMMARY

The culmination of the research project is found in its write-up. The writing stage is often perceived as the most difficult and time-consuming part of the research. Writing, however, is important because it allows the researcher to review his or her findings and ensure that the logic and focus of the study are appropriate. Additionally, the writing stage often yields unexpected dividends in the form of new insights and alternative explanations. In writing the research report or proposal, a general form that includes an introduction, a literature review, a method section, a results section, and finally, a discussion and interpretation of the findings should be followed. Style manuals or style sheets have different requirements, but all follow the same basic outline. The actual style of the report may be dictated by the audience for whom the report is written.

GENERAL REVIEW OF THE RESEARCH PROCESS

The purpose of this final section is to review the process of research. In Part One of this book we examined the relationships between theory and research. Part Two introduced the various methods researchers use to answer the research questions generated in the quest to further understand human communication and its effects. And, in Part Three, we examined how researchers make sense out of the quantitative data they gather as the research study is conducted. The purpose of research, in the end, is to add knowledge to what we already know about human behavior. In this case, of course, we are examining *human communicative behavior.*

Research begins with the identification of some area of communication that is both important and of interest to the researcher. As should be gathered by now, there are many areas of interest from which we can pose significant research questions. Throughout the book we have tried to indicate as many areas of interest as possible; the chapter Probes were written in such a way as to get you—the reader—involved in areas of your particular interest. Once an area of potential interest has been identified we move to the next step in the research process.

All research requires an understanding of previous study and thought. This stage of the research process consists of reading all material—books, journal articles, papers, and so forth—relevant to the area of interest. Here, of course, we are talking about library research and a review of the previous literature. At this stage we sometimes formalize our study by writing a prospectus, proposal, or area paper. All this work culminates in the *literature review,* which sets both the theory and tone of the research project being considered. From this literature review the research questions and hypotheses are generated, perhaps the most critical step in the research process.

The research question determines which method is selected to conduct the research. Selection of the most appropriate method is an important step. Here the researcher must decide his or her approach to the study, based, of course, on the type of question being asked. If the researcher is interested in assessing the communication from a particular event, person, or time, then an historical and/or critical method is most appropriate. On the other hand, if the researcher is interested in the examination of an ongoing event, describing how people perceive an event or communication, or attempting to understand the relationships between communication variables, he or she will choose one of the following methodologies: participant-observation, content analysis, survey, or experimental. Whatever the method a researcher chooses, however, it is important to remember that the research question should suggest the method, not the other way around.

Once the method has been chosen, procedures for conducting the study must be established. Regardless of methodology employed, creation of research procedures are critical to the study's success. Here we are talking about the plan of attack, the identification of materials necessary to conduct the research (documents in some instances, creation of scales in others). At this stage of the research process the social scientist must make some important decisions. How will the study be conducted? Where? What amount of control is necessary? How many people will be questioned or participate in the study? At this stage the researcher must create the instruments for the collection of data; whether that data comes from participant-observation or experiments, it must be assessed for validity and reliability. For the survey or experimental study, questions and scales must be created and tested. Confederates and/or interviewers must be trained and actual procedures tested. Finally, the sample must be selected or the random assignment of participants to conditions must be established. Once all this planning, pretesting, and testing has been completed the researcher can move to the next step in the process: data collection.

Depending on the research method selected, collecting the materials from which to draw conclusions may take a day, a week, or a year. Regardless of the method employed, data collection is an exciting, if not the most exciting stage of research. The data from which the research questions or hypotheses are tested or answered are assembled during this stage of the process.

In the experiment at least two additional features of the data collection stage must be addressed. First, as noted above, research participants must be chosen. These participants must be apprised of the study through the *consent form.* They must be provided a way out of the study if they so desire. Second, participants who complete the study must be debriefed. Both steps are crucial to a well-conducted and ethical experiment. In conducting survey research the researcher may offer copies of the findings to the participants at a later time. This information must be sent after the study has been completed.

Once all the data has been collected the research has entered the analysis process. At this stage the researcher uses whatever analytical procedures and tools are available to make sense out of the data acquired. In some methods this typically requires that the data be coded into the computer and statistical analyses computed. In others, the acquired data may be compared against some theoretical model, assessed against what others have found, and their logic employed in drawing their conclusions, or compared against certain aesthetic principles. Regardless of method, however, all data—for example, observations, scales, documents—must be analyzed before any meaningful conclusions can be drawn from the research.

Once the study has been conducted, the data analyzed, and conclusions drawn about the research questions the results must be made public. Here the researcher, according to the conventions of his or her discipline, writes the research report. This report establishes a rational for the research, reviews previous literature, states the research questions and hypotheses, describes the method employed in the collection of the data and the results, and then discusses the research. This stage of the process is extremely important. Here the researcher contributes to knowledge generation, to theory construction. The final report, in whatever way made public, ultimately will end up impacting on someone else and may provide the data necessary for their examination of communication behavior. The final report also identifies future areas of research based on the findings of this study and its limitations and qualifications.

Is the research process now over? No. This project should set the stage for the next. The next project will set the stage for another. Research is a true process, it never ends. Conducting research is an exciting adventure in understanding how and why people communicate. It is also hard but rewarding work.

By now you should have the necessary information and skills to conduct a research project in your particular interest area. It is hoped, too, that you can now make critical analyses of others' research, assessing where the method and procedures were good and where they were bad. We hope that your study of research methods will, in the end, make you a more informed and educated consumer of the ever-increasing amounts of research being disseminated daily. We also hope that some of you will be bitten by the research bug and go on to examine significant problems and areas of interest in your area of communication.

NOTES

1. Raymond K. Tucker, Richard L. Weaver, II, and Cynthia Berryman-Fink, *Research in Speech Communication* (Englewood Cliffs, N.J.: Prentice-Hall, 1981), 231–232.
2. In many instances the researcher reports, via a footnote, that the materials are available from him or her or offers more information about the construction of the measure or the operationalization of the manipulations.

Index